RESEARCH METHODS IN THE SOCIAL SCIENCES

RESEARCH METHODS IN THE SOCIAL SCIENCES

LEE ELLIS
Minot State University

Brown & Benchmark PUBLISHERS

Madison, Wisconsin • Dubuque, Iowa • Indianapolis, Indiana
Melbourne, Australia • Oxford, England

Book Team

Editor *Roger Wolkoff*
Developmental Editor *Sue Pulvermacher-Alt*
Production Editor *Karen A. Pluemer*
Visuals/Design Developmental Consultant *Marilyn A. Phelps*
Visuals/Design Freelance Specialist *Mary L. Christianson*
Publishing Services Specialist *Sherry Padden*
Advertising Manager *Nancy Milling*

WCB Brown & Benchmark

A Division of Wm. C. Brown Communications, Inc.

Executive Vice President/General Manager *Thomas E. Doran*
Vice President/Editor in Chief *Edgar J. Laube*
Vice President/Sales and Marketing *Eric Ziegler*
Director of Production *Vickie Putman Caughron*
Director of Custom and Electronic Publishing *Chris Rogers*

Wm. C. Brown Communications, Inc.

President and Chief Executive Officer *G. Franklin Lewis*
Corporate Senior Vice President and Chief Financial Officer *Robert Chesterman*
Corporate Senior Vice President and President of Manufacturing *Roger Meyer*

Cover design and illustration by Tessing Design, Inc.

Copyedited by Karen Dorman

To the world's social scientists,
from whom I have learned so much.

CONTENTS

Chapter 9 Nonquestionnaire Data: Direct Qualitative Observations

119

Chapter 10 Nonquestionnaire Data: Quantitative Observations

135

Chapter 11 Indirect Observational Data

149

Chapter 17 Multivariate Statistical Studies   257

Chapter 18 Ethical Issues in the Social Sciences, I: Responsibilities
to Subjects and to Fellow Social Scientists   277

PREFACE

The overall objective of this book is to share with students a basic understanding and appreciation of the research methods that lie at the heart of social science. Students will be able to use what they have learned not only to conduct research, but to intelligently and critically read research material as well. Throughout this text, emphasis has been placed on making both the technical know-how and the intellectual and practical importance of social science research apparent to the reader. A concerted effort has also been made to define and illustrate each new term that is used.

Among the hallmark features of this text are numerous examples of actual research studies, which are used to illustrate various points. Through these examples, students should begin to sense both the rich history and vibrant contemporary reality of social science research. A high proportion of these examples are extremely current, and may serve as inspiration for students wishing to contribute to the social science pool of knowledge. The examples should also make students aware of the dizzying pace at which research in the social sciences is being conducted and published.

In this, more than any other text currently available, examples and illustrations are drawn from all of the social sciences as well as from numerous related disciplines (as outlined in Chapter 1). Students will become acquainted with scientific investigations not only of humans living in a wide variety of societies, but also of nonhuman animals who exhibit behavior that helps us to better understand our own. Above all, throughout this text, an effort was made to avoid the false impression that social science research is only conducted in North America, or even in Western societies. Instructors who use this text will want to supplement its examples with ones that are more specific to their own particular discipline.

Another fairly unusual feature of this text is that it tightly interlinks the learning of research methods with a basic understanding of statistics. This integration is provided in three early chapters (Chapters 3, 4, and 5), which introduce students to basic statistical concepts at an essentially nonmathematical level. After reading these three chapters, you will understand these basic statistical concepts when they are used later in descriptions of various research methods.

Whereas many of today's texts in social science research methods are written specifically for one social science, this text is written for use in all of the social sciences—to the degree that the scientific method (a topic discussed in Chapter 1) is employed. Even students in allied disciplines such as education, journalism, marketing, psychiatry, or public health will find that this text covers basic concepts needed for developing competent research skills.

This text rests on the basic premise that students of social science (and related disciplines) should be familiar with the research methods that have come to typify the social sciences worldwide. In fact, creating either the impression or the reality of entirely unique research methods for each social science is both misleading and disruptive of valuable cross-disciplinary communication.

Special Comments to Students

Many social science students look forward to their first course in research methods without much enthusiasm. Not only does a course title that includes words ''Research Methods'' sound dry and technical, but the idea that statistical concepts are tightly interwoven with research methods (which they are) can make such a course intimidating, especially if you happen to have not yet had a course in statistics.

Although I may not be able to assure you that learning research methods is easy, I did make a serious effort in writing this text to keep students foremost in mind. I have tried to state each point clearly and provide interesting examples for illustration.

You are probably curious about how your learning will be tested. Test questions have been provided to most instructors to use at their discretion. The examination questions are designed to test your understanding of the main points made in each chapter. Some questions will ask you about the meaning of terms, while others will challenge you to combine terms to derive reasonable conclusions. Although you should read the summaries of studies used to illustrate major points, you will not find test questions specifically about those studies (unless your instructor states otherwise).

Whether we make it clear to students or not, we instructors learn a great deal from teaching. Much of this learning comes almost unconsciously from the feedback and questions that students provide. Most instructors will appreciate your asking questions when things are not clear to you. Also, if you have any criticisms or suggestions that I can use to improve future editions of this text, I would welcome your letters.

Some Comments to Instructors

The chapters in this text have been organized so that you can expect students to be able to read rudimentary research within three to four weeks after beginning the course (even if they have not had a course in statistics). Students should then be better able to model their own research efforts after actual studies they have read rather than simply what they have learned secondhand.

Thus, it is recommended that you assign students to read some fairly simple research reports. This text has a companion workbook containing such assignments. The main purpose of these out-of-class assignments is to give students more hands-on familiarity with social research (e.g., locating literature on a specific topic, reading and analyzing actual research reports, planning and carrying out their own rudimentary research project).

If you discover any technical inaccuracies or other deficiencies in this text, please bring these to my attention. In addition, if you know of any interesting examples of research studies that could be used to illustrate points made in future editions of this text, please send me a copy of the material.

Acknowledgments

Many people helped make this text possible. I thank Sue Pulvermacher-Alt of Brown & Benchmark for helping me through each phase of writing this text. The reviewers who carefully read and critiqued the book provided me with many helpful suggestions for improving it, and I thank them very sincerely:

Raymond Matura
University of Rio Grande

Linda Mealey
St. Johns University

Larry Wood
Brigham Young University

Concetta Culliver
Murray State College

Kandi Stinson
Xavier University

Mary Kite
Ball State University

Julia Hall
Drexel University

Bennett Judkins
Meredith College

James Iaccino
Illinois Benedictine College

C. Neil Bull
University of Missouri–Kansas City

I would also like to acknowledge the help of Alan Widmayer and Rhonda Kostenko, who diligently read and critiqued most of the chapters in various stages of drafting. The copyediting of Karen Dorman is also greatly appreciated. Others who generously took time to assist in the preparation of this text were Myrna Nelson, Bonnie Peterson, Duane Sweep, and Carla McDaniel.

I am very grateful to the hundreds of students over the years who have taken my research methods classes for bearing with me as a teaching style slowly developed. With their tolerance and feedback, I have been able to settle into a teaching format that seems to convey a clear picture of both the technical aspects of research methods and the sense of wonder and accomplishment that comes from their use. Finally, I must apologize to my wife and two daughters for shirking so many of my domestic responsibilities over the past four years.

CHAPTER 1

The Social Sciences and the Scientific Method

A re children from small families more or less likely to be delinquent and criminal than those from large families? Who can tolerate more pain, males or females? Just for fun, jot down what you think are the answers to these two questions; later, you can compare your guesses to the results of scientific research.

The two questions just posed are among the countless thousands of questions that social scientists have attempted to answer over the past century and a half (which is roughly the amount of time that the scientific method has been applied to the study of human behavior). And it so happens that these questions are among a relatively few questions for which there are numerous studies that have all come to essentially the same conclusions. Before looking at the evidence, imagine how you might gather relevant scientific evidence to these questions.

For example, how would you measure delinquent and criminal behavior, or pain tolerance? Where would you locate people willing to provide you with the necessary information, and how many individuals would you have to study? What would you do with the information after it had been collected? Are there ethical issues that should be considered before undertaking the necessary research? Even though your questions usually pertain to humans, would it be relevant to also consider evidence from other animal species?

The above questions reflect the issues that social scientists face when conducting research. You will find that, while there are rarely absolute answers to any questions faced by social scientists, usually there is a fairly narrow range of options to guide them in their work.

In reading this text, you will gradually come to understand the reasoning that underlies scientific research. In addition, you will become acquainted with the concepts needed to begin conducting social science research on your own. Through it all, you will come to appreciate that, while a text such as this one can teach you the basics, a high level of proficiency in social science research only comes through years of practice. In fact, it is safe to say that those who conduct scientific research on a regular basis learn new things about the research process every time they conduct a study. Nevertheless, many basics are best learned by reading about them, rather than through trial and error.

Now, let us return to the two questions posed in the first paragraph. Both of these questions have been extensively investigated, and the results of the numerous studies were recently reviewed (Ellis, 1986, 1988).[1] In brief, here is what the scientific evidence indicates:

How does the number of siblings one has relate to an individual's likelihood of being delinquent and criminal? At least 32 studies have been conducted in many parts of the world since the 1930s. All but one of these studies found that persons with the fewest number of siblings (including those with no siblings at all) had lower rates of delinquency and crime than persons who came from larger families (Ellis, 1988:531). The one exceptional study simply failed to find a significant relationship between family size and delinquency. Generally, the tendency for the number of siblings in one's family to be related to delinquency and crime was more pronounced in the case of extensive serious offense histories than in the case of mere trivial offenses.

Concerning pain tolerance, 17 studies of humans and 10 studies of other animals (mainly rats and mice) have looked for evidence of average sex differences. In humans, the comparisons usually involved having subjects do such things as pressing their bare feet or the palms of their hands against a pointed object attached to a pressure sensitive instrument for as long and as hard as the subjects could stand to do so, or to dip their arms in a vat of near-freezing water until the pain was no longer tolerable. Studies of pain tolerance in other animals have generally required subjects to withstand electric shock from the floor of their cages in order to reach food sources. All 17 studies of humans and all 10 studies of other animals were remarkably consistent in indicating that, on average, males tolerated pain to a greater degree than females (Ellis, 1986:530; also see Feine et al., 1991; Fowler-Kerry & Lander, 1991). There was, however, substantial variation within each sex, so that there were many females who exceeded the male average in pain tolerance.

Of course, finding average differences and explaining them are not the same thing. You could assume that sex role training would account for why men on average tolerate more pain than women, although this would not explain why similar average sex differences have been found in other species. Experiments with laboratory animals have been conducted to find out why they exhibit average sex differences in pain tolerance. These experiments have implicated exposure of the brain to sex hormones, especially testosterone (the main "male sex hormone") (Beatty & Beatty, 1970; Redmond et al., 1976:322), and the effects of this hormone on the body's natural opiate system (Kavaliers & Innes, 1990) as the primary cause of the average sex difference in response to pain. Whether the same factors are responsible for human sex differences in pain tolerance remains to be determined. However, evidence from humans that female pain tolerance fluctuates according to phases of the menstrual cycle and in conjunction with taking oral contraceptives (reviewed by Feine et al., 1991:260) suggests the involvement of sex hormones.

The research evidence just cited helps to illustrate that advancement in scientific knowledge rarely comes from a single study. Rather, such gains in scientific knowledge typically are only noticeable over decades of work by dozens of independent researchers carefully checking and rechecking one another's findings.

Although at first you may have difficulty with the terminology used by social scientists to conduct research and communicate their findings, you will see that it can be mastered with some serious effort. Also, you will find that the research methods used by social scientists depend largely upon common sense, even though what is discovered through the application of these methods will often seem to defy common sense.

This introductory chapter has two purposes: First, it introduces all the major social sciences as well as what will be called the **near social sciences** and **allied disciplines.** Second, it presents the basic characteristics of the scientific method, and how this method is used (and sometimes not used) in the various social sciences.

Circumscribing the Social Sciences

The term **social science** will be used throughout this text to refer to disciplines whose primary objective is to help understand behavioral and social phenomena. While the main social sciences typically focus their attention on the human species, branches within the social sciences specialize in studying the behavior and social phenomena of other species.

When did social science begin? The answer to this question depends on which social science you are discussing. Nevertheless, science historians agree that during the 1700s (i.e., the 18th century), ideas that eventually led to the development of such disciplines as anthropology, economics, psychology, political science, and sociology slowly began to emerge in parts of Europe (Brittain, 1990:105). It was not until the end of the 1800s, however, that professionalization of the social sciences became apparent. This professionalization primarily took the form of establishing special university departments in the various social science disciplines (with full-time faculty), and the publication of specialized social science journals.

While the social sciences are quite diverse, they all focus on some aspect of behavior and social life and on the institutions, technology, ideas, and aesthetic creations emanating from social interactions. Some social scientists even come full circle by reflecting upon the complex sociocultural processes which have given rise to science itself. Other social scientists extend their interests in behavior and social living to nonhuman animals, either for the purpose of gaining insights into human behavior, or as areas of study in their own right.

As you read through the descriptions of the major social science disciplines below, notice how each makes a valuable contribution to the understanding of the richness and wonder of the human species and of its extraordinary social and cultural accomplishments. The main social science disciplines are listed in alphabetical order, and there is no intention to suggest that one is somehow more important than another by the amount of space devoted to briefly describing each one. Some disciplines are simply more easily characterized than others.

Anthropology

Anthropology literally means the study of humankind. It began to form in the mid-1800s as intellectuals in Europe became increasingly interested in human origins and in studying the various races of humans and their diverse cultures (Lieberman, 1989:680). There are at least two major branches of anthropology recognized: physical and cultural (Lieberman, 1989:680). Physical (or biological) anthropology primarily attempts to piece together fossil evidence of the physical evolution of humans (Birdsell, 1987:2).[2] It also tries to link the emergence of the human species from several extinct ancestral forms of human-like creatures that have been discovered, some of whom lived several million years ago (Campbell, 1985:161; Barnouw, 1989:138). Physical anthropologists are also very interested in both the physical features and the genetic makeup of the various nonhuman primates (monkeys and apes) that still exist, and scientists hope to someday determine when nonhuman primate ancestors and human ancestors first diverged (Larsen, Matter, & Gebo, 1991; Relethford, 1990:190).

Cultural anthropologists specialize in studying the full diversity of human cultures and social customs as exhibited by people in thousands of human societies, both large and small, throughout the world (Haviland, 1991:13; Peoples & Bailey, 1991; Scupin & DeCorse, 1992:8). Cultural anthropologists often work closely with sociologists in studying contemporary industrialized societies.

In recent years, a number of anthropologists have taken up the study of social behavior of nonhuman primates, especially apes (Campbell, 1985:119; Richard, 1985). This work has made it possible to probe the similarities and differences that exist between humans and other primates. One of the foremost researchers has been Jane Goodall (1990), whose observations of wild chimpanzees over the past 30 years have provided tremendous insights into the behavior of man's closest living relative. Anthropologists such as Goodall who specialize in studying nonhuman primate behavior are often called **primatologists.**

Criminology/Criminal Justice

Scientific attempts to understand criminal behavior (and the sociolegal system which has been designed to help control criminal behavior) go back to the early 1800s in Europe. Various intellectuals began to suggest that instead of demons and other supernatural forces being responsible for crime, the causes might be found within each individual offender and/or within the societies where the crimes occurred (Masters & Roberson, 1990:54). Out of these ideas have emerged a variety of theories of criminal behavior.

Until the 1960s, most courses in criminology/criminal justice were taught under the disciplinary umbrella of sociology. Although there were a few colleges offering specialized degrees in criminology/criminal justice in the early part of this century, doing so became common in American colleges and universities by 1970 (see Adams, 1976). Today, while nearly all sociology departments still offer courses in criminology, the field of criminal justice (under various names) has emerged as a major social science in its own right. Programs which specialize in criminology emphasize attempts to understand the causes of criminal behavior, whereas criminal justice programs focus more on studying the criminal justice system.

Economics

The discipline of economics began taking shape near the end of the 19th century. Economists study all aspects of economic processes, from individual and family financial well-being (sometimes called microeconomics), all the way to the financial affairs of states and nations (often referred to as macroeconomics). Economics is closely related to the fields of business and finance, but it has ties with the fields of political science and sociology as well.

Geography

Geography literally means "measurement of the earth." However, as the discipline has developed, it has focused more on how political and economic processes impact, and are affected by, features of the earth at or near the earth's surface. While it is generally considered a social science, geography has close ties with geology, a discipline which directly studies the physical features of the earth and how those features have formed.

History

History is widely regarded as "the first social science," although it may actually share that distinction with philosophy and/or political science, since all these disciplines trace their roots back at least as far as the classical period of Greece. Building on the word story, history means learning from an account or a written record. Because the first forms of writing began to appear only about 6 to 7 thousand years ago (Lewin, 1988:1129), events preceding that time are referred to as **prehistoric.** When compared to all the other social sciences, history tends to be most similar to anthropology, especially a branch of anthropology called historic archaeology.

As will be explained later, history has a special function among the social sciences in its focus on the causes of unique events rather than on broad categories of events. For this reason, there is continual debate about whether history should be considered a science in the strictest sense of the term (Carr, 1962:70).

Philosophy

The prefix *philo* means "to love" and suffix *sophia* denotes wisdom or knowledge. Philosophy has its roots in ancient Greece and refers to intellectual efforts to understand the meaning of life, the nature of good and evil, and the limits to human knowledge. While some believe that philosophy is better classified as a humanity than as a social science, there can be no doubt that philosophy forms the foundation upon which all science has been built. Accordingly, some of the philosophical underpinnings of scientific methods will be discussed later in this chapter. Even today, most scientists who are awarded doctorate degrees receive PhDs (doctorates of philosophy) rather than degrees specifically naming their own disciplinary specialization.

Political Science

With his book *Politics,* Aristotle is often regarded as the first political scientist. As a recognized discipline, however, political science did not appear until the late 1700s, as the European Enlightenment witnessed the replacement of various monarchies with constitutional democracies.

Today, political scientists study all aspects of government and the political process. These include the inner workings of various branches of government, the analysis of voting patterns and shifts in public opinion, and the dynamics of international relations. Political science issues are often closely interwoven with issues in economics, geography, sociology, and history.

Psychology

Psychology began to form as a discipline apart from philosophy in the 1700s. It literally means study of the mind (or the human psyche or spirit). By the 1800s, this mentalistic concept of psychology had become a source of controversy which led to various attempts to make psychology a more objective discipline (Brozek, 1990). Since the turn of the 20th century, psychology has usually been defined primarily as the study of behavior, and secondarily as the study of cognitive processes such as thoughts and emotions (Dewsbury, 1984:244; Cooper, Heron, & Herward, 1987:7).

A recent survey of psychological literature revealed that over the past century, psychologists have increasingly turned their attention to studies of the brain and its functioning as key factors underlying behavior, thoughts, and emotions (Ellis, Miller, & Widmayer, 1988). This trend has increasingly linked psychology with biology, especially neurology and neurochemistry (Davis et al., 1988). Nevertheless, psychology still retains close ties to "mainstream" social science, particularly in terms of research methodology (Bunge, 1990).

Many psychologists concentrate on studying the behavior of nonhuman animals more than they study the behavior of humans. This is especially true of those specializing in such subdisciplines as *experimental psychology* and *comparative psychology*.

Social Work

Social work is a specialized discipline for helping a society's poor, disabled, and disadvantaged citizens. Social workers attempt to restore and maintain the lives of their clients at levels of well-being and self-sufficiency that would otherwise be unlikely. As a discipline, social work is similar to criminal justice in having a more practical orientation than most other social sciences. Also like criminal justice, social work began to become formally separated from sociology in the 1960s.

Sociology

Sociology began to be recognized as a major social science in the mid-1800s. A few decades earlier, a French philosopher and scientist named Auguste Comte argued that a special science was needed to study human societies and social relationships. Comte championed the idea that all matter evolves through major stages, starting with inorganic matter, proceeding through simple life-forms, and advancing further to life-forms in which large numbers of cells collectively form complex living creatures (i.e., multicellular plants and animals). Eventually, Comte contended, some of these creatures organize themselves into collectives, called "super organisms" or societies, and a special discipline is needed to study these entities.

Today, sociology is probably best defined as the study of social behavior, social institutions, and societies in general. While most sociologists are exclusively interested in social phenomena exhibited by humans in modern industrial societies, a few sociologists also study humans living in nonindustrial societies. In addition, some sociologists overlap with sociobiologists (discussed below) because of their interest in social phenomena among nonhuman animals (Collias, 1991).

The Near Social Sciences

In order to get a complete picture of the breadth and scope of the social sciences, five other disciplines should be mentioned: education, ethology, psychiatry, public health, and sociobiology.

Education

As a discipline, education involves studying the process of accumulating and transmitting information, usually in an academic setting. Many educators engage in research to improve teaching techniques, and to determine why students vary in learning abilities and interests. The research methods that they use are the same as those used in social science.

Ethology

Ethology literally means the study of "character," "habit," or a thing's "intrinsic property" (Dewsbury, 1984:11). One should not confuse *ethology* and *ethnology;* the latter refers to the study of human cultures that is at the foundation of cultural anthropology (this will be described in Chapter 9). Ethology began forming in the 1930s in Germany, and its major founders were eventually awarded the Nobel Prize for their scientific work. Ethologists attempt to study the behavior of all animals (including humans) primarily in naturalistic settings. In this way, ethologists try to understand how various behavior patterns may have contributed to animal adaptation.

Psychiatry

Literally, psychiatry means "correction of mental processes." As practiced, psychiatry involves efforts to treat persons with mental illness. Psychiatrists typically have a background both in medicine and in psychology. Thus, their treatment can include psychological counseling as well as prescribing drugs and performing surgery. Most psychiatric research methods are very similar to those used in the social sciences, although some methods are more closely allied to medical research.

Public Health

Public health is a discipline which, like psychiatry, is closely allied with medicine. Nevertheless, public health officials work closely with the social sciences and generally utilize the same research methods.

Sociobiology

Sociobiology is generally regarded as the most recent science of social behavior, tracing its roots back to the mid-1970s (Wilson, 1975; Dawkins, 1976). The discipline is oriented toward identifying the biological underpinnings of social behavior, both in humans and in other social species.

Other Disciplines That Utilize Social Research Methods

Finally, there are three disciplines whose practitioners fairly often employ social science research methodology: journalism, advertising and marketing, and home economics. Their use of social research methodology is as follows:

Increasingly, people in the fields of journalism, communications, and public relations are conducting, analyzing, and interpreting various types of social science data (e.g., Cameron, Lariscy, & Sweep, 1992). This is especially true of public opinion survey data. In addition, people in these professions are being called upon to digest social science research for popular consumption. A recent study, in fact, indicated studies that did receive popular press coverage were more likely to be subsequently cited in the scientific literature than studies that did not receive such coverage (Phillips et al., 1991). Consequently, persons being trained in fields such as journalism will benefit from an understanding of scientific research methods.

Persons in advertising and marketing have increasingly come to utilize surveying research methodology, particularly in the form of marketing surveys. Like their journalism counterparts, advertising students stand to gain from knowing how to select samples that are representative of a target population, how to phrase questions in ways that elicit meaningful responses, and how to interpret the responses they obtain.

Home economists have interests that extend into all aspects of family and home functioning. Growing numbers of home economists, therefore, utilize social science research methodology in their efforts to lay a scientific foundation upon which to build their understanding of the dynamics of family living and domestic relationships.

Features of the Scientific Method

Now that the broad scope of social science, along with its allied disciplines, has been identified, let us consider a simple question: What is it that makes a discipline "scientific"? Basically, the answer boils down not to the questions that are asked, but to the methods that are used in seeking answers. Therefore, the degree to which a social science is truly scientific depends upon the extent to which its practitioners use what is called the scientific method.

The characteristics of the scientific method can be grouped in various ways, but basically, seven characteristics can be identified.

Empirical

Ultimately, all things with which science can deal are empirical phenomena. Such phenomena are those which can be sensed, i.e., seen, heard, felt, tasted, or smelled (Dickinson, 1971). There are instances in which scientists hypothesize the existence of things that have not yet been sensed, at least not directly. These would include things that are too small (like various subatomic particles), too remote (such as black holes), or things that may exist but for which our methods of measurement have not yet been adequately developed (life on other planets). Nevertheless, all phenomena with which scientists can deal are at least *conceivably* empirical.

Before leaving the issue of empiricism, take note that there is no way of *proving* that our senses are not deceiving us about what exists. Thus, science rests upon an unprovable philosophical assumption (and, as we will see, this is not the only one).

Verifiable

The characteristic of verifiability assumes that we can use our senses to confirm or refute the empirical observations made by others, and that they, in turn, can check ours. For various reasons, mistaken observations are occasionally reported. Gradually, such an observation will be followed by attempts to replicate the finding until it is apparent that the original report was in error.

Cumulative

Isaac Newton was once asked by a student how he came up with all his ideas. He was said to have paused for a moment and replied, ''If I've seen far, it's because I've stood on tall shoulders.'' Newton's response reflects the cumulative nature of scientific knowledge. One of the most exciting features of the scientific method is that you need not start from scratch when attempting to understand something. Instead, you find out what others have already learned, and add to this base. Of course, if you feel unsure about some reported observations, then you often attempt to verify them before adding something new to the store of knowledge.

Self-Correcting

Science is considered self-correcting because when errors in observations are made, sooner or later the mistakes will be identified (Stokes, 1974; Silberner, 1982:41). Ultimately, no statement about scientific observations is ever excluded from the possibility of being in error, although from a practical standpoint many statements can be considered proven. Because science is self-correcting by always leaving all statements about reality open for further investigation, you will find most scientists do not say statements are either ''true or false.'' Instead, they will use such terms as ''The evidence strongly suggests . . .'' or ''Studies have shown. . . .'' The self-correcting and the verifiable and cumulative features of science methodology are closely linked (Fuchs & Turner, 1986:143).

Deterministic

Determinism is another unprovable philosophical assumption that scientists implicitly make in attempting to explain why things happen. Basically, this assumption is that any explanation given for a phenomenon must entail only empirical (or natural), as opposed to supernatural, factors (Encyclopedia of Sociology, 1981:282). Although there is no way to prove that supernatural entities (God, the devil, etc.) are not responsible for whatever is being observed, by removing the supernatural factor from consideration, scientists can at least hope to find the causes. If supernatural forces are controlling events that scientists are trying to understand, then they are unlikely to understand the phenomenon using scientific methodology. Consequently, scientists normally *assume* that causes are all natural in origin (natural in this sense would also include social causes).

There is little controversy any more in applying the assumption of determinism to the study of physical or even biological phenomena. When applied specifically to the study of behavior, however, the determinist assumption also implies that, in the strictest sense, there is no "free will" underlying human actions. People feel very uncomfortable applying this assumption, and there is a long-standing controversy over "free will" vs. determinism in the social sciences (Ruse, 1987; Russell, 1945; Viney, 1986). This controversy will not be debated here. Students of research methods only need to understand that (a) determinism is ultimately an unprovable assumption, and (b) it does not deny that humans (or other animals) make choices. The assumption simply postulates that all choices any living creature makes can be ultimately explained in terms of some combination of natural (including social) factors (see Harcum, 1991).

Ethical and Ideological Neutrality (Value Free)

The ethical neutrality of the scientific method does not mean that scientists must divest themselves of all moral principles and political beliefs in order to conduct research. In fact, two entire chapters later in this text will discuss many of the important ethical issues facing social scientists (Chapters 18 and 19). Ethical and ideological neutrality merely means that scientists should not allow such things as ethics and ideology to influence what is being empirically observed and reported.

There is a long-standing controversy as to whether it is possible for scientists, especially social scientists, to ever be completely objective, especially when studying people with cultural backgrounds unfamiliar to the observer (Brittain, 1990:108; Mahoney, 1987). One example of apparent social science bias has come from studies of sex differences in behavior. Overall, male researchers were found to report greater sex differences in various behavior patterns than were female researchers (Eagly & Carli, 1981). Which sex is closer to being correct still remains to be determined.

The best insurance against observational biases is to, first, never take a single study's results as proof. This means that social scientists should conduct numerous **replication studies** (using a variety of methodologies and samples before asserting that a particular finding is well-established) (Bornstein, 1990). The second way to avoid unintentional biases is to make social science a worldwide endeavor. Fortunately, people in nearly all countries have an interest in objectively studying social phenomenon (Brittain, 1990:108). This gives one reason for being optimistic about social scientists gradually becoming a universal human enterprise.

Statistical Generalizability

The scientific method usually involves subjecting information to statistical analyses. Sometimes the statistics involved are very simple, such as finding averages and calculating percentages, and other times the statistics are exceedingly complex. The view underlying this text is that no student can grasp social science research methods without a rudimentary knowledge of statistics. In Chapters 3, 4, and 5, you will learn various ways statistics are used by social scientists to generalize about their research findings.

In sum, seven interrelated characteristics of the scientific method can be identified. Although they are all important, you should not assume that scientists—even good scientists—necessarily adhere to the scientific method without exception. Less tangible qualities of the scientific process sometimes take precedence. These include individual motivation, inspiration, lucky hunches, and even stubborn defiance of prevailing opinion. About the only characteristic that is diametrically opposed to the spirit of science is insistence upon any single set of unquestionable dogmatic beliefs. In the following section, we will consider how and why the social sciences vary in the degree to which they utilize the scientific method.

Social Science Adherence to the Scientific Method

Without delving deeply into the question of what exactly is "knowledge" (this is done in Chapter 19), we can safely say that there are many ways we humans acquire it quite apart from the scientific method. Much knowledge comes from discussions with others and from reading what others have written based on casual observations. Other knowledge may come from inspiration, exploration, and creative thought.

Having described the social sciences and the basic features of the scientific method, we can now address another question: To what degree do the various social sciences normally utilize the scientific method? To answer this question in a completely objective way, a survey would need to be conducted among persons trained in each of the social sciences in which they would be asked detailed questions about the methods they use. Even without this empirical information, however, two social sciences can be identified as minimally utilizing the scientific method: philosophy and history (Carr, 1962:70; Brittain, 1990). This is *not* to imply anything about the value of these two disciplines, but simply to recognize some of the unique features of these two social sciences.

Philosophy, as was noted earlier, lies at the foundation of all science, and certain unprovable philosophical assumptions must be made (at least implicitly) for any science to get under way. Although it is true that, over the centuries, science has gradually encroached upon "philosophical territory"—such as scientific discoveries about the evolutionary origins of humankind (Ruse, 1982)—there are still numerous philosophical issues that the scientific method is poorly equipped to confront. For these reasons, philosophy must to some degree rely on methods that are beyond those used by scientists.

Empirical research is fundamental to history, but the questions that historians address make the scientific method inadequate for their work. As mentioned earlier, historians ask questions about the causes of unique events, whereas other social scientists seek causes of entire categories of events. For example, political scientists and sociologists might generalize about the causes of war, but historians would more typically focus on the causes of a *particular* war.

Another difference between historians and most other social scientists is the minimal use that historians make of statistics. Nevertheless, historians seem to be increasingly utilizing information that can be statistically analyzed (see Rowney & Graham, 1969; Jarausch & Hardy, 1991). A couple examples: Historical research in recent decades has statistically analyzed documents to calculate the ratios of males and females arrested for various crimes in England during the 18th century (Beatie, 1975). Another historical study was undertaken to determine what characteristics distinguished persons who did and did not join Germany's Nazi Party around the time of the Second World War (Kater, 1983). Overall, while most historical research does not rely heavily on the scientific method, there appears to be trends in this direction.

Summary

This introductory chapter contains basic descriptions of the social (and related) sciences and the methods they utilize. Social science includes the following disciplines: anthropology, criminology/criminal justice, economics, geography, history, philosophy, political science, psychology, social work, and sociology. The near social sciences consist of education, ethology, psychiatry, public health, and sociobiology. In addition, three disciplines that are not considered social sciences, although they have increasingly come to incorporate social science methodology, are journalism, advertising and marketing, and home economics.

Seven characteristics of the scientific method were identified to help distinguish the scientific method from all other ways of acquiring human knowledge. The scientific method is (1) empirical, (2) verifiable, (3) cumulative, (4) self-correcting, (5) deterministic, (6) ethically neutral, and (7) statistically generalizable.

Briefly, empirical refers to those things that can be seen, felt, heard, tasted, and smelled. Verifiable means that others are assumed to have the same abilities to make empirical observations as oneself. Cumulative refers to the tendency to go to new questions after several studies have verified the answers to old ones. The self-correcting nature of science means that errors made in empirical observations are eventually identified as such. Determinism is the unprovable assumption that natural, rather than supernatural or by free-will, forces are responsible for whatever it is that scientists set out to understand. Ethical neutrality means that scientists strive not to allow their moral beliefs to bias their empirical observations. Statistical generalizability refers to the tendency by scientists to describe what they have observed using widely agreed-upon statistical rules.

Two of the social sciences utilize the scientific method to a lesser degree than the others: philosophy and history. This does not, however, diminish the important roles that these two disciplines play in understanding the human condition. Philosophy does not rely on the scientific method because it provides the assumptional foundation upon which all knowledge, including scientific knowledge, is based. History does not rely heavily on the scientific method because it focuses on unique aspects of major human events, and does not ordinarily attempt to draw statistical generalizations about numerous similar events.

Notes

[1] Names and dates will appear throughout this text to offer documentation for points that are being made. This is a common practice in scientific writing. Details about these citation practices are described in Chapter 6. The tests will not require you to know the names of any persons cited within parentheses (unless your instructor states otherwise). Names mentioned outside parentheses, however, should be noted for test purposes.

[2] Physical anthropology is sometimes called paleoanthropology (Anonymous, 1992). The prefix *paleo* means very old.

References

Adams, R. (1976). Criminal justice: An emerging academic profession and discipline. *Journal of Criminal Justice, 4,* 303–314.

Anonymous. (1992). Paleoanthropologists launch a society of their own. *Science, 256,* 1281.

Barnouw, V. (1989). *Physical anthropology and archaeology* (5th ed.). Chicago: Dorsey.

Beatie, J. M. (1975). The criminality of women in eighteenth-century England. *Journal of Social History, 9,* 80–116.

Beatty, W. W., & Beatty, P. A. (1970). Hormonal determinants of sex differences in avoidance behavior and reactivity to electric shock in rats. *Journal of Comparative and Physiological Psychology, 73,* 446–455.

Birdsell, J. B. (1987). Some reflections on fifty years of biological anthropology. *Annual Review in Anthropology, 16,* 1–12.

Bornstein, R. F. (1990). Publications politics, experimenter bias and the replication process in social science research. *Journal of Social Behavior and Personality, 5,* 71–81.

Brittain, J. M. (1990). Cultural boundaries of the social sciences in the 1990s; new policies for documentation, information and knowledge creation. *International Social Science Journal, 41,* 105–117.

Brozek, J. (1990). Contributions to the history of psychology, XVII. Early uses of the term "objective psychology." *Perceptual and Motor Skills, 70,* 377–378.

Bunge, M. (1990). What kind of discipline is psychology: Autonomous or dependent, humanistic or scientific, biological or sociological? *New Ideas in Psychology, 8,* 121–137.

Cameron, G. T., Lariscy, R. W., & Sweep, D. D. (1992). Predictors of systematic public relations research in higher education. *Journalism Quarterly, 69,* 466–470.

Campbell, B. G. (1985). *Humankind evolving* (4th ed.). Boston: Little, Brown.

Carr, E. H. (1962). *What is history?* New York: Knopf.

Collias, N. E. (1991). The role of American zoologists and behavioural ecologists in the development of animal sociology, 1934–1964. *Animal Behavior, 41,* 613–631.

Cooper, J. O., Heron, T. E., & Herward, W. L. (1987). *Applied behavior analysis.* Columbus, Ohio: Merrill.

Davis, H. P., Rosenzweig, M. R., Becker, L. A., & Sather, K. J. (1988). Biological psychology's relationship to psychology and neuroscience. *American Psychologist, 43,* 359–371.

Dawkins, R. (1976). *The selfish gene.* New York: Oxford University Press.

Dewsbury, D. A. (1984). *Comparative psychology in the twentieth century.* Stroudsburg, PA: Hutchinson Ross.

Dickinson, W. R. (1971). Letter to the editor. *Science, 173,* 1191–1192.

Eagly, A. H., & Carli, L. L. (1981). Sex of researchers and sex-typed communications as determinants of sex differences in influenceability: A meta-analysis of social influence studies. *Psychological Bulletin, 90,* 1–20.

Ellis, L. (1986). Evidence of neuroandrogenic etiology of sex roles from a combined analysis of human, nonhuman primate, and nonprimate mammalian studies. *Personality and Individual Differences, 7,* 519–552.

Ellis, L. (1988). The victimful-victimless crime distinction, and seven universal demographic correlates of victimful criminal behavior. *Personality and Individual Differences, 9,* 525–548.

Ellis, L., Miller, C., & Widmayer, A. (1988). Content analysis of biological approaches in psychology: 1894 to 1985. *Sociology and Social Research, 72,* 145–149.

Encyclopedia of Sociology. (1981). Guilford, CT: DPG Reference.

Feine, J. S., Bushnell, M. C., Miron, D., & Duncan, G. H. (1991). Sex differences in the perception of noxious heat stimuli. *Pain, 44,* 255–262.

Fowler-Kerry, S., & Lander, J. (1991). Assessment of sex differences in children's and adolescents' self-reported pain from venipuncture. *Journal of Pediatric Psychology, 16,* 783–793.

Fuchs, S., & Turner, J. H. (1986). What makes a science 'mature'?: Patterns of organizational control in scientific production. *Sociological Theory, 4,* 143–150.

Goodall, J. (1990). *Through a window.* Boston: Houghton Mifflin.

Harcum, E. R. (1991). Behavioral paradigm for a psychological resolution of the free will issue. *Journal of Mind and Behavior, 12,* 93–114.

Haviland, W. A. (1991). *Anthropology* (6th ed.). Fort Worth, TX: Holt, Rinehart & Winston.

Jarausch, K. H., & Hardy, K. A. (1991). *Quantitative methods for historians: A guide to research, data, and statistics.* Chapel Hill: University of North Carolina Press.

Kater, M. (1983). *The Nazi Party: A social profile of members and leaders, 1919–1945.* New York: Oxford University Press.

Kavaliers, M., & Innes, D. G. L. (1990). Developmental changes in opiate-induced analgesia in deer mice: Sex and population differences. *Brain Research,* 516, 326–331.

Larsen, C. S., Matter, R. M., & Gebo, D. L. (1991). *Human origins: The fossil record* (2nd ed.). Prospect Heights, IL: Waveland.

Lewin, R. (1988). Linguists search for the mother tongue. *Science, 242,* 1128–1129.

Lieberman, L. (1989). A discipline divided: Acceptance of human sociobiological concepts in anthropology. *Current Anthropology, 30,* 676–682.

Mahoney, M. J. (1987). Scientific publication and knowledge politics. *Journal of Social Behavior and Personality, 2,* 165–176.

Masters, R., & Roberson, C. (1990). *Inside Criminology.* Englewood Cliffs, NJ: Prentice-Hall.

Peoples, J., & Bailey, G. (1991). *Humanity: An introduction to cultural anthropology* (2nd ed.). St. Paul: West.

Phillips, D. P., Kanter, E. J., Bêdnarczyk, B., & Tastad, P.L. (1991). Importance of the lay press in the transmission of medical knowledge to the scientific community. *New England Journal of Medicine, 325,* 1180–1184.

Redmond, D. E., Baulu, J., Murphy, D. L., Loriaux, D. L., & Zeigler, M. (1976). The effects of testosterone on plasma and platelet monoamine oxidase (MAO). *Psychosomatic Medicine, 38,* 315–326.

Relethford, J. (1990). *The human species: An introduction to biological anthropology.* London: Mayfield.

Richard, A. F. (1985). *Primates in nature.* New York: W. H. Freeman.

Rowney, D. K., & Graham, J. Q., Jr. (Eds.). (1969). *Quantitative history: Selected readings in the quantitative analysis of historical data.* Homewood, IL: Dorsey.

Ruse, M. (1982). *Darwinism defended: A guide to the evolution controversies.* Reading, MA: Addison-Wesley.

Ruse, M. (1987). Darwinism and determinism. *Zygon, 22,* 419–442.

Russell, B. (1945). *A history of western philosophy.* New York: Simon & Schuster.

Scupin, R., & DeCorse, C. R. (1992). *Anthropology: A global perspective.* Englewood Cliffs, NJ: Prentice-Hall.

Silberner, J. (1982, August). Cheating in the labs. *Science Digest, 90,* 38–41.

Stokes, J., III. (1974). "Purity" of science. *Science, 185,* 399.

Viney, D. W. (1986). William James on free will and determinism. *Journal of Mind and Behavior, 7,* 555–565.

Wilson, E. O. (1975). *Sociobiology: The modern synthesis.* Cambridge, MA: Harvard University Press.

Suggested Reading*

American Association for the Advancement of Science. (1989). *Social and behavioral sciences: A project 2061 panel report.* Washington, DC: AAAS. (This brief book provides educators and students with a possible view to social and behavioral science education in the next century.)

Boas, M. (1962). *The scientific renaissance, 1450–1630.* New York: Harper & Row. (Presents an easy-reading history of Western scientific thought, including social science thought, as Europe emerges out of the Middle Ages.)

Brittain, J. M. (1990). Cultural boundaries of the social sciences in the 1990s; new policies for documentation, information and knowledge creation. *International Social Science Journal, 41,* 105–117.

Gordon, S. (1991). *A history and philosophy of social science.* London: Routhledge.

Goodall, J. (1990). *Through a window.* Boston: Houghton Mifflin. (Continuing a tradition begun with her bestselling book, *In the shadow of man,* Jane Goodall gives her account of efforts to understand the complex social lives of chimpanzees living in the African rain forest. This is insightful nontechnical reading for any student of social science.)

Ross, D. (1991). *The origins of American social science.* New York: Cambridge University Press. (This book provides an account of how social science developed in America, with a primary focus upon sociology, economics, and political science.)

Sinnott, E. W. (1950). *Cell & psyche*: *The biology of purpose.* New York: Harper & Row. (For students who would like to read a provocative scientific classic that explores some extraordinary possibilities about how the human mind may work, this short book is highly recommended.)

---

*Every chapter of this text contains a suggested reading list of special books and articles, and sometimes entire journals, for those who might want to pursue chapter topics in greater depth. Some of these books and articles are annotated; the others are self-explanatory.

CHAPTER 2

Methods for Locating Research on Specific Topics of Interest

The purpose of this chapter is to acquaint you with the methods available to social scientists for locating research relevant to some topic. To accomplish this, however, you must be familiar with one of the most fundamental concepts in science—the concept of a **variable.** Then you need to know about the four levels at which variables can be measured (or calibrated). Once these two basic notions have been explored, you will be ready to find out how social scientists conduct literature searches on topics of interest.

The Nature of Scientific Variables

Nearly all the phenomena scientists deal with can be boiled down to relationships between variables. *Variables* are empirical phenomena that take on different values or intensities. Any phenomenon that always takes on the same value or intensity is called a **constant** and constants are usually not very interesting to study. A few examples of broad categories of variables that are of major interest to social scientists are attitudes, parenting activities, mental health, personality traits, religiosity, and social status. All these categories of variables take on different values not only between people but within people over time. For example, by any measure of religiosity, some people are more religious than others. Using a variety of measures, studies have shown that, on average, persons in their teens and early twenties tend to be less religious than those in their fifties and sixties (Francis & Pearson, 1987:147).

It is important to know the name of one widely used class of social science variable, those called **demographic variables.** These are variables that pertain to basic human characteristics such as age, sex, marital status, years of education, and income. Demographic variables are a special focus of governmental agencies such as the United States Bureau of the Census and the Canadian Census Bureau. The boundaries defining demographic variables are not precisely drawn. Thus, such variables as religious affiliation, race/ethnicity, and even political party affiliation would often be included as demographic variables, although many governmental agencies do not routinely ask citizens to report such information. This is not only because of the personal nature of such questions, but also because this kind of information has been misused by politicians and governmental policy implementers in the past.

Another important category of variables is *behavioral variables.* These variables pertain to behavior exhibited by humans and other animals. *Emotional, attitudinal, cognitive,* and *mental health/illness* are types of variables closely related to behavior, and usually must be inferred from behavior, but are nonetheless given separate consideration.

Sociocultural variables is another major category of social science interest. These are variables which emanate from behavior, although they are often considered apart from the behavior which produced them. The distinctive feature of sociocultural variables is that they are made possible by two or more organisms interacting rather than from individual activities.

Two more points should be made about variables of interest to social scientists. One is that, while most social scientists are primarily interested in human beings, many are at least secondarily interested in other animals. Second, many social scientists are not simply interested in demographic, behavioral, emotional, attitudinal, cognitive, mental health/illness, and sociocultural variables. They are also interested in variables which, strictly speaking, fall outside the realm of social science. These would include variables relating to physical health, the physical environment, and the food we eat, all of which may affect or be affected by the variables that social scientists primarily study.

In addition, social scientists have become increasingly interested in biological variables, such as those involving the brain (Ellis, Miller, & Widmayer, 1988). The reason for this growing social science interest in the brain is increased recognition of its role in controlling behavior (Leger, 1992).

Conceptual versus Operational Definitions of Variables

Scientists tend to be concerned about carefully defining their variables. To understand this concern, consider the following problem: Two researchers conduct separate studies of some phenomenon and come to inconsistent conclusions. One of the researchers finds that males have more of Variable X than females do, and the second researcher finds the sexes equal with respect to Variable X. Hoping to settle the issue, both researchers conduct new studies, and both confirm their own original findings. What could account for their continued failure to agree with one another? Although there are several possibilities, one of the most basic is that what they both were calling Variable X was actually not the same variable.

To illustrate that such problems can and do arise, imagine that you wanted to determine how many people in some population had one or more forms of mental illness. Or, say you wanted to compare people in terms of their emotional states under various conditions. How could you do so, and then how could you explain your methods in sufficient detail that other researchers could replicate what you found? But, you might say, I'm not really interested in how to measure these variables; I'm much more interested in what causes them. Unfortunately, there is no way to scientifically confirm the causes of something if you can not measure it. Therefore, the challenge of accurately measuring every variable can not be escaped.

Scientists recognize two fairly distinct types of definitions for variables: conceptual definitions and operational definitions. **Conceptual** (also occasionally called **nominal**) **definitions** are typically found in dictionaries. Such definitions normally use familiar terms to describe a word (or phrase) that is unfamiliar. The other type of definition used in science, an **operational definition,** specifies in empirical terms precisely what should be done to observe variations in some variable.

The difference between conceptual and operational definitions can be illustrated by considering a variable used in the physical sciences. Almost everyone has learned that the hardest known substance is the diamond. Consider how such a conclusion was reached. If you looked up the definition of "hardness" in a dictionary, you would find that hardness refers to the degree to which a substance is solid and firm, difficult to break, mold, etc. There is nothing in the conceptual definition of hardness to indicate that, of the millions of substances in the world (including thousands of hard metal alloys), diamonds would be the hardest.

The discovery that diamonds are the hardest of all substances resulted from agreement by physical scientists that the most appropriate way to gauge hardness would involve a simple empirical operation: Scratch a flat surface of one object with an angled corner of another object. In other words, physical scientists have agreed to operationalize "hardness" as follows: Take several objects that all have a flat surface and an edge at the same angle; using identical pressure, run the angled edge of each object along the flat surface of all the other objects. By inspecting the groove made on the surface of each object (usually with a microscope), scientists designate the relative hardness of each object according to the depth of each groove. Thus, hardness can be operationally defined (or operationalized) with a prescribed set of operations that anyone else could replicate and verify. While hardness is not a variable of major interest to social scientists, it does provide a simple and clear example of how scientists think about every variable they study.

Consider for a moment a variable that is of great interest to social scientists, especially those specialized in the study of social stratification (e.g., economists and sociologists)—the variable of "wealth." Conceptually, people comprehend the meaning of wealth; but if you wanted to precisely compare individuals or families, how might you operationalize wealth?

There are, of course, extreme examples in which it would not be necessary to ask people whether they were wealthy. However, since most people are somewhere in a broad middle range, few social scientists would want to trust appearance for assessing people's wealth.

As an alternative to using subjective impressions of wealth, you could operationalize wealth in terms of people's self-reported annual income. There are problems with this approach, however. In addition to the possibilities that some people will decline to answer and others will even lie, there are other serious drawbacks. For example, people who have major land holdings or corporate stock investments may not have earned much in a particular year. Also, what about college students whose annual incomes may be zero, but whose parents are paying all their expenses? There are obviously problems with simply using annual income to measure wealth.

Another operational measure of wealth might involve asking subjects to rate themselves on a 10–point scale where 1 equals extreme poverty and 10 equals extreme wealth. One problem with this method is that people may use different standards for their judgments. For instance, those who come from a small town situated in a poor rural area of the country might be close to 10 from their perspective, but closer to 5 from the standpoint of an economically prosperous urban community.

If the measurement of wealth sounds complicated, imagine the difficulty you would have measuring such concepts as social status and social class. These latter concepts (sometimes used interchangeably, and sometimes not) not only include the concept of wealth, but include other variables such as years of education and occupational prestige (Ellis, 1993:16).

We will be returning to issues in measuring social science variables, especially in Chapters 7 and 8. For now the primary point is that even though you may have a clear conceptual definition in mind for a particular variable, a clear operational definition may be difficult to devise. Both, of course, are important in science.

One last note: no scientific definition is fixed in stone. If a researcher has a good reason for either conceptually or operationally defining a term in a new way, there is no rule or authority in science to prevent it. The criteria that are used to judge the merit of new definitions for variables (especially operational definitions) have to do with how "useful" they happen to be. These matters will be readdressed in Chapter 7.

Levels of Measurement

Any operational definition of a variable must specify how its variability is to be measured. This requires that crucial decisions be made about **levels of measurement** (or **levels of calibration**). According to work pioneered by S. S. Stevens (1946), four levels of measurement may be distinguished. A basic understanding of these levels is important for choosing statistics that are most appropriate for a given set of observations. As these four levels are presented, notice that their order begins with the least complex and ends with the most complex.

The first level of measurement is called **nominal.** Measuring a variable at this level merely involves naming the calibrating units. Examples of variables that are most often measured at this level would be sex, religious preference, political affiliation, college major, and place of birth.

The second level of measurement is called **ordinal.** Measurement at this level involves arranging the calibrating units into a logical order or rank. There are not many clear examples of variables that are measured at this level, but one example is to rank people according to various criteria such as rank in the military or occupational prestige. The key feature of ordinal measurement is that there is an order in the calibrations without any assumption that the distances between each calibrating unit are equal. For example, in academically ranking one's graduating class, there is no reason to assume that the grade point average separating 1st and 2nd place is the same as the grade point average separating 10th and 11th place.

Interval level measurement is the third level. It involves not only having an order to the calibrating units (as in ordinal measurement), but also involves specifying a distance (usually an equal distance) between each successive unit. Many social science variables are measured or assumed to be measured at this level. Examples include time of day, scores on academic achievement tests, and self-rated degree of loneliness on a scale from 1 to 10.

The fourth and most complex level of measurement is **ratio** measurement. It not only specifies a distance between each successive calibration unit, but it also assumes that there is a point at which the variable literally does not exist, and designates this point as zero. Variables such as height and weight are examples.

Measuring variables at the interval or ratio levels has definite advantages over measurement at either the ordinal or nominal level, although not all variables can be measured at the interval or ratio level (Wang & Mahoney, 1991:53). The main advantage is that precise averages can be calculated and compared (along with a number of other statistical operations) on interval and ratio level data, but these calculations cannot be routinely performed on ordinal or nominal variables. To illustrate, answer this question: What was the average sex for the students in your high school graduating class? Such a question is nonsense because sex is measured at a nominal level and the concept of average is not really applicable at this level. (In Chapter 3, more will be said about the concept of average.)

It is important to distinguish levels of measurement from the closely related concepts of **discrete** and **continuous variables.** A discrete variable is one that exists in two or more segments (regardless of how researchers decide to measure it). For example, the variable of sex exists in two segments, and the variable of religious preference exists in terms of the number of religious denominations that there happens to be in a population under study. Normally, discrete variables are measured at either the nominal or the ordinal level.

A continuous variable is one that does not exist in segments, but instead varies gradually from low to high, weak to strong, etc. Examples of continuous variables are age, academic ability, and the degree to which one loves chocolate. Researchers can measure continuous variables at any of the four levels. For example, age could be measured in terms of the categories infant, child, adolescent, and adult (an ordinal level of measurement). This would obviously be cruder than measuring age at the interval level (e.g., years of age). Measuring continuous variables at the interval or ratio levels is more exact and lets researchers apply more precise statistics than measuring continuous variables at the ordinal or nominal levels.

More will be said about these measurement options later. For now, bear in mind that the concept of discrete vs. continuous variables refers to how variables actually exist out there in the real world, whereas the four levels of measurement (or calibration) refer to how variables may be measured. Later, you will see that measurement decisions are based in part on whether a variable is discrete or continuous.

Locating Information on a Topic of Interest

Now that you have a basic understanding of the concept of a variable and of the options scientists have for measuring variables, imagine what you would do if you were interested in knowing more about a particular variable. Say you want to learn more about a variable that social scientists have been studying for years. How would you find out what has already been investigated regarding this variable? To answer this question, you need to become acquainted with scientific abstracts.

Abstract Publications in the Social Sciences

Many students will be amazed by the scientific publications called **abstracts.** These publications contain brief (usually one paragraph) summaries of thousands of articles appearing annually in all the major science disciplines. (It should be noted that each summary itself is also called an abstract.) What is astonishing about these publications is how voluminous and diverse they are in the subjects they cover.

No one really knows how many articles are published in the social sciences every year, partly because the boundaries surrounding the social sciences are fuzzy. Nevertheless, there are thousands of periodicals (usually called **journals**) currently being published worldwide in the social sciences, and these journals publish several dozen articles each year. Most of these articles are summarized in one or more social science abstract publications.

Using the Abstracts

Suppose that you are interested in locating research pertaining to the following simple question: Are teenage mothers more likely to abuse their children than older mothers? If you are not familiar with abstracts, you might attempt to find an answer to this question in the following ways. First, you look through the card catalog or the library's computer files for books on the subject. The main problem with this kind of source is that book titles tend to be general. You would probably find books both on teenage motherhood and on child abuse, but you are not likely to find specific books on how child abuse relates to age of the mother.

Another source for research is a general indexing periodical such as the *Reader's Guide*. This is a useful source for information about articles in popular, general readership magazines. You might find citations in the *Reader's Guide* to articles about maternal age and child abuse. You are likely to be disappointed, however, to find that the articles consist of unsubstantiated opinion, a few anecdotal accounts, and maybe one or two brief quotes from interviews with "experts." If you are interested in reports by people who actually have conducted research on the relationship between maternal age and child abuse, neither card catalogs nor indexes for popular magazines are likely to be of great help.

Few people in the general public are familiar with scientific abstracts; for social scientists, being familiar with them is essential. Any social science abstract that you consult will contain information directing you to the results of research on very specific topics. The abstracts normally consist of twelve monthly installments, called issues, which are bound into a volume at the end of each year along with an annual index. Because the major abstracts cost hundreds of dollars per year, nearly all subscribers are libraries rather than individual scientists.

The most widely used abstract publications in the social sciences are the *Psychological Abstracts* and the *Sociological Abstracts*. Some of the more specialized abstract publications include *Child Development Abstracts, Criminal Justice Abstracts, Education Resource Information Clearinghouse (ERIC), Psychopharmacology Abstracts, Social Work Abstracts,* and *Women's Studies Abstracts.*

There is some overlap in the journals covered by the various abstract publications. In other words, most social science articles will be abstracted in more than one abstract publication. This is especially true of articles published in the interdisciplinary social science journals (for examples, see Appendix A).

There are two ways to search the abstracts. First you will learn to do a manual search (i.e., search the actual bound volumes). Then you will learn to conduct what are called electronic (or computer) searches.

Manual Searches of Abstract Publications

All abstract publications consist of two main parts: the abstracts (or article summaries) themselves and the indexes. One index is by author and will not concern us here, and the other index is by subject matter.

Let's go back to the question about whether child abuse is more common among teenage mothers than among older mothers. To search the abstracts for relevant information, you would begin by identifying the key terms (or variables) in your question. For this particular question, there are two variables: child abuse and maternal age (or age of mother). Variables like these are identified in the index of most abstract publications. They typically appear as a heading, which is followed by a number of subheadings. The subheadings refer to variables related to the heading. For example, you might find child abuse listed as follows:

> *Child Abuse* (also see Child Neglect)
>   Alcohol use by the parent, 5643
>   Childhood conduct disorders, 647
>   Divorce, custody disputes, 15331
>   Maternal age, 835
>   Poverty, 12243
>   Stepparents, 1186
>   Teenage pregnancy, 5958

The number following each subheading refers to a specific abstract, and thereby an article which linked that particular subheading to child abuse. Notice that you would want to jot down two numbers: the one following maternal age and the one following teenage pregnancy. It might also be worthwhile to check the child neglect heading, and see if there is a heading for maternal age as well, before turning to the abstract entries themselves.

Locate one of the abstract entries whose number appeared in the index and read through the abstract to confirm (or disconfirm) that it is of relevance to your question. If the article appears relevant, you may want to obtain a copy so you can read more of the details. The most common procedures for getting copies of articles will be outlined after a brief discussion of electronic searches.

Other publications used in the social sciences for identifying articles of interest are called **index publications.** Index publications differ from abstract publications in that there are no article summaries in index publications; thus, only the title is available to give you an indication of an article's coverage. The main index publication in the social sciences is called the Social Science Index.

Electronic Searches of Abstract and Index Publications

Since the mid-1980s, many abstract and index publications are being "published" either on large mainframe computers or on laser disks (called CD ROM) that can be accessed by computers. Either system electronically scans with lightning speed for both single or multiple key phrases, much as you would do visually in a manual search. Electronic searches of the abstracts can be carried out more rapidly than manual searches. The downside with electronic searches, however, is that they may overlook options that often catch a researcher's eye as he or she is visually scanning a manual index.

You can imagine how electronic searches work by thinking of an entire abstract publication existing as microscopic electronic impulses on high density laser disks. Then imagine an incredibly rapid and fine scanner canvassing one of these disks for key phrases. Each time it locates a key phrase, it has made a "hit," and the abstracts corresponding to each hit are electronically duplicated in a special temporary memory storage cell in the computer. At the end of the search (which usually takes less than a minute), the user is told how many hits were made; the user can then ask to see each of the abstracts, either on the computer terminal screen or printed out on paper (called a hard copy).

As the technology surrounding electronic searches continues to improve, manual abstract publications may become a thing of the past. For now, however, all social science students should have some experience conducting manual searches. If you have access to equipment for conducting electronic searches, get some experience with this, too. (You may need a few minutes of help from a reference librarian the first time you conduct an electronic search.)

The main electronic searching systems currently available are:

British Education Index
Criminal Justice Periodicals Index
ERIC (Educational Resources Information Clearinghouse)

Expanded Academic Index
Family Resources
National Criminal Justice Resources Services (NCJRS)
PAIS (Public Affairs Information Service) International
Population Bibliography
PsychINFO
Religion Index
Social Science Index
Sociological Abstracts
U.S. Political Science Documents

It is likely that your college or university library allows student access to their available computerized systems. All of the systems identified above cover referenced (as opposed to popular) articles and books, and they are all controlled by similar command procedures.

Scientists who are active in research sometimes use a recently developed alternative to both manual and electronic abstracts. They subscribe to a weekly publication called *Current Contents for the Social and Behavioral Sciences.* This publication presents the Table of Contents for over 1,300 journals throughout the world, plus subject and author indexes. The author index contains addresses, allowing users to write to authors for copies of their articles.

How to Get Copies of Articles of Interest

There are three main ways to get copies of scientific articles. The most obvious method is to locate the article in the periodical section of your library. If necessary, check with the librarian about the procedure; you will find that most libraries have a master list of all the periodicals to which they subscribe.

If your library does not subscribe to the journal you want, you may get a copy of the article through what is called interlibrary loan. To secure articles (or books) through interlibrary loan, just complete a form giving your name and address, the author and title of the article being requested, and the name of the journal as well as the year of publication, volume number, and page numbers. Ask any college or university librarian for a form.

The third method is one that you should not routinely use, especially for class projects. Nevertheless, it is good to be aware of it as you begin your professional career. This method is to request copies of articles directly from the authors. These copies are called **reprints.** Technically, reprints are printed tearsheets of an article printed by the publisher of the journal in which the article appeared, but in a broader sense, reprints also include photocopies of articles that authors send to interested fellow scientists. We will use reprint here in the broader sense.

Soon after publishing an article in a scientific journal, the author (or the senior author of an article by multiple authors) may begin receiving reprint requests from other researchers (often from remote parts of the world). It is customary, although certainly not mandatory for authors to comply with these requests, especially if the article appeared in a journal which is not readily available in many small libraries. Sending out these reprints ensures that persons who are interested in the research can read the article; many times it also helps to initiate communication between researchers with common interests.

Corresponding with a researcher may be easier than you think. In most cases, all that is needed is the name of the university at which the author is located. The city, state, and zip code for domestic universities can be obtained from any library, and are often listed in the back of dictionaries. Campus mail rooms may also prefer to have a department listed, but this is not a necessity.

If the institutional affiliation happens to be a government agency, you can indicate the name of the agency following the researcher's name, and then write "State Office Building" followed by the name of the state and the state's capital city.

Summary

This chapter has been designed to familiarize you with basic terminology and procedures used in social science: the nature of scientific variables, and how to locate specific information about those variables.

Two types of definitions for variables were distinguished: conceptual definitions and operational definitions. The former refers to "dictionary" definitions, and the latter refers to "empirically verifiable" definitions. Together, these two types of definitions help to ensure that the same variables are under scrutiny in different studies. When two studies ostensibly fail to agree upon a finding, one of the first possibilities to consider is that the studies were not working with the same variable in operational terms.

There are four levels at which variables may be calibrated (measured or scaled). The simplest (or lowest level) is nominal calibration. All that is required at this level is to name the calibrating units without making any assumptions about how they should be arranged relative to one another. In ordinal measurement of a variable, the calibrating units are arranged in an order relative to one another, but without concern for the varying distances which may exist between each unit. Interval measurement requires that an equal distance exist between each of the calibration units. And ratio measurement meets the requirement of interval measurement, plus it assumes that zero represents the complete absence of the variable.

The final topic of this chapter pertained to locating scientific information on a specific variable or on a specific relationship between two or more variables. You were introduced to abstract publications and shown how to consult them for citations to articles published on many different variables. This chapter also discussed three ways that you can obtain scientific articles of interest: from the library, via interlibrary loan, and from the author(s).

References

Ellis, L. (1993). Operationally defining social stratification in human and nonhuman animals. In L. Ellis (Ed.), *Social stratification and socioeconomic inequality: A comparative biosocial analysis.* (pp. 15–35). New York: Praeger.

Ellis, L., Miller, C., & Widmayer, A. (1988). Content analysis of biological approaches in psychology: 1894 to 1985. *Sociology and Social Research, 72,* 145–149.

Francis, L. J., & Pearson, P. R. (1987). Empathic development during adolescence: Religiosity, the missing link? *Personality and Individual Differences, 8,* 145–148.

Leger, D. W. (1992). *Biological foundations of behavior.* New York: HarperCollins.

Stevens, S. S. (1946). On the theory of scales of measurement. *Science, 103,* 677–680.

Wang, M., and Mahoney, B. (1991). Scales and measurement revisited. *Health Values, 15,* 52–56.

Suggested Reading

Barzun, J., & Graff, H. F. (1970). *The modern researcher.* New York: Harcourt Brace Jovanovich.

Bogardus, E. S. (1960). *The development of social thought* (4th ed.). New York: David McKay.

CHAPTER 3

Univariate Statistics: Measures of Central Tendency and Variable Dispersion

W hen you were in junior high school, would you have been affected by the way a teacher dressed? For example, would you have been more likely to pay attention in class or do your homework for, say, a male teacher who regularly wore a suit and tie rather than jeans and a T-shirt? A recent study was conducted in Canada in which 200 junior high students reported on what they thought "a friend" would do under these two conditions (Davis et al., 1992). After exploring some fundamental statistical concepts, it will be possible to carefully consider the findings from this study.

This and the next two chapters will acquaint you with statistical concepts that are vital for learning how to conduct social science research. For those who have already had a course in statistics, these three chapters will reiterate and extend concepts you have already learned. If you have not yet taken a course in statistics, these chapters will outline a number of essential concepts with which you need to become familiar in order to grasp the role of statistics in social science research methodology.

Strictly speaking, mathematics is not a science. Whereas science fundamentally deals with empirical phenomena (as discussed in Chapter 1), mathematics deals mainly with ideas, principally in the form of numbers and functional relationships between numbers. Science and mathematics have become intimately linked over the past few centuries because mathematical concepts are useful for describing many aspects of the empirical world. The mathematical concepts that social scientists use the most are referred to as **statistics.**

Becoming familiar with basic statistical concepts without actually learning the formulas is not as difficult as it may seem. It is like learning how to drive an automobile without ever finding out exactly how the engine works. The statistical concepts that are the focus of this chapter are **univariate statistics.** These are statistics in which a single variable varies along a single dimension.

Measures of Central Tendency

The word **average** is in every English-speaking person's vocabulary, but few people outside of science and mathematics are aware that the term has at least three distinct meanings. Because of the term's different meanings, people are sometimes misled when discussing averages. To give an example, the average income of workers in the United States during the mid-1980s was more than $30,000 per year even though only about one third of the American workers earned an income that high (U.S. Bureau of the Census, 1984; also see Smith, 1991, p. 128). This may sound like double talk, but once you understand the differences in the concept of average, this seemingly contradictory statement can be easily explained. We will return to it later in this chapter.

An average can be defined as a measure of central tendency. This concept can be most meaningfully applied to variables that are measured at an interval or ratio level. The term may be relevant to some ordinal data, but rarely is it applied to nominal data. To comprehend the concept of average, think about variables distributed within a graph called a **frequency distribution curve.** The characteristics of a frequency distribution curve are simple: Along the vertical axis (called the **Y-axis**) is represented the number of observations (or sometimes the percentage of a population), and along the horizontal axis (called the **X-axis**), the different values of some variable are represented. Figure 3.1 represents a frequency distribution curve in which a special kind of curve—called a **normal** (or **bell-shaped**) **curve**—is represented.

A frequency distribution curve allows you to determine how many subjects got a particular score. Thus, in Figure 3.1, you can see that at Point A, 75 subjects got a score of 1.5 and at Point B, 125 subjects got a score of 3.3. Few frequency distribution curves have a shape that is so perfectly normal as this one, but many are sufficiently close to such a bell shape as to warrant assuming that, if they had been based on very large samples (i.e., many thousands of subjects), they would be normally distributed. Within the context of various frequency distribution curves, three types of averages can be delineated.

■ FIGURE 3.1

A frequency distribution curve based on hypothetical data.

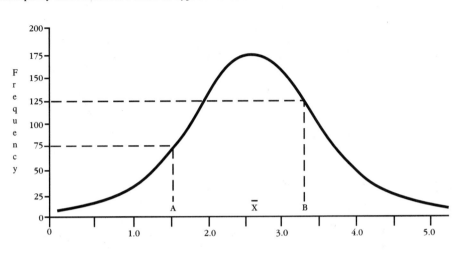

The Mean

The concept of average that people are most familiar with is called the **mean.** It is defined as the result of adding up the values (or scores) of some variable for a group of subjects, and then dividing the total by the number of subjects. Another name for this type of average is the **arithmetic average.** In a normal distribution (such as the one in Figure 3.1), the mean would be located at the highest point in the middle of the curve, directly above the **X** with a bar over it (sometimes the capital letter **M** is also used).

The Mode

The second type of average (or measure of central tendency) is called the **mode.** Mode means "hump" or "peak." (When you order pie *a la mode,* you have not asked for pie with "ice cream on top," but literally for pie with "a hump on top".) The mode is defined as the most frequently observed score (or set of scores, if similar scores are grouped together) in a distribution curve. Obviously, for a curve that is normally distributed (as in Figure 3.1), the mode would be in the same location as the mean. So you may wonder why there are separate concepts if the mode and the mean are in the same place. The answer is that not all distribution curves are normally distributed (bell-shaped).

Look at the frequency distribution curve in Figure 3.2. This curve is **bimodal** because it has two modes rather than one. Let's say that you conduct a survey among persons attending a convention comprised of professional racehorse jockeys and

■ **FIGURE 3.2**

A bimodal frequency distribution curve based on hypothetical data.

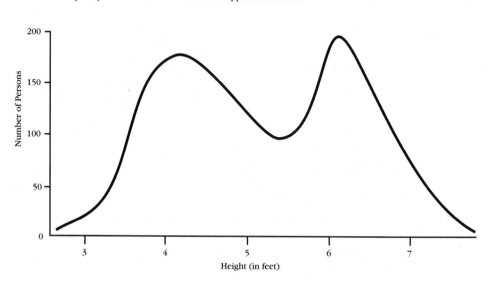

basketball players. If you ask all the attendees their heights and plot the results on a frequency distribution curve, you will probably get a distribution that is bimodal (i.e., has two peaks).

If you calculate the mean height for this population, it will be somewhere around 5'5". This figure will obviously be misleading to anyone who associates "average" with what is most typical of a population. In this case, you would tell readers that, for this population, the sample was bimodally distributed, and that one peak was at 4.1 and the other was at 6.2.

Although the example of a convention of racehorse jockeys and basketball players is obviously contrived, there are times when variables are bimodally distributed within real populations. In the field of evolutionary biology, for example, as two new species or breeds begin to diverge from a common ancestral stock, there is a time during the transition when some of the traits for the diverging population will take on a bimodal distribution. Also, at least one study found females exhibited a bimodal distribution in a test of spatial reasoning (Kail, Carter, & Pellegrino, 1979).

The Median

The third type of average commonly recognized in science is the median. It is simply defined as the 50th percentile (or the midpoint) in a set of numbers that have been arranged in ascending order. More technically, the median is the point along the X-axis above which and below which one half of the distribution is found. Referring back to Figure 3.1, you can see that the point above which and below which half of

■ **FIGURE 3.3**

Distribution in annual income for United States workers, 1982. (From U.S. Department of Commerce, 1984.)

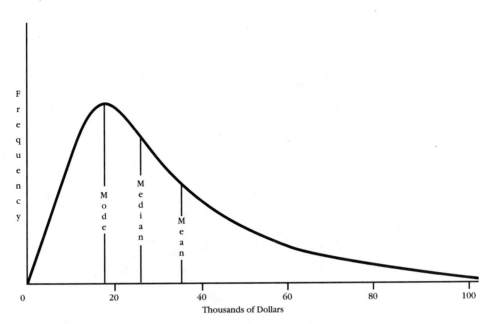

the sample is located on the X-axis would be at exactly the same location as the mean and mode. So again you may wonder why this third type of average is necessary. The answer is that there are certain types of distribution curves for which neither the concepts of the mean nor the mode are appropriate.

Figure 3.3 is an example of a distribution curve that is better described in terms of a median than either of the other two measures of central tendency. This curve is said to be **skewed**, and the direction of the skew is toward the higher values, where the curve tapers off more gradually. Although it is true that the central tendency for this figure could be described in terms of the mode, modes have a tendency to be unstable in that values can be easily shifted higher or lower by a relatively few chance observations.

Remember the seemingly contradictory statement made earlier about how the average income of U.S. workers during the 1980s was more than $30,000, even though fewer than one third of the U.S. workers had incomes this high? Figure 3.3 shows how this statement can be and, in fact, is true. For skewed distributions, the mean is substantially higher than the median. If you take all the money earned in a given year in the U.S. and divide it by the number of wage earners, you will find that a relatively few workers making large salaries (e.g., those making over $100,000 per year) would cause the mean to be pulled to the right to a substantial degree relative to the median and especially relative to the mode.

■ **FIGURE 3.4**

Duration of marriages that ended in divorce in the United States in 1979. (Data from U.S. Department of Health and Human Services, 1984; Graph adapted from Fisher, 1991:111.)

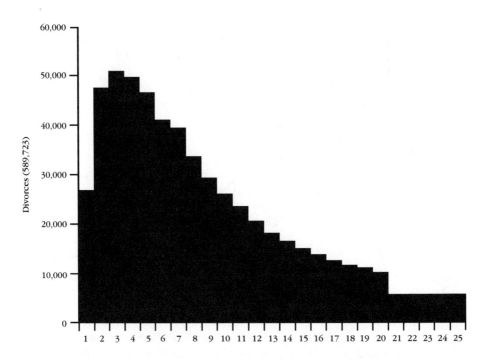

The mode, on the other hand, might be easily shifted from one year to the next by changes in minimum wage laws. This is why most government officials use the median as the best way to represent average income. It is derived by arranging all earnings in ascending order, and then counting either forward or backward until you reach one half of the work force.

Frequency distribution curves that are at least slightly skewed are fairly common, although they are less common than normally distributed curves. Variables linked to age—such as the age distribution of persons in most countries, or the age distribution of persons involved in crime—are nearly always skewed distributions.

Figure 3.4 presents a second example of a skewed distribution. It is based on records of divorces granted in the United States in 1984, and shows the number of years people were married before they divorced.

Based upon Figure 3.4, what would you tell someone who asked you, "What was the average number of years of marriage for persons who got divorced in 1984?" Obviously, you would need to inform the person who asked you that the distribution was substantially skewed, and that the answer depended on what they meant by average. If the person was trained in social science, you could then explain that the mode was at three years, the median was around seven years, and the mean

■ **FIGURE 3.5**

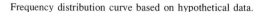

Frequency distribution curve based on hypothetical data.

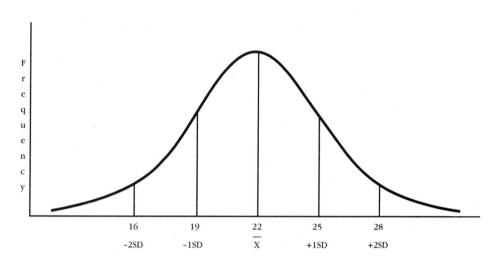

was in the vicinity of ten years. If the person who asked you was not trained in social science, it would probably be best if you just said that roughly half the divorces were obtained before seven years, and the other half after that time.

Incidentally, the preceding paragraph helps to illustrate an important general point: Always keep your audience in mind when you are providing scientific information. Your purpose should *not* be to show how much you know about a topic, but to convey as much information as possible, given the level at which your audience will understand that information.

Concepts of Dispersion

The other major feature of a frequency distribution curve is called **dispersion.** This concept refers to the degree to which scores are tightly or loosely scattered about the measure of central tendency (i.e., mean, mode, or median). Various ways of measuring dispersion have been developed. The most widely used by far is standard deviation.

Standard Deviation

For variables that are normally distributed, a useful shorthand way of describing dispersion has been devised. Because normally distributed variables are so prevalent, this standardized measure of dispersion has numerous statistical applications.

To perceive a standard deviation, look at Figure 3.5, and imagine that it is a slide and you are located at its summit (the mean). Notice that, as you descend down the slope (in either direction), you would reach a point when the curve stops bending

■ **FIGURE 3.6**

A frequency distribution curve based on hypothetical data.

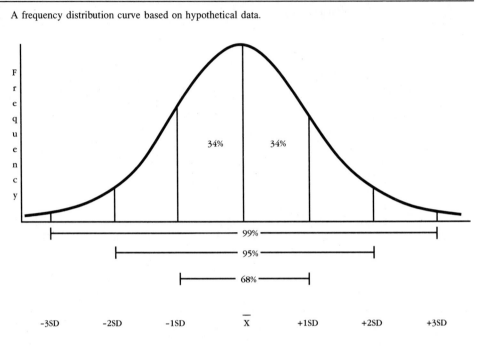

outward (convexed) and begins bending inward (concaved). If you draw a vertical line through that point so that the line intersects the X-axis, the distance between that line and the mean is called **standard deviation.**

The most common symbols used to represent the standard deviation are **s, SD,** and σ. In statistics, there are rules for differentiating these symbols that are not relevant to the present discussion. For this text, we will use the symbol SD. There are specific mathematical formulas in statistics that are used to calculate the standard deviation. However, for purposes of this text, you only need to have a mental picture of standard deviations.

Using the numbers shown along the X-axis of Figure 3.5, note that the mean is at approximately 22, and the standard deviation is about 3. Thus, if you start at the mean and begin counting up, you encounter **+1SD** at 25, **+2SD** at 28, etc. Similarly, counting back from the mean (i.e., to the left), you encounter **–1SD** at 19, **–2SD** at 16, etc.

To understand the power of standard deviation in conjunction with the mean, you should know that it is possible to construct any normal curve simply by knowing the curve's mean and standard deviation. Figure 3.6 makes this point clear. Mathematically, it had been determined that 34% (one third) of an entire population will get a score between the mean and the first standard deviation on either side of the mean. Thus, two thirds of the scores for a normally distributed variable will fall between the first standard deviation on both sides of the mean. Close to 95% of the scores will fall within the first two standard deviations. And, for all practical purposes, all scores for a normally distributed variable are captured by three standard deviations (although theoretically, a normal curve of distribution never intersects with the X-axis).

By knowing the few numbers represented in Figure 3.6, it is possible to make a number of deductions about scores for any normally distributed variable simply from knowing the mean and standard deviation. Consider the following simple illustration. You read an article which reports that the mean was 30 and the standard deviation was 5 for scores on a social science exam. If 200 students took the test, you can now figure out how many students got a score higher than 40. The answer is roughly 2½% of 200, or 5. You get this answer by plugging in 30 as the mean of your normal curve, and noting that 40 would come at the second positive standard deviation (since the standard deviation is 5). Because only 2½% of the population remains beyond the second standard deviation, you multiply .025 times 200 students. Of course, because a variable may not be perfectly normally distributed, you may find that there were actually a few more or a few less than 5 students who got scores higher than 40. See if you can determine how many of these 200 students got scores below 25, and got scores between 25 and 30.

The mean and standard deviation are fundamental concepts in social science that you will find in nearly every research report that you read. In fact, many statistics used in the social sciences (and the biological sciences as well) are rooted in these two concepts.

Other Measures of Dispersion

There are other measures of dispersion that you will encounter when reading research reports. One is called the **range.** If the variable is being measured at the interval or ratio level, the range is defined as the top value for a variable minus the bottom value. This simple concept of dispersion has limited utility because it is quickly altered by one unusually high or low value. Any extremely unusual score in a variable's distribution is called an **outlier.**

Another measure of dispersion is called the **variance.** It is defined as the standard deviation squared. Scientists use the concept of variance as a conservative indicator of the entire spread of a population with respect to scores on a variable.

Describing the dispersion of scores for variables that are skewed, bimodally distributed, or otherwise not bell-shaped is less standardized than for normally distributed variables. The most common measure of dispersion of nonnormally distributed variables divides the distribution into **quartiles.** Quartiles are calculated by arranging all the scores in order, and then counting until you reach the interval containing one fourth, one half, and three fourths of the population. If this sounds reminiscent of procedures used to determine the median, it is because the median and the second quartile are the same thing, i.e., the 50th percentile. While quartiles are a cruder measure of dispersion than the standard deviation (and the variance), the concept of quartiles can be applied in meaningful ways to a diversity of irregularly shaped distribution curves.

Illustrating the Concepts of Averages and Dispersions

Below are a couple examples of studies whose findings can be reasonably well interpreted with nothing more than the concepts of mean and standard deviation in mind. The first example was alluded to at the beginning of this chapter.

Students' Responses to How Teachers Are Dressed

To assess how dress might alter the respect male teachers get from students, 200 junior high school students were shown one of two different photographs of the same male teacher. In one photograph the teacher was formally dressed in business suit and tie, and in the other photograph he was casually dressed in a T-shirt and jeans. The answers from 12 of the students were not used because they did not fill out the questionnaire properly, making the final sample 92 students who saw the teacher formally dressed and 96 students who saw him casually dressed.

The students were asked 12 specific questions about how they thought a good friend or classmate would respond to the teacher whose picture they were shown. The questions included "Would your friend do assignments given by him?," "Make smart remarks to him?," "Disrupt the class?," "Pay attention in his class?," etc. Students answered each question on a 5-point scale ranging from "definitely not" to "definitely."

In coding the returned questionnaires, the researchers assigned numbers from 1 to 5 to the responses (with 5 meaning more respect) and then summed these 12 responses as a final index of respect. Thus, the scores on each student's respect rating ranged from a low of 12 to a high of 60. A summary of the results is presented in Table 3.1.

Try to answer the following two questions based upon Table 3.1: Which type of dress elicited the greatest overall respect score from the students? What percentage of students rated the casual dress with a respect score over 40? Hint: Go back to Figure 3.6 and write 33.6 at the mean and 39.9 (which you get by adding 7.3 to 33.6) at the first standard deviation.

The answer to the first question should be obvious. Although there was not much difference, formal dress elicited a respect score three points higher than the casual dress.

Table 3.1 Average "Respect" Score for Junior High School Teacher Who Was Formally versus Casually Dressed

	Formal Dress	*Casual Dress*
Mean	36.6	33.6
Standard Deviation	6.6	7.3
N	92	96

■ **FIGURE 3.7**

Frequency distributions of total conservatism scores for males and females. (Adapted from Sidanius & Ekehammar, 1980:20.)

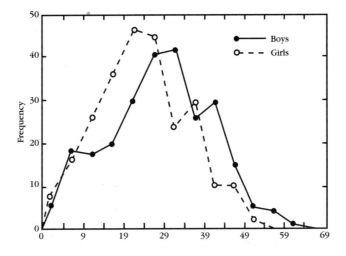

We are assuming in the second question that the responses were normally distributed. First you can deduce that 50% of the subjects gave the photograph of casual dress a 33.6 or higher. Recall that 34% of a sample on a normally distributed variable will score between the mean and the first standard deviation (each way). This leaves 16% of the sample beyond the first standard deviation. By adding the mean of 33.6 plus the standard deviation of 7.3, you get 39.9; and you can say that 16% of the students gave the photograph of casual dress a respect score higher than 40.

Sex Differences in Attitudinal Conservatism

To further solidify your thinking about averages and dispersions, consider results from a study conducted a few years ago among a group of high school students in Sweden. These students were asked questions designed to assess sex differences in attitudinal conservatism (Sidanius & Ekehammar, 1980). While females were found to be more conservative than males on some topics, overall there was a slightly greater tendency for males to respond conservatively than females. This slight difference is shown in Figure 3.7.

The distribution curve in Figure 3.7 is based on a sample size of 254 males and 253 females. Notice how both the distribution curves approximate normality.

To test your understanding up to this point, examine Figure 3.7 and then circle your answers to the following questions (answers are at the end of the chapter):

1. Without doing any addition or division, visually estimate the mean for the male sample. Do not actually calculate the mean. (Hint: It helps to draw a line where the mean is located.)
   A. 28.65
   B. 5.45
   C. 46.87
   D. 39.11
   E. 14.24

2. Again, without doing any calculations, guess the mean for the female sample.
   A. 18.19
   B. 24.43
   C. 8.98
   D. 58.10
   E. 34.44

3. Which of the two curves is slightly skewed, and what is the direction of the skew?
   A. There appears to be no difference.
   B. The male distribution curve is slightly more positively skewed than that of the female.
   C. The female distribution curve is slightly more positively skewed than that of the male.
   D. The male distribution curve is slightly more negatively skewed than that of the female.
   E. The female distribution curve is slightly more negatively skewed than that of the male.

4. What is the standard deviation for males, assuming that the curve is normally distributed? (Hint: It may be helpful to draw a line where you envision the first positive and the first negative standard deviations to be, and then use the average distance of those two points from the mean to locate the correct answer.)
   A. 4.11
   B. 1.44
   C. 23.31
   D. 12.63
   E. 33.89

5. What is the standard deviation for females? Assume normality for the female distribution curve, albeit this is less justified than in the male distribution curve.
   A. 3.01
   B. 38.54
   C. 24.19
   D. 49.06
   E. 11.02

Summary

This chapter has been designed to familiarize you with the basic logic of certain fundamental statistical concepts without taking you through the underlying mathematics. In particular, this chapter has explored basic statistical concepts that are used to give scientists a snapshot picture of the variables they deal with in a study. The focus has been on two statistical concepts: central tendencies and dispersion. Fortunately, most variables are sufficiently close to being normally distributed that scientists are justified in limiting their attention to means and standard deviations.

The mean is derived by adding up all the scores obtained for a variable and then dividing the sum by the number of individuals in the study. This is the preferred measure of central tendency as long as the variable under consideration is close to being normally distributed. Nearly all variables that are not normally distributed are either skewed and/or multimodal. For variables with skewed distributions, the median and the mode are the preferred measures of central tendency. For multimodal distributions, the researcher identifies where the major modes are located.

Regarding *standard deviation,* students should remember that roughly one third of any normally distributed population will be found within the first standard deviation on *each* side of the mean, and that about 95% of the population will be found within the first two standard deviations on *both* sides of the mean. In statistics courses, students learn how to precisely calculate these and many other proportions of the population under normal curves of distribution.

The concepts introduced in this chapter make it possible for you to understand some of the most common statistics used in research reports. The next two chapters will continue to acquaint you with the basic ways that social scientists use statistical concepts.

References

Davis, B., Clarke, A. R. B., Francis, J., Hughes, G., MacMillan, J., McNeil, J., & Westhaver, P. (1992). Dress for respect: The effect of teacher dress on student expectations of deference behavior. *Alberta Journal of Educational Research, 38,* 27–31.

Fisher, H. (1991). Monogamy, adultery, and divorce in cross-species perspective. In M. H. Robinson and L. Tiger (Eds.), *Man & beast revisited* (pp. 95–126). Washington, DC: Smithsonian.

Kail, R., Carter, P., & Pellegrino, J. (1979). The locus of sex differences in spatial ability. *Perception and Psychophysics, 26,* 182–186.

Sidanius, J., & Ekehammar, B. (1980). Sex-related differences in socio-political ideology. *Scandinavian Journal of Psychology, 21,* 17–26.

Smith, S. A. (1991). Sources of earnings inequality in the black and white female labor forces. *Sociological Quarterly, 32,* 117–138.

United States Department of Commerce, Bureau of the Census. (1984). *Current population reports, series P-60, no. 142. Money income of households, families and persons in the United States: 1982.* Washington, DC: U.S. Government Printing Office.

United States Department of Health and Human Services. (1984). *Vital statistics of the United States, 1979. Volume 3: Marriage and divorce.* Hyattsville, MD: U.S. Government Printing Office.

Suggested Reading

Hacking, I. (1991). *The taming of chance.* New York: Cambridge University Press. (Highly recommended to students who are interested in a delightful account of how probability theory and the concept of a normal curve of distribution developed over the past few centuries.)

Zeisel, H. (1968). *Say it with figures.* New York: Harper & Row. (Provides useful advice on how to clearly convey basic statistical information to readers.)

Correct answers to the multiple choice questions: 1. A; 2. B; 3. C; 4. D; 5. E.

Bivariate Statistics and the Concept of Correlation

In societies where it is not illegal to have more than one wife, what do you think is the best predictor of how many wives a man will have? In industrialized countries, are couples who have no children, or only a few, more or less likely to divorce than couples who have many children? Is being abused as a child related to the probability of abusing (or at least using) drugs later in life? These are some of the questions that will be addressed in this chapter. But first you need to become acquainted with one of the most widely used statistical concepts in social science.

The types of statistics outlined in Chapter 3 are used by social scientists to describe how single variables are distributed. However, what if you wanted to talk about how one variable is related to a second variable? In this case, simply knowing about averages and measures of dispersion would not be sufficient. What you would need is a type of statistic that permits you to compare the degree to which two variables have something in common. These statistics are called **bivariate statistics,** and they are exemplified by **correlations.**

This chapter will explore this widely used type of statistic, which researchers use to depict how two variables relate. As the concept of correlation is described, look for the beauty contained in the simplicity and power of this statistic. As in Chapter 3, the emphasis here will be on the logic and the use of correlations in research, not on the formulas needed in their calculation.

Background

In the mid-1700s, a French philosopher-mathematician named Rene Descartes (pronounced de cart') deduced that it was possible to describe geometric shapes with equations. This helped to bring about such fields of mathematics as algebra and calculus. It also laid some of the intellectual foundation for statistics that can show how variables are related to one another. These are called **correlational statistics.** As this chapter will show, correlation converts numbers derived from empirical observations into a single number that can then be meaningfully interpreted (provided some notes of caution are kept in mind).

Two English social scientists are credited with developing the most popular correlational statistic used today. The first of the two scientists was Francis Galton. Late in the 1800s, he began working with ways of describing relationships between variables. A few years later, Galton's work was elaborated and refined by a former student, Karl Pearson. Pearson devised the formula that is still used today for representing relationships between variables.

The Concept of a Scattergram

A **scattergram** is a graph that can be used to represent how two variables measured at the interval or ratio levels are related to one another. To envision the construction of a scattergram, imagine that you were desperate for something to do and decided to conduct a study to find out whether people's shoe size and age are related. Because sex is related to shoe size, assume that you confined your study to males, and that you were very anxious to know the results so you stopped collecting data after five subjects. Say that you got the following results:

Subjects	Shoe Size	Age
Sam	8	15
Bill	13	20
Mike	5	10
Jim	5	13
Dave	10	18

To represent this simple set of data in a scattergram, you first draw the axes for a graph, and assign one of the variables (say shoe size) to the Y-axis (vertical axis) and the other variable (age) to the X-axis (horizontal axis). Next you calibrate each axis to include the entire range of scores for the two variables. This is shown in Figure 4.1. Also shown in this graph is the data plotted with the name of each subject beside the point representing his location with reference to the two variables. (The number appearing after the "r" can be ignored for the moment. It will be explained later in this chapter.)

■ **FIGURE 4.1**

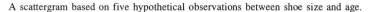

A scattergram based on five hypothetical observations between shoe size and age.

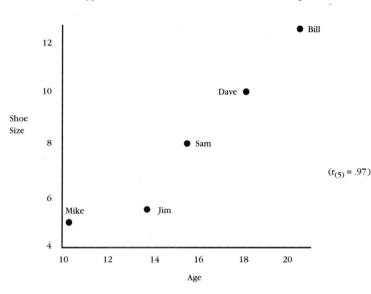

From this scattergram, consider the following question: Does there appear to be a relationship between shoe size and age? An affirmative answer comes from inspecting Figure 4.1 and noticing that there is a strong tendency for those who scored low on the variable of shoe size (Mike and Jim) to have also scored low on the variable of age. Likewise, those who scored high on shoe size (Dave and especially Bill) also scored high on age. This sort of pattern is referred to as a **positive relationship** (or a **positive correlation**). More formally, a positive relationship is one in which increasing values of one variable are associated with increasing values of another variable.

Let us now turn to another set of hypothetical data, this time going directly to the scattergram instead of beginning with a table of numbers showing the actual observations. Figure 4.2 represents the relationship between Variable M and Variable N. As with Figure 4.1, the question you should answer after examining this graph is: Does there appear to be a relationship between these two variables? Your answer again should be yes. However, notice that in Figure 4.2 subjects who scored high on Variable M are scoring low on Variable N and vice versa. This relationship is said to be **negative** (or **inverse**). Stated more formally, an inverse (or negative) correlation is one in which increasing values of one variable are associated with decreasing values of the other variable.

Something else is noteworthy about Figure 4.2: All five observations fall *perfectly* along a straight line (as opposed to simply coming close as in Figure 4.1). When this occurs, the correlation is said to be perfect.

■ FIGURE 4.2

A scattergram based on five hypothetical observations of scores on Variables M and N.

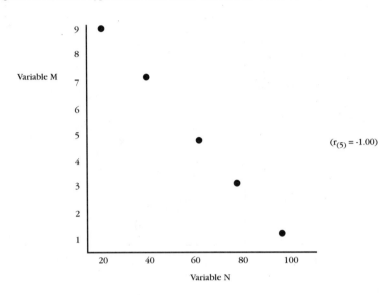

Converting Scattergrams into Correlation Coefficients

Numbers used to represent correlations are called **correlation coefficients.** The coefficient used to represent a perfect negative correlation is −1.00, and for a perfect positive correlation, a +1.00 (the plus sign is normally just understood rather than specified). As one might suspect, there are few perfect correlations in the "real world."

As illustrated below, all correlations range from 1.00 to −1.00, with 0.00 marking the midway point and representing the complete absence of a relationship between two variables:

Entire Range of Correlation Coefficients

−1.00	0.00	+1.00

Figure 4.3 shows how a scattergram would look with a set of data represented by a 0.00 correlation. The points on this graph might be compared to a shotgun blast. Notice that how subjects scored on one variable has no relationship with how they scored on the other variable. To keep things simple, the axes on Figure 4.3 have had the calibrations omitted. Instead, arrows are used to represent increasing values for Variables X and Y.

■ **FIGURE 4.3**

A scattergram based on 47 hypothetical observations of scores on Variables Y and X.

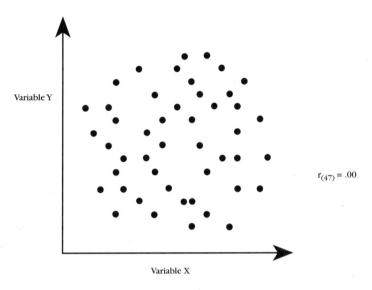

The Concept of a Regression Line

The set of points in Figure 4.3 suggests no correlation between the variables because the figure lacks what is called a **regression line.** This is defined as the line that comes closest to intersecting all the points in a scattergram. Notice that in Figures 4.1 and 4.2, you could easily approximate where the regression line would traverse. In Figure 4.3, however, it is difficult even to decide whether the regression line should run in a positive or negative direction.

In statistics, students learn two formulas for determining regression lines, but here it is only necessary for you to be able to visually estimate these lines. From this, you can estimate the numbers used to represent the configuration of points in scattergrams, as we will do in the next section.

Estimating Correlation Coefficients from Scattergrams

Although every scattergram can be represented by a correlation coefficient, the only way to determine the coefficient accurately is by a statistical formula. This chapter will not teach you the formula, but it will teach you how to interpret correlation coefficients when you encounter them. Correlation coefficients in scientific literature are rarely accompanied by scattergrams.

■ **FIGURE 4.4**

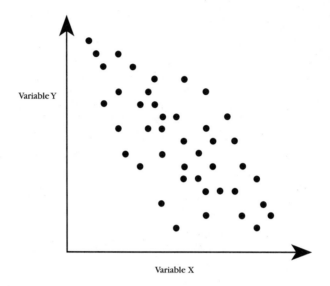

A scattergram of the relationship between Variables Y and X, based on 43 hypothetical observations.

Variable Y

Variable X

The symbol used to represent correlation coefficients is **r.** Sometimes this symbol is followed with a subscript indicating the size of the sample upon which it is based. For example, Figure 4.1 is represented as $r_{(5)}$, since there were five subjects in the study.

You have seen three scattergrams thus far; each would be associated with a different correlation coefficients. If you look back on Figure 4.1, you will see that it represents a strong positive correlation, with a correspondingly strong (nearly perfect) correlation coefficient (r = .97). Figure 4.2, of course, represents a perfect negative correlation (r = −1.00), and Figure 4.3 reflects the essential absence of a correlation (r = .00).

To challenge your current comprehension of correlations, attempt to estimate the correlation coefficient for Figure 4.4. In other words, estimate how well these data points cluster along a regression line as opposed to being randomly scattered. Your first step should be to eliminate half the possible coefficients automatically by deciding whether the correlation is positive or negative. Figure 4.4 is obviously negative because the high values for Variable Y are associated with low values for Variable X and vice versa. Therefore, the correlation must be somewhere between 0.00 and −1.00. In narrowing your estimate further, try to answer the following question: Is the pattern created by the points more like a random scattering, i.e., a shotgun blast, or more like a straight line? This should tell you whether the coefficient is above .50 (closer to a straight line) or below .50 (closer to a shotgun blast); and if you really cannot decide, the coefficient is probably close to .50 itself. Do not read the following paragraph until you have made your guess.

■ **FIGURE 4.5**

A scattergram of the relationship between Variables 1 and 2, based on hypothetical data.

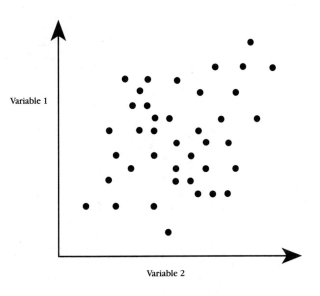

The answer is r = −.65. This would be considered a strong correlation, though it is still far from perfect, as in Figure 4.1. (Pay no attention to the different numbers of observation points in the two graphs.)

If your guess was between −.50 and −.80, you made a good guess and probably understand the basic concept. If your guess was outside that range, or you were afraid to even try, go back to Figure 4.4 and pencil in a regression line. Notice that the points are distinctly packed about the line; they are definitely far from being randomly scattered (like a shotgun blast). This tells you that the correlation coefficient is in excess of .50.

Let's do one more: Estimate the correlation coefficient for Figure 4.5. Again, your first step should be to eliminate half the possibilities by determining whether the direction of the scatter is positive or negative. Do this by visualizing the regression line. Then determine whether the scattering of points better conforms to the regression line or to a shotgun blast. If the former, the correlation coefficient is probably above .50; if the latter, it is probably below .50. Make your estimate before reading any further.

The correlation coefficient for Figure 4.5 is .32. If your estimate was close to this value, you are understanding the basic concept of correlation, at least as it relates to **linear relationships.** The following section introduces you to the concept of linearity.

■ FIGURE 4.6

A scattergram representing the relationship between Variables M and N, based on hypothetical data.

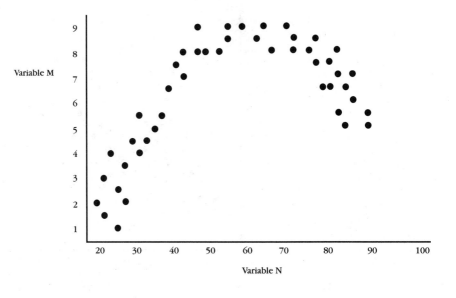

Curvilinear versus Linear Correlations

Our discussion of correlations so far has followed a basic assumption: that the best fitting regression line for a set of points is straight. This is called a linear assumption, and there are cases in which such an assumption is inappropriate. Fortunately, most of the variables considered by social scientists (at least within their ranges of variation) warrant a linear assumption. If in doubt, however, the safest thing to do is to look at the scattergram. By applying the most common correlational formula (i.e., Pearson correlation) to a set of data, you assume that the best fitting regression line is straight.

To appreciate the significance of the assumption of linearity, consider Figure 4.6. If you draw the best fitting straight line through these points, your best attempt would be a line ascending at about a 30° angle along the Y-axis starting at about 4. If you calculate the correlation coefficient for these data points based on this straight regression line, you would get a low positive correlation ($r = .25$). In fact, the relationship between Variable M and N is much stronger than .25. The problem lies with the assumption that a straight regression line is appropriate for this set of data.

When relationships are curvilinear rather than linear, researchers typically present the data in a scattergram rather than with a correlation coefficient. Nevertheless, there are special correlational formulas that can be applied to a wide variety of curved lines. There is no need for students in introductory research methods to know how to interpret nonlinear correlations, but it is helpful to know that they exist.

■ FIGURE 4.7

Samples of the most common shapes of curvilinear correlational patterns.

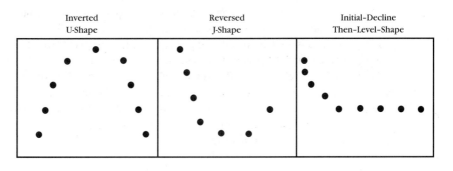

The most common shapes of nonlinear relationships are U-shape, J-shape, and ''initial rise (or decline) then level'' shape, all of which can be inverted. These are illustrated in simplified form in Figure 4.7.

One example of a U-shape relationship is between the number of children a couple has and the couple's marital stability. Specifically, couples with no children and those with the greatest number of children have been shown to have greater probabilities of divorce than couples with one or two children (Thornton, 1977:531; Maneker & Rankin, 1987).

Another example of a U-shape relationship is between alcohol consumption and mortality rates due to heart disease. People who are most likely to die from heart disease either report that they are abstainers or that they are among the heaviest drinkers (reviewed by Marmot, 1984; Moore & Pearson, 1986). This U-shape correlation has been interpreted as showing that moderate consumption of alcohol is helpful in preventing diseases of the cardiovascular system (e.g., Turner, Bennett, & Hernandez, 1981). However, a recent review of the evidence points out that, compared to moderate drinkers, many abstainers are formerly heavy drinkers and that their death rates from heart disease are even higher than that of currently heavy drinkers, mainly because they are older (Sharper, 1990). This plus other evidence raises questions about the beneficial effects of moderate levels of alcohol consumption in preventing heart disease, although the detrimental effects of heavy drinking appear to be well established. Besides being an example of a curvilinear relationship, this line of research also illustrates a point that will be made later in this chapter—you should be extremely cautious in making deductions about causation based solely on correlational data.

An example of an initial decline, then level curve is the relationship between a mother's age when pregnant and her chances of having a low birth weight infant (Ketterlinus, Henderson, & Lamb, 1990). The average birth weight of babies born to mothers between the ages of 13 and 15 was lower than babies born to mothers older than 16. Beyond the age of 16, however, teenaged mothers were no more likely to give birth to low birth weight infants than mothers in their 20s.

The concept of curvilinearity helps to underscore a point made earlier: Correlational statistics, like all statistics, are based on assumptions, and the researcher who conducts a study has to make sure that the data being analyzed match those assumptions. In Figure 4.6, for instance, there is clearly a strong relationship between Variables M and N. The fact that a Pearson correlational formula assumes linearity, however, means that it would yield only a slight positive correlation coefficient when applied to Figure 4.6. Note that had the measurement of Variable N stopped at 60, the Pearson correlation coefficient would have been much stronger (i.e., r = .94).

The Pearson correlation also assumes that variables were measured at interval or ratio levels. There are other types of correlational formulas, however, and there are ways of adapting Pearson correlation for use with nominal level variables, but these issues will not be covered in this text.

Interpreting Descriptions of the Strength of Correlations

Research reports using correlations are often accompanied by narrative accounts with statements such as "A strong relationship was found between this variable and that variable." What does a researcher mean when making such statements? Here are some general guidelines:

A. Correlation coefficients that are .80 or higher would reflect very strong relationships (regardless of whether the coefficients were positive or negative).
B. Coefficients in the .60s and .70s would be considered strong or quite strong.
C. Coefficients in the .40s and .50s would be regarded as moderate to substantial.
D. Those in the .20s and the .30s would be termed weak to modest.
E. Finally, coefficients in the teens or below would usually be of little or no practical importance, even if they happen to be statistically significant because of very large sample sizes. (The importance of sample size in interpreting correlations is discussed in Chapter 5.)

These ranges are not presented for you to memorize; they merely expound on the obvious. In other words, no researcher would ever be justified in describing a correlation coefficient of .25 as very strong, or a coefficient of .93 as modest.

Variability and Correlations

As a rule, researchers will seek to maximize the variability in each variable that is correlated. By so doing, they increase the chance of observing any relationship that may exist between variables. Figure 4.8 illustrates this point by presenting a

■ **FIGURE 4.8**

A scattergram of the relationship between Variables A and B, based on hypothetical data.

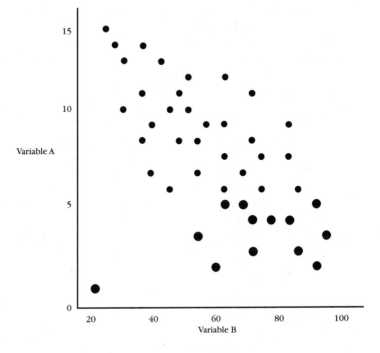

scattergram with a substantial negative correlation between variables A and B (i.e., $r_{(44)} = -.61$). However, if the variability in Variable A is confined to 0 to 5 instead of 0 to 15 (i.e., just the bold points), the correlation would be virtually zero, and would switch from negative to positive ($r_{(13)} = .12$).

One more feature of Figure 4.8 is that it contains one observation point that would be termed an outlier. As mentioned in Chapter 3, this term refers to any observation that is extremely deviant relative to the overall pattern of observations. The outlier in Figure 4.8 is located at 1 on the Y-axis and at 20 on the X-axis. The magnitude of a correlation coefficient is affected more by outliers than by observations which fall within the general pattern of points. The more points there are that conform to the general pattern, however, the less of an effect one or two outliers have on a correlation coefficient. In Figure 4.8, the coefficient is depressed from $r_{(43)} = -.67$ to $r_{(44)} = -.61$ by the inclusion of the outlier. Although researchers should never remove observations without explicitly stating that they have done so, sometimes extreme outliers are removed in a separate analysis in order to show the relationship for the bulk of the sample (e.g., Scott & Schwalm, 1988).

Variance and Correlations

The concept of variance in correlation coefficients is given more attention in statistics courses than in research methods courses, but is still worth mentioning here. Besides linearity, another assumption of Pearson correlation is that the variables being correlated are roughly normally distributed (Hodge & Treiman, 1968:725). In other words, it is assumed that most scores on both variables being correlated will conform to a normal curve of distribution.

You may recall from Chapter 3 that, for normally distributed variables, variance is defined as the square of the standard deviation (see p. 39). A mathematical extension of that definition allows for the concept of variance within a scattergram as well. Correlational variance may be defined as the square of the correlation coefficients (Rodin & Rodin, 1972:1166). Thus, a correlation coefficient of r = .75 is said to account for 56% of the variance in the variables being correlated (and is often expressed as $r^2 = .56$).

Correlational variance is often referred to as **shared variance** (or **common variance**). The full significance of the concept of shared variance cannot be described here, but keep the basic definition in mind for use in more advanced applications of correlational statistics (some of which will be described in Chapter 17).

Correlation versus Causation

The last issue in this chapter reflects a fundamental point that needs to be made about research based on correlations. It is summarized by the old social science adage: "Correlation ≠ causation" (e.g., Ezekiel, 1941:451; Alland, 1967:208; Kagan & Freeman, 1970:514; Games, 1990). This adage means that you should not be fooled into thinking you have found a cause-and-effect relationship when you find that two variables are correlated, no matter how logical the connection may seem.

Consider the following example: Researchers have repeatedly shown that there is a substantial correlation between how much people are subjected to physical abuse as children and their probabilities of abusing drugs (including alcohol) later in life (Young, 1964; Green, 1976; Cohen & Densen-Gerber, 1981; Wright, 1985). Since it is impossible to argue that drug abuse in adolescence or adulthood could cause persons to be abused as children, you might conclude that child abuse must lead to drug abuse later in life.

No matter how logical this argument sounds, it contains a flaw that you need to recognize. The flaw is sometimes referred to as the **third variable problem.** This phrase refers to the possibility that one or more "third variables" (which may not have even been included in the study) were responsible for the relationship that was found.

In the case of child abuse and later drug abuse being related, one possibility involves the fact that alcoholism and drug abuse generally tend to run in families (either because of genetic factors or because of "bad examples," or both) (Oreland et al., 1985:99). If so, and if parents who are drug abusers are more likely to be physically abusive (such as when they are drunk or high), the relationship between being abused as a child and becoming a drug abuser later in life may not be reflecting any real causal influence of the child abuse per se.

More will be said in later chapters about the important concept of **causation.** For now, suffice it to say that the task of sorting out cause-effect relationships is considerably more complex than simply documenting that some type of relationship exists between two or more variables. Despite the warning against equating correlation with causation, you should know that it is customary to put the antecedent (and *possible* causal) variable on the X-axis and the subsequent (and *possible* effect) variable on the Y-axis (Howell, 1989:101). In the case of child abuse and drug abuse, for example, child abuse would normally appear on the X-axis, and drug abuse on the Y-axis.

Interpreting Correlation Coefficients: An Actual Example

Now consider some results from a recent study in anthropology. The study was undertaken to answer the following question: Do wealthy males have more wives and more children than poor males? This study was conducted among a tribal people living in Kenya, Africa, known as the *Kipsigis* (pronounced kip' sig is) (Borgerhoff Mulder, 1988). Marriage and birth records among the Kipsigis have been maintained for decades by a local missionary. Like most human societies (industrial societies being the most notable exception), polygyny—the practice of males having more than one wife—is fairly common among the Kipsigis.[1]

Using the missionary records, the researcher correlated two indicators of wealth among the Kipsigis males (size of landholdings and number of cows owned) with both the number of wives and number of surviving offspring each male had. Since there may have been changes over time, the correlations were performed for three so-called marriage cohorts.

The term **cohort** is used often in the social sciences; it refers to a group of subjects with some significant life event in common (in this case, when the males first got married). One cohort consisted of males who were first married between 1918 and 1929, the second cohort were those first married between 1930 and 1939, and the third cohort were those first married between 1940 and 1953 (Borgerhoff Mulder, 1988:423).

Before reading the next paragraph, try to guess what this study found. Do you think it found a relationship between either of the two measures of wealth and either the number of wives or the number of children these males had?

Table 4.1 Correlation between Wealth (Measured by Size of Landholdings and Number of Cows Owned) and Reproductive Success for Males (Measured by Number of Wives and Number of Surviving Offspring)

Measure of Reproductive Success	Marriage Cohorts				
	1918–29	1930–39		1940–53	
	Acres	Acres	Cows	Acres	Cows
Number of wives	.70**	.91***	.84***	.49**	.62**
Number of surviving offspring	.72***	.92***	.86***	.42**	.50**
N	11	25	25	37	34

**p < .01; ***p < .001 (Adapted from Borgerhoff Mulder, 1988:420.)

Not all of the findings of this study are presented here, but the key findings relevant to the basic question are provided in Table 4.1. From this table you can see that, for all three cohorts, there are fairly strong positive correlations between male reproductive success and wealth. In fact, most of the correlations are very strong, suggesting that, at least in societies where polygyny is practiced, wealth is positively correlated both with the number of wives a male has and with the number of offspring he has.

Three additional features of this table are worth mentioning before bringing this chapter to a close. First, for the time being, ignore both the asterisks and the footnote to Table 4.1. These symbols have to do with the "statistical significance" of the findings, a concept that will be the focus of Chapter 5. Second, note that the number of subjects used to derive each correlation is presented at the bottom of the table beside the letter **N** (for "number of subjects"). Third, for the earliest cohort (1918–29), information on the number of cows owned was not available; thus, only size of landholdings could be correlated during this period.

Summary

The concept of correlation developed out of a desire by social scientists to have a standardized mathematical shorthand for describing how variables relate to one another. Although caution must be exercised in applying the concept to the study of relationships between variables (especially if the relationship is not linear or the variables are not measured at least at the interval level), correlational analyses are widely used in the social sciences.

To learn how correlation coefficients are calculated, you need to have training in statistics. However, to interpret correlation coefficients, you only need to understand the following basic principles:

1. A correlation coefficient is a number ranging from −1.00 to 1.00, with .00 representing the complete lack of a relationship.
2. A coefficient at or near −1.00 indicates a relationship in which increases in the value of one variable are strongly linked to decreases in the value of the other variable. This would be termed a strong negative correlation (or relationship).
3. Conversely, a coefficient at or near 1.00 denotes a relationship in which increases in the value of one variable are strongly associated with increases in the value of the second variable. This would be termed a strong positive correlation.

You must not assume that a correlation between two variables necessarily means that one of these variables caused the other. One or more third variables (which may not have even been measured) could be responsible for the relationship.

Notes

[1] The term of polygamy refers to either a man or a woman having more than one spouse. Polygamy includes both polygyny and polyandry, the latter being the rare practice of women having more than one husband (see Lancaster & Kaplan, 1992).

References

Alland, A. (1967). *Evolution and human behavior.* London: Tavistock.

Borgerhoff Mulder, M. (1988). Reproductive success in three Kipsigis cohorts. In T. H. Clutton-Brock (Ed.), *Reproductive success* (pp. 419–438). Chicago: University of Chicago Press.

Cohen, F. S., & Densen-Gerber, J. (1981). A study of the relationship between child abuse and drug addiction in 178 patients: Preliminary results. *Child Abuse and Neglect, 6,* 383–387.

Ezekiel, M. (1941). *Methods of correlational analysis* (2nd ed.). New York: Wiley.

Games, P. A. (1990). Correlation and causation: A logical snafu. *Journal of Experimental Education, 58,* 239–246.

Green, A. H. (1976). A psychodynamic approach to the study and treatment of child abusing parents. *Journal of Child Psychiatry, 15,* 414–420.

Hodge, R. W., & Treiman, D. J. (1968). Social participation and social status. *American Sociological Review, 33,* 722–740.

Howell, D. C. (1989). *Fundamental statistics for the behavioral sciences.* Boston: PWS-KENT.

Kagan, J., & Freeman, M. (1970). Relation of childhood intelligence, maternal behavior, and social class to behavior during adolescence. In H. E. Fitzherald and J. P. McKinney, *Developmental psychology, studies in human development* (pp. 508–521). Homewood, IL: Dorsey Press.

Ketterlinus, R. D., Henderson, S. H., & Lamb, M. E. (1990). Maternal age, sociodemographics, prenatal health and behavior: Influences on neonatal risk status. *Journal of Adolescent Health Care, 11,* 423–431.

Lancaster, J. B., & Kaplan, H. (1992). Human mating and family formation strategies: The effects of variability among males in quality and the allocation of mating effort and parental investment. In T. Nishida, W. C. McGrew, P. Morley, M. Pickford, & F. deWaal (Eds.), *Topics in primatology*, (Volume 1, pp. 21–33). Tokyo, Japan: University of Tokyo Press.

Maneker, J. S., & Rankin, R. P. (1987). Correlate of marital duration among those who file for divorce: Selected characteristics in California, 1966–1976. *Journal of Divorce, 10,* 97–107.

Marmot, M. G. (1984). Alcohol and coronary heart disease. *International Journal of Epidemiology, 13,* 160–166.

Moore, R. D., & Pearson, T. (1986). Moderate alcohol consumption and coronary artery disease: A review. *Medicine, 65,* 242–267.

Oreland, L., von Knorring, L., von Knorring, A. L., & Bohman, M. (1985). Studies on the connection between alcoholism and low platelet monoamine oxidase activity. *Progress in Alcohol Research, 1,* 83–117.

Rodin, M., & Rodin, B. (1972). Student evaluations of teachers. *Science, 177,* 1164–1166.

Scott, J. E., & Schwalm, L. A. (1988). Rape rates and the circulation rates of adult magazines. *Journal of Sex Research, 24,* 241–250.

Sharper, A. G. (1990). Alcohol and mortality: A review of prospective studies. *British Journal of Addiction, 85,* 837–847.

Thornton, A. (1977). Children and marital stability. *Journal of Marriage and the Family, 39,* 531–540.

Turner, T. B., Bennett, V. L., & Hernandez, H. (1981). The beneficial side of moderate alcohol use. *Johns Hopkins Journal, 148,* 53–63.

Wright, L. S. (1985). High school polydrug users and abusers. *Adolescence, 20,* 853–861.

Young, L. (1964). *Wednesday's children: A study of child neglect and abuse.* New York: McGraw-Hill.

Suggested Reading

Thorndike, R. M. (1976). *Correlational procedures for research.* (This book presents a relatively math-free discussion of correlations and guidelines for their use in social science.)

CHAPTER 5

The Concept of Statistical Significance, and Various Tests of Statistical Significance

Who do you think are more religious, males or females? Consider the results of a recent study carried out among more than a thousand high school students in Northern Ireland (Francis & Greer, 1990). Religiosity was measured in this study by summing the answers to a series of questions pertaining to beliefs in traditional Christian doctrines and values. The average score by the males was 85.3, whereas the average for the females was 92.2. Obviously, females scored higher in religiosity than males. However, what if someone said that this rather small difference was nothing more than a chance event, such as when you toss a coin 20 times and sometimes get more than 10 heads? Given that the sample exceeded a thousand, you might say it is hard to believe that this much of a difference would have occurred by chance (which is in fact what the researchers concluded). But how do scientists get beyond simply arguing about such issues? Is there an objective way of deciding whose opinion is most reasonable?

These questions will be the focus of this chapter. This is the third and last chapter designed to acquaint you with how statistics are fundamentally interwoven with research methods.

The Concept of Chance

If you tossed a coin 100 times and got heads 51 times and tails 49 times, would you suspect that there was something wrong with the coin? Most likely, you would attribute this small deviation from the expected 50/50 ratio to chance (or random error).

However, if you tossed a coin 100 times and got heads 92 times, you would probably consider this too far from 50/50 to be dismissed as chance. Now, where would you draw the line between these two extremes?

Questions similar to this frequently arise in scientific research. For example, say a researcher finds that 64 out of 100 males felt a certain way about an issue, while 54 out of 100 females felt the same way. Does this indicate that the sexes differ from one another? The question in essence is this: What is the likelihood that this small sex difference in results occurred by chance?

In the process of becoming familiar with scientific research methods, it is important to address questions like these in accordance with certain procedures. As you read articles written by social scientists, you will see these procedures repeatedly utilized in a variety of ways.

The Concept of Statistical Significance

In science, the concept that is most central to separating "real" from "chance" observations is known as **statistical significance** (sometimes merely called significance). The word significance in ordinary language implies that a subjective judgment is being made, but in scientific terminology, statistical significance refers to judgments that are made according to agreed on mathematical rules of probability. The bottom line is that some observed differences and relationships between variables are so great that they are deemed statistically significant, while other differences and relationships are too small to be considered statistically significant.

When conducting research, you must understand how judgments are made about statistical significance. This understanding can be accomplished by introducing you to three underlying concepts: **statistical probability, sample size,** and the **normality of many probability outcomes.** These are discussed below.

The Concept of Statistical Probability

Statistical probability refers to mathematical estimates of the likelihood of various events taking place. Usually, estimates of statistical probability begin with simple events whose probability is intuitively obvious. As we consider these probability events, keep in mind that the lowest probability of an event happening is 0.00 (0%) and the highest probability is 1.00 (100%).

An example of an intuitively obvious line of reasoning is dice throwing, where the probability of any one side turning up each time the die is thrown is 1/6 (or .167). Certain basic rules of probability have been developed that combine the outcomes of these simple events to make more complex predictions.

One widely used rule of probability is the **multiplicative rule.** In its simplest form, it states that the probability of two or more like events, such as rolling a die two or more times, is equal to the probability of each event multiplied by all the others. Thus, the chance of a 1 turning up on two consecutive throws is equal to $1/6 \times 1/6$, or $1/36$. Stated in decimal terms, this would be $.167 \times .167$, which equals .0278 (or 2.78%). Thus, there is a less than 3% chance that a 1 will turn up on any two throws of a die. The probability of rolling "snake eyes" with two dice would be the same.

Another basic rule of probability is the **additive rule.** This rule states that the probability of two or more mutually exclusive events is equal to the sum of their independent probabilities. Thus, the likelihood of a 1 or a 2 turning up on any throw of a die is equal to $1/6 + 1/6$, or $1/3$. In decimal terms, this would be $.167 + .167$, or .334 (33%).

Such simple rules of probability can be easily expanded beyond just two events. They can also be combined to make some astonishing predictions. For example, if you are in a class with more than 30 students, there is an almost 100% probability that two of those 30 students will have the same birthday (disregarding the year they were born).

Here is how the multiplicative and additive rules can be combined to make this prediction: First, imagine that you pick 2 of these 30 students at random. The probability that they will have the same birthday is very low: $1/365$ or .0027 (i.e., 1/4 of 1%) However, both these students have this same probability of matching up with the remaining 28 students in class; thus $.0027 \times 28 = .0810$ (or 8.1%). If you pick a third student at random, there is a $.0027 \times 26$ probability that he or she will have the same birthday as the remaining 26 students, i.e., .0756. Add this to .081 for a sum of .1566. Then the fourth student you pick has a $.0027 \times 25$ probability of having the same birthday as the remaining 25 students. When you finish multiplying and adding all these probabilities, you will come very close to 1.00.

Skeptical? Test it empirically. If your class has fewer than 30 students, have some students also include a birthday of a parent or spouse. Ask how many were born in January, and then ask each of them the precise day. Do this for each month, and see if you end up with at least one match.

The Concept of Sample Size

Another concept that illustrates statistical significance is sample size. In social science, sample size normally refers to the number of subjects in a study. As we will discuss again in Chapter 12, the more subjects there are in a study, the more confidence you can have in the findings (all else being equal).

Sample size invokes another law of probability, known as the **law of diminishing returns.** This law states that the more subjects a sample already contains, the less impact each additional subject will make on the confidence you can have in your findings. By extension, adding 100 more subjects to a sample of 100 will do considerably more to increase confidence in your findings than will adding 100 more subjects to a sample of 10,000.

■ FIGURE 5.1

Frequency distribution curve showing the probabilities for various outcomes each time two dice are rolled. (Adapted from Hinkle, Weirsma, & Jurs, 1988:157.)

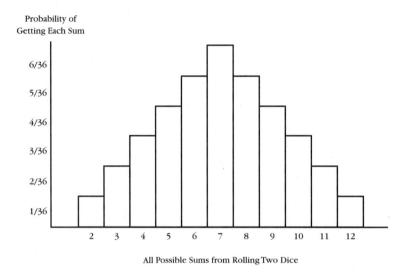

All Possible Sums from Rolling Two Dice

The Near Normality of Many Probability Outcomes

The probable outcome of many events, including something as simple as rolling dice, has been shown to resemble a normal curve of distribution. To illustrate this, assume again that you have two dice, and want to know the probability of every possible outcome each time they are thrown. In other words, how many times are you likely to get snake eyes, 3, 4, 5, etc.? The answer is displayed in Figure 5.1. It shows that the probability of getting snake eyes is 1/36, the same as the probability of getting two 6s. The outcome with the highest probability is 7 (a 1 and a 6, a 2 and a 5, or a 3 and a 4).

Notice how Figure 5.1 resembles a normal curve of distribution (as discussed in Chapter 3). When a graph is made for all possible outcomes of rolling three dice at a time, the resulting curve comes even closer to the familiar bell shape. And graphs showing the possible outcomes of rolling four or more dice at a time resemble almost perfectly normal curves of distribution.

Applying the Concept of Probability to Correlations

You now have a basic idea of how probability statements are made about both simple events (such as the throwing of a die) as well as complex events (such as the likelihood of a group of people having the same birthday). You have also seen that as simple events become more complex (such as throwing several dice at a time), their outcomes often resemble normal curves of distribution. Now we are ready to integrate the concept of probability with the concept of correlations.

Say that you wanted to estimate the likelihood that one of the scattergrams presented in Chapter 4 occurred by chance. Recall that a scattergram with no relationship between the two variables would resemble a shotgun blast of points, and would be represented by r = .00. As a correlation between two variables gets stronger, the initial shotgun blast tends to collapse into a more elliptical shape until, finally, all the points fall along a single regression line. To estimate the likelihood of a scattergram being due to chance, you must decide when the configuration of points has flattened to such a degree that the probability of the pattern having occurred by chance is too low to be a reasonable possibility.

Estimates of chance have been applied to correlations; note that the most widely used formula for calculating correlations (i.e., Pearson correlations) has a built-in assumption that both variables being correlated are roughly normally distributed. This assumption allows the formula for calculating Pearson correlations to build on logic surrounding the probability of normal curves of distribution. Thus, even though data represented by a scattergram may seem to have nothing to do with simple rules of probability, in fact they do. Correlational formulas effectively reduce all possible sets of observations down to certain basic rules of probability.

Representing Statistical Significance in Correlations

Because the mathematical formula for calculating Pearson correlations is rooted in certain basic rules of probability, every coefficient that is calculated has a specific probability of having occurred by chance. The probability is dependent on the sample size. The underlying logic is this: As either the correlation coefficient or the sample size (or both) gets larger, the probability that the correlation was due to chance decreases.

Tables are located in the back of many statistics texts for converting combinations of correlation coefficients and sample sizes to their corresponding probabilities of having occurred by chance. In addition, most computer programs that calculate correlations for a set of data also automatically calculate, and print out, the probability of each coefficient having been due to chance.

As mentioned earlier, all estimates of chance range from between a low of 0 to a high of 1 (not to be confused with correlation coefficients themselves, which range from −1.00 to 1.00). The probability of a finding being due to chance is often called the **probability of error.**

In many research reports where correlational data are used, the coefficients are followed by the symbol **p** (often called the **p-value**). This symbol is then followed by one of four additional symbols, whose meaning you should recognize. They are as follows:

p < "the probability is less than"
p = "the probability is equal to"
p ≤ "the probability is equal to or less than"
p > "the probability is greater than"

One feature of statistical significance that takes getting used to is called **levels of significance.** In describing the probability of a finding being due to chance, researchers describe *low* probabilities of error as making the finding *highly* significant. In other words, a researcher would consider p = .01 more significant than p = .05. After a little practice, you will become accustomed to thinking that way also.

How Much Probability of Error Should Be Tolerated?

No scientific finding based on a sample is ever associated with a zero probability of having occurred by chance, although many scientific findings based on large samples come close (e.g., p < .0001). Because every finding derived from a sample is associated with *some* probability of error, a researcher must decide how much error to risk.

The convention is that scientists will risk no more than .05 probability of error when declaring a finding statistically significant (for an exception, see Dancey, 1990:447). Thus, if a particular correlation coefficient is p < .03, most researchers would declare the relationship statistically significant. Most researchers, however, would not consider a correlation associated with p = .06 as statistically significant, although they would probably note that the result came close to significance. If a finding has less than a .01 risk of being due to chance, almost all researchers will declare the finding statistically significant.

Cutoff points for declaring findings statistically significant are sometimes referred to as **tolerance limits,** because these points refer to how much error is being risked. Tolerance limits are set by the researcher who undertook the study.

Statistical significance of findings are presented either as part of the written text of the report or as part of a statistical table. When statistical significance is indicated in a table, it is customary for researchers to identify the findings considered statistically significant with one or more asterisks. Usually a single asterisk indicates findings that meet the minimum requirement for statistical significance (usually the .05 level), and additional asterisks are used to designate findings that exceed other cut off levels (such as .01). A legend at the bottom of the table indicates these precise cutoff points.

If you turn back to Table 4.1 (p. 58) in the preceding chapter, you will find that it illustrates this point. At least two asterisks follow each of the correlation coefficients. At the bottom of the table, you can see that two asterisks indicate that the coefficient has less than a .01 probability of being due to chance, and that three asterisks indicate that the coefficient has less than .001 probability of being due to chance. Thus, in Table 4.1, even though the sample sizes are all fairly low (the highest one being an N of 37), the probability of the coefficients being due to chance is sufficiently low as to be declared statistically significant. Had one of the coefficients been only .12, for example, it would not have been considered statistically significant, because the probability of error would have exceeded .05.

■ FIGURE 5.2

Two scattergrams representing the results of two independent attempts to determine the correlation between Variables Y and X, based on hypothetical data.

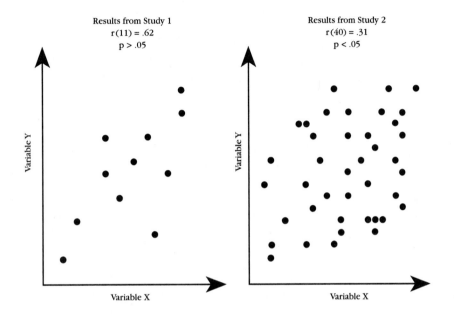

Results from Study 1
r(11) = .62
p > .05

Results from Study 2
r(40) = .31
p < .05

Variable Y

Variable X

Variable Y

Variable X

Further Illustrating the Concept of Statistical Significance within the Context of Correlations

Now consider the two scattergrams in Figure 5.2. Let's say that they reflect the results of two independent studies, and let's assume that the researchers who conducted these two studies used exactly the same procedures. As you can see, the results of Study 1 indicate that there is a strong positive correlation between Variables X and Y (r = .62), whereas Study 2 suggests that the correlation is positive, but not nearly as strong (r = .31).

Which of these two studies are you more likely to trust, and why? Your answer should be that you have more confidence in the results of Study 2 than Study 1 because Study 2 is based on a larger sample size. Even though the magnitude of the correlation coefficient happens to be greater in the case of Study 1, the fact that the sample for Study 2 is almost four times larger means that it has a lower probability of error. To be more precise, notice that the results of Study 1 do not even reach statistical significance. This is because r = .62 for a sample size of 11 has more than a .05 risk of sampling error. Study 2, on the other hand, is considered statistically significant because an r = .32 based on a sample size of 40 has less than a .05 probability of sampling error. Had the researcher who conducted the second study only wanted to risk a .01 probability of sampling error, however, he or she would not have been able to declare even Study 2 statistically significant.

Let us now examine the results of an actual study. Some time ago, a small number of subjects were given a questionnaire to assess the relationship between a personality trait called sensation seeking and a type of human attitude known as dogmatism-authoritarianism (Kish & Donnenwerth, 1972). The researchers correlated the scores for these two variables for the male subjects and the female subjects separately.

The analyses revealed one relationship that was statistically significant and one that was not. To be more precise, among the 13 males in the study, a correlation of $r_{(13)} = -.81$ (p < .01) was obtained; whereas, for 29 females, the relationship was only $r_{(29)} = -.29$ (p > .05). Let us further analyze what was found:

A. There was obviously a strong tendency for males who were most prone toward sensation seeking to be least dogmatic and authoritarian. Even with just 13 subjects, the probability of an $r = -.81$ being observed by chance is less than 1/100. Therefore, the researchers declared this relationship statistically significant.

B. The correlation between the scores on the sensation seeking measure and the scores on the dogmatism-authoritarianism measure were much weaker for the 29 females in the study ($r = -.29$). The researchers found that the probability of such a correlation being due to chance was greater than 5%. Since 5% is the maximum amount of error most scientists will risk when declaring a finding statistically significant, it was concluded that a statistically significant correlation between sensation seeking and dogmatism-authoritarianism was not found in the case of females.

The Concept of the Null Hypothesis

As will be explained more in Chapter 14, a **hypothesis** is a tentative statement about empirical reality, which may or may not be true. A **null hypothesis** simply posits that no relationship or no difference exists in whatever is being studied. In other words, when researchers put forth a null hypothesis about two or more variables, they are hypothesizing that the variables are not related to one another, or that there are no differences between two or more groups with reference to the variables under scrutiny.

The null hypothesis is most often implied rather than stated. Thus, even though a researcher does not explicitly state the null hypothesis, it looms as an implied alternative to any hypothesis that the researcher does state. Researchers normally state (and) test what are called **alternative** or **research hypotheses.** These hypotheses assert that there are relationships or differences among whatever variables are under study.

To illustrate the null versus the alternative hypothesis, let us return to the personality-attitude study (Kish & Donnenwerth, 1972). Recall that the researchers found a significant relationship between sensation seeking and dogmatism-authoritarianism for males, but not for females. What these researchers found can now be said a different way: The null hypothesis was rejected in the case of males, but it could not be rejected in the case of females. Since the null hypothesis is normally only implied, researchers often speak of "retaining it" or "failing to reject it." Saying that the null hypothesis is "accepted" is also considered proper.

Until the null hypothesis is taken up again in Chapter 14, understand that when reading a research report in which an alternative hypothesis (e.g., X is bigger than Y) was rejected, by implication, the null hypothesis was retained. Conversely, when some research hypothesis (e.g., A is negatively associated with B) was accepted, the implication is that the null hypothesis was rejected.

Applying the Concept of Statistical Significance to Noncorrelational Data

Thus far, we have illustrated the concept of statistical significance with correlational research. Let's turn attention now to research that does not entail correlating one variable with another. First, we will consider how the concept is used in comparing two normally distributed populations. Second, we will apply the concept of statistical significance to the comparison of proportions.

Statistical Significance When Comparing Means and Normal Distributions

Who do you think do better in college statistics courses, men or women? Despite the stereotype, if you guessed men the evidence is not on your side! Two studies have addressed this question in recent years. In terms of final grades, one study found no significant sex difference (Buck, 1985), and the other found that females received significantly higher grades than males (Brooks, 1987).

Let us consider how the differences in these two studies were assessed from a statistical standpoint. The most widely used method for comparing means (such as comparing average grades for males to average grades for females) is known as the **t-test.** (It is also sometimes referred to as the **student's t-test,** because it was first developed by a graduate student.) We will not be discussing the mathematics underlying the t-test (a basic statistics course will show you the formula and how to solve it). However, it is important that you know the logic surrounding the t-test so you can intelligibly read articles that utilize this statistical test.

In the second of the two studies just cited, the researcher consulted the grade sheets he had kept in his ten years of teaching college statistics. Using A = 4.0, B = 3.0, etc., he noted the sex of each student and the final grade given. The mean grade for the 154 male students was 2.21, and the mean for the 168 female students was 2.74. The researcher then had to consider whether the difference was more than what might have occurred by chance.

As a tool for addressing just such a question, the t-test essentially considers three things: What is the magnitude of the mean difference? How much variation is there within each of the two means? And, how many subjects were there in the study? Based on the combination of these three factors, the t-test formula provided an estimate of the probability that 2.21 and 2.74 are statistically different. The t-test indicated to the researcher that if he considered the two means to be different (in other words if he rejected the null hypothesis), his risk of doing so erroneously was $p < .001$ (or 1/1000). What do you think he concluded? As noted earlier, his conclusion was that females performed significantly better than males in his statistics courses over the years (Brooks, 1987).[1]

Another widely used test for comparing means is more complicated, although it is also more flexible. It is called **analysis of variance (ANOVA).** It permits you to compare several means all at once (Howell, 1989:220).

Consider the following simple example of a study that used ANOVA (although a t-test would have sufficed for the limited results that are reported here). A study was undertaken to find out if one sex was better than the other in accurately judging family relatedness (Nesse, Silverman, & Bortz, 1990). The researchers presented 100 males and 100 females with 48 photographs showing 24 pairs of closely related persons (e.g., siblings). What do you think their results showed?

The basic findings were as follows: The mean number of photographs correctly paired by the female subjects was 14.99 and the mean number correctly paired by the male subjects was 14.53. Thus there was a slight difference in favor of the females. Do you think the difference was sufficient to be considered significant? An ANOVA revealed that if the researchers said the differences were significant, they would be risking a 19% probability of error (i.e., $p \leq .19$). In other words, 19 times out of 100, such a small difference (given the sample size) would have occurred by chance. What do you think they concluded?

Your guess should be that they could not reject the null hypothesis in this case. In other words, this study reached the conclusion that no significant sex difference was found in the ability to judge family relatedness by viewing photographs of people.

Statistical Significance and Differences in Proportions

Say you were interested in knowing whether teenagers and adults differed in their tendency to endorse a particular political statement. Assume that you interviewed 100 persons between 13 and 19 and 100 persons between 23 and 29, and found that 36 of the teenagers endorsed some political statement and 33 of the adults did so. Now you must decide whether you found a significant difference. In other words, is 36 out of 100 as opposed to 33 out of 100 more than would be likely to occur by chance? Note that 36 and 33 are not averages (as was the case in examples discussed earlier). Rather, each of these two numbers is one part of a fraction. Both 36 and 33 are numerators that can be divided by 100 (the denominator) to obtain a proportion, i.e., .36 and .33, respectively. Thus, the basic question behind this hypothetical example

"...So as you see, it's six of one and a half-dozen of the other."

is whether .36 (or 36%) is significantly different from .33 (or 33%). Based on your common sense, what do you think will be concluded when an objective statistical test is applied to these proportions?

The most widely used statistical test for assessing whether two or more proportions can be regarded as significantly different is called **chi-square (X^2).** Without considering the specific mathematics involved in calculating chi-square, applying it to these data reveals that if you were to reject the null hypothesis, you would be risking more than a .05 probability of doing so erroneously. Therefore, scientists would nearly always decide not to reject the null hypothesis in this case, thereby concluding that the two proportions were not significantly different.

Had the results revealed that 56 of the 100 teenagers and only 13 of the 100 adults endorsed the political statement, however, the chi-square test would have indicated that less than 1 in 1000 times ($p < .001$) would such a great difference have occurred by chance. Thus, the null hypothesis would have been rejected in favor of an alternative hypothesis: Teenagers are more likely to endorse the political statement than are adults.

The next chapter will present an example of a simple study which used the chi-square test (Lester, Brockopp, & Priebe, 1969). Before you read the actual article, let us briefly consider it here. The study was designed to determine whether there was a significant tendency for suicides to occur more frequently around the full moon than at other times of the year. To find out, the researchers determined when 399 suicides occurred relative to the four phases of the 28–day lunar cycle (each phase consisting of 7 days).

How many of the 399 suicides would have occurred by chance in each of the four phases of the lunar cycle? The answer, of course, is 99.25. Therefore, if the full moon phase is actually linked in some way to the incidence of suicides, you would expect that particular phase to exceed 99.25. As the study reveals, 102 suicides occurred during the full moon phase of the lunar cycle. Do you think this was sufficiently different from 99.25 to be considered statistically significant? You will find out in the next chapter.

Concluding Remarks about Statistical Significance

At this point, you may wonder exactly how statistical significance can be determined. The short answer is that most statistics texts contain conversion tables. These tables present ranges of t-test and ANOVA values, correlation coefficients, or chi-square values (usually across the top) and sample sizes (usually down the side). After getting a particular t-test score, ANOVA score (symbolized by the letter **F**), chi-square value, or a particular correlation coefficient in a study, you consult the table to identify the probability that the result is due to chance given the sample size used in the study. (Nowadays, most statistical computer programs automatically calculate and print out these probabilities.) The more complete answer to the question of how probabilities of error are determined cannot be given here except to say that they have been derived from the work of statistical specialists and based largely on **probability theory.**

You should be aware that there are other tests besides t-tests, ANOVAs, correlations, and chi-squares to which the concept of statistical significance can be applied. Some will be discussed in later chapters.

Finally, it should be said that only with practice can you become completely accustomed with concepts surrounding statistical significance. To help you, we will return to these issues in Chapter 14 and build on them.

Summary

Before beginning to read social science research reports (let alone write them!), you must be aware of how statistical concepts are used in the research process. This chapter has concentrated on the concept of statistical significance, one that provides researchers with a way of estimating the probability that a particular finding was due to chance. All probabilities range from .00 to 1.00, and the lower the probability that a finding is due to chance, the more significant is the finding.

Rarely will a researcher declare a finding statistically significant if it has more than a .05 (i.e., 5%) probability of having been due to chance. Various statistical procedures have been developed for determining these probabilities. These procedures are based on some simple rules of probability and on the fact that probability estimates often can be represented by normal curves of distribution.

Fundamental to decisions about statistical significance is the concept of the null hypothesis. This hypothesis asserts that there is no difference or no relationship among the variables being studied. It is seen as an implied alternative to the hypothesis that a researcher is really seeking to test (called an alternative or research hypothesis). In other words, a researcher may determine whether the null hypothesis can be rejected with little risk of error in order to effectively test an alternative hypothesis.

This chapter has discussed the concept of statistical significance at different levels. At a fundamental level, you can think of statistical significance in terms of different outcomes when rolling dice. More complex illustrations come from noting that many outcomes of dice rolling take on distributions resembling the familiar bell-shaped curve. This has allowed statisticians to devise formulas that can be applied to many different empirical phenomena.

The concept of statistical significance was illustrated with examples involving correlations, tests of differences between means and distributions, and tests of differences between proportions. When correlation coefficients are presented in a research report, they are usually followed by a number, called a p-value, which indicates the likelihood of the coefficient having been due to chance. The p-value depends on both the magnitude of the coefficient itself and the size of the sample involved in the study.

Two types of statistical tests of differences between means and distributions were described—t-tests and ANOVA (analysis of variance). Both of these tests allow researchers to estimate the likelihood of two groups of subjects (or the same subjects under different conditions) having obtained different average scores by chance. The degree to which two means are significantly different from one another depends upon the magnitude of the difference, the degree of dispersion within each group tested, and the size of the sample in each group.

To determine if two proportions (including percentages) are significant, the most widely used test is chi-square. The mathematical rational behind this test is somewhat different from the rational surrounding Pearson correlations, the t-test, and ANOVA in that chi-square makes no assumptions about the normality of the variables under study. Chi-square calculations depend on the magnitude of the difference in two or more proportions.

There are many statistical concepts that cannot be given attention here, but you should now have an idea of how social scientists (in fact, all scientists) make decisions about the statistical significance of the data they collect. Some additional statistical concepts will be presented later in this text.

Notes

[1] Finding such sex differences and explaining them are two different things. It needs to be mentioned that, in fact, males have been found to do better in mathematics than females, especially when nonverbal spatial reasoning is required (Wood, 1976; Bradberry, 1989). The types of mathematical tasks at which females do as well or better than males are ones which place a premium on following strict rules and entering values into specific formulas (Wood, 1976:156). Statistics courses may be taught from this latter perspective to a greater degree than are other mathematics-related courses.

References

Bradberry, J. S. (1989). Gender differences in mathematical attainment at 16+. *Educational Studies, 15,* 301–314.

Brooks, C. I. (1987). Superiority of women in statistics achievement. *Teaching of Psychology, 14,* 45–46.

Buck, J. L. (1985). A failure to find gender differences in statistics achievement. *Teaching of Psychology, 12,* 100.

Dancey, C. P. (1990). The influence of familial and personality variables on sexual orientation in women. *Psychological Record, 40,* 437–449.

Francis, L. J., & Greer, J. E. (1990). Measuring attitudes towards Christianity among pupils in Protestant secondary schools in Northern Ireland. *Personality and Individual Differences, 11,* 853–856.

Hinkle, D. E., Weirsma, W., & Jurs, S. G. (1988). *Applied statistics for the behavioral sciences* (2nd ed.). Boston: Houghton Mifflin.

Howell, D. C. (1989). *Fundamental statistics for the behavioral sciences* (2nd ed.). Boston: PWS-Kent.

Kish, G. B., & Donnenwerth, G. V. (1972). Sex differences in the correlates of stimulus seeking. *Journal of Consulting and Clinical Psychology, 38,* 42–49.

Lester, D., Brockopp, G. W., & Priebe, K. (1969). Association between a full moon and completed suicide. *Psychological Reports, 25,* 598.

Nesse, R. M., Silverman, A., & Bortz, A. (1990). Sex differences in ability to recognize family resemblance. *Ethology and Sociobiology, 11,* 11–21.

Wood, R. (1976). Sex differences in mathematics attainment at GCE ordinary level. *Educational Studies, 2,* 141–160.

Suggested Reading

Mohr, L. B. (1990). *Understanding significance testing.* Beverly Hills, CA: Sage.

CHAPTER 6

The Structure of a Research Report, and Styles for Citing and Referencing

Y ou may dread the thought of plowing through some technical scientific report, especially if it is loaded with statistics. But as this chapter will show, understanding such material is easier than you think. Among the secrets are knowing how research reports are structured, and not starting off with the most complicated examples. Once you get experience reading simpler reports of social science research, you will be able to read more technical ones. From there you will acquire the expertise needed to prepare research reports of your own.

This chapter addresses two main topics: the structure of most research reports, and the styles used for referencing and citing relevant research that others have conducted.

The Basic Format for a Research Report

There is a logical structure that characterizes most scientific research reports. Familiarity with this structure not only will help you read research reports, but can also serve as a guide for writing them. The following outline depicts the components of most scientific research reports.

Immediately following the title and author in a scientific article is a one-paragraph **abstract** (or summary). (Even though many research reports are written by more than one author, for simplicity throughout the remainder of this chapter, "author" will be used to refer to one or multiple authors.) The abstract gives readers a basic picture of the study, usually in less than 200 words. The abstract is a useful feature of scientific research reports (and other scientific articles), but it is not considered a part of the *body* of a scientific report. In fact, short scientific reports (those less than a page or two in length) often have no abstract.

Introduction

The first component of the body of a research report is the introduction. It is typically divided into two subparts: the **Review of Literature** and the **Statement of the Problem** (or the **Hypothesis**).

In the literature review, the author describes the results of prior research that is considered pertinent to the study at hand. The literature review section also often includes an outline of theoretical ideas that may have lead a researcher to undertake the study. (More will be said in Chapter 14 about how theory and research mutually complement one another.) In addition, the literature review often offers a practical justification for the study. A clear sign that you are reading the literature review: the author is focusing on studies conducted by others in the past rather than on any aspect of the study at hand.

The other component of the introduction—the statement of the problem—is normally only a sentence or two in length (rarely more than a paragraph). The statement of the problem tells readers precisely why this study was undertaken. Although the literature review often points out where gaps still exist in the understanding of some phenomenon, the author of a research report will end the introduction with a succinct statement of what gaps he or she will specifically attempt to help fill. The statement of the problem serves to narrow the reader's focus onto exactly what the present study was designed to accomplish. Watch for such phrases as "The purpose of this study . . ." or "This study was undertaken to . . .".

Sometimes, instead of giving a statement of the problem, the author will state a formal hypothesis. As alluded to in Chapter 5, a hypothesis is a statement about what a researcher expects to find, rather than simply what question will be addressed. In other words, a hypothesis is more formal and definite than a statement of a problem. A researcher who is relatively uncertain as to what will be found usually offers a mere statement of the problem, but if he or she has strong beliefs about what will be found (often based on some theory), a formal hypothesis will be made.

Methods

Like the introduction, the methods section of a research report consists of two distinguishable parts. The first part is a description of the **sample** (or the subjects) included in the study. The second part offers an account of what was done to the subjects, and is called the **procedures.** Each of these two subsections is described in more detail below.

In describing a sample, the author discloses who the subjects were in specific terms, so if any readers want to replicate the study, they can locate a similar group of subjects and confirm the findings. This subsection usually refers to demographic information, e.g., how many of each sex, their average age, education levels, the geographical region in which the subjects lived. Other distinctive features of the sample that would be important for researchers interested in replicating the study should also be included (e.g., how the subjects were recruited).

The procedures subsection of the methods provides an account of how the study was carried out, as well as a description of any research instruments that were used. **Research instrument** is a general term referring to a tangible object used to collect scientific data. The most common research instruments used in the social sciences are questionnaires (their design will be discussed in Chapter 8). As is seen in the sample, a researcher should tell the reader enough about the procedures so that it is possible for anyone to replicate the study.

Many times, a questionnaire is so lengthy that only a sketch of it is presented. This is because journals have guidelines for limiting the length of articles. If some important features of the research instrument cannot be fully explained in a report, it is appropriate and fairly common to include a notation in the methods section that interested readers may contact the author for a copy of the questionnaire. Of course, the disadvantage of this procedure is that, as time passes, it becomes increasingly difficult to locate authors.

The methods section sometimes contains a short subsection near the end that tells the reader what statistical analyses were applied to the data and why. In other studies, however, the types of analyses are sufficiently obvious as to require no special explanation in the methods section.

Results

In the results (or findings) section, readers are told what was discovered with reference to the problem or hypothesis posed in the introduction. The results section may have several parts, all uniquely tailored to the various aspects of the study being reported. This section of a research report tends to be the most technical from a statistical standpoint. It is common to find tables or graphs in the results section.

Conclusions

In this section (also called the **Discussion** or **Discussion and Conclusions**), the author reflects on his or her findings and their overall significance. Shortcomings and pitfalls may be discussed so that future researchers can avoid them. In the conclusions section, the author comes back to the problem or hypothesis posed in the introduction and tells the reader what new insights were achieved.

The body of a scientific report is followed by a reference section and occasionally by an appendix. The reference section will be discussed in detail later in this chapter.

Identifying the Parts of a Research Report

Following is a short research report that was published some years ago to explore the possibility that suicides are more likely to occur during the full moon. The short report will be examined in detail to illustrate how a report is sectioned. As you read the article, notice that like most completed research reports, this one is written in the past tense. Because most research reports are considerably longer than this one, they actually will identify the main sections with specific headings; this short article does not do so. With or without headings, however, it is important for you to be able to develop an ''intuitive'' recognition of the components of a research report.

While reading the ''Suicide-Moon'' article, you will notice that it refers to chi square, which is one of the statistical tests described in the preceding chapter (pages 70–71). The researchers who conducted this study—Lester and his associates—used the chi square test to help them determine what proportion of the 399 suicides they sampled occurred during the full moon. The full moon is one of the four moon phases, each of which lasts 7 days (for a total of 28 days).

To follow the reasoning of the researchers, note that by chance, one fourth of the suicides (i.e., 99.25 suicides) should have occurred during the full moon. This was designated the expected number of suicides. When they examined the recorded dates of each suicide, Lester and his coresearchers found that 102 of the suicides occurred during the full moon lunar phase. Their question then was whether this obviously small difference (99.25 vs. 102) should be considered statistically significant (i.e., beyond what would occur simply by chance). Using the chi square test, the researchers' calculations revealed that, were they to declare 102 significantly different from 99.25, they would be risking a .25 probability of error. As we noted in Chapter 5, this amount of error is much more than the .05 level that most researchers tolerate when they declare a finding statistically significant. Thus, the study concluded that there was no significant tendency for suicides to occur more often during the full moon than during the moon's remaining three phases.

As you read this research report, keep in mind that the sections and subsections appear in the order in which they were described above. This is typical (although not universal) of all research reports. Some minor wording changes have been made in the article to maximize its clarity for the introductory reader, and, of course, the article did not originally appear with each sentence starting on a separate line. Also, unlike most research reports, this one was so short that it did not warrant an abstract. While reading this article, focus on understanding why each sentence has been assigned to the part of the research report identified in the right hand margin.

This article provides a clear example of how scientists attempt to slowly remove the shroud from nature's many secrets, and how they communicate their discoveries. Upon reading such reports, other researchers are sometimes inspired to conduct additional research on the topic. Now that you have read a brief research report with an eye toward recognizing its structure and organization, let's look at how research reports are cited and referenced.

Psychological Reports, 1969, 25, 598.	Journal, yr, volume, page
Association Between a Full Moon and Completed Suicide*	Title of Report
David Lester, G.W. Brockopp, and K. Priebe	Authors
Pokorny (1964) investigated whether a sample of completed suicides in Texas was clustered around the incidence of a full moon rather than a new moon. He found no association for the total sample, or for subgroups by sex and race.	Literature Review
It was felt to be of interest to examine this association in a northern state, since there could be geographical differences.	Statement of the Problem
A list of all 399 completed suicides recorded in Erie County, New York from 1964 to 1968 was obtained.	Sample
The sex of each suicide victim was identified and the date of the suicide was recorded. The number of suicides occuring in the 7 days centering around the full moon was compared with the number expected by chance (one-fourth).	Procedures
During the 7 days of the full moon, 102 suicides occurred. The number expected by chance would have been 99.25. The difference, although in the predicted direction, did not reach statistical significance ($X_2 = 1.07$, df=1, p > .25).	
The data were examined for males and females separately and the differences failed to reach statistical significance for either sex (for males: $X^2 = .22$; for females: $X^2 = 1.41$, df = 1, p > .10).	Results
Overall, the present results support the conclusion of Pokorny in indicating that no significant association exists between phases of the moon and incidence of completed suicides.	Conclusions
Reference Pokorny, A. D. (1964). Moon phases, suicide, and homicide. American Journal of Psychiatry, 121, 66–67.	Reference Section

* Used by permission of authors and the journal. (The wording of this report has been slightly modified relative to the original publication.)

Citation and Referencing Styles in Social Science Publications

Two of the features of the scientific method are that it is cumulative and self-correcting. These features are made possible by researchers accurately relating not only what they found but also what others have found (and who those other researchers were). Researchers are obliged to inform readers about the location of reports that they cite. For example, in the research article discussed in the preceding section, Lester and his associates indicate in the introduction that one prior study—one conducted by Pokorny—already failed to find a link between suicidal tendencies and the phases of the moon. Readers who wanted to read Pokorny's study for themselves (perhaps to find out more about the sample size or the procedures) could go to the end of the article by Lester and his associates and find the complete reference to Pokorny's study (which appeared in the *American Journal of Psychiatry* in 1964). From this referenced information, an interested reader can locate and read the Pokorny report.

It is important at this point to distinguish between a reference and a citation. A **reference** is a listing of information about an article or book, which can be used to locate the publication in a library (or any other place it might be stored). A **citation,** on the other hand, is a statement or notation in a body of a report, which refers a reader to a reference. In the "Suicide-Moon" report, the study by Pokorny is *cited* in the first sentence, and is *referenced* at the end of the article.

Styles for citing and referencing articles vary somewhat from one scientific journal to another, but researchers are expected to follow certain rules and practices that are required by almost all scientific journals. These rules and practices are outlined below, first for referencing styles, and then for citation styles.

Referencing Styles

The following items of information are required of nearly all references to a scientific article:

> Author(s)
> Year of publication
> Title of the article
> Journal in which the article appeared
> Volume (and sometimes issue)
> Pages

For most scientific articles, it is not necessary to identify the issue because, unlike popular magazines (where each issue begins with page 1), in scientific journals the paging runs consecutively throughout each volume (in most journals, a new volume is begun each year).

Occasionally, popular magazine articles are referenced in scientific publications. The most common practice is to reference them just like a scientific article except that the issue would be identified (usually directly following the volume and according to the week or month the issue was released).

The required information for referencing books in scientific publications are as follows:

Author(s)
Year book was published
Title
City in which the book was published
Publisher

Many books are edited rather than authored throughout by the same person (or persons). This means that each chapter is authored by one or more separate writers. In edited books, you would reference specific chapters rather than the book as a whole. In referencing a specific chapter in an edited book, the necessary items of information are:

Author(s) of the chapter
Year book was published
Title of the chapter
Editor(s) of the book
Title of the book
Pages covered by the chapter (sometimes omitted)
City in which the book was published
Publisher

The above items for referencing articles, books, and chapters in books reflects the information that you would use to locate this material in a library or order it through interlibrary loan. These items of information are given in nearly all references, but the precise style and order in which they are presented varies from one publication to another. For example, there are variations in (a) whether the first names of the author(s) are spelled out or indicated only by their initials, (b) rules for capitalizing titles of books and articles, and (c) underlining and italicizing the titles of journals and books.

It is important for you to be familiar with at least one of the common ways that references and citations are written. As shown in Appendix B, referencing and citation styles vary from one social science journal (and book publisher) to another. Because it is far easier to illustrate referencing styles than it is to present all the rules for each style, Appendix B contains examples of the most widely used referencing styles in the social sciences. Your instructor will probably instruct you to become familiar with at least one of these styles.

Citation Styles

Within the body of a scientific report (especially the literature review section), readers will encounter citations. Citations inform readers where they can find the detailed information to support a particular argument or conclusion, because all the articles and books cited will be referenced. You should know the two main citation styles: the author-date style and the numbering style.

Author-Date Citation Style

The most common citation style currently used in the social sciences is the author-date citation style. The "Suicide-Moon" study discussed earlier provides an example of this citation style. Notice that the first passage of this article states the following:

> Pokorny (1964) investigated whether a sample of completed suicides in Texas was clustered around the incidence of a full moon rather than a new moon. He found no association for the total sample, or for subgroups by sex and race.

To confirm this interpretation of Pokorny's study, you might want to read the article that Pokorny published in 1964. This or any other scientific article can be obtained from most college and university libraries, either in bound form, on microfiche, or through interlibrary loan.

A variation on the author-date citation style would involve rewriting the first sentence of the above passage as follows:

> A study conducted in Texas found no significant association between suicide rates and incidences of the full moon (Pokorny, 1964).

Note that the only substantive difference between the two versions is that the latter form focuses attention more on the nature of the finding rather than on who conducted and reported the study. Either of these two versions of the author-date citation style are acceptable.

Some articles have numerous authors, and it would be cumbersome to include them all in a citation. When citing studies with multiple authors, there are slight rule variations from one journal (or book publisher) to another. With two authors, both authors are indicated, and they are usually separated with an ampersand [e.g., (Smith & Jones, 1988)], although some journals use and [e.g., (Smith and Jones, 1988)]. Of course, if the authors are referred to in the body of the sentence, you would always use *and* instead of the ampersand [e.g., Smith and Jones (1988) contended . . .].

Most journals stipulate that when there are more than two (and especially when there are more than three) authors, that the first author's last name should be indicated, followed by the notation, *et al.* (literally meaning "and all the others"). Thus, an article published by Smith, Jones, Carter and Davis in 1978 would be cited as Smith et al., 1978. In the 1980s, the American Psychological Association (APA) adopted the policy of citing all of up to eight authors the first time an article is cited, but to use et al. following the name of the first author in all subsequent citations of that reference. However, this cumbersome practice has now been abandoned by many journals that otherwise adhere to the APA referencing and citation style.

There are a number of minor variations in the author-date referencing style. Some publications use brackets instead of parentheses, and some do not insert commas between the author(s) and the date in their citations.

A lingering controversy surrounds whether to indicate pages in citations. While all agree that the page should be indicated for any direct quotation, opinions vary on whether page citations are appropriate for merely assisting the reader in locating where the most pertinent support to a particular statement can be found. The advantage of directing readers to a specific page, especially in a book or a lengthy review article, is that it often saves readers considerable time trying to verify a particular point. Also, it is much easier to determine that a citation was made erroneously if a specific page was referenced than if it was not. A safe practice is to include page citations unless you know that the journal or book publisher that will publish your manuscript has specific policies to the contrary. These page citations can be easily dropped at any point before a manuscript goes to press, but they are difficult to locate and add if they were not included initially.

The author-date citation style uses two forms of page citations. One is to follow the date with a colon and then the page number [e.g., Smith and Jones (1988:45) or (Smith & Jones, 1988:45)]. The other style is to follow the date with a comma, a space, a ''p.'', a space, and the page number [e.g., Smith and Jones (1988, p. 45) or (Smith & Jones, 1988, p. 45)]. In some instances, the writer will indicate several consecutive pages [e.g., (Smith & Jones, 1988:45–51)], but the more common practice for a passage spanning several pages (such as would be required to explain a theory or a complex research project) is to merely indicate the page on which the relevant passage begins.

Finally, it should be mentioned that special kinds of notations are sometimes made within an author-date citation. For example, if a cited article is a review article rather than a research report, the citation might read: (reviewed by Smith & Jones, 1988). Also, if a writer was unable to get a copy of a particular article that some other researcher cited, the finding from the unobtainable reference might be cited as follows:

> A study by Adams (cited by Smith and Jones, 1988:47) found that. . . .

Numbering Citation Style

Compared to the author-date citation style, the numbering style has the advantage of not being as disruptive when you are reading. If research activities have been intense in a particular area, you may find many sentences in the literature review containing five or six citations. To readers who are primarily interested in following the arguments rather than in knowing all the appropriate citations supporting each argument, the author-date citation style can be a bit of a distraction.

There are two different versions of the numbering citation style: one for when references are listed alphabetically in the reference section, and one for when references are listed according to the order in which they appear in the text. In the former case, you might read a sentence which has three numbers directly behind it, usually in superscript (e.g. [4,7,14]). These numbers refer the reader to entries in the reference section, which are usually alphabetized by the senior author's last name. With the second version of the numbering citation style, the references are numbered sequentially according to the order in which citations to them appear in the text.

Footnoting and Endnoting

The oldest citation style—footnoting—is rarely used anymore in the social sciences. Therefore, the citation rules to follow for footnoted references will not be reviewed here (instead see Turabian, 1965:18).

Even though footnoted references are rare in scientific writing, footnotes are still used to make an occasional important qualifying statement that is nonetheless tangential to the central theme or line of reasoning in the body of an article. In some cases, these qualifying statements are printed at the end of the body of an article (usually just before the reference section) rather than at the bottom of a page. In this case, they are called endnotes instead of footnotes. When footnotes or endnotes are used, they are cited according to a numbering citation style.

Summary

This chapter has dealt with three interrelated topics. The first topic was the basic format or organization of research reports. In most scientific research reports, specific items of information need to be presented. Although there is plenty of room for variation, most research reports consist of the following sections and subsections:

1. In the introduction the reader is (a) informed of the current state of knowledge and theorizing about a topic (review of the literature), and then is (b) told how the present study will try to advance the knowledge and/or clarify the theorizing (statement of the problem).
2. The reader is told in the methods section how the study was designed and executed in two important respects: (a) the choice of subjects and (b) the procedures that were employed to obtain the data, including both the instruments that were used and the way subjects were treated during the study. By providing this information, the methods section makes it possible for any reader to replicate or extend the study.

3. In the results (or findings) section, readers are informed of all findings that the writer considers relevant to the statement of the problem.

4. The final section in the body of a research report is the conclusions (or discussion and conclusions). Here readers should be given a general picture of what was found and how it is relevant to the aim of the study (even without carefully reading the methods and results sections). In addition, readers should get an idea of what questions remain, and even what mistakes to avoid should they attempt to pursue the topic further.

The second subject of this chapter was referencing styles. As you become familiar with the wide diversity of social science journals, you will find that there are innumerable minor variations in referencing styles. Nevertheless, the information needed for referencing the three main types of publications—articles, authored books, and chapters in edited books—is essentially identical in every style utilized. For articles, the following items of information are needed: Author(s), year of publication, title of the article, name of journal, volume, and pages. The required items of information for authored books are: Author(s), year of publication, title, city, and publisher. And for edited books, the items included in the majority of references are: Author(s), year of publication, chapter title, book editor(s), book title, pages covered by the chapter, city, and publisher.

Citation styles were the third focus of this chapter. Social scientists no longer use footnoting for citing or referencing. Instead, references are all arranged in the back of the article or book (usually alphabetically), and cited in the body of the report with either a numbering citation method or, more commonly, an author-date citation method.

References

Lester, D., Brockopp, G. W., & Priebe, K. (1969). Association between a full moon and completed suicide. *Psychological Reports, 25,* 598.

Turabian, K. L. (1965). *A manual for writers of term papers, theses, and dissertations.* Chicago: University of Chicago Press.

Suggested Reading

American Psychological Association. (1984). *Publication manual of the American Psychological Association* (3rd ed.). Washington, DC: American Psychological Association. (This is the most widely used style manual for social science. Many journals besides those published by the American Psychological Association follow the guidelines for writing and referencing set forth in this manual. It is often simply referred to as the APA Manual.)

Brown, R. H. (1992). *Writing the social text: Poetics and politics in social science discourse.* (Social scientists are not all of one mind about what is appropriate, either in subject matter or approach. These differences in opinion manifest themselves in part in the social science publications. This edited book provides readers with insights into the ideological, and even political, maneuvering that is a part of publishing in the social sciences.)

Cuba, L. J. (1988). *A short guide to writing about social science.* (This brief guide is very useful to anyone who is serious about developing his or her skills in writing for social science audiences.)

CHAPTER 7

The Concepts of Reliability, Validity, and Precision in Measuring Variables

A distinction was made in Chapter 2 between conceptually defining and operationally defining variables. To review, a conceptual definition uses other words to convey the meaning of a concept, whereas an operational definition refers to a set of empirical operations that may be performed in order to measure a variable. In other words, operational definitions are distinguished by the methods used in their measurement. Thus, scientists sometimes speak about ''operationalizing concepts'' and ''operational measures'' for variables.

A major focus in this chapter will be on how to determine the degree to which operational definitions are accurate reflections of their corresponding conceptual definitions. To cite a simple example, have you ever wondered why some people habitually use their left hand instead of their right hand? (Perhaps you, like the writer of this text, are one of those ''lefties.'') Realizing that variables must be objectively measured in order to be scientifically studied, let us consider how the variable of ''handedness'' might be measured (or operationalized).

Initially, you might think that the best way to measure handedness would be to simply ask people whether they are right-handed or left-handed. However, studies have shown that some people are not consistent in hand usage, even for fairly specific types of tasks (Annett, 1970; Steenhuis et al., 1990:929). Therefore, you might decide to include a third response choice for your subjects: ambidextrous (or mixed-handed). Although better than just giving subjects two possible choices, allowing them three choices still would not accommodate those who always use their left-hand for writing but always use their right hand for cutting with a scissors. Not to be discouraging, but these are the types of problems social scientists frequently encounter when they begin to explore the complexities of behavior, especially human behavior.

Increasingly, researchers interested in handedness have come to measure this variable by giving subjects a list of several tasks that people usually perform with their hands. Subjects are asked to report what proportion of time they use each hand for performing each of these tasks (e.g., Dawson, 1977; Coren, Porac, & Duncan, 1979; Dean, 1982; Ellis & Ames, 1989; Steenhuis et al., 1990; Williams, 1991).

To give an example, a study was recently undertaken to look for subtle cross-cultural differences in handedness in a number of North and South American countries (Ardila et al., 1989). The researchers administered a test of handedness to large numbers of subjects in each country studied. The test consisted of the following five hand task-related items:

Drawing or writing
Using a toothbrush or a comb
Throwing a ball or stone
Using scissors or cutting with a knife
Holding a match while striking it

For each item, subjects were given five response choices: Always right, usually right, no preference, usually left, and always left. To determine the overall handedness of each subject, the researchers assigned consecutive numbers to these response choices (+2 through –2), and then added the five numbers (one for each of the handedness tasks) together for a final handedness score (potentially ranging from +10 through –10).

More will be said in the next chapter about how researchers decide what questions (or items) to use and what response options to offer. Here, it is only important to note that the concept of handedness can be measured in a variety of ways; nearly all handedness measures are more refined than just asking people whether they are right- or left-handed. Therefore, although we still talk about left-handers and right-handers, scientists now recognize that handedness exists along a continuum with the majority of people heavily concentrated near the right end of that continuum (Steenhuis et al., 1990). Incidentally, this tendency for most humans to be biased toward right-handedness has been documented in almost all human societies ever studied (both past and present), although not exactly to the same degree (reviewed by Harris, 1990).

You may recall the distinction made in Chapter 2 between continuous variables and discrete variables, the former referring to variables with gradual variability, and the latter referring to variables with a limited number of categories. It is common to speak of people as being either right- or left-handed (with mixed-handers usually considered left-handed), but because of the real variability that has now been documented, and because that variability has now been associated with many traits (including ones related to brain function) (see Coren, 1990), it is more appropriate to treat handedness as a continuous variable. (More will be said about the difference between continuous and discrete variables later in this chapter.)

Reliability, Validity, and Precision:
The Three Aspects of Measurement Accuracy

To outsiders, it may seem trivial for scientists to spend time worrying about how accurately each variable in a study is being measured. However, many erroneous conclusions have been drawn from scientific research because one or more variables were not measured correctly. Questions about how best to measure variables are, in fact, among the most fundamental and enduring questions that scientists face. These questions plague all fields of science, but they are particularly acute in the social sciences where so many variables are relatively intangible and difficult to quantify. Imagine, for example, the difficulty researchers have studying such variables as creativity, morality, political attitudes, reading ability, or social status.

Accuracy in measuring a variable can be broken down into three interrelated features: **reliability, validity,** and **precision.** In measurement terms, reliability is essentially synonymous with ''stability,'' validity is synonymous with ''appropriateness'' of a particular measurement procedure, and precision refers to the degree to which a measure is ''fine-grained'' rather than ''coarse-grained.''

Reliability is the tendency for the measurement of a variable to remain stable over time. To give a simple example, say that every day you weighed yourself on your bathroom scale, and from one day to the next it registered a weight that varied as much as twenty pounds. This is substantially more variation in body weight than could ever actually occur. You would obviously suspect that this particular scale was unreliable and in need of repair or replacement. It may seem odd to think of a bathroom scale as an operational definition of weight, but it is exactly that. Most bathroom scales are designed to give their users a measure of the degree to which some type of spring is being depressed. The measure of this spring depression constitutes an observable operational definition of weight.

Validity refers to the degree to which you are measuring what you intend to measure. To give an absurd example, say you tried to measure people's occupational interests by having them stand on a bathroom scale. No matter how *reliable* the readings were, such a procedure would not be a *valid* measure of occupational interests.

The precision of an operational measure may vary independently of its reliability and validity. To see this, imagine again that you tried to measure occupational interests with a bathroom scale. Even if the precision of the scale were increased by increasing the fineness of its calibration (say, to tenths of a pound instead of each whole pound), neither the reliability nor the validity would be altered.

Precision simply refers to how well variations in a variable can be discerned, whereas both reliability and validity are more challenging to assess. In fact, there are four specific ways of assessing reliability and validity, and we turn our attention now to these assessment procedures.

Ways of Assessing Reliability

Although there is no way to determine with certainty whether or not a variable is being measured in the most reliable way possible, there are four methods for making reasonable judgments about reliability. These methods are known as **test-retest reliability, cross-test reliability, inter-item** (or **intra-test**) **reliability,** and **inter-rater reliability.**

Test-retest (or consistency) reliability assesses how consistently similar scores are obtained with a specific testing procedure or instrument. For instance, Zuckerman (1979) developed a questionnaire designed in part to measure people's variations in boredom susceptibility. He found that when the same group of subjects were given the questions about their boredom tendencies twice, separated by a three-week interval, their overall scores on these questions were highly correlated (r = .70). In a recent attempt to develop a set of questions for measuring boredom proneness, an even higher test-retest correlation was obtained (r = .83) among a group of undergraduates enrolled in an introductory psychology class, albeit after only a one-week interval (Kass and Vodanovich, 1990:9). Both studies support the view that people's tendencies to be bored are fairly stable, at least over the course of a few weeks. If not, the reliability of the questions being used would be in doubt.

A well-known example of studies undertaken to assess reliability have involved tests of intelligence or basic academic ability. Their reliability has been convincingly demonstrated in numerous test-retest studies by giving groups of subjects the same test at two or more points in time. These test-retest studies have shown that, except when testing children under school age (when scores are very unstable), subjects' scores tend to correlate very highly with their scores later in life, even when several years have lapsed between the two testing dates (Anastai, 1976:251; Hunt, 1983:141). More precisely, researchers have typically obtained coefficients exceeding r = .85 when correlating standardized IQ test scores by subjects who take a test at 8 years of age and then repeat it a decade later (reviewed by Sattler, 1982:58). Note that although these findings bode well for the reliability of standardized IQ tests, they leave open questions about the tests' validity.

Cross-test reliability correlates the results of two different operational measures of the same variable. If subjects who score high on one measure also score high on the other measure, and vice versa, the researcher is encouraged to believe that both tests are reliable. An example of this would be to have a group of subjects take the two main tests used for college admission—the Scholastic Achievement Test (SAT) and the American College Test (ACT). If the two correlated to only a small degree (e.g., r = .20), the reliability of at least one of these two tests would be called into question.

One study involving cross-test reliability had to do with the accuracy of people's self-reported weight. Several weeks after a group of subjects had completed a questionnaire sent to them in the mail (which included a question about their weight), they were invited to visit a medical clinic for further information (Charney et al., 1976). At the clinic, their weight was determined with a conventional scale. The correlation between what the subjects had reported on the questionnaire and their weight according to the scale was exceedingly similar (r = .96). You can see that this gave the researchers great confidence in self-reported weight.

Inter-item (intra-test) reliability compares scores on part of a measure of some variable with scores on another part of the same measure. The most widely used form of this method is called the **split-half method.** To understand this method, imagine that you have 50 true-false items in a questionnaire designed to measure people's knowledge of world affairs. To assess the split-half reliability of the items in this questionnaire, you randomly choose half of the items (e.g., all of the even numbered questions) and determine each subject's score on these 25 items. If you then do the same for the odd numbered questions and determine each subject's score, you can correlate the two scores. To the degree your measure of knowledge of world affairs is a reliable test, scores derived from the two halves of the test should be strongly correlated (of course, in a positive direction).

The fourth way of assessing reliability is called **inter-rater** (or **inter-judge**) **reliability.** Its use is restricted to measures of variables that involve the judgments of two or more raters (or judges). If you were interested in knowing if various social problems such as crime and drug abuse were related to a country's commitment to a free market economy (capitalism), you might have no other way of measuring the relative commitment of countries to capitalism, except by asking a group of experts (e.g., economists and political scientists) to rate a list of countries on a 10–point scale of free enterprise commitment. As a check on reliability, the ratings made by each rater could be correlated with those made by all the other raters.

How Reliable Does Reliability Have To Be?

A widely accepted rule of thumb is to consider correlation coefficients exceeding .75 to .80 as indicative of high reliability, at least for behavioral or social variables (Rossi & Freeman, 1989:242). In other words, using any of the four methods for assessing reliability, if you can ''repeat'' a score for a group of subjects to the point that a correlation of .80 or greater can be obtained, scientists would conclude that the reliability of your test has been impressively demonstrated.

If you fail to come close to a .80 correlation in assessing reliability, however, you should not assume that the measure is unreliable. Many reliable tests fail to yield a .80 test-retest correlation because people's scores from one point in time to another are undergoing change. People's attitudes toward political candidates and current events, for example, may change at least a little from one news broadcast to another. Likewise, you would probably be suspicious of a test that found a .80 correlation between people's moods from one day to the next simply because moods are recognized as unstable. If you try numerous operational measures for a variable, and the best reliability you can achieve is a .35, you would still use the measure until a more reliable measure is developed.

Consider a study undertaken to measure the prevalence of disruptive and anti-social behavior exhibited by male institutionalized delinquents (Kelley, 1981). The researcher had dormitory counselors rate each juvenile twice, first at the end of one week and again at the end of three weeks of observations. She found that the average rating given by the counselors between these two time frames was r = .50. Even though this coefficient is considerably less than .80, it is still indicative of acceptable reliability, given (a) the difficulty of each counselor to observe the subjects at the same time, and (b) the fact that presumably all subjects observed were on the high end of the disruptive-antisocial behavior continuum to begin with. In other words, had the rating method been used on a group of subjects exhibiting a wider range of disruptive-antisocial behavior, the correlation probably would have been higher (see pages 54–55 on restricted variability in variables).

Ways of Assessing Validity

There are basically four methods for determining if a variable is being validly measured. They are as follows: **face** (or **content**) **validity, concurrent** (or **comparative**) **validity, predictive** (or **criterion**) **validity,** and **construct** (or **theoretical**) **validity.**

Before explaining each of these types, a special comment needs to be made about terminology. Unfortunately, the terminology surrounding measurement validity has never been completely standardized, so that different words are used to refer to the same type of validity. The policy adopted here is to mention the two main terms applied to each of the four types of validity. The end of this section contains a suggestion on how you can remember the difference between each type.

Face (or content) validity refers to judgments about validity made on the basis of overall appearance. Remember our example of using a bathroom scale to measure occupational interests? Everyone would recognize that this is absurd on the face of it. In other words, without even bothering to undertake a serious investigation, the "bathroom scale" measure of occupational interests can be dismissed as invalid.

Before leaving the issue of face validity, it should be mentioned that scientists should never completely close the door on a novel way of measuring a variable, even if it seems outrageous. Some items used on various standardized personality tests, for example, appear to have little to do with personality. However, when responses to these questions are combined with others, they sometimes provide enlightening information (see Eysenck & Eysenck, 1975; Graham, 1990). The point is that face validity is important to consider, but should rarely be the sole criterion used in assessing the validity of an operational measure.

Concurrent (comparative) validity compares apparent validity of a new operational measure to an established, more widely used operational measure. For example, if you are interested in measuring academic aptitude with some new method (say brain wave patterns), one way to determine if this is a valid measure of academic aptitude is to correlate the scores with some already established paper-and-pencil measures of academic aptitude.

Another example brings us back to the variable of handedness. Coren, Porac, and Duncan (1979) were able to demonstrate a high degree of consistency between "behavioral measures of handedness" (as judged by a researcher while interacting with subjects), and self-reported measures given by the subjects themselves on a written questionnaire. The latter is the more established measure for handedness.

One more example of concurrent validity concerns a phenomenon known as proximics (or spacing behavior). This is the tendency that people (and other animals) have to prefer varying distances between themselves and others when socially interacting. Since the late 1950s when the first investigations of proximics began to be reported, researchers have used at least three different methods for observing this phenomenon. These observational methods are covered more in later chapters, but they are briefly described here: One involved the use of hypothetical sketches of a person in a room, and subjects were asked to indicate how much distance they would prefer to be from various people in this room (a paper-and-pencil measure). Another method involved asking people to "role-play" in an actual room in which one or more persons would stand at various distances from a subject (a role-playing measure). The third method involved observing people in malls or courtyards and estimating the distances they were from one another (a "real world" measure).

Once social scientists had developed more than one distinct method for measuring people's spacing preferences, it was appropriate to ask how valid (and reliable) each method is relative to the other measures. One study addressed this question by comparing the same group of subjects on two of the measures: the paper-and-pencil measure and the role-playing measure. The researchers found that the two measures strongly correlated with one another. The r's in their study ranged between .50 and .80 and were highly significant (Duke & Norwicki, 1972). However, a later study compared all three measures, and reached different conclusions. First, it failed to confirm that the paper-and-pencil measure and the role-playing measure yielded similar results. Most of the r's in this study involving these two measures were below .15 and failed to be statistically significant. In addition, this second study obtained only modest correlations between the real world observations and both the paper-and-pencil measure and the role-playing measure. Most of the r's here were between .00 and .30 (Slane, Petruska, & Cheyfitz, 1981).

Based on their findings, the later researchers reasoned that the real world observations were probably the most accurate, since spacing behavior is conceptualized as something spontaneous among people who interact socially. Since neither the paper-and-pencil method nor the role-playing method yielded results closely correlating with those in the real world, their validity was questionable.

Not only does the example cited above on proximics illustrate the concept of concurrent validity, but the studies also point to the slow ongoing process surrounding scientists' efforts to get a firm fix on a variable's valid measurement. It should not surprise you to find that decades often go by while scientists wrangle over how best to measure some variable. If you are a person who wants the answers and wants them now, you should probably not choose social science as a profession. We will take up issues surrounding attempts to measure spacing preferences again in Chapter 10.

Predictive (or criterion) validity involves assessing the validity of an operational measure by attempting to determine how well values (or scores) from an operational measure predict what they ought to predict. To give an example of predictive validity, say you are interested in measuring risk-taking tendencies, and you develop some questionnaire items that seem to focus on such tendencies. To increase your confidence, you might give the questionnaire to a group of subjects who had been admitted to the emergency room at least twice in the past year and to another group of subjects who had never been admitted. If the scores of these two groups fail to show any average difference, the validity of your items as a measure of risk-taking tendencies would be suspect.

Another example comes from putting yourself in the place of those who first developed the academic achievement tests that are taken by most high school students planning to attend college. Imagine that you are one of the researchers developing the first of these tests. After devising the first test prototype, you administer it to 500 high school seniors and then correlate their scores with their grade point average (GPA). What would you conclude about the prototype's validity if there is no significant relationship between the students' test scores and their GPA? What would you conclude if you get a negative correlation? In both cases, the validity of your prototype test looks questionable.

The key to assessing criterion validity is that the researcher identifies one or more variables that should be associated with, or predicted by, the variable he or she has attempted to operationalize.

Theoretical (or construct) validity is a type of validity that is not of great concern to social scientists. This is because most social science theories have not reached the level of theoretical sophistication where this type of validity is highly relevant. Basically, a well-designed theory will spell out how its key variables should be interlinked with one another. Therefore, if you have valid measures of each of the variables involved, they should intercorrelate just as the theory predicts. If they do not intercorrelate as the theory states, the validity of one or more of the operational measures is questioned. This type of validity is used primarily in the physical sciences, but as the social sciences mature in theoretical terms, this may change.

For the student trying to remember the difference between these four methods of assessing validity, it is unfortunate that all four are sometimes called by names beginning with the letter "c." When confronted with lists such as this that are difficult to distinguish, it is sometimes helpful to use a pneumonic device (i.e., some rhyme or nonsense phrase which aids recall). You may want to memorize the following nonsense phrase: "Face/content, concurrent/compare, predict/criterion, construct/theory."

Finally, even though scientists often speak of operational measures as being either "reliable" or "unreliable," or as "valid" or "invalid," it is closer to reality to think of these qualities in terms of varying degrees, rather than in either/or terms.

Assessing Precision

The precision in measurement of a variable can vary from extremely fine (or precise) to very coarse. To illustrate, consider the variable of age. Social scientists consider it sufficiently precise to measure age according to years, unless they are interested in the age of infants (then months or weeks of age might be used). Although it would certainly be more precise to measure the age of adults by asking them how many months, weeks, or even days old they are rather than just how many years old they are, it is doubtful that the extra precision would accomplish much, especially when balanced against the extra time (and irritation) it would impose on those asked to provide the information.

Some cases, however, may require more than the ordinary degree of precision. One example was discussed at the beginning of this chapter—handedness. Another example has to do with people's sexual orientation. In many studies where this variable has been measured, subjects have simply been asked whether they are heterosexual, homosexual, or bisexual (see Shively, Jones, & DeCecco, 1984; Van Wyk & Geist, 1984). Other studies do not even include the category of bisexuality (e.g., Craig, 1987). Recent studies, however, have used much more precise measures of sexual orientation. In these studies, subjects were asked to indicate what percentage of their sexual fantasies or sexual experiences involved members of the same and the opposite sex, and subjects were given a continuum along which to respond, ranging from 0 to 100 percent (Ellis, Burke, & Ames, 1987; McConaghy & Blaszczynski, 1991). (More will be said in Chapter 8 about this and other response options.)

In describing measurement precision, keep in mind the distinction between discrete and continuous variables. If you are measuring a discrete variable (such as sex or religious preference), your main concern in calibrating the variable is to be exhaustive in specifying all of the categories. On the other hand, if you are measuring a continuous variable (such as handedness or sexual orientation), your most precise measurement strategy is to allow subjects a wide range of response options, not just two or three.

Subject Anxiety and Mood as Factors Affecting Measurement Accuracy

As you might expect, many unintended factors can diminish the accuracy of a researcher's attempts to measure a variable. Some factors are specialized to particular types of research designs, and will be discussed in later chapters. However, one factor that is unavoidable has to do with the basic mood and attitudes people have as they are participating in a research project. In particular, people are likely to have at least some anxiety when serving as subjects, wondering in the back of their minds whether they are responding foolishly or possibly being deceived in some way.

An example of subject anxiety significantly affecting the measurement of a variable comes from a phenomenon known as "white coat hypertension." This refers to evidence that subjects undergoing a simple blood pressure test often exhibit significantly higher blood pressure when tested by a physician dressed in a lab coat than when tested by a plainclothes technician (Pickering et al., 1988).

A recent study demonstrated that in a routine screening of college students for evidence of high blood pressure, both the tester's sex and the subject's sex affected the objective measurement of blood pressure (McCubbin et al., 1991). Specifically, the study found that female college students who were tested by male testers registered significantly higher blood pressure than females tested by females. Similarly, although the differences were not as great, male college students who were tested by female testers registered significantly higher blood pressure than males tested by members of their own sex.

It may be reasonable to argue that "real" blood pressure is that which occurs under the least anxiety-provoking circumstances, but ultimately such an issue is impossible to settle. All that a researcher (or clinician) can do is to be aware that testing conditions will affect the observations that are made. It may also be appropriate to test some subjects (i.e., those who are borderline hypertensive) under more than one set of testing conditions.

Some Closing Remarks About Reliability, Validity, and Precision

If a variable is not being measured reliably, validly, and precisely, it is said to contain **measurement error** (Skog, 1992). This type of error stands in opposition to **sampling error,** a type of error that will be described more in Chapter 13.

As this chapter has revealed, there are few ironclad rules to follow in assessing reliability, validity, and precision in measurement. Reasonable judgments are an indispensable part of devising and assessing appropriate measures for scientific variables. Another point that needs to be emphasized is that there are no perfectly reliable, valid, or precise ways to measure any variable, although some measures come closer than others. For example, variation in such variables as age, sex, marital status, height, and body weight can be measured with high degrees of accuracy, especially from the standpoint of reliability and validity (Wing et al., 1979; Jackson et al., 1990). However, such things as people's behavior, attitudes, and emotions almost always warrant serious concern over their measurement reliability, validity, and precision (see Fishbein & Ajzen, 1975; Eiser & van der Pligt, 1988).

Finally, the concepts of reliability, validity, and precision in measurement are overlapping and complementary concepts in the sense that increases in one often means increases in the other two. Together, these three concepts comprise what scientists call measurement accuracy, and all three are vital considerations in conducting social science research. This does not mean that you should not conduct a study simply because you are unsure of the accuracy of one or more of your operational measures. It merely means that (a) you should be aware that some measures of a variable are likely to be more accurate than others, (b) efforts should be made to establish a measure's relative accuracy, and (c) once established, the more accurate measures should be used instead of the less accurate measures.

Summary

Imagine that two studies attempt to answer the same question, and that they come to inconsistent conclusions. Say that one study finds a positive correlation between two variables, and the other study finds a negative correlation. Let us consider the most likely explanations: First, it is conceivable that data were miscoded or erroneously interpreted in one of the two studies. Second, perhaps the researcher in one of the studies actually faked his or her findings, a phenomenon which has occasionally been documented (see Chapter 18). A third possibility, the focus of this chapter, is that one or both of the key variables in one of the two studies was measured inappropriately.

There are three interrelated forms of inappropriate or inaccurate operational measures of a scientific concept: reliability, validity, and precision. No one can ever expect perfection, but every effort should be made in scientific studies to achieve a high degree of accuracy.

Reliability refers to the degree to which an operational measure can be reproduced under reasonable conditions. For example, since people's interest in sports is fairly stable over time, you would expect a reliable measure of sports interest to yield a strong correlation among a group of subjects from one month to another. If subjects who had a strong interest one month tended to not indicate a strong interest the following month, you would have to doubt the reliability of the questions that were used. This is an example of test-retest (or consistency) reliability. The other three main forms of reliability utilized in the social sciences are cross-test, inter-item, and inter-rater reliability. Cross-test reliability compares two tests designed to measure the same variable. Inter-item reliability compares scores for a portion of the items comprising a multi-item test with scores for another portion. Inter-rater reliability is when raters (or judges) must be used to measure a variable, and it usually involves determining how much agreement there is between two or more raters asked to judge the extent of some characteristic in a group of subjects.

The second feature of an accurate operational definition, validity, refers to the degree to which an operational measure is, in fact, measuring what it is purported to measure. For instance, even if your measure of "interest in sports" yields fairly consistent responses from a group of subjects at two points in time, there still may be reason to doubt that "interest in sports" is actually what you are measuring. Four criteria are used to assess the validity of a measure. These are known as face (or content) validity, concurrent (or comparative) validity, predictive (or criterion) validity, and construct (or theoretical) validity.

Precision is the third feature of measurement accuracy. This means that variation in a variable can be measured (or calibrated) in a fine-grained or a coarse-grained manor. Fine-grained measures are more precise than coarse-grained measures, and continuous variables are best measured in a fine-grained manner. More will be said in the next chapter about ways to calibrate the measurement of variables.

References

Anastasi, A. (1976). *Psychological testing*. New York: Macmillan.

Annett, M. A. (1970). Classification of hand preference by association analysis. *British Journal of Psychology, 61,* 303–321.

Ardila, A., Ardila, O., Bryden, M. P., Ostrosky, F., Rosselli, M., & Steenhuis, R. (1989). Effects of cultural background and education on handedness. *Neuropsychologia, 27,* 893–897.

Charney, E., Goodman, H., McBridge, M., Lyon, B., & Pratt, R. (1976). Childhood antecedents of adult obesity: Do chubby infants become obese adults? *New England Journal of Medicine, 295,* 6–9.

Coren, S. (Ed.). (1990). *Left-handedness: Behavioral implications and anomalies*. Amsterdam: North-Holland.

Coren, S., Porac, C., & Duncan, P. (1979). A behaviorally validated self-report inventory to assess four types of lateral preference. *Journal of Clinical Neuropsychology, 1,* 55–64.

Craig, R. J. (1987). MMPI-derived prevalence estimates of homosexuality among drug-dependent patients. *International Journal of the Addictions, 22,* 1139–1145.

Dawson, J. L. B. (1977). Alaskan Eskimo hand, eye, auditory dominance and cognitive style. *Psychologia, 20,* 121–135.

Dean, R. S. (1982). Assessing patterns of lateral preference. *Clinical Neuropsychology, 4,* 124–128.

Duke, M. P., & Norwicki, S. Jr. (1972). A new measure and social-learning model for interpersonal distance. *Journal of Experimental Research in Personality, 6,* 119–132.

Eiser, J. R., & van der Pligt, J. (1988). *Attitudes and decisions*. London: Routledge.

Ellis, L., & Ames, M. A. (1989). Delinquency, sidedness, and sex. *Journal of General Psychology, 116,* 57–62.

Ellis, L., Burke, D., & Ames, M. A. (1987). Sexual orientation as a continuous variable: A comparison between the sexes. *Archives of Sexual Behavior, 16,* 523–529.

Eysenck, S. B., & Eysenck, H. J. (1975). *Manual of the Eysenck Personality Questionnaire: Adult version and children's version*. London: University of London Press.

Fishbein, M., & Ajzen, I. (1975). *Belief, attitude, intention and behaviour: An introduction to theory and research*. Reading, MA: Addison-Wesley.

Graham, J. R. (1990). *MMPI-2: Assessing personality and psychopathology*. New York: Oxford University Press.

Harris, L. J. (1990). Cultural influences on handedness: Historical and contemporary theory and evidence. In S. Coren (Ed.), *Left-handedness: Behavioral implications and anomalies* (pp. 195–258). Amsterdam: North-Holland.

Hunt, E. (1983). On the nature of intelligence. *Science, 219,* 141–146.

Jackson, J., Strauss, C. C., Lee, A. A., & Hunter, K. (1990). Parent's accuracy in estimating child weight status. *Addictive Behaviors, 15,* 65–68.

Kass, S. J., & Vodanovich, S. J. (1990). Boredom proneness: Its relationship to type A behavior pattern and sensation seeking. *Psychology, 27,* 7–16.

Kelley, C. (1981). Reliability of the behavior problem checklist with institutionalized male delinquents. *Journal of Abnormal Child Psychology, 9,* 243–250.

McConaghy, N., & Blaszczynski, A. (1991). Initial stages of validation by penile volume assessment that sexual orientation is distributed dimensionally. *Comprehensive Psychiatry, 32,* 52–58.

McCubbin, J. A., Wilson, J. F., Bruehl, S., Brady, M., Clark, K., & Kort, E. (1991). Gender effects on blood pressures obtained during an on-campus screening. *Psychosomatic Medicine, 53,* 90–100.

Pickering, T. G., James G. D., Boddie, C., Harshfield, G. A., Blank, S., Laragh, J. H. (1988). How common is white coat hypertension? *Journal of the American Medical Association, 259,* 225–228.

Rossi, P. H., & Freeman, H. E. (1989). *Evaluation: A systematic approach* (4th ed.). Newbury Park, CA: Sage.

Sattler, J. M. (1982). *Assessments of children's intelligence and special abilities* (2nd ed.). Boston: Allyn & Bacon.

Shively, M. G., Jones, C., & De Cecco, J. P. (1984). Research on sexual orientation: Definitions and methods. *Journal of Homosexuality, 9,* 127–136.

Skog, O. (1992). The validity of self-reported drug use. *British Journal of Addiction, 87,* 539–548.

Slane, S., Petruska, R., & Cheyfitz, S. (1981). Personal space measurement: A validational comparison. *Psychological Record, 31,* 145–151.

Steenhuis, R. E., Bryden, M. P., Schwartz, M., & Lawson, S. (1990). Reliability of hand preference items and factors. *Journal of Clinical and Experimental Neuropsychology, 12,* 921–930.

Van Wyk, P. H., & Geist, C. S. (1984). Psychosocial development of heterosexual, bisexual, and homosexual behavior. *Archives of Sexual Behavior, 13,* 505–506.

Williams, S. M. (1991). Handedness inventories: Edinburgh versus Annett. *Neuropsychology, 5,* 43–48.

Wing, R., Epstein, L., Ossip, D., & LaPorte, R. (1979). Reliability and validity of self-report and observer's estimates of relative weight. *Addictive Behaviors, 4,* 133–140.

Zuckerman, M. (1979). *Sensation seeking: Beyond the optimal level of arousal.* Hillsdale, NJ: Erlbaum.

Suggested Reading

Carmines, E. G., and Zeller, R. A. (1979). *Reliability and validity assessment.* Beverly Hills, CA: Sage. (This brief book provides useful information to those interested in refining their skills in measuring variables.)

Kirk, J., and Miller, M. L. (1986). *Reliability and validity in qualitative research.* Beverly Hills, CA: Sage.

Journals which specialize in articles on measurement issues in the social sciences are the following:

Behavior Research Methods, Instruments and Computers
Educational and Psychological Measurement
Measurement and Evaluation in Counseling and Development

Data Based on Self-Reports: Guidelines for Constructing and Administering Questionnaires

N o one knows the precise figure, but it is safe to say that most social science data are collected by way of human subjects providing responses to questionnaires. As the term has come to be used in social science, a **questionnaire** refers to any research instrument through which human beings provide information about their lives and behavior (and sometimes the lives and behavior of others they know, such as family members). This information is provided either by directly responding to written questions, or via questions presented during a telephone conversation or a face-to-face interview.

A **research instrument** refers to any physical thing (including a questionnaire) that is used to collect scientific data. In the broadest sense of the term, a questionnaire can even include research instruments that are completed by trained observers without actually interviewing subjects (for example, when observers record direct observations of behavior). In general, however, questionnaires are research instruments in which persons without specialized training in data collection play a central role in providing the information about themselves.

Questionnaires are fundamental to social science research, and thus it is important for you to be familiar with the principles and guidelines for designing and administering questionnaires. This chapter will focus on the design of questionnaires. The fact that persons who generally have no formal training in social science provide most of the ''raw data'' upon which most social science knowledge is based underscores the importance of questionnaire design.

Basic Terminology

Before describing how to design a research questionnaire, some basic terminology needs to be introduced. First, a distinction should be made between a research **subject** and a **respondent.** The term respondent refers to a person who provides asked-for information on a questionnaire or in an interview. The concept of a subject in science includes respondents, although it also refers to any biological organism (human or otherwise) that is part of a scientific study (other than the researchers).

A basic concept in the context of a questionnaire is that of the **question** (or **questionnaire item**). A question or item refers to anything that elicits linguistic or numeric responses (in either written or oral form) from a respondent. Questions in a research questionnaire need not be phrased literally in the form of a question. For example, respondents might be asked to respond to the following statements:

> I consider it important that whomever I marry share my religious beliefs.
> As a child, I was very hyperactive.

Both of these statements could constitute questions or items in a questionnaire. Sometimes questions in a questionnaire consist of incomplete sentences. For example, subjects might be instructed to indicate how they perceive themselves with respect to the following adjectives and phrases:

> Outgoing personality
> Superstitious
> Impulsive

Each of these phrases would be considered a question or item as long as subjects were permitted to make some sort of response to each one. Before saying more about the wording of questions, attention will be given to the response options that can be offered to subjects.

Response Options for Questions

Response options refer to the range of options given to subjects with regard to a question. These options are important to a researcher because they have a major influence on the type of data that will eventually be available for analysis. Response options fall into four general categories: open-ended, fill-in-the-blank, end-anchored, and all-points-anchored. There are several forms of each of these general types.

Open-Ended Response Options

Items that present a question (or make a statement) without giving any constraints on how subjects can respond are called open-ended. Examples of items providing open-ended response options include:

> What do you think of war?
> In what ways is your family important to you?

Controversy has long surrounded the advisability of using open-ended questions (see Lazarfeld, 1944), with most researchers opting for closed-ended response options (described below). The main drawback to open-ended response options is that they tend to be time-consuming to code (Geer, 1991). **Coding** refers to the process of deciding how data will be entered into a standard format for analysis. Not only is a considerable amount of time involved in reading and then deciding how best to code each response, but responses to many open-ended questions are sometimes ambiguous and impossible to decipher.

Studies that have used open-ended questions (e.g., Geer, 1991) have found that these items are particularly helpful in exploring areas of research that have received little prior attention. For example, following the growing concern that Americans had with sexual harassment in the workplace and on college campuses, subjects were asked to report, in an open-ended format, any incidences of sexual harassment that they knew about (Till, 1980). This was useful to the researcher and his associates in delineating people's varying conceptions of what constitutes sexual harassment. Concerns that open-ended questions often cause subjects to go off on irrelevant tangents have been largely discounted provided the questions are clearly phrased (Geer, 1991).

Fill-in-the-Blank Response Options

Questions asking subjects to respond by writing in or uttering a limited number of words (usually one or two) are called fill-in-the-blank items. Examples of fill-in-the-blank questions are:

> Religious preference (if Protestant, specify denomination) _____
> Place of birth _____

Items with fill-in-the-blank response options are often used for variables measured at the nominal level. Often, they will be coded into categories (e.g., a dozen or so religious groups or geographical regions) by the researcher.

End-Anchored Continuum Response Options

The distinguishing feature of end-anchored continuums is that subjects are allowed to respond along a continuum in which only the two extreme values have specific meaning. There are three forms of this response option: the **demarcated linear form** and two **numeric forms.**

To give an example of the demarcated linear form, say you are interested in attitudes toward capital punishment. You might ask the following question:

> To what degree do you believe that it is appropriate for the state to execute persons convicted of murder?
>
> Extremely   Extremely
> Inappropriate   Appropriate
>
> |___|___|___|___|___|___|___|___|

The best known example of the demarcated linear form of the end-anchored continuum is called the **semantic differential scale.** Developed in the 1950s (Osgood, Suci, & Tannenbaum, 1957), these scales arrange numerous polar opposite adjectives at each end of a linear continuum (usually demarcated into seven response options), and ask subjects to respond to a single noun or phrase (e.g., murderers, the elderly, political liberals) by putting an "X" in the appropriate space. Examples of the adjectives might include: Competent-Incompetent, Strong-Weak, Selfish-Generous, Good-Bad (Monette, Sullivan, DeJong, 1990:379; Neuman, 1991:163).

In the numeric form of the end-anchored continuum, the questions may be asked in the same way, but in place of the linear continuum, subjects are instructed to answer by writing in or circling a number. For the **write-in end-anchored response option**, the question might be stated as follows:

> To what degree do you approve of the state executing persons convicted of murder? (Answer anywhere from 1 to 9, with 1 representing strongly approve, and 9 representing strongly disapprove) _____

An actual example was a study designed to more precisely measure homosexuality than by simply asking subjects whether they are homosexual, heterosexual, or bisexual (Ellis, Burke, & Ames, 1987). The question allowed subjects to answer from 0 to 100, and was phrased as follows:

> When imagining sexual relationships, the individual with whom you imagine interacting is
>
> a member of the opposite sex _____ % of the time
> a member of the same sex _____ % of the time

The **circled end-anchored response option** of the question on the death penalty would normally appear as follows:

To what degree do you approve of the state executing persons convicted of murder?

Strongly Disapprove								Strongly Approve
1	2	3	4	5	6	7	8	9

Both the numeric forms are often more compact and quicker to transcribe for computerized data entry than is the demarcated line form.

All-Points-Anchored Response Options

The fourth type of response option involves anchoring all the response options with words (usually adjectives or adverbs). Although there are no hard-and-fast rules for the number of words used, the most common scales have five points and follow this form:

SA—Strongly Agree (or Strongly Approve)
A—Agree (or Approve)
N—Neutral
D—Disagree (or Disapprove)
SD—Strongly Disagree (or Strongly Disapprove)

This form is called the **Likert scale,** after one of the first social scientists to use it (Likert, 1932). To refer to other types of all-points-anchored scales, the term **Likert-type** is sometimes used (e.g., Stuart & Jacobson, 1979:245). Likert-type scales have 4, 6, or 7 response options instead of 5, or offer response continuums such as "extremely good performance," "good performance," "average performance," "poor performance," and "extremely poor performance" (Wyatt, 1989).[1]

Deciding Which Response Options to Use

A researcher has several things to consider in deciding on which response option to offer subjects for each question asked. The following four points are particularly important:

(1) *Try to minimize the amount of coding.* Generally, the fewer items that must be read, interpreted, and coded by a researcher (or coding assistant), the better. Of the four main types of response options just outlined, the latter two require no coding and are therefore generally preferred over the first two types.

(2) *Try to measure variables at least at the interval level.* Whereas end-anchored continuum scales almost always meet the assumption of interval measurement, all-points-anchored scales are less certain in this regard. You can not be as sure that the adjectives used to anchor each point in a scale will be interpreted by subjects in equal-interval fashion as you can be when consecutive numbers are used.

(3) *Avoid frequently switching from one type of response option to another.* This can be accomplished by organizing questions so all those with similar response options appear together.

(4) *Give subjects considerable latitude in their responses.* Probably the most frequent error made in constructing items for research questionnaires is that of allowing insufficient response options for subjects. This deficiency can often be remedied simply by changing a question requiring a yes/no (or an agree/disagree) response to one that allows subjects to indicate "to what degree" they have a particular characteristic or attitude on a scale from 1 to 10. Consider the following:

What percentage of people do you think believe in ESP (extrasensory perception)? This question has been studied extensively in Canada in recent years (Gray, 1990). One group of studies found that more than 80% of Canadians believe in ESP (Gray, 1990:174), whereas other studies have found that less than half of Canadians believe in ESP (a percentage similar to this has also been reported for the United States) (Messer & Griggs, 1989:189).

What would account for a discrepancy of more than 30%? The questions are phrased in similar ways, but the response options are substantially different. In the studies that have obtained the lower percentages, respondents are given only two choices: either they believe in ESP or they do not. The studies that have found 80% of Canadians believing in ESP ask subjects *to what degree* do they believe in or doubt the reality of ESP. Subjects are allowed to respond on a nine-point scale ranging from +4 (meaning extremely convinced that ESP actually occurs) to –4 (meaning extremely doubtful that ESP actually occurs).

Notice that the second of these two options allows respondents who are only slightly open to the possibility that ESP really occurs to answer a "+1" or possibly "+2." However, in responding to the either/or response option, many of these "slightly open" respondents would say that they do not believe in ESP.

Another example of how subtle phrasing of questions can affect people's responses comes from a 1980 CBS-New York Times poll on abortion (Reiss, 1981:272). At two different points in the interview, respondents were asked the following contradictory questions:

> Do you think there should be an amendment to the Constitution prohibiting abortion, or shouldn't there be such an amendment?

> Do you believe there should be an amendment to the Constitution protecting the life of the unborn child, or shouldn't there be such an amendment?

To the first question, 29% agreed and 62% disagreed (with 9% uncertain). To the second question, 50% agreed and 39% disagreed (with 11% uncertain). It is obvious that substantial percentages of respondents will express contradictory opinions simply because of the way the questions were phrased. There is even evidence that the order in which certain questions on such controversial issues as abortion are asked will affect many people's responses (Tenvergert et al., 1992).

In constructing response options, researchers should keep in mind the tremendous variability that exists in most human social behavior (and attitudes). Given this variability, researchers should construct their questions in ways that capture this variability. Otherwise, they force subjects to distort accounts of their views and behavior.

Of course, providing a limited number of response options is appropriate for many discrete variables (such as a respondent's sex or political party affiliation). Also, there are times in the analysis of data when a researcher will be justified in collapsing some of the response options. For example, if you only have 30 subjects in a study, and they responded to a question on a 20-point scale, you may want to collapse the responses to a considerable degree (e.g., from 1 to 5, 6 to 10, 11 to 15, and 16 to 20). However, it is rarely advisable to restrict the response options for subjects answering questions about continuous variables to a point that the real diversity in the behavior can not be gaged.

Although not all social scientists would agree on this point, my advice is that researchers use end-anchored continuum scales as much as possible when measuring continuous variables. It used to be recommended that in telephone and personal interview surveys, no more than four all-points-anchored categories be given to subjects (because of the difficulty people would have in remembering the name of each response category as the questions were being presented). However, with end-anchored continuums, subjects only need to remember the names of the two ends of the continuum and how many segments exist between the two ends. Thus, even with surveys based upon telephone and personal interviews, end-anchored continuum scales appear to be increasingly utilized (Loken et al., 1987).

Guidelines for Item Construction

Most advice given by seasoned researchers about questions to ask on questionnaires falls within the realm of common sense. For example, questions should be easy to understand, and the questionnaire itself should be well-organized and simple to follow.

About the only rules that can be set out with no fear of contradiction are that the person designing the questionnaire should (a) put himself or herself in the place of the person completing the questionnaire, and (b) **pretest** any questionnaire before making copies for final distribution (Fowler & Mangione, 1990). Pretesting is administering a questionnaire to would-be subjects before giving it to actual subjects.

It is best to pretest in more than one or two phases. I recommend using all four of the following steps, with revisions in your questionnaire after each phase:

Self-Test Phase: If possible, every questionnaire should first be taken by the person who designed it. After the questionnaire has been completed, it should be set aside for a few days (so that it is no longer fresh in the designer's mind). Then a copy should be printed out and completed by the designer as though he or she were an actual respondent. In completing the questionnaire, the designer should try to assume the role of a subject who will actually be surveyed.

Informed Pre-Subject Phase: Copies of the questionnaire should be given to three or four people who are aware of the basic purpose of the study. These pre-subjects should be asked to critique each question for clarity and likelihood of eliciting responses relevant to the study's purpose.

Uninformed Pre-Subject Phase: Up to a dozen or so copies of the revised questionnaire should be administered to people who are given no more details about the purpose of the study than the final group of subjects who will eventually be sampled. This group of pre-subjects should be asked to complete the questionnaire in its entirety without critiquing it. After completing the questionnaire, these pre-subjects should be debriefed and asked to identify any problems with the wording of the questions. Since the designer of the questionnaire is often tempted in these debriefing sessions to correct the pre-subjects about how they *should* have interpreted the questions, it is better to have someone other than the questionnaire's designer performing these interviews. None of these completed questionnaires will be used in the study.

Early Actual Subject Phase: Assuming that the questionnaires do not all have to be administered at one time, it is a good idea to conduct one final pretest of the first 10 to 25 questionnaires actually administered. Unless some serious problems arise, the data from these questionnaires will be included in the study.

Pretesting of questionnaires is very important, whether the questionnaires are completed directly by respondents or by trained interviewers.

Types of Questions to Avoid

Even though no ironclad rules can be made regarding exactly how to design and phrase questionnaire items, six recommendations can be stated:

(1) *Avoid rhetorical and leading questions.* Leading questions are stated in such a way as to "beg" for a particular response. Rarely should items that are rhetorical or leading be included in a questionnaire (unless a questionnaire is being used as a propaganda tool instead of for scientific research).

Especially when studying people's attitudes on some subject, a researcher may be tempted to try to "open their minds." As a result, questions are likely to be argumentative or have a "preachy" tone to them. The following two questions are essentially rhetorical in character:

Wouldn't you say it is high time that women in this country receive equal treatment under the law?
How much justification can you see in the way people on welfare are being treated in today's society?

The rhetorical nature of these questions may elicit affirmative responses from significant numbers of subjects who would not have responded affirmatively to neutrally phrased questions. However, the value of this information as reflections of peoples real attitudes will have been compromised.

(2) *Avoid conjunctive items.* Conjunctive items ask subjects to respond to more than one issue at a time. For example, if your question is intended to determine how favorable people's attitudes are toward a country's current president, you might ask whether subjects consider the president to be an honest and competent leader. Although both of these personal qualities would be seen as favorable by most people, some respondents might consider the president honest but not competent, or vice versa. Normally, if you are interested in someone's overall attitudes toward something rather than in how they would objectively assess various qualities of something, your questions should be phrased in a straightforward way, e.g., What is your overall impression of the current president?

(3) *Avoid "yeasaying" items.* Social scientists have discovered that certain types of statements often elicit what are called yeasaying responses from a substantial proportion of subjects (Goldsmith, 1987). Basically, these items have a philosophical-sounding "tone" that seems to compel many respondents to affirm them. Here are two examples:

These days, a person does not really know who he can count on.
With the way things look for the future, it is hardly fair to bring children into the world.

What makes these items noteworthy is that they were among the items used for years to measure **anomie,** a widely used concept roughly meaning "without social identity" (Durkheim, 1951). In the early 1970s, the validity of such items for measuring anomie was called into question when it was discovered that many subjects who agreed with these two statements also agreed with their exact opposite (sometimes even within the same questionnaire!) (Carr, 1971). Here are examples:

These days, a person knows who he can count on.
With the way things look for the future, it is a good time to be bringing children into the world.

Items such as these have a quality about them that seems to "ring true" for many people regardless of any objective meaning they may convey. Other examples of yeasaying items come from studying the way people express their views on highly emotional issues such as the earlier example on abortion. Unless the specific purpose of a study is to measure yeasaying tendencies, items that tend to elicit yeasaying responses should be avoided.

(4) *Avoid questions containing a kernel of truth, particularly if they are obviously condescending (i.e., insulting).* Examples of these questions are:

> The elderly are a burden to society.
> Ex-convicts can not be trusted.

Both of these statements would put many respondents in a quandary as to how to respond. They would feel uncomfortable grossly generalizing about people in ways that are obviously derogatory. Nevertheless, they might also feel that both the elderly and ex-convicts as *groups* do differ from people *in general* as the statements assert.

(5) *Avoid questions that have ambiguous words or phrases.* Even though the following items at first glance seem to be clear, they could be taken in a variety of ways:

> Do you believe that prisons are effective?
> Are you a drug user?

For example, the concept of *prison effectiveness* could be interpreted in several ways. It could be interpreted in the sense of keeping convicted prisoners from committing crime as long as they are behind bars, committing new crimes after prison release, or even holding down a job and staying off the welfare roles after leaving prison. Regarding the question of drug use, would not the type of drugs, the amount, and the time frame involved all be important?

No matter how much experience you have at constructing questionnaires, you should always be on guard against ambiguous questions. A recent article cited a number of examples of ambiguously worded questions located in questionnaires administered by professional government and academic agencies (Fowler, 1992).

(6) *Avoid questions about behavior that are not bounded by time (and sometimes by place).* For example, the following question would be difficult for subjects to answer if their church-attending behavior had recently changed:

> How often do you go to church? _____

To make this question more meaningful, it might be bounded as follows, assuming that the researcher is primarily interested in recent church attendance:

> Over the past year, how many times did you attend church services? _____

If church-attending behavior in childhood is of primary interest, then the question might be phrased as follows:

> As you were growing up, about how many times did you attend church services in an average year? _____

Or, if both childhood and current church attendance are of interest, the question might be phrased as follows:

> Please indicate about how many times you attended church services *in an average year* during the following times in your life:
>   From age 1 to 10 _____
>   From age 11 to 18 _____
>   From 19 to present (if applicable) _____

Some Examples of Poorly Phrased Questions

Although many questionnaire items can only be meaningfully critiqued within the context of the overall purpose of the study for which they were designed, some items are so obviously flawed that they should not be used for any research study. Read each of the following four examples, and see if you can spot problems with them:

1. What is the size of your family? _____
2. Do you get along with your parents? _____
3. If a women says no to sex, she means no. _____
4. Is peer pressure a result of your drinking? _____

Below are brief critiques and more suitable alternatives for each of these four questions.

(1) *What is the size of your family?* Some subjects answering this question might assume that the researcher is only interested in knowing how many brothers and sisters (siblings) they have, while others would probably include their parents *plus* their siblings in the count. Subjects whose parents are divorced might not know whether to include both parents or just one. Also, those with older siblings no longer living at home would probably not know whether to include them or not. This question is simply too vague.

Most of the ambiguities could be avoided by asking subjects: *How many brothers and sisters do you have?* Of course, a researcher interested in more detailed aspects of various family arrangements might instead ask whether all family members were presently in the home, or whether the subjects had any half-siblings (either in or outside the home).

(2) *Do you get along with your parents?* This question has two problems. First, it asks for an either/or answer to a question that many subjects would want to give an intermediate answer to. The second problem is that the question is not bounded in

time (i.e., within the past year, the past five years, throughout childhood). Obviously, parent-child relationships are dynamic and almost certain to vary over time. A better question might be:

> On a scale from 1 to 10 (with 1 being the worst, and 10 being the best imaginable), how would you rate your relationship with your parents during the following periods of your life?
>
> From early childhood to age 12 _____
> From ages 13 to 18 _____
> Beyond 18 (if applicable) _____

(3) *If a woman says no to sex, she means no.* This statement seems straightforward. However, research has shown that a substantial minority of women self-report that they sometimes say no to a male's sexual advances in dating situations when they are in fact willing to have sex (Muehlenhard & Hollabaugh, 1988). Members of either sex who are aware of (or at least suspect) this possibility will be hard-pressed to give an unqualified response to the statement.

Depending on the exact purpose for including this item in a research questionnaire, a better phrasing might be as follows:

> To what degree do you feel that, in a dating situation, if a woman says she does not want to have sex, her date has no right to push the issue further? Answer from 0 to 10, with 0 meaning that her date has no right to pressure her, and 10 meaning that he has a right to pressure her until he gets his way. _____

(4) *Is peer pressure a result of your drinking?* Among other things, this question is poorly phrased. Presumably, the researcher who proposed it wanted to know to what degree subjects who drank did so because of peer pressure (rather than because they liked its taste, were becoming addicted, or wanted to for some other reason).

This question might be better broken into the following two questions:

> In the past year or so, how often have you consumed alcohol? (circle one)
> never
> seldom
> occasionally
> fairly often
> very often
>
> If you do drink, indicate which of the following best explains why you do so?
> (Assign a 1 to the main reason and a 2 to the second most important reason)
> _____ Because my friends are doing it
> _____ Because I enjoy the taste
> _____ Because I am (or may be becoming) addicted
> _____ Because I was encouraged to do so at home
> _____ Because I like the way it makes me feel
> _____ Other (specify) _____

Combining Two or More Items for Difficult-to-Measure Variables

If a variable can be reliably and validly measured with a single item, there is little justification for including more than one question about it in a questionnaire. For example, researchers do not need to develop more than one item for measuring sex and age of subjects. However, for variables that are difficult to measure accurately (as many variables pertaining to behavior, emotions, and attitudes are), researchers often ask more than one question within the same questionnaire and then combine the responses to these items into a single score. These measures are called **multi-item scales,** and have been shown to substantially improve the reliability of difficult-to-measure variables (Sax, 1980:271; Rushton, Brainerd, & Pressley, 1983; Mould, 1988:332; Neston & Safer, 1990).

An example of a multi-item scale was discussed at the beginning of Chapter 7. Readers will recall that in recent years the measurement of handedness has often entailed asking subjects to indicate how frequently they use each hand in performing several dexterity tasks, not just one. Researchers normally derive a single handedness score for each subject by adding up the responses given to each of several dexterity items. Thus, if there were 10 items comprising a handedness scale (hand used in writing, hand used in throwing a ball, etc.), and subjects could respond to each item anywhere from 1 (nearly always right) to 5 (nearly always left), then on the final scale, each subject could score anywhere from 10 (extremely right-handed) to 50 (extremely left-handed).

Another example of multi-item scales to which all students can relate are examination scores. Rather than assigning grades to students on the basis of how well they answered a single question, instructors typically ask numerous questions throughout the term and then designate the ''amount learned'' according to the *proportion* of questions that each student answers correctly.

Here are some guidelines to keep in mind when devising multi-item scales:

(1) *Make sure that all the items used in a given scale are relevant to the variable targeted for measurement.* Unfortunately, determining the relevance of items to a variable is not always easy or obvious, even for experienced researchers. Because intuitive methods of judging whether questions are really relevant to a particular variable can sometimes be incorrect (especially when dealing with complex intellectual and attitudinal variables), many researchers supplement their intuition with a special statistical technique—called *factor analysis.* Basically, factor analysis is an extension of correlational statistics (see Chapter 4) that makes it possible to locate subtle patterns in the way subjects respond. From these patterns, researchers are able to group questionnaire items into categories corresponding to different variables (Thompson, 1962). More will be said about factor analysis in Chapter 17.

(2) *The items comprising a scale are usually equally weighted.* This means that no question has more influence on the final scale score than any other question. To give each item equal weight, the structure and number of response options for each item should all be the same.

(3) *Whenever possible, researchers should measure continuous variables* (the opposite of discrete variables) *at the interval or ratio levels.* Continuous variables measured at the nominal and ordinal levels make it difficult for a researcher to treat the results in statistically meaningful ways. In particular, only variables measured at the interval or ratio levels allow you to calculate means and standard deviations.

(4) *In deriving individual scores on a scale, researchers should* **reverse score** *any items that are negatives of other items comprising the scale.* For example, say you used the following two items to measure the degree to which adults exhibited hyperactive-disruptive symptoms in childhood:

> To what degree do you recall being disruptive in grade school? (Answer from 1 to 9, with 1 representing "not at all" and 9 representing "to an extreme degree")
> _____ .

> When you were a child, to what degree did you enjoy playing quietly by yourself or with a friend, rather than engaging in boisterous, rowdy play? (Answer from 1 to 9, with 1 representing "not at all" and 9 representing "to an extreme degree")
> _____ .

In order for the possible scores on this two-item scale to range as they should from 2 to 18, you need to invert the score for one of them. Since this is a scale for measuring childhood hyperactivity and disruptiveness, which of the two items should be reverse scored? The answer is the second one.

Scenario Items

Some questionnaire items consist not simply of a question or brief statement, but describe a series of hypothetical social circumstances to which subjects are asked to respond. These are called **scenario items** (or **scenarios**).

Scenario items have been used in recent years to study circumstances associated with aggression, both sexual (e.g., Tetreault & Barnett, 1987; Bridges & McGrail, 1989) and nonsexual (Ellis, Hoffman, & Burke, 1990). In this latter study, subjects were given the following scenario:

> You loaned $100 more than a year ago to someone who is now avoiding you. You look the person up, and remind him/her that the money has not yet been paid back. The person laughs and says he/she did return it several months ago, and tells you that you are lying about not remembering. What would you most likely do?
> _____

Subjects were asked to respond on a five-point scale, ranging from "Say nothing and/or walk away" to "Physically attack the person."

Scenario items can be used to look for both subtle and complex variations in responses to social environmental factors. Little research has yet been conducted, however, to determine how closely responses to scenario items correspond to people's actual behavior when confronted with circumstances resembling the scenarios.

Final Comments on Constructing Social Science Questionnaires

In measuring variables, it is wise to employ operational measures that have already been developed and shown to be reliable and valid according to criteria presented in Chapter 7. For this reason (as well as others), if you are not familiar with the literature in an area, you should try to find help from someone who has done prior work in the area.

Having made the point in favor of using already tried-and-true operational measures when they exist, it should be quickly added that, if you are familiar with a field and feel you have a good reason for defying convention, do so. Often, the biggest breakthroughs in science come from novel innovations in the operationalization of some key variable (Kennedy, Sherman, & Lamont-Havers, 1972:602).

Additional closing remarks center around never abusing the goodwill of those who agree to serve as subjects in a study. One of the heartwarming rewards of social science research comes from finding how willing most people are to cooperate as research subjects. This willingness to help is greatest, of course, when the time involved seems reasonable, when they have reason to believe that the results will be worthwhile, and when they are treated courteously and in accordance with the golden rule ("Do unto others as you would have them do unto you"). Also, people are more inclined to be subjects in a research project if the questions are stated clearly and concisely, and the response options are appropriate and simple to understand.

Another general point has to do with the phrasing of questionnaire items. Sometimes fairly subtle changes in the wording of questions can have substantial effects upon response patterns. For a case in point, consider a recent study in which 42% of college males self-reported having coerced a female into sexual behavior (Craig, Kalichman, & Follingstad, 1989). This percentage is nearly three times higher than what all other studies of males have found (reviewed by Ellis, 1989:4). In discussing these findings, the investigators speculated that the difference may have been due to the unique way they phrased their question. Instead of asking subjects "Have you ever . . . ," Craig et al. (1989:430) asked them "How many times have you ever. . . ." If this simple change in wording is responsible for their unusual findings, it still leaves open the issue of which is the more valid way to phrase such questions.

Finally, it should be noted that not all data in the social sciences are collected via questionnaires. In particular, a number of social science studies have been based on direct observations. These data collection methods are given attention in the next two chapters.

Summary

This chapter has dealt with issues and options having to do with the construction of social science research questionnaires. No one knows exactly what proportion of social science data are derived from questionnaires (either directly by having respondents read and respond to questions, or less directly by having them respond to questions asked by an interviewer), but it is safe to say that most social science data is obtained in this way. The advantages of this method of data collection, compared to direct observation by trained researchers, is that massive amounts of data can often be collected cheaply and quickly. However, the main potential disadvantage is that the quality of the data is often justifiably suspect. Unless the questions and response options are carefully phrased and pretested, and the subjects are motivated to provide honest and thoughtful answers, the results can be very misleading.

Three major topics about questionnaire construction were addressed in this chapter. The first had to do with the types of response options that can be presented to respondents. These options were subsumed under the following four categories: open-ended, fill-in-the-blank, end-anchored (both linear and numeric), and all-points-anchored. Each option has legitimate uses in the social sciences. Many factors need to be weighed by researchers in deciding which response option to use, including the degree of precision desired, the age and educational background of the subjects, and the audience for which the final report of results is being prepared.

The second topic of this chapter dealt with ways of phrasing items in a questionnaire. A number of guidelines were offered while recognizing that sometimes there are legitimate reasons for deviating from one or all of them. About the only guideline that should never be ignored has to do with pretesting questionnaires. Ideally, questionnaire pretesting should consist of four phases: a self-test phase, an informed pre-subject phase, an uninformed pre-subject phase, and an early actual subject phase.

The third topic of this chapter pertained to the formation of multi-item scales by combining the results of two or more individual questions that are intended to measure the same variable. This procedure can serve to broaden the variation in scores as well as increase the reliability of your measurement of the variable in question.

Before making some final comments about the art of questionnaire construction, scenario items were discussed. These are items in which hypothetical social circumstances are presented to a subject, and the subject is asked to reveal how he or she would respond to those circumstances.

Notes

[1] Unfortunately, terminology is not entirely standardized with respect to what does and does not constitute a Likert, or Likert-type scale. For example, one report recently described a 10-point end-anchored continuum as a "Likert format" (Pelham et al., 1992:284).

References

Bridges, J. S., & McGrail, C. A. (1989). Attributions of responsibility for date and stranger rape. *Sex Roles, 21,* 273–286.

Carr, L. G. (1971). The Strole items and acquiesce. *American Sociological Review, 36,* 287–293.

Craig, M. E., Kalichman, S. C., Follingstad, D. R. (1989). Verbal coercive sexual behavior among college students. *Archives of Sexual Behavior, 18,* 421–434.

Durkheim, E. (1951). *Suicide.* Glencoe, IL: Free Press.

Ellis, L. (1989). *Theories of rape: Inquiries into the causes of sexual aggression.* New York: Hemisphere.

Ellis, L., Burke, D., & Ames, A. (1987). Sexual orientation as a continuous variable: A comparison between the sexes. *Archives of Sexual Behavior, 16,* 523–529.

Ellis, L., Hoffman, H., & Burke, D. M. (1990). Sex, sexual orientation, and criminal and violent behavior. *Personality and Individual Differences, 11,* 1207–1212.

Fowler, F. J., Jr. (1992). How unclear terms affect survey data. *Public Opinion Quarterly, 56,* 218–231.

Fowler, F. J., Jr., and Mangione, T. W. (1990). *Standardized survey interviewing: Minimizing interviewer-related error.* Newbury Park, CA: Sage.

Geer, J. G. (1991). Do open-ended questions measure "salient" issues? *Public Opinion Quarterly, 55,* 360–370.

Goldsmith, R. E. (1987). Two studies of yeasaying. *Psychological Reports, 60,* 239–244.

Gray, T. (1990). Questionnaire format and item content affect level of belief in both scientifically unsubstantiated and substantiated phenomena. *Canadian Journal of Behavioural Science, 22,* 173–180.

Kennedy, T. J., Jr., Sherman, J. F., & Lamont-Havers, R. W. (1972). Factors contributing to current distress in the academic community. *Science, 175,* 599–607.

Lazarfeld, P. F. (1944). The controversy over detailed interviews—an offer for negotiation. *Public Opinion Quarterly, 8,* 38–60.

Likert, R. (1932). A technique for the measurement of attitudes. *Archives of Psychology, 21* (40), 1–55.

Loken, B., Pirie, P., Virnig, K. A., Hinkle, R. L., Salmon, C. T. (1987). The use of 0–10 scales in telephone surveys. *Journal of the Market Research Society, 29,* 353–362.

Messer, W. S., & Griggs, R. A. (1989). Student belief and involvement in the paranormal and performance in introductory psychology. *Teaching of Psychology, 16,* 187–191.

Monette, D. R., Sullivan, T. J., & DeJong, C. R. (1990). *Applied social research: Tool for the human services.* Fort Worth, TX: Holt, Rinehart, & Winston.

Mould, D. E. (1988). A critical analysis of recent research on violent erotica. *Journal of Sex Research, 24,* 326–340.

Muehlenhard, C. L., and Hollabaugh, L. C. (1988). Do women sometimes say no when they mean yes? The prevalence and correlates of women's token resistance to sex. *Journal of Personality and Social Psychology, 54,* 872–879.

Neston, P. G., & Safer, M. A. (1990). A multi-method investigation of individual differences in hemisphericity. *Cortex, 26,* 409–421.

Neuman, W. L. (1991). *Social research methods: Qualitative and quantitative approaches.* Boston: Allyn & Bacon.

Osgood, C. E., Suci, G. J., & Tannenbaum, P. H. (1957). *The measurement of meaning.* Urbana, IL: University of Illinois Press.

Pelham, W. E., Murphy, D. A., Vannatta, K., Milich, R., Gnagy, E. M., Greenslade, K. E., Greiner, A. R., & Vodde-Hamilton, M. (1992). Methylphenidate and attributions of boys with attention-deficit hyperactivity disorder. *Journal of Consulting and Clinical Psychology, 60,* 282–292.

Reiss, I. L. (1981). Some observations on ideology and sexuality in America. *Journal of Marriage and the Family, 43,* 271–283.

Rushton, J. P., Brainerd, C. J., & Pressley, M. (1983). Behavioral development and construct validity: The principle of aggregation. *Psychological Bulletin, 94,* 18–38.

Sax, G. (1980). *Principles of educational and psychological measurement and evaluation* (2nd ed.). Belmont, CA: Wadsworth.

Stuart, R. B., with Jacobson, B. (1979). Sex differences in obesity. In E. S. Gomberg and V. Franks (Eds.), *Gender and disordered behavior* (pp. 241–256). New York: Brunner/Mazel.

Tenvergert, E., Gillespie, M. W., Kingma, J., & Klasen, H. (1992). Abortion attitudes, 1984–1987–1988: Effects of item order and dimensionality. *Perceptual and Motor Skills, 74,* 627–642.

Tetreault, P. A., & Barnett, M. A. (1987). Reactions to stranger and acquaintance rape. *Psychology of Women Quarterly, 11,* 353–358.

Thompson, J. W. (1962). Meaningful and unmeaningful rotation of factors. *Psychological Bulletin, 59,* 211–223.

Till, F. J. (1980). *Sexual harassment: A report on the sexual harassment of students.* Washington, DC: National Advisory Council on Women's Education Programs.

Wyatt, G. E. (1989). Reexamining factors predicting Afro-American and white American women's age at first coitus. *Archives of Sexual Behavior, 18,* 271–298.

Suggested Reading

Labaw, P. (1980). *Advanced questionnaire design.* Cambridge, MA: Abt Books.

Schuman, H., & Presser, S. (1981). *Questions and answers in attitude surveys.* New York: Academic Press.

Sudman, S., & Bradburn, N. M. (1982). *Asking questions.* San Francisco: Jossey-Bass.

True, J. A. (1989). *Finding out: Conducting and evaluating social research* (2nd ed.). Belmont, CA: Wadsworth. (Part II of this book provides many examples of how social science data may be collected, including how questions should be phrased and organized.)

CHAPTER 9

Nonquestionnaire Data: Direct Qualitative Observations

The preceding chapter focused on the issues of constructing questionnaires. Although it would be difficult to exaggerate the importance of questionnaires in social science research, it is also important to be aware that a considerable amount of social science research does not come from questionnaires. Besides studies of non-human animals—none of which are based on questionnaires—substantial numbers of studies of humans also come from non-questionnaire sources.

This chapter and the one that follows will identify the main methods of social science observation without the use of questionnaires. The alternatives fall into two categories: **qualitative observations** and **quantitative observations.** The present chapter will deal with the first of these alternatives, and Chapter 10 will deal with the second.

Qualitative observations basically involve recording events as they happen rather than as a result of purposely setting out to record specific variables. Reports based on qualitative observations are unique in that they rarely follow the strict reporting format described in Chapter 2. Qualitative studies often resemble the work of a newspaper reporter rather than that of a scientist intent on observing a few specific variables. Consequently, qualitative research tends to be individually tailored around the unique circumstances of the people (and sometimes other animals) being observed.

Persons and animals observed in qualitative studies are called **subjects.** However, many qualitative studies of humans obtain information from a special category of subjects called **informants.** These are individuals who intentionally provide data to a researcher other than by structured questionnaire or interview, thereby making them distinct from **respondents** (as discussed in Chapter 8, p. 102).

Data from qualitative observations may be subsumed under six overlapping categories: **participant observations, ethnographic observations, case studies, archaeological** and **historiographic data, focus group studies,** and **qualitative animal studies.** Each one of these is described below.

Participant Observations

Studies based on participant observation are those in which a researcher becomes enmeshed in the social processes that he or she is observing (Lofland, 1971:93; Bogdan & Taylor, 1975:5; Sommer & Sommer, 1991:55). Becoming a participant observer may occur strictly by accident, or it may result from a researcher intentionally infiltrating and becoming a part of some social process (either surreptitiously or with the knowledge of the other members of the social group).

Such studies have been conducted on numerous topics, including the following: homeless men (Anderson, 1961), large city gangs (Thrasher, 1936; Matza, 1969), a doomsday cult (Festinger, Rieken & Schacher, 1956), police officers patrolling their beat (Kirkham, 1975), sexual encounters among gay men (Humphreys, 1970), and even patrons of a laundromat (Kenen, 1982). (For a more extensive list, see Neuman, 1991:337.)

The methodology surrounding participant observation is largely unstructured and must be tailored to fit individual circumstances. For this reason, few guidelines will be given in this chapter as to exactly how to conduct this or other forms of qualitative research. More will be said about the nature of participant observations after a closely related type of qualitative research, called ethnography, is described.

Ethnographic Observations

The prefix *ethno* means people or ''folks,'' and *graphy* refers to measurement or description (Neuman, 1991:340). Ethnographic research probably constitutes the majority of qualitative research by social scientists; it is especially common among cultural anthropologists (Hammersley, 1992:11). In fact, some have even equated ethnology and cultural anthropology (e.g., Scupin & DeCorse, 1992:8). Normally, however, the following distinction is made: Whereas cultural anthropology is the study of human culture (and the behavior which makes culture possible), ethnology refers to knowledge resulting from ethnographic observations. The methodology commonly used in obtaining ethnographic data is to directly observe and record impressions of the lives and customs of specific groups of people without the use of structured questionnaires or other research instruments (Ember & Ember, 1988:203). It is among the oldest and most colorful research in the social sciences.

Ethnographic research can be traced back many centuries to written accounts by long-distance traders and explorers about their encounters with people inhabiting strange lands. As far as accounts written by persons specially trained in this form of research, ethnography is about 150 years old. Because ethnographic research is largely descriptive in nature, it rarely makes use of complex statistics.

Probably the best known ethnographic research in contemporary times is that of the Yanomamo (pronounced Ya' no ma mo), an Indian tribe in South America's Amazon rain forest, by Napoleon Chagnon (see Scupin & DeCorse, 1992:11). Although some statistical studies of the Yanomamo's reproductive behavior have also been reported (Chagnon, 1988), most of the information has been qualitative in nature. The Yanomamo have had a violent history, with deadly raids and battles among neighboring tribal bands having been commonplace.

Other examples of ethnographic research are ones of hunter-gatherers in western Africa (Lee, 1984), of communal farmers in China (Chance, 1984), of a herding society in northern Africa (Goldschmidt, 1976), and of feuding among tribal groups in the former Yugoslavia (Boehm, 1984). It is sad to note a sense of urgency on the part of ethnographers to study the remaining inhabitants of technologically simple societies because their way of life is rapidly disappearing (Bodley, 1988; Linden, 1991). Virtually all pre-agrarian life styles—which is reminiscent of how all humans lived until roughly 10,000 years ago—is literally vanishing in our midst. Not only is this resulting in the disappearance of enormous amounts of fascinating social science knowledge, but more importantly, we are losing forever a vital link to our essential humanity.

One term that is central to ethnographic research is that of ethnocentrism. This refers to the tendency to judge the worth (or goodness) of other societies on the basis of how closely they resemble the observer's own society (Schusky & Culbert, 1987:216). Ethnographers make a concerted effort not to hold, and certainly not to reveal, any condescending attitudes toward the customs they witness. Certain exceptions are sometimes made to this basic policy, however, as will be discussed in Chapter 18.

The term ethnographic research is sometimes used interchangeably with participant observations (see Rensberger, 1983; Schusky & Culbert, 1987:101). However, this should be discouraged since at least three distinctions can be made:

First, unlike participant observations, many ethnographic accounts do not entail the observer becoming integrated into the sociocultural network he or she is trying to study. While it is certainly advisable for an ethnographer to learn the language, eat the food, and at least respect (if not take part in) the customs of those being studied, differences in physical appearance virtually ensures that ethnographers will be seen as "outsiders."

A second distinction between participant observation and ethnographic research is that the latter typically focuses on relatively small nonindustrial cultures, whereas participant observations usually take place in subcultures or institutions comprising some large industrial society.

Third, most ethnographic research is carried out by persons trained in anthropology, whereas those who conduct most participant observations are either sociologists or social psychologists.

All three of these differences are, of course, only matters of degree, and it is certainly true that there are major commonalities between ethnographic observations and participant observations. These commonalities include the following: First, they often rely on hearsay information from one or two key informants. Second, the standard research reporting format described in Chapter 2 is not generally adhered to. Third, a researcher's subjective impressions about what is worth reporting play a more central role in these and other forms of qualitative research than in most quantitative research.

Because of the impressionistic nature of qualitative research methods, they are more subject to errors in judgment and to varying interpretations than are quantitative research methods. This has been found to be especially true of some of the earlier ethnographic accounts (Barnard, 1983:196). Three examples will help to illustrate this point.

First, would you say that humans who live a foraging (or hunter-gatherer) way of life are more likely to be violent than people living in more technologically advanced societies? While the question seems simple, the ethnographic evidence is mixed, even for the most widely studied hunter-gatherers, the San of Kalahari, Namibia. Whereas some researchers have described the San as harmless and noncombative (Thomas, 1959; Marshall, 1976), others have concluded that their rates of interpersonal violence may actually exceed those of most countries where an established criminal justice system maintains actual records of violent offenses (Lee, 1979, 1984; Christiansen & Winkler, 1992). Ultimately, there are many problems in attempting to assess the level of violence among small nomadic bands, including sample size, the absence of written records, and the fact that even minor injuries may be lethal in societies where emergency medical services are not in easy reach.

Second, in the 1920s, an ethnographic account was written about village life in central Mexico (Redfield, 1930). About 20 years later, another ethnographer visited the same village and wrote quite a different account (Lewis, 1951). The first account described an "idyllic rural setting in which people were happy, healthy, and well integrated" (Friedl & Whiteford, 1988:93). However, the second account was of a village steeped in suspicion, tension, and little cooperation. Although it is possible that the village underwent a radical transformation between the two visits, the descriptions of the external features of the village suggests that little had changed. In hindsight, it seems most likely that both researchers were somewhat biased, at least in the sense of being incomplete and selective in what they reported (Friedl & Whiteford, 1988:93; Murphy, 1989:252).

The third example is of an ethnographic account that has been shown to be in substantial error; it involved one of the most famous cultural anthropologists of the 20th century, Margaret Mead. In the early part of this century, Mead (1928) spent nearly a year living among the inhabitants of a village in the main Pacific island of Samoa. She was especially interested in finding out how adolescents in the village made the transition from childhood to sexual maturity. Mead's research brought her to conclude that the transition among the Samoans was much less repressive and not nearly as traumatic as the transition made by adolescents in industrial societies such as the United States.

Nearly half a century later, a researcher attempted to verify Mead's basic conclusions, and in doing so documented several serious and fundamental errors (Freeman, 1983). For example, Mead reported that because Samoan society was very casual about adolescent sexuality, it was virtually free of all forms of sexual aggression. To the contrary, crime statistics have shown that rape rates in the Samoan Islands are actually higher than those of the United States (Marshall, 1983:1044), a country which has the highest known rape rate among industrial nations (Ellis, 1989a:7).

In fairness to Mead (who died a few years before these criticisms of her work were published) (Rensberger, 1983), it should be noted that official crime statistics were largely unavailable in the 1920s. It is also possible that the particular village she studied was atypical with respect to its sexual customs. Also, it should be said that Mead's research techniques have rarely been cited as exemplary of ethnographic research (Goodenough, 1983; Brady, 1991:497). Even so, her findings continue to be alluded to in support of dubious conclusions about the degree to which adolescent sexuality varies among cultures (Brown, 1991:20).

The above three examples underscore the importance of having more than one researcher collecting ethnographic data in a given society. Unfortunately, as noted earlier, the rapid rate at which isolated human cultures are being disrupted and absorbed by technologically advanced societies is making these verification efforts increasingly difficult.

Despite their value, ethnographic data appear to be more susceptible to errors, and, once made, these errors are more difficult to detect than in most quantitative forms of social science research. Nevertheless, the importance of such data would be difficult to overestimate. Fortunately, as will be discussed in Chapter 11, it has become possible to combine the results of numerous ethnographic accounts for the same or similar societies, and thereby treat these accounts as quantifiable data.

Case Study Observations

Observations conducted under the name case studies (or case histories) are qualitative observations that focus on single individuals, groups, agencies, or episodes (Mason & Bramble, 1989:39). Case studies often resemble participant observations in the degree of intimacy and rapport that is established between the observer and the observed. However, there are three notable differences. One has to do with the number of subjects being observed. Case studies often involve observing only one subject, especially at any given time, whereas participant observations usually entail observing several subjects at a time. Second, in case studies the researcher normally does not attempt to become socially absorbed into what is being observed. Third, case studies are often carried out as part of the process of clinical or institutional treatment, whereas participant observations are rarely linked to any treatment efforts.

Among examples of case study observations are these: An account was recently written of a few 3- and 4-year old-children who appear to have learned to read on their own (Anbar, 1986). A man with a long history of voyeurism was recently treated with a prescription drug originally developed for treating obsessive-compulsive disorders, with some encouraging results (Emmanuel, Lydiard, & Ballenger, 1991). After a criminal conviction, many states allow (or even mandate) that a case study be prepared by a probation officer for the judge to use before pronouncing a final sentence (Hood & Sparks, 1970:164; Glueck & Glueck, 1974:189; Council of Europe, 1977:148; Carter, 1978). Recently, an article was written reviewing numerous psychiatric and psychological case studies of people diagnosed with kleptomania, a compulsion to steal especially in the form of shoplifting (Goldman, 1991:988).

Archaeological and Historiographic Data

Archaeological data consist of artifacts and physical remains (either fossilized or not) of people who are no longer living (Wallace, 1983; Fagan, 1986:13). Artifacts are any natural objects or material that have been intentionally fashioned or modified for some useful or aesthetic purpose.

Fossils are mineralized or physical traces of formerly living things. Mineralized traces of living things—usually only their hard body parts (such as teeth and bones)—sometimes form after long periods of time if the body was quickly sequestered from scavengers and microorganisms following death. Natural events that are conducive to fossilization include deposits of silt after a flood and layers of ash following a volcanic eruption. Gradually, the organic hard body parts are replaced by more stable minerals which can still be distinguished from the surrounding earth or rock (Schiffer, 1976).

Most archaeological data are of such a unique character that they can only be adequately described in qualitative terms. However, as individual collections of archaeological data are accumulated (such as in museums), categorizing and comparing them in quantitative terms becomes possible (Watson, LeBlanc, & Redman, 1984). For example, recent work with the bones of still largely unfossilized pre-Columbian American aborigines have provided considerable insight into their eating habits, diseases, and trading practices (Levy, 1992).

Historiographic data consist primarily of written records (and other symbolic communication) that can be used to reconstruct some aspects of the lives of people who lived in literate societies (i.e., societies in which writing was common). Examples of historiographic data include diaries and letters written by societal members, newspaper accounts, and numerous types of administrative documents and official proclamations.

Like archaeological data, most historiographic data is most adequately characterized in qualitative terms. However, there are also examples of historiographic data that lend themselves to quantification. For example, a historiographic study was recently conducted in which rates of out-of-wedlock births in Sweden were traced from 1680 to 1839, and shown to parallel trends in prosecutions for extramarital (including premarital) sexual behavior (Sundin, 1992). Specifically, as out-of-wedlock births rose, so too did the number of prosecutions, especially of women.

THE FAR SIDE By GARY LARSON

"Anthropologists! Anthropologists!"

As this study illustrates, even though historiographic data is usually qualitative in nature (e.g., records of significant individual events), social scientists can sometimes quantify such data simply by counting the number of such records in a given year or geographical area. For this reason, the use of historiographic records will be more fully described in Chapter 11 under the heading of **archival data** (also see Jarausch & Hardy, 1991).

Data Derived from Focus Groups

Research based on focus groups provides a relatively new but already popular type of qualitative research methodology (Bartos, 1986; Bers, 1989). In this research, investigators bring together up to several dozen persons to discuss some topic. Although data from focus groups are often partially quantitative in nature, and sometimes include completion of a structured questionnaire, participants are normally asked to "speak their minds" on a topic in an unstructured format. The comments made by the participants are either coded by the researcher on the spot, or are tape recorded for analysis later (Stewart & Shamdasani, 1990).

Focus groups originated as a marketing research tool, and are still used for determining ways of selling commercial products or promoting political candidates (Bartos, 1986). For example, participants in a focus group might be asked to try some product and then return with comments. They also might be shown two or three possible promotional campaigns, and asked to comment on the advantages and disadvantages of each campaign. Data from focus groups are used to help uncover strengths and weaknesses in marketing approaches to a commercial product or political candidate, and to identify persons who are most and least likely to purchase a product or vote for a candidate. Focus groups may be convened several times throughout a marketing cycle or a campaign, so as to identify changes that may be taking place in people's perceptions.

Focus groups are not used simply for marketing commercial products and developing campaign strategies for political candidates. They have also been used to develop better ways of informing women about how to detect and prevent cervical cancer (Dignan, Michielutte, & Sharp, 1990), more effective approaches to reducing cigarette use by adolescents (Sussman, Burton & Dent, 1991), and new techniques for soliciting funds by nonprofit organizations (Krueger, 1988).

Qualitative Animal Data

Qualitative accounts of nonhuman animal behavior have enriched the social sciences for more than a century. As an early example, Charles Darwin (1872/1965) provided a detailed comparison of the facial and bodily expressions of various emotions, such as anger, sadness, and happiness, made by mammals, including humans (also see van Hooff, 1969).

Most of the qualitative research on nonhumans is conducted by social scientists with major training in comparative psychology, ethology, and primatology (generally considered a branch of physical anthropology) (see Snowdon, 1983; Nishida, 1987). Social scientists who conduct qualitative studies of nonhuman animals are referred to as **naturalists** (although many naturalists also conduct studies in which quantitative data are collected). Basically, naturalistic observations in nonhuman animals would be analogous to ethnographic observations of humans. Below are a few examples.

Qualitative studies by naturalists have revealed evidence of rudimentary cultural learning in various species of primates. The earliest of these studies reported that Japanese macaques (a species of monkey native to Japan) sometimes learned new food preparation techniques by imitating one another (Kawai, 1965; Itani, 1958). Qualitative studies have also provided evidence of culturelike variations in food preparation techniques as well as in social structure, among wild-living chimpanzees (reviewed by Chivers, Wood, & Bilsborough, 1984; Nishida, 1987; Gibbons, 1992). These variations have been of special interest to social scientists because of the genetic similarity between chimpanzees and ourselves (e.g., they have 24 pairs of chromosomes, we have 23 pairs, and many of the chromosomes appear to be all but interchangeable) (Bogart & Benirschke, 1977; Lewin, 1987; Miyamoto, Slightom, & Goodman, 1987; Mereson, 1988).

Other naturalistic observations by social scientists of a largely qualitative nature have had to do with the formation and maintenance of dominance hierarchies (Chase, 1980; Pollock, 1979), the use of nonlinguistic vocal communication (Fossey, 1974; Snowdon & Cleveland, 1984), the display of sexual behavior and preferences (McGinnis, 1979), play behavior especially among the young (Cheney, 1978), food sharing (Kavanagh, 1972), the formation of social alliances (Cheney & Seyfarth, 1986; Cheney, 1977), and the maintenance of social organization (Neville, 1968; Rhine, 1972; Nash, 1976).

Qualitative animal studies have also been conducted that are very similar to case studies in humans. One area that has been especially fascinating deals with the use of symbolic communication. Specifically, the American Sign Language (ASL) has been taught to three different species of apes: the common chimpanzee (Gardner & Gardner, 1975; Seyfarth, 1987), the pygmy chimpanzee (Savage-Rumbaugh, Rumbaugh, & McDonald, 1985; Savage-Rumbaugh et al., 1986), and the gorilla (Patterson, 1978, 1981). Nevertheless, there is considerable controversy about how similar their use of sign language is to human usage (Terrace, 1985; Seyfarth, 1987). From a quantitative standpoint, no ape has yet mastered more than 400 words, a feat surpassed by most humans long before entering kindergarten.

Other examples of qualitative animal research of a case study nature have been the result of **serendipitous observations.** This refers to any worthwhile scientific evidence which "falls into a researcher's lap," rather than being something he or she set out to discover.

Serendipitous case studies of various primate species have documented instances of infant killing (Goodall, 1979; Kawanaka, 1981; Newton, 1984) and even cannibalism (Goodall, 1979; Norikoski, 1982). Examples of homosexual behavior have also been documented (Edwards & Todd, 1991). Nonhuman primates have even been seen teaching their young "cultural" behavior. Specifically, langur monkeys (who are native to India) were seen training their young in ways of attacking snakes (Srivastava, 1991).

Another case study among nonhumans described an odd instance of rivalry between mated pairs of two species of birds (robins and sparrows). After the robins had meticulously built a nest and laid eggs in it, the pair of sparrows badgered them until they abandoned the nest. When the sparrows took over, they ejected the robins' eggs, eventually replaced them with their own eggs, and brooded them (Ellis, 1989b).

The animal counterpart to human ethnographic data would be long-term detailed studies of groups of nonhuman animals living in natural (or near-natural) habitats. The best known example of this has been research by Jane Goodall (1979, 1990). In the early 1960s, she began observing a specific band of chimpanzees in southeast Kenya, and has continued this to the present time (now with the assistance of many other researchers) (e.g., Goodall et al., 1979). Her efforts have documented instances of crude tool use (and even tool making), hunting and eating of small mammals, and brutal intergroup gang attacks among chimpanzees (Goodall, 1990).

A Special Note on Field Research

Before concluding this chapter, let's look at the concept of **field research** (or **field studies**) Field research is research conducted in the environment in which the subjects being studied normally live (as opposed to studying subjects in artificial environments such as a laboratory) (Dooley, 1990:276). As a rule, those who conduct field research try to avoid disturbing the normal flow of activities being observed (Emerson, 1988; Mason & Bramble, 1989:41), except in the case of what are called **field experiments** (experimentation will be the focus of Chapter 15).

Some writers treat qualitative research and field research as virtually synonymous (Mason & Bramble, 1989:41; Neuman, 1991:336). Doing so is inadvisable, however, since many field studies also involve the collection of quantitative data, as will be discussed in the next chapter. Basically, it is safe to say that most qualitative observations are based on field research. As will be shown in the next chapter, however, quite a number of quantitative studies are also conducted in the field.

The main advantage of field research compared to research that takes place in artificial settings is that it tends to provide the most realistic picture of the complexity and dynamics of the events being studied. The main disadvantage is that the context in which behavior occurs in the field is often so complex that the true causes of specific behavior patterns are often impossible to identify and document. Another disadvantage of field research is that the behavior under study may be so infrequent that the researcher almost never observes it.

Summary

While most social science research is based on people's responses to questionnaires, a substantial proportion is not. This chapter has categorized and described the main qualitative alternatives that social scientists have to collecting data via questionnaires.

Six sources of qualitative observations were identified: participant observations, ethnographic accounts, case studies, archaeological and historiographic sources, focus groups, and qualitative animal studies. Participant observations are observations made by individuals who become intimately involved in a subculture or an institution within a society. Ethnographic accounts are narrative descriptions that social scientists provide based on visits that they make to a foreign (usually nonindustrial) society. Case studies (or case histories) are accounts which focus on a single individual or a single incident, and attempt to describe the circumstances which bore most heavily on the individual or incident. Archaeological and historiographic sources of qualitative data come either from artifacts and fossils or from written records, and both provide insights into the lives of people who are no longer living. In focus groups, a group of persons are brought together by a researcher to discuss some topic of interest such as a new commercial product or political candidate.

From their discussion, perceived strengths and weaknesses of products and candidates can be identified. Qualitative animal studies involve observations of the behavior of nonhuman animals. The methods used to make these observations are usually similar to ethnographic research with humans, except that verbal communication with those being studied is not possible.

The last concept introduced in this chapter was that of field research. Basically, all research conducted in a naturalistic setting (as opposed to a laboratory or classroom setting) would constitute field research. Field research can be both qualitative and quantitative.

References

Anbar, A. (1986). Reading acquisition of preschool children without systematic instruction. *Early Childhood Research Quarterly, 1,* 83–87.

Anderson, N. (1961). *The hobo: The sociology of the homeless man.* Chicago: University of Chicago Press.

Barnard, A. (1983). Contemporary hunter-gatherers: Current issues in ecology and social organization. *Annual Review of Anthropology, 12,* 193–214.

Bartos, R. (1986). Qualitative research: What it is and where it came from. *Journal of Advertising Research, 26,* RC-3–RC-6.

Bers, T. H. (1989). The popularity and problems of focus-group research. *College and University, 64,* 260–268.

Bodley, J. H. (Ed.) (1988). *Tribal people & development issues: A global overview.* Mountain View, CA: Mayfield.

Boehm, C. (1984). *Blood revenge.* Lawrence: University of Kansas Press.

Bogart, M. H., & Benirschke, K. (1977). Chromosomal analysis of the pygmy chimpanzee (*Pan paniscus*) with a comparison to man. *Folia Primatologica, 27,* 60–67.

Bogdan. R., and Taylor, S. J. (1975). *Introduction to Qualitative research methods: A phenomenological approach to the social sciences.* San Francisco: Jossey-Bass.

Brady, I. (1991). The *Samoa Reader*: Last word or lost horizon? *Current Anthropology, 32,* 497–500.

Brown, D. (1991). *Human universals.* New York: McGraw-Hill.

Carter, R. M. (1978). *Presentence report handbook.* Washington, DC: U.S. Government Printing Office (#027–000–00577–2).

Chagnon, N. A. (1988). Life histories, blood revenge, and warfare in a tribal population. *Science, 239,* 985–992.

Chance, N. A. (1984). *China's urban villagers: Life in a Beijing commune.* New York: Holt, Rinehart & Winston.

Chase, I. D. (1980). Social process and hierarchy formation in small groups: A comparative perspective. *American Sociological Review, 45,* 905–924.

Cheney, D. L. (1977). The acquisition of rank and the development of reciprocal alliances among free-ranging immature baboons. *Behavior, Ecology, and Sociobiology, 2,* 303–318.

Cheney, D. L. (1978). The play partners of immature baboons. *Animal Behaviour, 26,* 1038–1050.

Cheney, D. L., & Seyfarth, R. M. (1986). The recognition of social alliances among verbet monkeys. *Animal Behaviour, 34,* 1722–1731.

Christiansen, K., & Winkler, E. M. (1992). Hormonal, anthropometrical and behavioral correlates of physical aggression in !Kung San men of Namibia. *Aggressive Behavior, 18,*
  271–280.

Chivers, D. J., Wood, B. A., and Bilsborough, A. (Eds). (1984). *Food acquisition and processing in primates.* New York: Plenum Press.

Council of Europe. (1977). *International exchange of information on current criminological research projects.* Strasbourg, France: European Committee on Crime Problems.

Darwin, C. (1965). *The expression of the emotions in man and animals.* Chicago: University of
  Chicago Press. (Original work published 1872)

Dignan, M. B., Michielutte, R., & Sharp, P. (1990). The role of focus groups in health education for cervical cancer among minority women. *Journal of Community Health, 15,*
  369–375.

Dooley, D. (1990). *Social research methods* (2nd ed.). Englewood Cliffs, NJ: Prentice-Hall.

Edwards, A. A., & Todd, J. D. (1991). Homosexual behaviour in wild white-handed gibbons
  (*Hylobates lar*). *Primates, 32,* 231–236.

Ellis, L. (1989a). *Theories of rape: Inquiries into the causes of sexual aggression.* New York:
  Hemisphere.

Ellis, L. (1989b). Usurping a newly built robin's nest by a pair of sparrows: A case report.
  Journal of Evolutionary Psychology, 9, 110–111.

Ember, C. R., & Ember, M. (1988). *Anthropology* (5th ed.). Englewood Cliffs, NJ: Prentice-
  Hall.

Emerson, R. M. (Ed.). (1988). *Contemporary field research: A collection of readings.* Prospect
  Heights, IL: Waveland.

Emmanuel, N. P., Lydiard, R. B., & Ballenger, J. C. (1991). Fluoxetine treatment of voyeurism.
  American Journal of Psychiatry, 148, 950.

Fagan, B. M. (1986). *People of the earth* (5th ed.). Boston: Little, Brown.

Festinger, L., Rieken, H. W., & Schacher, S. (1956). *When prophecies fail.* Minneapolis: University of Minnesota Press.

Fossey, D. (1974). Vocalizations of the mountain gorilla (*Gorilla gorilla*). *Animal Behaviour,
  20,* 36–53.

Freeman, D. (1983). *Margaret Mead and Samoa: The making and unmaking of an anthro-
  pological myth.* Cambridge, MA: Harvard University Press.

Friedl, J., & Whiteford, M. B. (1988). *The human portrait: Introduction to cultural anthropology.* Englewood Cliffs, NJ: Prentice-Hall.

Gardner, R. A., & Gardner, B. T. (1975). Evidence for sentence constituents in the early utter-
  ances of child and chimpanzee. *Journal of Experimental Psychology: General, 194,*
  244–267.

Gibbons, A. (1992). Chimps: More diverse than a barrel of monkeys. *Science, 255,* 287–288.

Glueck, S., & Glueck, E. (1974). *Of delinquency and crime.* Springfield, IL: Charles C. Thomas.

Goldman, M. J. (1991). Kleptomania: Making sense of the nonsensical. *American Journal of
  Psychiatry, 148,* 986–996.

Goldschmidt, W. (1976). *Culture and behavior of the Sebei.* Berkeley: University of California
  Press.

Goodall, J. (1979). Life and death at Gombe. *National Geographic, 155,* 593–620.

Goodall, J. (1990). *Through a window.* Boston: Houghton Mifflin.

Goodall, J., Bandora, A., Bergmann, E., Busse, C., Matama, H., Mpongo, E., Pierce, A., & Riss,
  D. (1979). Intercommunity interactions in the chimpanzee population of the Gombe Na-
  tional Park. In D. A. Hamburg & E. R. McCown (Eds.), *The great apes.* Menlo Park, CA:
  Benjamin Cummings.

Goodenough, W. (1983). Margaret Mead and cultural anthropology. *Science, 220,* 906–908.

Hammersley, M. (1992). *What's wrong with ethnography?* London: Routhledge.

Hood, R., & Sparks, R. (1970). *Key issues in criminology.* New York: McGraw-Hill.

Humphreys, L. (1970). *Tearoom trade: Impersonal sex in public places.* Chicago: Aldine.

Itani, J. (1958). On the acquisition and propagation of new food habits in the troop of Japanese monkeys at Takasakiyama. *Primates, 1,* 84–98.

Jarausch, K. H., & Hardy, K. A. (1991). *Quantitative methods for historians: A guide to research, data, and statistics.* Chapel Hill: University of North Carolina Press.

Kavanagh, M. (1972). Food sharing behavior in a group of douc langurs (*Pygathrix nemaeus*). *Nature, 239,* 406–407.

Kawai, M. (1965). Newly acquired protocultural behavior of the natural troop of Japanese monkeys on Koshima islet. *Primates, 6,* 1–30.

Kawanaka, K. (1981). Infanticide and cannibalism in chimpanzees—with special reference to the newly observed case in the Mahale Mountains. *African Studies Monograph, 1,* 69–99.

Kenen, R. (1982). Soapsuds, space and sociability: A participant observation of a laundromat. *Urban Life, 11,* 163–184.

Kirkham, G. L. (1975). Doc cop. *Human Behavior, 4* (May), 19–25.

Krueger, R. A. (1988). *Focus groups: A practical guide for applied research.* Newbury Park, CA: Sage.

Lee, R. B. (1979). *The !Kung San: Men, women, and work in a foraging society.* Cambridge, England: Cambridge University Press.

Lee, R. B. (1984). *The Dobe !Kung.* New York: Holt, Rinehart & Winston.

Levy, D. (1992). The wide world of geography turns in Washington: Tales from the burial mounds. *Science, 257,* 1210.

Lewin, R. (1987). My close cousin the chimpanzee. *Science, 238,* 273–275.

Lewis, O. (1951). *Life in a Mexican village: Tepozlan restudied.* Urbana: University of Illinois Press.

Linden, E. (1991). Lost tribes, lost knowledge. *Time, 138* (September 23), 46–56.

Lofland, J. (1971). *Analyzing social settings: A guide to qualitative observation and analysis.* Belmont, CA: Wadsworth.

Marshall, E. (1983). A controversy on Samoa comes of age. *Science, 219,* 1042–1045.

Marshall, L. (1976). *The !Kung of Nyae Nyae.* Cambridge: Harvard University Press.

Mason, E. J., & Bramble, W. J. (1989). *Understanding and conducting research,* (2nd ed.). New York: McGraw-Hill.

Matza, D. (1969). *Becoming deviant.* Englewood Cliffs, NJ: Prentice-Hall.

McGinnis, P. R. (1979). Sexual behaviour in free-living chimpanzees: Consort relationships. In D. A. Hamburg & E. R. McCown (Eds.), *The great apes.* Menlo Park, CA: Benjamin Cummings.

Mead, M. (1928). *Coming of age in Samoa: A psychological study of primitive youth for western civilization.* New York: William Morrow.

Mereson, A. (1988). Monkeying around with the relatives. *Discover, 9* (March), 26–27.

Miyamoto, M. M., Slightom, J. L., & Goodman, M. (1987). Phylogenetic relations of humans and African apes from DNA sequences in the globin region. *Science, 238,* 369–372.

Murphy, R. F. (1989). *Cultural and social anthropology: An overview* (3rd ed.). Englewood Cliffs, NJ: Prentice-Hall.

Nash, L. T. (1976). Troop fission in free-ranging baboons in the Gombe Stream National Park, Tanzania. *American Journal of Physical Anthropology, 44,* 63–78.

Neuman, W. L. (1991). *Social research methods: Qualitative and quantitative approaches.* Boston: Allyn & Bacon.

Neville, M. K. (1968). A free-ranging rhesus monkey troop lacking males. *Journal of Mammalology, 49,* 771–778.

Newton, P. N. (1984). Infanticide and social change in forest grey langurs, *Presbytis entellus,* in Kanka Tiger Reserve, India: *International Journal of Primatology, 5,* 366.

Nishida, T. (1987). Local traditions and cultural transmission. In B. B. Smuts, D. L. Cheney, R. M. Seyfarth, R. W. Wringham, & T. T. Struhsaker (Eds.), *Primate societies* (pp 462–474). Chicago: University of Chicago Press.

Norikoski, K. (1982). One observed case of cannibalism among wild chimpanzees of the Mahale Mountains. *Primate, 23,* 66–74.

Patterson, F. G. (1978). Conversations with a gorilla. *National Geographic, 154,* 438–465.

Patterson, F. G. (1981). Ape language. *Science, 211,* 86–87.

Pollock, J. I. (1979). Female dominance in *Indri indri. Folia Primatologica, 31,* 143–164.

Redfield, R. (1930). *Tepoztlan, A Mexican village.* Chicago: University of Chicago Press.

Rensberger, B. (1983). Margaret Mead: The nature-nurture debate. *Science 83,* 4 (April).

Rhine, R. J. (1972). Changes in the social structure of two groups of stump-tail macaques. *Primates, 13,* 181–194.

Savage-Rumbaugh, R., Rumbaugh, S., McDonald, K., Sevcik, R. A., Hopkins, W. D., & Rubert, E. (1986). Spontaneous symbol acquisition and communicative use by pygmy chimpanzees (*Pan paniscus*). *Journal of Experimental Psychology: General, 115,* 211–235.

Savage-Rumbaugh, S., Rumbaugh, D. M., & McDonald, K. (1985). Language learning in two species of apes. *Neuroscience & Biobehavioral Reviews, 9,* 653–665.

Schiffer, M. (1976). Towards the identification of site formation processes. *American Antiquity, 48,* 675–706.

Schusky, E. L., & Culbert, T. P. (1987). *Introducing culture* (4th ed.). Englewood Cliffs, NJ: Prentice-Hall.

Scupin, R., & DeCorse, C. R. (1992). *Anthropology: A global perspective.* Englewood Cliffs, NJ: Prentice-Hall.

Seyfarth, R. M. (1987). Vocal communication and its relation to language. In B. B. Smuts, D. L. Cheney, R. M. Seyfarth, R. W. Wringham, & T. T. Struhsaker (Eds.), *Primate societies* (pp 440–451). Chicago: University of Chicago Press.

Snowdon, C. T. (1983). Ethology, comparative psychology and animal behavior. *Annual Review in Psychology, 34,* 63–94.

Snowdon, C. T., & Cleveland, J. (1984). "Conversations" among pygmy marmosets. *American Journal of Primatology, 7,* 15–20.

Sommer, B., & Sommer, R. (1991). *A practical guide to behavioral research.* New York: Oxford University Press.

Srivastava, A. (1991). Cultural transmission of snake-mobbing in free-ranging hanuman Langurs. *Folia Primatologica, 56,* 117–120.

Stewart, D. W., & Shamdasani, P. N. (1990). *Focus groups: Theory and practice.* Newbury Park, CA: Sage.

Sundin, J. (1992). Sinful sex: Legal prosecution of extramarital sex in preindustrial Sweden. *Social Science History, 16,* 99–128.

Sussman, S., Burton, D., & Dent, C. W. (1991). Use of focus groups in developing an adolescent tobacco use cessation program: Collective norm effects. *Journal of Applied Social Psychology, 21,* 1772–1782.

Terrace, H. S. (1985). On the nature of animal thinking. *Neuroscience & Biobehavioral Reviews, 9,* 643–652.

Thomas, E. M. (1959). *The harmless people.* New York: Knopf.

Thrasher, F. M. (1936). *The gang.* Chicago: University of Chicago Press.

van Hooff, J. A. (1969). The facial displays of the catarrhine monkeys and apes. In D. Morris (Ed.). *Primate ethology* (pp. 9–88). New York: Doubleday.

Wallace, R. L. (1983). *Those who have vanished: An introduction to prehistory.* Homewood, IL: Dorsey.

Watson, P. J., LeBlanc, S., & Redman, C. J. (1984). *Archeological explanations: The scientific method in archeology.* New York: Columbia University Press.

Suggested Reading

Gibbons, A. (1992). Chimps: More diverse than a barrel of monkeys. *Science, 255,* 287–288. (This brief article provides an interesting account of largely qualitative primatological research on some of the amazing diversity in the "cultural" behavior patterns of chimpanzees living in more than 30 diverse populations throughout Africa.)

Hammersley, M. (1990). *What's wrong with ethnography?* New York: Routhledge, Chapman & Hall. (This book takes a careful look at ethnographic research methodology, and argues that it needs to be better integrated with the rest of social science research methods.)

Lorenz, K. (1966). *On aggression.* New York: Bantam. (This insightful book is for anyone who wants to learn about how other animals interact socially and exhibit emotional feelings toward one another. It is a classic example of qualitative observations written by a famous social scientist.)

Rose, D. (1990). *Living the ethnographic life.* Newbury Park, CA: Sage. (This book provides much practical information to those interested in pursuing a career in ethnography.)

Wolcott, H. F. (1990). *Writing up qualitative research.* Newbury Park, CA: Sage. (A useful guide for writing up the results of qualitative research.)

Journals that specialize in publishing articles on qualitative research are *Ethnography, Journal of Contemporary Ethnography,* and *Qualitative Sociology.* Among the journals specializing in publishing naturalistic research involving nonhuman subjects are *Animal Behaviour, Auk, Ethology,* and *Primates.* In these latter journals, you will find both qualitative and quantitative data utilized.

CHAPTER 10

Nonquestionnaire Data:
Quantitative Observations

In the preceding chapter, qualitative methods for observing social science data were outlined as an alternative to using questionnaire data. This chapter describes another alternative: quantitative observations. **Quantitative observations** are direct observations made by a researcher (or a trained assistant) of phenomena that can be expressed in some type of specific codable (usually numeric) form. Qualitative observations, on the other hand, are difficult to depict except in linguistic, nonnumeric form. In fact, the distinction between quantitative and qualitative observations must often be made rather arbitrarily (Lieberson, 1992:3).

Quantitative observations can be divided into two categories: **laboratory observations** and **field** (or **naturalistic**) **observations**. An intermediate category—**semifield** (or **semi-natural**) **observations**—can also be identified, although here it will be discussed simply as a subcategory of field observations.

Laboratory Observations

Observations in a laboratory are those in which a researcher confines his or her investigation to a physical space that is under his or her control. Although we often think of a laboratory as consisting of test tubes and mechanical gadgets, some laboratories used by social scientists have been as simple as an ordinary classroom.

It should be noted that laboratory observations are often part of an important type of research design called **experimental research,** which will not be discussed until Chapter 15. At this juncture, all you need to know about experimental research is that it has a unique feature: In it, a researcher actually *manipulates* one or more variables under study, rather than simply observing and measuring the variables.

The degree of control that a researcher can have in laboratory settings has advantages and disadvantages. One advantage is that it reduces the confounding influences of many factors totally extraneous to a researcher's interests that inevitably complicate field studies. Another advantage is that technical equipment can be used with greater ease than in most field studies. The main disadvantage to conducting research in a laboratory is that such settings can be so contrived and artificial that the findings have little relevance to the "real world."

Physiological and Biochemical Observations

There are many examples of observations made by social scientists in a laboratory setting. A number of these involve measuring either physiological variables (such as brain waves or muscular tension) or biochemical variables (such as hormones or neurotransmitters) (reviewed by Asberg, Traskman, & Thoren, 1976; Raleigh et al., 1980; von Knorring, Oreland, and Winblad, 1984; Ellis & Ames, 1987; Gove & Wilmoth, 1990).

Such work by social scientists has become especially prevalent since the 1960s (Ellis, Miller, & Widmayer, 1988). Many social scientists have sought to discover what effect physiological or biochemical variables have on behavior. Also, sometimes physiological and biochemical variables can be used to make inferences *about* behavior. It is only in this latter sense that physiological and biochemical variables will be discussed here.

One example of a biochemical technique used to make inferences about human behavior is urine analysis. It has been employed by social scientists to detect the use of various drugs (Adler & Cowan, 1990; McAllister & Makkai, 1991). Aside from its use in criminal investigations and in the monitoring of parolees (Visher & McFadden, 1991), urine analysis has been a part of several recent studies of expectant mothers (Frank, Zuckerman, & Amaro, 1988; Chasnoff, Landress, & Barrett, 1990; Neuspiel & Hamel, 1991). In addition, in a study of heart disease patients wanting help in breaking their addiction to cigarettes, urine analysis was used to monitor progress (Wilcox, Hughes, & Roland, 1979). Analysis of hair samples has also been used to monitor the use of certain drugs (Mieczkowski et al., 1991).

Since the use of drugs can be more easily measured just by asking subjects, why would social scientists go to the trouble of using urine or hair analysis? The answer is that, even when there is no risk of criminal prosecution, many persons using drugs do not disclose this in interview situations (how much they do on anonymous questionnaires is unknown). For example, one study revealed that 24% of the women seeking prenatal care services at a public hospital in Boston who tested positive for cocaine through urine tests denied using cocaine in the screening interview (Frank et al., 1988).

Another example of social scientists using laboratory instruments to infer behavior (or, in this case, emotions) involves sexual arousal. A pressure sensitive device has been developed which fits around the male penis to detect even slight erectile responses. It can be monitored electronically in an adjoining room (Annon, 1988). Such devices have been used extensively in recent years for evaluating the effectiveness of various clinical programs for treating rapists, exhibitionists, and other sex offenders (e.g., Quinsey et al., 1975; Maletzky, 1980; Earls, 1988; Proulx, 1989; Flor-Henry et al., 1991). It must be noted that these devices are not foolproof (Hall, Proctor, & Nelson, 1988). Nevertheless, their validity in assessing sexual arousal among convicted sex offenders is almost certainly higher than self-report measures, especially when paroling decisions are partially dependent on evidence that an individual will not reoffend.

Incidentally, similar devices have been developed for measuring female sexual arousal (Cooper et al., 1990). However, because females have much lower probabilities of committing sex offenses than males (Oliver, 1967:27; O'Connor, 1987), the clinical use of such devices has been minimal.

Another category of physiological measures used to make inferences about human behavior deals with polygraphs (or "lie detectors"). This will be discussed in Chapter 13.

In archaeology, various laboratory techniques have been used to determine the eating habits of humans over tens of thousands of years. Measuring (a) the chemical composition of fossilized bones (Dorozynski & Anderson, 1991), (b) microscopic scratches and wear patterns on teeth (Shipman & Rose, 1983), (c) the types of bones located in butchering sites (White, 1992), and (c) even the residual composition of fossilized feces (Pfeiffer, 1985:116; Feder & Park, 1989:72) have allowed archaeologists to decipher the basic dietary habits of ancestral hominids. For example, a recent study based on these techniques found substantial evidence of frequent cannibalism among the Anasazi, inhabitants of southwest North America centuries before the arrival of Europeans (White, 1992).

Mechanical and Electrical Observations

Various mechanical and electrical observational instruments have been developed for use in the social sciences. Among those that are used often in laboratory research with humans are ones that measure response speed (e.g., pressing a button) to various stimuli (e.g., the flash of a light). Typically, subjects will be asked to sit at a table and press a button as soon as they see a light come on, or hear a particular sound. With other instruments of this type, subjects will be required to press a particular sequence of buttons depending on the stimuli they are presented.

Such reaction time studies have provided researchers with a variety of interesting findings. For example, differences according to age and sex have been found (McKeever, Gill, & VanDeventer, 1975; Bashore, Nydegger, & Miller, 1982; Giambra & Quilter, 1989). Studies indicate that persons who are prone toward psychopathy (pronounced psy cop′ ath e), a condition closely linked to criminal behavior, have quicker but less accurate reaction times than nonpsychopaths (Raine & Venables, 1988). Persons with high intelligence (as assessed by paper-and-pencil tests) tend to be faster and more accurate in reacting to most stimuli than those of low intelligence, especially if complex contingent-type responses must be made by the subjects, rather than responses requiring few discriminatory judgments (Lunneborg, 1977; Jensen, 1982; Schweizer, 1989).

Observations Made Under Deceptive Laboratory Conditions

Although most laboratory observations by social scientists have involved instrumentation, some have not. Many laboratory observations that involve no instrumentation are conducted in laboratories in order to mislead subjects about the real purpose of a study.

The most famous set of laboratory observations involving deception was a series of studies undertaken in the 1960s and 1970s by Stanley Milgram (1963, 1974). In most of these studies, subjects were told that they were in a learning experiment requiring two subjects. One subject would be the "trainer" and the other would be the "learner." The trainer (who was actually the only real subject) was given a list of words to teach to the learner, and each time the learner failed to repeat the list accurately, the trainer would be instructed to punish the learner with volts of electricity.

In reality, the learners in Milgram's studies were **confederates,** persons who merely play a role to help conduct an experiment. The confederates in Milgram's experiments were not really being shocked, although the subjects thought they were. The basic purpose of the studies was to determine what was required to get people to comply with orders given by someone in authority (in this case, the experimenter) (see Seamon & Kenrick, 1992:636).

Another instance of laboratory research involving deception was in a series of studies undertaken to document what came to be called the "MUM effect." The typical design of the study was as follows: Subjects were asked to verbally convey an item of either good news or bad news to another person (again a confederate). As you might guess, these studies showed that nearly all the subjects were more likely to avoid conveying bad news (e.g., a parent had just died) than good news (e.g., they had just won a lottery) (Rosen & Tesser, 1972; Tesser, Rosen, & Conlee, 1972; Conlee & Tesser, 1973).

Studies involving the so-called **bogus pipeline** provide still another example of social science investigations involving deception. Subjects were connected by electrodes to a sophisticated-appearing device described as a newly developed computerized brain scanner, and were led to believe that even slight distortions of the truth would be detected (Jones & Sigall, 1971). Researchers were able to compare the answers given when subjects thought they were being monitored by these seemingly infallible "lie detectors" (which were in fact completely bogus) to answers given under normal testing conditions. Substantial differences were found, especially when subjects were asked about their attitudes toward very sensitive issues (Evans, Hansen, & Mittelmark, 1977; Quigley-Fernandez & Tedeschi, 1978; Bray, Hill, & Henderson, 1979).

Looking back on this section, you may notice that most of the references to studies involving deception of subjects were published in the 1960s and 1970s. By the 1980s, most social science studies involving overt deception by researchers were brought to a halt. More will be said about why in Chapter 18.

Quantitative Laboratory Observations of Nonhumans

Laboratory observations are very common in social science research with nonhuman subjects. Animals used most often in such research are various species of rodents, especially domesticated strains of rats and mice. These species are popular primarily because they are easily maintained in confined spaces, and because they reproduce rapidly. Of course, one disadvantage to using rodents is that they are not as closely related to humans as are several other species of laboratory animals, i.e., nonhuman primates. As a rule, the less related that species are to one another, the less confidence you can have that whatever you find out about one species is generalizable to the other. Of course, no matter how closely related a species may be to humans, scientists must still be cautious in generalizing (Rajecki, 1983). More will be said about this point in Chapter 14 in a section on **animal models.**

Among the most commonly used devices for measuring behavior in laboratory animals are various types of mazes. Mazes used in animal research vary in complexity from those that are similar to the paper-and-pencil mazes that humans trace for amusement (e.g., Seamon & Kenrick, 1992:222) to very simple mazes, such as the T-maze and the Y-maze. In the T-maze and the Y-maze, animals are placed at the base of the T or the Y, and the researcher notes their tendency to turn either right or left when they reach the juncture. By making various incentives and disincentives contingent on the choices animals make, researchers have been able to find out much about animal behavior (Hilgard, Atkinson, & Atkinson, 1975:208; Seamon & Kenrick, 1992:213).

Another instrument used frequently in research with laboratory animals is a type of cage, or testing chamber, called a Skinner box. It is so called because it was invented and first used by B. F. Skinner, a famous 20th century psychologist (Bourne & Ekstrand, 1979:122). The Skinner box is equipped with a lever (or, for birds, a pecking disk) that is connected to a reward (usually food) dispenser (Seamon & Kenrick, 1992:210). Hundreds of studies have been conducted over the past half century, primarily by psychologists, to determine how animals respond to a wide variety of reward (and sometimes punishment) schedules that are made contingent upon their behavior (see Hilgard, Atkinson, & Atkinson, 1975:208; Wortman, Loftus, & Marshall, 1992:173).

Studies based on behavior exhibited by animals in various types of Skinner boxes have also provided evidence of group differences in response patterns apart from the reward or punishment schedules utilized. For example, certain strains of rats respond differently to the same reward contingencies (Harrington, 1979). Sex differences in rat response patterns have been clearly demonstrated (Cales & Guillamon, 1986; van Hest, van Haaren, & van de Poll, 1989; Guillamon et al., 1990). Although the cause of strain differences remains to be identified, the sex differences in response patterns have been traced to sex differences in the degree of brain exposure to testosterone (Cales & Guillamon, 1986; van Hest, van Haaren, & van de Poll, 1989).

An even more sophisticated electrically controlled instrument has been used in research with nonhuman primates. Recall that the preceding chapter described case study observations in which chimpanzees were taught to communicate with the American Sign Language. These largely qualitative studies have recently been augmented with more quantitative observations of other chimpanzees who have learned to communicate on a computerized console. The console covers one wall of the cage and contains numerous buttons. Each button has a different symbol, which the chimpanzees use as words in their artificial language.

These machines have made it possible for social scientists to quantitatively determine how nonhuman primates acquire and use at least rudimentary language (Rumbaugh, 1981). The research indicates that the vocabularies of chimpanzees remain exceedingly limited compared to what most humans accomplish even within the first few years of life (Seyfarth, 1987:442). Thus, the prospect of chimpanzees ever providing social scientists with data via a questionnaire is still remote!

Finally, it should be mentioned that the distinction between instrument-aided and simple visual laboratory observations have become blurred with the availability of video cameras. Increasingly, researchers who study laboratory animals over extended periods of time do so by panning their living space with a video camera. The tapes are viewed at a later time (e.g., Blanchard & Blanchard, 1989). This allows researchers to not only fast forward through segments of tape when little of interest is happening, but also to play back particularly significant events as many times as they want.

Quantitative Field Observations

Quantitative field (or naturalistic) observations are used by social scientists to answer numerous questions. The main advantage of such observations over laboratory observations is that subjects will be seen behaving more naturally in the field than in most laboratories. While the value of observing subjects behaving normally is obvious, it can also be a source of frustration. In particular, if the behavior of interest happens only rarely under field conditions, more time may be required than a researcher can justify devoting to a study.

As noted earlier, some observations take place in environments that fall somewhere between a field and a laboratory setting. These are called semi-field observations. This term usually refers to studies of nonhuman animals that are made in fenced-in enclosures much larger than a normal cage (e.g., Eaton, 1976; de Waal, 1982). In these enclosures, subjects have considerable freedom to roam about as they would under natural conditions.

The concept of field observations was introduced on page 128, since it is also closely tied to qualitative observations. In fact, field observations can be either qualitative or quantitative in nature.

One of the earliest examples of a study involving quantitative field observations was reported by Francis Galton (1908:315). (You may recall his name appearing in Chapter 4 in connection with the concept of correlation.) During travels to various parts of England, Galton gave subjective ratings to hundreds of women that he happened to pass. He eventually calculated the average ratings given in several geographical regions, and concluded that women in London were more attractive than those elsewhere in the country.

While the scientific value of Galton's field study can certainly be questioned, it gives you an example of how social scientists sometimes take advantage of quite ordinary opportunities to collect data. Below are some other examples.

Have you ever noticed that people vary in the way they usually carry their books? Disregarding those using a backpack or briefcase, watch your fellow students the next time you stroll between classes. Notice in particular how most males carry their books down to one side, and how females frequently carry their books close to the chest with either one or two arms. Such differences have been documented on college campuses in many parts of the world (Jenni, 1976; Jenni & Jenni, 1976; Rekers & Mead, 1979).

A study of book-carrying styles conducted in the primary and secondary grades found the same type of sex differences in book-carrying styles, although to a lesser degree than among college students (Rekers & Mead, 1979). Why such sex differences exist, and why they would become more pronounced with age (at least up to early adulthood), no one yet knows. Because the patterns appear to be worldwide, however, at least one researcher has suggested that some biological factors may be involved (Jenni, 1976).

Another example of quantitative field observations has involved seat belt usage by motorists. Studies have found a number of factors (e.g., age, sex, and nationality) associated with such usage (see Anonymous, 1989). One field study has shown that inducements given out by a fast food restaurant were effective in increasing seat belt usage, at least temporarily (Cope, Moy, & Grossnickle, 1988).

One more example of field observations was briefly discussed in Chapter 7. It pertains to proxemics, the study of tendencies to maintain a preferred distance from those with whom one socially interacts (Sommer, 1959; Hall, 1968). You may recall the discussion of proxemics in connection with validity (p. 93). Because there are three rather distinct operational measures of spacing preferences—a paper-and-pencil method, a role-playing method, and a real life measure—researchers have been able to compare them. Differences in proximal preferences have been associated with such variables as sex, age, race, nationality, and social status (Hayduk, 1978).

Many examples can be cited of quantitative field observations of nonhumans. Ethologists and other naturalists have documented how various species of birds and nonhuman primates behave under both natural and seminatural conditions (see Gould, 1982; Smuts et al., 1987).

Among the examples of field experiments by social scientists are ones involving communication behavior. One fascinating series of field studies involved recording and then playing back amplified sounds made by vervet monkeys (a species of primates native to southern Africa) (Cheney & Seyfarth, 1982; Seyfarth & Cheney,

1984). Among other things, the studies showed that these animals learn to transmit and understand the meaning of specific calls alerting one another to different predators. With high levels of statistical significance, the vervets were found to look up when researchers played warning calls for eagles and look down when they played warning calls for snakes.

Probably the most widely studied behavior patterns in field observations of non-humans are of aggression and dominance. There are many forms of aggression (Moyer, 1968, 1982), but most aggression is operationalized in one of two ways: by actually witnessing physical attacks or inferentially by counting the number of physical wounds sustained by various animals (e.g., Catlett, 1961; Brain & Poole, 1974; Singleton & Hay, 1982).

Dominance, on the other hand, tends to be more subtle and difficult to measure than aggression, both in the field as well as in laboratory studies (Ellis, 1993). Although dominance and aggression are often related, they can not be equated (Kemper, 1990:29). Dominance is usually measured in terms of access to some resource (e.g., food, territory). Aggression is only one of the means used by animals to obtain and retain such access.

The Overlap Between Questionnaire Data and Direct Observations

Before closing this chapter, you should note that there are times when it is difficult to clearly distinguish between questionnaire data and qualitative and quantitative observations. For example, studies have been conducted in which the behavior of children has been measured based on evaluations given by their teachers (e.g., Janes et al., 1979; Whalen, Henker, & Dotemoto, 1981) or by their parents (e.g., Buss, Iscoe, & Buss, 1979; Barkley et al., 1985). How would these observations be classified? The reason this is difficult to answer is that most questionnaire data are about a respondent's own behavior and background, and most direct observations are made by researchers or trained assistants. When teachers or parents provide information about a child, they are not only functioning as questionnaire respondents but also as observers, albeit not professionally trained.

You should also be aware that questionnaire data and direct observations are sometimes combined in the same study. For instance, laboratory studies have been undertaken in which employer-employee relationships are role-played (or simulated) to gain insight into what may actually occur on the job. In these studies, the "employer" might be asked to fill out a questionnaire about the "employee's" work performance during a short experimental session (e.g., Spencer & Taylor, 1988). Another example comes from laboratory studies designed to determine the effects of exposing males to various forms of pornography. In some of these studies, subjects watch one or more pornography films, and then complete questionnaires in which they describe their attitudes toward women and/or assess their probability of behaving aggressively (including the commission of rape) (e.g., Donnerstein & Hallam, 1978; Malamuth & Check, 1983, 1985).

Although there are some instances in which direct observational data and data obtained via questionnaires overlap, and other instances in which they are used together in the same study, distinguishing between these two types of data is still important. The main point of this chapter and the preceding two chapters is that you recognize the wide array of options social scientists have for studying behavior and social phenomenon. In the next chapter, you will learn about a final set of observational methods, called **indirect observations.**

Contrasting Qualitative and Quantitative Research Methods

Also before bringing this chapter to a close, we should note that qualitative and quantitative data were often viewed in adversarial terms. Many social scientists were almost compelled to choose one or the other (Hammersley, 1992:161).

In point of fact, there are advantages and disadvantages to each. The main disadvantage to qualitative research methods is that they often lack scientific rigor. Because no standardized set of questions and response options are presented to subjects, there is a substantial risk that a researcher will reach erroneous conclusions (Barnard, 1983:196; Palmer, 1989:2; Knauft, 1991:405). On the other hand, many aspects of human behavior and culture are so complex that quantitative data are inadequate for capturing the full breadth and color of what social scientists are trying to comprehend.

In the final analysis, qualitative and quantitative research designs should be viewed as complementary, rather than as antagonistic (Hammersley, 1992). Social science has certainly been enhanced by findings from both of these broad categories of social science research methods.

Summary

This chapter has explored ways of collecting social science data via quantitative observations. Such observations involve a researcher (or a trained assistant) tabulating the frequency or intensity of one or more variables, and then subjecting these measures to statistical analysis. Contrary to quantitative observations, qualitative observations are difficult to statistically analyze.

Quantitative observations were divided into two categories: laboratory observations and field (or naturalistic) observations. (An intermediate category, called semi-field observations, was also delineated, although it was treated as a variation on field observations.) One advantage to laboratory observations is that they maximize the degree of control that a researcher has over the environment within which a study takes place. This control provides some assurance that extraneous and unforeseen factors were not responsible for the findings. Another advantage is that laboratory observations allow a researcher to use technical instruments with greater precision than in most field observations. Numerous examples were given of quantitative observations made in laboratory settings. These were subsumed under four headings: (a) physiological and biochemical measures of behavior, (b) mechanical and electrical measures of behavior, and (c) observations involving deception, and (d) studies conducted primarily on nonhuman animals.

The main advantage of field observations (which, incidentally, can be either qualitative or quantitative in nature) is that the behavior under study tends to be more spontaneous and natural than behavior in a laboratory. Several examples of field observations were presented, involving research with both humans and other species.

References

Adler, M. W., & Cowan, A. (Eds.). (1990). *Testing and evaluation of drugs of abuse.* New York: Wiley.

Annon, J. S. (1988). Reliability and validity of penile plethysmography in rape and child molestation cases. *American Journal of Forensic Psychology, 4,* 11–26.

Anonymous. (1989). Seat belts: Americans won't, Japanese will. *Psychology Today, 22* (November), 18.

Asberg, M., Traskman, L., & Thoren, P. (1976). 5–HIAA in the cerebrospinal fluid: A biochemical suicide predictor? *Archives of General Psychiatry, 33,* 1193–1197.

Barkley, R. A., Karlsson, J., Pollard, S., & Murphy, J. V. (1985). Developmental changes in the mother-child interactions of hyperactive boys: Effects of two dose levels of Ritalin. *Journal of Child Psychology and Psychiatry, 26,* 705–715.

Barnard, A. (1983). Contemporary hunter-gatherers: Current issues in ecology and social organization. *Annual Review of Anthropology, 12,* 193–214.

Bashore, T. R., Nydegger, R. V., & Miller, H. (1982). Left visual field superiority in a letter-naming task for both left- and right-handers. *Cortex, 18,* 245–256.

Blanchard, R. J., & Blanchard, D. C. (1989). Antipredatory defense behaviors in a visible burrow system. *Journal of Comparative Psychology, 103,* 70–82.

Bourne, L. E., & Ekstrand, B. R. (1979). *Psychology: Its principles and meanings* (3rd ed.) New York: Holt, Rinehart & Winston.

Brain, P. F., & Poole, A. E. (1974). Some studies on the use of standard opponents in intermale aggression testing in TT albino mice. *Behaviour, 102,* 96–109.

Bray, J. H., Hill, P. C., & Henderson, A. H. (1979, April). Increasing the validity of self-reports of drug use: Generalizability of a bogus pipeline procedure used to study cigarette smoking. Paper presented at the annual meeting of the Southeastern Psychological Association, San Antonio, TX.

Buss, A. H., Iscoe, I., & Buss, E. H. (1979). The development of embarrassment. *Journal of Psychology, 103,* 227–230.

Cales, J. M., & Guillamon, A. (1986). Sex differences and the early postnatal gonadal steroids effect in the free-operant behaviour of the rat. *Neuroscience Letter, Supplement, 26,* 249–251.

Catlett, R. H. (1961). An evaluation of methods for measuring fighting behaviour with special reference to *Mus musculus. Animal Behaviour, 9,* 8–10.

Chasnoff, I. J., Landress, H. J., & Barrett, M. E. (1990). The prevalence of illicit-drug or alcohol use during pregnancy and discrepancies in mandatory reporting in Pinellas County, Florida. *New England Journal of Medicine, 322,* 1202–1206.

Cheney, D. L., & Seyfarth, R. M. (1982). How vervet monkeys perceive their grunts: Field playback experiments. *Animal Behaviour, 30,* 739–751.

Conlee, M. C., and Tesser, A. (1973). The effects of recipient desire to hear on news transmission. *Sociometry, 36,* 588–599.

Cooper, A. J., Swaminath, S., Baxter, D., & Poulin, C. (1990). A female sex offender with multiple paraphilias: A psychologic, physiologic (laboratory sexual arousal) and endocrine case study. *Canadian Journal of Psychiatry, 35,* 334–337.

Cope, J. G., Moy, S. S., & Grossnickle, W. F. (1988). The behavioral impact of an advertising campaign to promote safety belt use. *Journal of Applied Behavior Analysis, 21,* 277–280.

de Waal, F. (1982). *Chimpanzee politics: Power and sex among apes.* New York: Harper & Row.

Donnerstein, E., & Hallam, J. (1978). Facilitating effects of erotica on aggression toward females. *Journal of Personality and Social Psychology, 36,* 1270–1277.

Dorozynski, A., & Anderson, A. (1991). Collagen: A new probe into prehistoric diet. *Science, 254,* 520–521.

Earls, C. M. (1988). Aberrant sexual arousal in sexual offenders. *Annuals of the New York Academy of Sciences, 528,* 41–48.

Eaton, G. G. (1976). The social order of the Japanese macaques. *Scientific American, 235* (4), 95–106.

Ellis, L. (1993). Operationally defining social stratification in human and nonhuman animals. In L. Ellis (Ed.), *Social stratification and socioeconomic inequality: Volume 1, A comparative biosocial approach* (pp. 15–35). New York: Praeger.

Ellis, L., & Ames, M. A. (1987). Neurohormonal functioning and sexual orientation: A theory of homosexuality-heterosexuality. *Psychological Bulletin, 101,* 233–258.

Ellis, L., Miller, C., & Widmayer, A. (1988). Content analysis of biological approaches in psychology: 1894 to 1985. *Sociology and Social Research, 72,* 145–149.

Evans, R. I., Hansen, W. B., & Mittelmark, M. B. (1977). Increasing the validity of self-reports of smoking behavior in children. *Journal of Applied Social Psychology, 62,* 521–523.

Feder, K. L., & Park, M. A. (1989). *Human antiquity.* Mountain View, CA: Mayfield.

Flor-Henry, P., Lang, R. A., Koles, Z. J., & Frenzel, R. R. (1991). Quantitative EEG studies of pedophilia. *International Journal of Psychophysiology, 10,* 253–258.

Frank, D. A., Zuckerman, B. S., Amaro, H. (1988). Cocaine use during pregnancy: Prevalence and correlates. *Pediatrics, 82,* 888–895.

Galton, F. (1908). *Memories of my life.* London: Methuen.

Giambra, L. M., & Quilter, R. E. (1989). Sex differences in sustained attention across the adult life span. *Journal of Applied Psychology, 74,* 91–95.

Gould, J. L. (1982). *Ethology: The mechanisms and evolution of behavior.* New York: Norton.

Gove, W. R., & Wilmoth, C. (1990). Risk, crime, and neurophysiologic highs: A consideration of brain processes that may reinforce delinquent and criminal behavior. In L. Ellis and H. Hoffman (Eds.), *Crime in biological, social and moral contexts* (pp. 261–293). New York: Praeger.

Guillamon, A., Cales, J. M., Rodriguez-Zafra, M., Perez-Laso, C., Caminero, A., Izquierdo, M. A., & Segovia, S. (1990). Effects of perinatal diazepam administration on two sexually dimorphic nonreproductive behaviors. *Brain Research Bulletin, 25,* 913–916.

Hall, E. T. (1968). Proxemics. *Current Anthropology, 9,* 83–108.

Hall, G. C. N., Proctor, W. C., & Nelson, G. M. (1988). Validity of physiological measures of pedophilic sexual arousal in a sexual offender population. *Journal of Consulting and Clinical Psychology, 56,* 118–122.

Hammersley, M. (1992). *What's wrong with ethnography?* London: Routhledge.

Harrington, G. A. (1979). Strain differences in free operant leverpress levels in the rat. *Bulletin of the Psychonomic Society, 13,* 153–154.

Hayduk, L. A. (1978). Personal space: An evaluative and orientating overview. *Psychological Bulletin, 85,* 117–134.

Hilgard, E. R., Atkinson, R. C., & Atkinson, R. L. (1975). *Introduction to psychology* (6th ed.). New York; Harcourt Brace Jovanovich.

Janes, C. L., Hesselbrock, V. M., Myers, D. G., & Penniman, J. H. (1979). Problem boys in young adulthood: Teachers' ratings and twelve-year follow-up. *Journal of Youth and Adolescence, 8,* 453–472.

Jenni, M. A. (1976). Sex differences in carrying behavior. *Perceptual and Motor Skills, 43,* 323–330.

Jenni, D. A., & Jenni, M. A. (1976). Carrying behavior in humans: Analysis of sex differences. *Science, 194,* 859–860.

Jensen, A. R. (1982). Reaction time and psychometric g. In H. J. Eysenck (Ed.), *A model for intelligence.* New York: Springer.

Jones, E. E., & Sigall, H. (1971). The bogus pipeline: A new paradigm for measuring affect and attitude. *Psychological Bulletin, 76,* 349–364.

Kemper, T. D. (1990). *Social structure and testosterone.* New Brunswick, NJ: Rutgers University Press.

Knauft, B. M. (1991). Violence and sociality in human evolution. *Current Anthropology, 32,* 391–428.

Lieberson, S. (1992). Einstein, Renoir, and Greeley: Some thoughts about evidence in sociology. *American Sociological Review, 57,* 1–15.

Lunneborg, C. E. (1977). Choice reaction time: What role in ability measurement? *Applied Psychological Measurement, 1,* 309–330.

Malamuth, N. M., & Check, J. V. P. (1983). Sexual arousal to rape depictions: Individual differences. *Journal of Abnormal Psychology, 92,* 55–67.

Malamuth, N. M., & Check, J. V. P. (1985). The effects of aggressive pornography on beliefs in rape myths: Individual difference. *Journal of Research in Personality, 19,* 299–320.

Maletzky, B. M. (1980). *Assisted covert sensitization in exhibitionism: Description, assessment and treatment.* New York: Garland.

McAllister, I., & Makkai, T. (1991). Correcting for the underreporting of drug use in opinion surveys. *International Journal of the Addictions, 26,* 945–961.

McKeever, W. F., Gill, K. M., & VanDeventer, A. D. (1975). Letter versus dot stimuli as tools for ''splitting the normal brain with reaction time.'' *Quarterly Journal of Experimental Psychology, 27,* 363–373.

Mieczkowski, T., Barzelay, D., Gropper, B., & Wish, E. (1991). Concordance of three measures of cocaine use in an arrestee population: Hair, urine, and self-report. *Journal of Psychoactive Drugs, 23,* 241–249.

Milgram, S. (1963). Behavioral study of obedience. *Journal of Abnormal and Social Psychology, 67,* 371–378.

Milgram, S. (1974). *Obedience to authority.* New York: Harper & Row.

Moyer, K. E. (1968). Kinds of aggression and their physiological basis. *Communications in Behavioral Biology, 2,* 65–87.

Moyer, K. E. (1982). Aggression theories. *Academic Psychology Bulletin, 4,* 415–423.

Neuspiel, D. R., & Hamel, S. C. (1991). Cocaine and infant behavior. *Journal of Developmental and Behavioral Pediatrics, 12,* 55–64.

O'Connor, A. A. (1987). Female sex offenders. *British Journal of Psychiatry, 150,* 615–620.

Oliver, B. J., Jr. (1967). *Sexual deviation in American society.* New Haven, CN: College and University Press.

Palmer, C. (1989). Is rape a cultural universal? A reexamination of the ethnographic data. *Ethnology, 28,* 1–16.

Pfeiffer, J. E. (1985). *The emergence of humankind* (4th ed.). New York: Harper & Row.

Proulx, J. (1989). Sexual preference assessment of sexual aggressors. *International Journal of Law and Psychiatry, 12,* 275–280.

Quigley-Fernandez, B., & Tedeschi, J. T. (1978). The bogus pipeline as lie detector: Two validity studies. *Journal of Personality and Social Psychology, 76,* 247–256.

Quinsey, V. L., Steinman, C. M., Bergersen, S. G., & Holmes, T. F. (1975). Penile circumference, skin conductance, and ranking responses of child molesters and ''normals'' to sexual and nonsexual visual stimuli. *Behavior Therapy, 6,* 213–219.

Raine, A., & Venables, P. H. (1988). Skin conductance responsivity in psychopaths to orienting, defensive, and consonant-vowel stimuli. *Journal of Psychophysiology, 2,* 221–225.

Rajecki, D. W. (Ed.). (1983). *Comparing behavior: Studying man studying animals.* Hillsdale, NJ: Erlbaum.

Raleigh, M. J., Brammer, G. L., Yumiler, A., Flannery, J. W., McGuire, M. T., & Geller, E. (1980). Serotonergic influences on the social behavior of vervet monkeys. *Experimental Neurology, 68,* 322–334.

Rekers, G. A., & Mead, S. (1979). Human sex differences in carrying behaviors and a replication and extension. *Perceptual and Motor Skills, 48,* 625–626.

Rosen, S., & Tesser, A. (1972). Fear of negative evaluation and the reluctance to transmit bad news. *Journal of Communication, 22,* 124–141.

Rumbaugh, D. M. (1981). Who feeds Clever Hans? *Annals of the New York Academy of Science, 364,* 26–34.

Schweizer, K. (1989). Relating reaction time components and intelligence. *Personality and Individual Differences, 10,* 701–707.

Seamon, J. G., & Kenrick, D. T. (1992). *Psychology.* Englewood Cliffs, NJ: Prentice-Hall.

Seyfarth, R. M. (1987). Vocal communication and its relation to language. In B. B. Smuts, D. L. Cheney, R. M. Seyfarth, R. W. Wringham, & T. T. Struhsaker (Eds.), *Primate societies* (pp. 440–451). Chicago: University of Chicago Press.

Seyfarth, R. M., & Cheney, D. L. (1984). Grooming, alliances, and reciprocal altruism in vervet monkeys. *Nature, 308,* 541–543.

Shipman, P., & Rose, J. (1983). Evidence of butchery and hominid activities at Torralba and Ambrona: An evaluation using microscopic techniques. *Journal of Archaeological Science, 10,* 465–474.

Singleton, G. R., & Hay, D. A. (1982). A genetic study of male social aggression in wild and laboratory mice. *Behavior Genetics, 12,* 435–448.

Smuts, B. B., Wrangham, R. W., Cheney, D. L., Seyforth, R. M., & Struhsaker, T. T. (Eds.) (1987). *Primate societies.* Chicago: University of Chicago Press.

Sommer, R. (1959). Studies in personal space. *Sociometry, 22,* 247–260.

Spencer, B. A., & Taylor, G. S. (1988). Effects of facial attractiveness and gender on causal attributions of managerial performance. *Sex Roles, 5/6,* 273–285.

Tesser, A., Rosen, S., & Conlee, M. C. (1972). News valence and available recipient as determinants of news transmission. *Sociometry, 35,* 619–628.

van Hest, A., van Haaren, F., & van de Poll, N. E. (1989). Perseverative responding in male and female Wiston rats: Effects of gonadal hormones. *Hormones and Behavior, 23,* 57–67.

Visher, C., & McFadden, K. (1991). *A comparison of urinalysis technologies for drug testing in criminal justice.* Washington, DC: U.S. Department of Justice (NCJ 12292).

von Knorring, L., Oreland, L., & Winblad, B. (1984). Personality traits related to monoamine oxidase activity in platelets. *Psychiatry Research, 12,* 11–26.

Whalen, C. K., Henker, B., Dotemoto, S. (1981). Teacher response to the methylphenidate (Ritalin) versus placebo status of hyperactive boys in the classroom. *Child Development, 52,* 1005–1014.

White, T. D. (1992). *Prehistoric cannibalism at Mancos 5MTUMR-2346.* Princeton, NJ: Princeton University Press.

Wilcox, R. G., Hughes, J., & Roland, J. (1979). Verification of smoking history in patients after infarction using urinary nicotine and cotinine measurements. *British Medical Journal, 6197* (2), 1026–1028.

Wortman, C. B., Loftus, E. F., & Marshall, M. E. (1992). *Psychology* (4th ed.). New York: McGraw-Hill.

Suggested Reading

Bickman, L., & Henchy, T. (1972). *Beyond the laboratory: Field research in social psychology.* New York: McGraw-Hill. (This book of readings provides a wide array of interesting examples of field studies carried out during the 1960s.)

Smuts, B. B., Cheney, D. L., Seyfarth, R. M., Wringham, R. W., & Struhsaker, T. T. (Eds.), *Primate societies.* Chicago: University of Chicago Press. (This book provides a nice overview of field research findings in primate behavior. While some of the evidence is qualitative in nature, most of it is quantitative.)

Among the journals which specialize in quanitative field research on nonhumans are *Animal Behaviour, Behaviour, Ethology,* and *Primates.* Journals that specialize in quanitative field research of humans include *Social Psychology Quarterly,* the *Journal of Personality and Social Psychology,* the *Journal of Social Issues, Social Problems,* and the *Journal of Experimental Social Psychology.*

CHAPTER 11

Indirect
Observational Data

C hapter 8 presented information about how questionnaires are used in the social sciences. In Chapter 9, you learned about one category of direct observations—qualitative direct observations. The other type of direct observations—quantitative observations—was the focus of Chapter 10. The remaining category of methods used by social scientists to obtain data will be the focus of this chapter—indirect observations.

Basically, **indirect observations** are data that the researcher performing the analysis was not responsible for collecting. In other words, if the data that Researcher A is to analyze and interpret for a particular study was collected by Researcher B, then Researcher A is analyzing data based upon indirect observations.

Indirect observations can be obtained from a variety of sources, but the main suppliers are fellow social scientists, along with governmental, educational, medical, religious, and business agencies. Sometimes indirect observations are originally collected via questionnaires (including government forms), sometimes by direct observations, and other times they may be contained in published documents. Three major categories of indirect observation will be discussed: **archival data, content analysis data,** and **meta-analysis data.**

Archival Data

Much social science research involves the analysis of archival data, particularly in the fields of economics, political science, and sociology. Archival data are quantitative data that have already been collected by someone (or some agency) other than the researcher who will analyze them (Mason & Bramble, 1989:50).

The term **secondary analysis** often refers to the analysis of archival data, although sometimes the same researcher who has collected a set of data may choose to perform a secondary analysis. Basically, a secondary analysis is any analysis of data for which the data were not originally collected (Hyman, 1972:1). In other words, if you gave out a large questionnaire for the purpose of testing a particular hypothesis, but later used the same data set to explore some additional hypotheses, all of your later analyses would be referred to as secondary analyses.

Archival data can be divided into two forms: institutional and noninstitutional. Institutional archival data includes data collected by organizations such as government agencies, churches, and businesses, often in the course of their basic recordkeeping. Examples are records kept by police agencies on the number of calls they receive about crimes, by welfare departments on the number of clients they have receiving various types of services, or by churches on marriage ceremonies performed.

Noninstitutional archival data include data compiled primarily by social scientists themselves for specific research purposes. It would also include surveys of public opinion sponsored by newspapers and television stations that were eventually subjected to a secondary analysis. In the course of research, it is not uncommon for social scientists to obtain information on numerous variables (and relationships between variables) that are never formally analyzed. If these data are made available to others for the purpose of performing a secondary analysis, the data then constitutes archival data. Secondary analyses of archival data have become increasingly feasible because of the ever-growing number of archival data sets being economically stored in computer-accessible formats.

Examples of Institutional Archival Data

Social scientists have uncovered fascinating examples of institutional archival data that are centuries old. For example, one study was able to estimate the average age at first marriage of people living in an English township dating back to the 12th century (Andorka, 1978:67). These data were discovered in the recesses of an old parish church. Elsewhere in England, old jail logs were retrieved that allowed researchers to determine the age and sex of hundreds of persons arrested and convicted for various crimes going back as many as five centuries (Beatie, 1975; Weiner, 1975; Cockburn, 1977).

There are also many examples of more contemporary institutional archival data. Some are quite simple and obvious, such as observations based on school records of academic achievement and absences (Robins, 1966; Cairns, Cairns, & Neckerman, 1989).

Other examples have involved data that few people have any idea exist. For instance, in the 1980s, the United States Congress authorized a detailed study of Vietnam War veterans to determine any long-term effect of various herbicides (e.g., Agent Orange) to which many soldiers were exposed. The final data set contained an enormous amount of post- discharge information on more than 4,000 middle-aged men on topics ranging from physical and mental health issues to their current socio-economic status, family relationships, etc. (U.S. Public Health Service, 1989; Ellis & Nyborg, 1992). Recently, this data set was used to look for associations between the sex hormone levels and occupational status attainment, and it suggested that male sex hormones may affect brain functioning in ways that ultimately influence career choices, and thereby social status (Dabbs, 1992).

There are literally thousands of large data sets derived from routine institutional recordkeeping and institutionally sponsored surveys that are now available on computer (Glenn, 1973; Inter-University Consortium, 1984). In recent years, it has become possible for researchers to avail themselves of these data sets almost instantaneously by calling special telephone numbers and asking that some or all of a data set be downloaded into their personal computer (via a modem). The only things to which researchers would not be given access, of course, would be names, addresses, or phone numbers of the persons who provided the information.

Besides the data stored on computer, there are numerous data sets that have been printed in various publications. For example, nearly all countries have a census bureau that can provide researchers with a wealth of information. Increasingly, the United Nations has become a repository for international archival data on such diverse topics as births, deaths, marriages, divorces (e.g., Fisher, 1991), and even various criminal offenses (e.g., Rahav & Ellis, 1990).

Another valuable source for international statistics is the World Health Organization (WHO). Based on statistics compiled by WHO, a recent study found some interesting patterns associated with societal murder rates (Lester, 1991).

With the increasing availability of large archival data sets, you might wonder why social scientists would even bother to collect their own original data. In fact, while some social scientists have become specialists in secondary analysis, most still prefer to tailor data collection for a specific purpose. It is not often that researchers can find already-collected data sets measuring all the variables that they want to study. Barring this limitation, however, secondary analysis of archival data sometimes makes it possible to carry out a scientific study in the matter of a few weeks or even days, instead of months and sometimes years.

Let's briefly consider how a typical secondary analysis might be undertaken: A researcher becomes aware of the existence of a large data set, and obtains from the person or agency that collected the data a list of what variables were measured. If not all of the variables of interest were measured, the researcher may simply change some or all of his or her questions to match the variables that were measured. There is nothing wrong with conducting research in this way although it is sometimes frowned on by ''purists.'' Traditionally, researchers formulate a question (or hypothesis), and then find data relevant to it, rather than finding the data and then formulating the question (or hypothesis) to fit the data.

Content Analysis Data

Especially in the past quarter of a century, numerous social science studies have been published based on the analysis of various written and/or published documents such as books, articles, and even photographs. Such studies are subsumed under the category of content analysis. Content analysis occasionally overlaps with the secondary analysis of archival data, but a distinction is usually apparent. Archival data nearly always begins in the form of quantitative data, whereas content analysis usually begins with data of a more qualitative nature that are then quantified in some way. Below are some examples.

A simple example of content analysis is a recent study about the proportion of books in the social sciences dealing with drinking patterns among Native Americans (Young, 1991). The number of books for various years was divided by the total number of books listed in the social sciences for each of those years. Using a similar method, a study was undertaken to look for trends in the proportion of articles about feminist issues that appeared in a popular girl's magazine (Peirce, 1990). Also, changes in the annual proportion of articles dealing with genetics and biology in psychology journals was traced from 1894 to 1984 as another example of content analysis (Ellis, Miller, & Widmayer, 1988). Even restroom graffiti has been subjected to content analysis (Innala & Ernulf, 1992). In nearly all content analyses, the statistics are confined to presenting and comparing proportions (such as percentages and rates per year).

More complex content analyses have involved efforts to identify long-term trends in the weight and body proportions of fashion models. Studies that have taken careful measurements of photographs appearing since the 1930s have consistently documented trends toward more slender fashion models. One review of these studies proposed that these trends may help to explain the increasing popularity of dieting among Western women, and also the apparent increase in anorexia (Morris, Cooper, & Cooper, 1989). These trends may also be related to increasing preferences for thin female shapes by people living in industrial societies (Anderson et al., 1992).

Several interesting content analyses have studied classified advertisements placed in the ''personal section'' of various newspapers and magazines. These studies have shown that ads placed by men were more likely to mention the man's financial status (Harrison & Saeed, 1977), whereas ads placed by women were more likely to mention their physical attractiveness (reviewed by Feingold, 1990:983). (For a theoretical explanation of such sex differences, see Buss, 1989.)

Other studies based on content analysis have looked for trends in the use of men's and women's body parts on magazine covers (Nigro et al., 1988), in portrayals of alcohol consumption on television (Pendleton, Smith, & Roberts, 1991), in the content of television commercials (Ferrante, Haynes, & Kingsley, 1988), in the content of children's readers (Purcell & Stewart, 1990), and even in the content of obituaries (Kirchler, 1992).

Cross-Cultural Content Analysis

Before leaving the discussion of content analysis, an important type warrants separate attention. Recall in Chapter 9 the discussion of ethnographic observations as a major form of qualitative data in the social sciences (pp. 120–123).

What if you were to take hundreds of these individual ethnographic accounts, and using a standardized coding scheme, combine them into a large data bank so that general cultural patterns could be detected? You could then consult the data bank to determine such things as whether the most warlike cultures were also the most aggressive in their child-rearing practices. Such a data bank has, in fact, been produced, and has made possible numerous cross-cultural studies by social scientists who may have never actually visited any of the societies studied (see especially Burton & White, 1987). As you might suspect, the social scientists who have made the greatest use of this data bank have been anthropologists.

The most extensive versions of this cross-cultural data bank are variously called the *Human Relations Area Files (HRAF),* the *Atlas of World Cultures,* and the *Ethnographic Atlas.* It was first compiled for general use in the 1950s and 1960s by anthropologist George Murdock (1957, 1967; Murdock & White, 1969). The file is now available in many university libraries in paper form, on microfiche (Murdock, 1981; Ember & Ember, 1988:202), and, most recently, on computer (Ferraro, 1992:75). With these files it is possible to look for combinations of more than 700 different cultural patterns and practices among more than 300 different cultures/societies throughout the world (Ferraro, 1992:74).

Let's look at a short history of the *HRAF.* Murdock (1937) was the first to conduct a content analysis of ethnographic data. This was before he decided to set up a central repository for such data and make it available for use by other social scientists. In his initial study, Murdock was interested in finding out how widespread were the tendencies for men and women to specialize in various occupations. His cross-cultural comparison of the ethnographic accounts brought him to conclude that there is a virtually universal tendency for men and women to gravitate toward distinct work activities, a finding that has been confirmed by subsequent cross-cultural analyses (e.g., Talmon, 1965; Brown, 1970; Murdock & Provost, 1973; White, Burton, & Dow, 1981). In nearly all human societies, males tend to specialize in hunting, heavy work with lumber and metal, and warfare. Females, on the other hand, tend to do most of the weaving, food preparation, and child care. There appear to be a few exceptional societies, and there are certainly numerous individual men and women within most societies who defy the general pattern (reviewed by Parker & Parker, 1979:293).

Another cross-cultural study based upon an early version of the *HRAF* discovered a strong relationship between types of family systems and the ways most members of a society make a living (Nimkoff & Middleton, 1960). For example, hunter-gatherers were more likely to live in monogamous nuclear families than were humans living in various early agrarian societies (where polygamous life-styles were more prevalent).

A third early HRAF study looked for geographical patterns in the length of time females normally waited to resume sexual intercourse after giving birth (Whiting, 1964). It found that women who lived in the tropics tended to wait longer than those living in temperate zones, a pattern that was tentatively attributed to nutritional factors.

The *HRAF* (occasionally supplemented with additional ethnographic data) (e.g., Broude & Greene, 1976) has been utilized in numerous other social science studies. These include studies designed to look for societal variations in the prevalence of warfare (Ross, 1985, 1986), the prevalence of rape (Sanday, 1981; Palmer, 1989), the sharing of power in marital relationships (Stephens, 1963:297), the degree of polygamy (D'Andrade, 1966), attitudes and customs surrounding sexual behavior (Minturn, Grosse, & Haider, 1969; Broude & Greene, 1976), marriage customs (Thornhill, 1991), rates of reproduction according to social status (Betzig, 1982), ownership and property rights (Rudmin, 1992), and sex differences in aggression (Rohner, 1976).

There are still methodological issues that remain unresolved in cross-cultural research based on ethnographic accounts, and much caution is called for in interpreting results from cross-cultural studies (see Burton & White, 1987; Ferraro, 1992:75). Besides variation in the quality of individual ethnographic accounts, one of the biggest methodological problems has involved variation in the **units of analysis.** In some ethnographic accounts, attention may have been confined to a small nomadic band within a larger tribe, whereas other accounts may pertain to the tribe as a whole. Despite these problems, cross-cultural studies based on ethnographic accounts have provided much insight into both the similarity and differences between humans living in vastly different cultures and time frames.

Meta-Analysis Data

The prefix *meta* means above or over. Accordingly, a meta-analysis presents an overview of the findings from a large number of related studies. Unlike articles (and books) which simply review the literature on some topic (and also provide an overview), a meta-analysis uses various methods that can "standardize" the findings of diverse individual studies to some common statistic (albeit always with some loss in precision) (Top, 1991:75; Wells & Rankin, 1991:76).

First developed in the 1970s (Glass, 1976), meta-analysis is a set of procedures for reducing the findings from numerous studies down to a common statistic for collective analysis (Hattie & Hansford, 1984:239, Mann, 1990:476; Kulik & Kulik, 1992). Depending on how carefully the original studies were conducted and reported, meta-analysis helps researchers suggest an overall conclusion to all studies dealing with a particular topic.

Although meta-analysis has become popular in recent years, not only in social science (Guzzo, Jackson, & Katzell, 1987:411) but in science as a whole (Mann, 1990:478), these studies have also been criticized. One criticism is that the conclusions reached from a meta-analysis can be altered simply by using different criteria in deciding which studies to include and exclude from the final pool of studies to be analyzed (Chalmers, 1989). Another criticism is that meta-analysis opens the door to the possibility of ''bad science'' outnumbering ''good,'' because most meta-analyses make few judgments about the quality of each study being analyzed, and allow each study to contribute to the final outcome according to its sample size (Wachter, 1988:1407). Some critics have also asserted that because meta-analysis involves pooling data, it tends to blur real differences that may exist from one sample to another (Holden, 1991:960). You should note that although meta-analysis is certainly a valuable method for combining the results of numerous studies, its own results are still not beyond question (see Cossette, Malcuit, & Pomerleau, 1991:175).

One of the biggest methodology challenges to conducting a meta-analysis (or a thorough literature review in general) is locating all the relevant studies before undertaking a collective interpretation. It is advisable to begin by conducting both a manual and a computerized search of the literature (as outlined in Chapter 2). Also, contact as many of the original researchers as possible to determine (a) whether they have conducted additional research that did not come to your attention, and (b) if they are aware of any other research that you may have overlooked (Armstrong & Lusk, 1987).

When determining what statistics to use, you should consult the main manuals currently available (e.g., Glass, McGaw, & Smith, 1981; Hedges & Olkin, 1985; Hunter & Schmidt, 1990) and several meta-analyses that have already been published (see below). Something else to keep in mind is that a meta-analysis can not make up for poor research designs in the original studies. Therefore, it should only be performed on studies that a researcher considers adequate from a design standpoint (Wortman, Loftus, & Marshall, 1992:52).

Meta-analysis has been conducted on many social science topics in recent years. These include questions such as how closely ''romantic partners'' resemble one another in physical attractiveness (Feingold, 1988), what factors are most associated with accident proneness (Arthur, Barrett, & Alexander, 1991), how academic performance relates to anxiety (Seipp, 1991), and how parental divorce affects the social well-being of children (Amato & Keith, 1991) and the probability of children becoming delinquent (Wells & Rankin, 1991). Other questions addressed by meta-analyses have been how class size affects student achievement (Glass & Smith, 1979), whether employment screening tests are equally valid for various racial groups (Hunter, Schmidt, & Hunter, 1979), and how effective are various forms of psychotherapy (Svartberg & Stiles, 1991).

The topic that has been the focus of more meta-analyses than any other is sex (or gender) differences in behavior. Since the late 1970s, meta-analyses have been directed toward determining whether the sexes differ in tendencies toward conformity (Cooper, 1979; Eagly & Carli, 1981), in overall activity levels (Eaton & Enns, 1986), in motor skills and coordination (Thomas & French, 1985), in verbal ability (Hyde & Lynn, 1988), in leadership styles (Eagly & Johnson, 1990), and in tendencies to smile and gaze (Hall & Halberstadt, 1986). In addition, meta-analyses have attempted to draw conclusions about how someone's sex affects other people's judgments about his or her intellectual abilities (Swim et al., 1989) and job qualifications (Olian, Schwab, & Haberfeld, 1988).

Summary

Indirect observations refer to data that are collected by someone (or some agency) other than the researcher who will be analyzing the data. Three categories of indirect observations were identified: archival data, content analysis data, and data used in meta-analyses.

Archival data refers to data that a researcher did not actively collect (although the researcher might have been instrumental in coding and keying the data into a computer). Most archival data still comes from governmental records, although other public and private sources are also being tapped. Primary analysis of archival data refers to the first time a data set is used by a researcher. If a data set has already been analyzed, and an analysis is later undertaken having little to do with why the data were originally collected, this analysis is referred to as a secondary analysis.

Data used in what is called a content analysis is usually written and/or published material. The analysis involves counting key words, phrases, or other features of a series of documents to identify trends or other patterns. A special type of content analysis involves the use of the *Human Relations Area File (HRAF)*. This file has been accumulated on the basis of hundreds of ethnographic accounts from all over the world, and has been used for dozens of cross-cultural studies by social scientists.

A meta-analysis refers to a "study of a set of individual studies." Data used in a meta-analysis are created by imposing a common statistic onto several individual studies that all addressed a specific question.

References

Amato, P. R., & Keith, B. (1991). Parental divorce and the well-being of children: A meta-analysis. *Psychological Bulletin, 110,* 26–46.

Anderson, J. L., Crawford, C. B., Nadeau, J., & Lindberg, T. (1992). Was the Duchess of Windsor right? A cross-cultural review of the socioecology of ideals of female body shape. *Ethology and Sociobiology, 13,* 197–227.

Andorka, R. (1978). *Determinants of fertility in advanced societies.* New York: Free Press.

Armstrong, J. S., & Lusk, E. J. (1987). Return postage in mail surveys. *Public Opinion Quarterly, 51,* 233–248.

Arthur, W., Barrett, G. V., & Alexander, R. A. (1991). Prediction of vehicular accident involvement: A meta-analysis. *Human Performance, 4,* 89–105.

Beatie, J. M. (1975). The criminality of women in eighteenth-century England. *Journal of Social History, 9,* 80–116.

Betzig, L. L. (1982). Despotism and differential reproduction: A cross-cultural correlation of conflict asymmetry, hierarchy, and degree of polygyny. *Ethology and Sociobiology, 3,* 209–221.

Broude, G., & Greene, S. (1976). Cross-cultural codes on twenty sexual attitudes and practices. *Ethnology, 15,* 409–429.

Brown, J. K. (1970). A note on the division of labor by sex. *American Anthropologist, 72,* 1073–1078.

Burton, M. L., & White, D. R. (1987). Cross-cultural surveys today. *Annual Review in Anthropology, 16,* 143–160.

Buss, D. M. (1989). Sex differences in human mate preferences: Evolutionary hypotheses tested in 37 cultures. *Behavioral and Brain Sciences, 12,* 1–19.

Cairns, R. B., Cairns, B. D., & Neckerman, H. J. (1989). Early school dropout: Configurations and determinants. *Child Development, 60,* 1437–1452.

Chalmers, T. C. (1989). Meta-analysis (letter). *Science, 243,* 283–284.

Cockburn, J. S. (Ed). (1977). *Crime in England—1550–1800.* Princeton, NJ: Princeton University Press.

Cooper, H. M. (1979). Statistically combining independent studies: A meta-analysis of sex differences in conformity research. *Journal of Personality and Social Psychology, 37,* 131–146.

Cossette, L., Malcuit, G., & Pomerleau, A. (1991). Sex differences in motor activity during early infancy. *Infant Behavior and Development, 14,* 175–186.

Dabbs, J. M., Jr. (1992). Testosterone and occupational achievement. *Social Forces, 70,* 813–824.

D'Andrade, R. G. (1966). Sex differences and cultural institutions. In E. D. Maccoby (Ed.), *The development of sex differences* (pp. 174–204). Stanford: Stanford University Press.

Eagly, A. H., & Carli, L. L. (1981). Sex of researcher and sex-typed communications as determinants of sex differences in influenceability: A meta-analysis of social influence studies. *Psychological Bulletin, 90,* 1–20.

Eagly, A. H., & Johnson, B. T. (1990). Gender and leadership styles: A meta-analysis. *Psychological Bulletin, 198,* 233–256.

Eaton, W. O., & Enns, L. R. (1986). Sex differences in human motor activity level. *Psychological Bulletin, 100,* 19–26.

Ellis, L., Miller, C., & Widmayer, A. (1988). Content analysis of biological approaches in psychology: 1894 to 1985. *Sociology and Social Research, 72,* 145–149.

Ellis, L., & Nyborg, H. (1992). Racial/ethnic variations in male testosterone levels: A probable contributor to group differences in health. *Steroids, 57,* 72–75.

Ember, C. R., & Ember, M. (1988). Anthropology (5th ed.). Englewood Cliffs, NJ: Prentice-Hall.

Feingold, A. (1988). Matching for attractiveness in romantic partners and same-sex friends: A meta-analysis and theoretical critique. *Psychological Bulletin, 104,* 226–235.

Ferrante, C. L., Haynes, A. M., & Kingsley, S. M. (1988). Image of women in television advertising. *Journal of Broadcasting & Electronic Media, 32,* 231–237.

Ferraro, G. (1992). *Cultural Anthropology: An applied perspective.* St. Paul, MN: West.

Fisher, H. (1991). Monogamy, adultery, and divorce in cross-species perspective. In M. H. Robinson & L. Tiger (Eds.), *Man & beast revisited* (pp. 95–138). Washington, DC: Smithsonian.

Glass, G. V. (1976). Primary, secondary, and meta-analysis of research. *Educational Researcher, 5,* 3–8.

Glass, G. V., McGaw, B., & Smith, M. L. (1981). *Meta-analysis in social research.* Beverly Hills, CA: Sage.

Glass, G. V., & Smith, M. L. (1979). Meta-analysis of research on the relationship of class-size and achievement. *Evaluation and Policy Analysis, 1,* 2–16.

Glenn, N. D. (1973). The social scientific data archives: The problem of underutilization. *American Sociologist, 8,* 42–45.

Guzzo, R. A., Jackson, S. E., & Katzell, R. A. (1987). Meta-analysis analysis. *Research in Organizational Behavior, 9,* 407–442.

Hall, J. A., & Halberstadt, A. G. (1986). Smiling and gazing. In J. S. Hyde & M. Linn (Eds.), *The psychology of gender: Advances through meta-analysis* (pp. 136–158). Baltimore: Johns Hopkins University Press.

Harrison, A. A., & Saeed, L. (1977). Let's make a deal: An analysis of revelations and stipulations in lonely hearts' advertisements. *Journal of Personality and Social Psychology, 35,* 257–264.

Hattie, J. A., & Hansford, B. C. (1984). Meta-analysis: A reflection on problems. *Australian Journal of Psychology, 36,* 239–254.

Hedges, L. V., & Olkin, I. (1985). *Statistical methods for meta-analysis.* Orlando: Academic Press.

Holden, C. (1991). Is "gender gap" narrowing? *Science, 253,* 959–1260.

Hunter, J. E., & Schmidt, F. L. (1990). *Methods of meta-analysis: Correcting error and bias in research findings.* Newbury Park, CA: Sage.

Hunter, J. E., Schmidt, F. L., & Hunter, R. (1979). Differential validity of employment tests by race: A comprehensive review and analysis. *Psychological Bulletin, 86,* 721–735.

Hyde, J. S., & Linn, M. C. (1988). Gender differences in verbal ability: A meta-analysis. *Psychological Bulletin,* 53–69.

Hyman, H. (1972). *Secondary analysis of sample surveys: Principles, procedures and potentialities.* New York: Wiley.

Innala, S. M., & Ernulf, K. E. (1992). Understanding male homosexual attraction: An analysis of restroom graffiti. *Journal of Social Behavior and Personality, 7,* 503–510.

Inter-University Consortium for Political and Social Research. (1984). *Guide to resources and services—1983–1984.* Ann Arbor: University of Michigan's Institute for Social Research.

Kirchler, E. (1992). Adorable woman, expert man: Changing gender images of women and men in management. *European Journal of Social Psychology, 22,* 363–373.

Kulik, J. A., & Kulik, C. C. (1992). Meta-analysis: Historical origins and contemporary practice. *Advances in Social Science Methodology, 2,* 53–79.

Lester, D. (1991). Murdering babies: A cross-national study. *Social Psychiatry and Psychiatric Epidemiology, 26,* 83–85.

Mann, C. (1990). Meta-analysis in the breech. *Science, 249,* 476–480.

Mason, E. J., & Bramble, W. J. (1989). *Understanding and conducting research* (2nd ed.). New York: McGraw-Hill.

Minturn, L., Grosse, M., & Haider, S. (1969). Cultural patterning of sexual beliefs and behavior. *Ethnology, 8,* 301–318.

Morris, A., Cooper, T., & Cooper, P. J. (1989). The changing shape of female fashion models. *International Journal of Eating Disorders, 8,* 593–596.

Murdock, G. P. (1937). Comparative data on the division of labor by sex. *Social Forces, 15,* 551–553.

Murdock, G. P. (1957). World ethnographic sample. *American Anthropologist, 59,* 644–687.

Murdock, G. P. (1967). *Ethnographic atlas.* Pittsburgh: University of Pittsburgh Press.

Murdock, G. P. (1981). *Atlas of world cultures.* Pittsburgh: University of Pittsburgh Press.

Murdock, G. P., & Provost, C. (1973). Factors in the division of labor by sex. *Ethnography, 12,* 203–225.

Murdock, G. P., & White, D. R. (1969). Standard cross-cultural sample. *Ethnology, 8,* 329–369.

Nigro, G. N., Hill, D. E., Gelbein, M. E., & Clark, C. L. (1988). Changes in the facial prominence of women and men over the last decade. *Psychology of Women Quarterly, 12,* 225–235.

Nimkoff, M. F., & Middleton, R. (1960). Types of family and types of economy. *American Journal of Sociology, 66,* 215–225.

Olian, J. D., Schwab, D. P., & Haberfeld, Y. (1988). The impact of applicant gender compared to qualifications on hiring recommendations: A meta-analysis of experimental studies. *Organizational Behavior and Human Decision Processes, 41,* 180–195.

Palmer, C. (1989). Is rape a cultural universal? A reexamination of the ethnographic data. *Ethnology, 28,* 1–16.

Parker, S., & Parker, H. (1979). The myth of male superiority: Rise and demise. *American Anthropologist, 81,* 289–309.

Peirce, K. (1990). A feminist theoretical perspective on the socialization of teenage girls through *Seventeen* magazine. *Sex Roles, 23,* 491–500.

Pendleton, L. L., Smith, C., & Roberts, J. L. (1991). Drinking on television: A content analysis of recent alcohol portrayal. *British Journal of Addiction, 86,* 769–774.

Purcell, P., & Stewart, L. (1990). Dick and Jane in 1989. *Sex Roles, 22,* 177–185.

Rahav, G., & Ellis, L. (1990). International crime rates and evolutionary theory: An application of the r/K selection concept to human populations. In L. Ellis & H. Hoffman (Eds.), *Crime in biological, social, and moral contexts* (pp. 115–120). New York: Praeger.

Robins, L. N. (1966). *Deviant children grown up: A sociological and psychiatric study of sociopathic personality.* Baltimore: Williams & Wilkins.

Rohner, R. P. (1976). Sex differences in aggression: Phylogenetic and enculturation perspectives. *Ethnos, 4,* 57–72.

Ross, M. H. (1985). International and external conflict. *Journal of Conflict Resolution, 29,* 169–192.

Ross, M. H. (1986). A cross-cultural theory of political conflict and violence. *Political Psychology, 7,* 427–469.

Rudmin, F. W. (1992). Cross-cultural correlations of the ownership of private property. *Social Science Research, 21,* 57–83.

Sanday, P. R. (1981). The socio-cultural context of rape: A cross-cultural study. *Journal of Social Issues, 37,* 5–27.

Seipp, B. (1991). Anxiety and academic performance: A meta-analysis of findings. *Anxiety Research, 4,* 27–41.

Stephens, W. N. (1963). *The family in cross-cultural perspective.* New York: Holt, Rinehart, & Winston.

Svartberg, M., and Stiles, T. C. (1991). Comparative effects of short-term psychodynamic psychotherapy: A meta-analysis. *Journal of Consulting and Clinical Psychology, 59,* 704–714.

Swim, J., Borgida, E., Maruyama, G., & Myers, D. G. (1989). Joan McKay versus John McKay: Do gender stereotypes bias evaluations? *Psychological Bulletin, 105,* 409–429.

Talmon, Y. (1965). Sex role differentiation in an equalitarian society. In T. E. Lasswell, J. H. Burma, & S. H. Aronson (Eds.), Life in society (pp. 144–155). Glenview, IL: Scott, Foresman.

Thomas, J. R., & French, K. E. (1985). Gender differences across age in motor performance: A meta-analysis. *Psychological Bulletin, 98,* 260–282.

Thornhill, N. W. (1991). An evolutionary analysis of rules regulating human inbreeding and marriage. *Behavioral and Brain Sciences, 14,* 247–293.

Top, T. J. (1991). Sex bias in the evaluation of performance in the scientific, artistic, and literary professions: A review. *Sex Roles, 24,* 73–106.

United States Public Health Service. (1989). *Health status of Vietnam veterans, Volumes 1 through 6.* Atlanta, GA: Center for Disease Control.

Wachter, K. W. (1988). Disturbed by meta-analysis? *Science, 241,* 1407–1408.

Weiner, C. (1975). Sex roles and crime in late Elizabethan Herefordshire. *Journal of Social History, 8,* 38–60.

Wells, L. E., & Rankin, J. H. (1991). Families and delinquency: A meta-analysis of the impact of broken homes. *Social Problems, 38,* 71–93.

White, D. R., Burton, M. L., & Dow, M. M. (1981). Sexual division of labor in African agriculture. *American Anthropologist, 83,* 824–849.

Whiting, J. W. M. (1964). Effects of climate on certain cultural practices. In W. H. Goodenough (Ed.), *Explorations in cultural anthropology* (pp. 511–544). New York: McGraw-Hill.

Wortman, C. B., Loftus, E. F., & Marshall, M. E. (1992). *Psychology* (4th ed.). New York: McGraw-Hill.

Young, T. J. (1991). Native American drinking: A neglected subject of study and research. *Journal of Drug Education, 21,* 65–72.

Suggested Reading

Burton, M. L., & White, D. R. (1987). Cross-cultural surveys today. *Annual Review in Anthropology, 16,* 143–160. (A well-written overview of the current breadth of cross-cultural research based on ethnographic accounts.)

Dale, A., Arber, S., & Procter, M. (1988). *Doing secondary analysis.* London: Unwin Hyman. (This book is written mainly for sociologists, but it can provide students in the social sciences with useful information on how to perform secondary analyses on large data sets.)

Glass, G. V., McGaw, B., & Smith, M. L. (1981). *Meta-analysis in social research.* Beverly Hills, CA: Sage. (The first book written on meta-analysis. The senior author originated this type of analysis in the mid-1970s.)

Hyman, H. (1972). *Secondary analysis of sample surveys: Principles, procedures and potentialities.* New York: Wiley. (This is the first book written on secondary analysis. Much has changed since this book was published, especially in the computer technology surrounding access to data for secondary analysis. Nevertheless, many useful ideas can still be gleaned from this book about how to perform and interpret one's results.)

One journal that has become especially prominent in the publication of meta-analyses is *Psychological Bulletin.* Among the journals that publish studies based on composite analyses of ethnographic records are the *American Anthropologist* and *Contemporary Anthropology,* and *Ethos.* See *Population and Development Review, Public Health Reports* and *Social Psychiatry and Psychiatric Epidemiology* for journals that publish articles based on archival data.

CHAPTER 12

Surveying and Sampling

Perhaps the most famous photograph in American history is of President Harry S. Truman holding up a copy of the *Chicago Daily Tribune* with headlines declaring that he had lost the presidency to his Republican rival, Thomas Dewey. Those in charge of the newspaper were so confident they knew the outcome of the election that they ran this headline the following morning without waiting for the official count. What gave the staff this confidence were several opinion polls leading up to the 1948 presidential election, all showing Dewey with a commanding lead (Bailar, 1988:1058). The confidence of the *Tribune*'s staff was apparently unshaken by the crudeness with which the samples in these polls had been obtained, or by the fact that several of the surveys indicated many voters were still undecided only a few days before the election (Babbie, 1973:75).

For many years following this erroneous *Tribune* headline people were understandably leery of election poll results. Today, with vastly improved sampling methodology, polls and other public opinion surveys are commonplace, and their results have become more trustworthy. Social scientists, newspaper reporters, politicians, and advertisers have learned how to conduct surveys that can be accurate to within a few percentage points of the true figures.

The Nature of Scientific Surveys

In science, the term **survey** is applied to any research study that examines some empirical phenomenon without fundamentally disturbing it. The term survey is particularly appropriate if the aim of the study is to determine the prevalence of some

President-elect Harry S. Truman holding up a copy of the Chicago Tribune the night after the 1948 election. © Bettmann Newsphotos.

phenomenon within a population over a specified time frame. As will be discussed extensively in Chapter 15, there are research designs—called **experiments**—whose purpose is to systematically alter a phenomenon, rather than to simply document its prevalence.

Surveys are conducted in virtually all the sciences. For example, astronomers survey the heavens for the positions of planets and the existence of previously unknown galaxies. Zoologists survey ecological habitats to count endangered species or to estimate insect infestations.

Thousands of surveys related to human behavior and culture are reported every year, not only by social scientists, but also by professionals in several allied fields such as education, journalism, advertising, and public planning. These surveys inquire into people's opinions, interests and voting patterns, their health and economic well-being, their criminal victimization, and numerous behavior patterns. Support for these surveys comes from government agencies, from nonprofit organizations, and from business enterprises of all types. Numerous other surveys are undertaken each year by academic researchers motivated by little more than personal curiosity about the fascinating diversity of human activities and attitudes.

Basic Terminology

In order to discuss surveying and sampling, it is important to be acquainted with some terminology. One of the basic terms is **population** (sometimes called a **universe**).[1] A population or universe refers to a naturally existing collection of some phenomenon (usually a collection of people living in a designated geographic area at a given point in time).

A **sample** is defined as a subset of some population. Normally, samples are very tiny fractions of the populations from which they are drawn. For example, 3,000 United States citizens constitute a large *number* of people, but they are far less than 1% of the entire U.S. population.

A **representative sample** is a fundamental concept in surveying. It refers to a sample whose members possess all characteristics in the same proportion as the population as a whole. For example, if the population you are studying is the student body at a particular university (Hypothetical U.), and 8% of the student body at Hypothetical U. are females under the age of 19 majoring in social work, a representative sample from that student body will contain 8% females under the age of 19 majoring in social work (and also contains all other characteristics of the student body as a whole). Basically, a representative sample is a "miniaturized reflection" of the population being targeted for study.

Students should bear in mind that a representative sample refers to an ideal or a goal that a researcher strives to approximate in a survey. This chapter will show that there are different sampling methods, researchers use to approximate representative samples. Some of these methods have taken social scientists many years to develop and refine while others are quite old and obvious.

A term that is related to but should not be confused with representative sample, is **random sample** (although some researchers carelessly use these terms interchangeably). A random sample is a sample that has been drawn from a population in which every member of the population had an equal chance of being picked. Whereas a representative sample is an ideal toward which most surveyors strive, a random sample is the result of certain procedures that allow a representative sample to be obtained.

Each individual comprising a sample is referred to as a **sampling unit.** All random samples of sufficient size (sample sizes will be discussed later) can be assumed to approximate a representative sample. However, as will be shown later, there are ways of obtaining representative samples that do not rely entirely on random sampling methods.

In order to obtain most random samples, you need to have access to what is called a **sampling frame** (Fowler, 1988:19). A sampling frame refers to a complete list of all members of the population. One reason random sampling procedures are not used more often is that obtaining complete lists of many populations of interest is often very difficult.

Another basic term used in connection with surveys is **census.** This refers to a survey that includes (or at least comes close to including) 100% of the members of a population, either directly or indirectly (such as through another household member). The word census got its name from the fact that most census surveys are conducted once every ten years (at the beginning of each new decade) in virtually all literate countries (i.e., societies in which most adult citizens are able to read and write). From these ''nearly 100% surveys,'' comes much information about human populations. As will be discussed later, census data can help determine the preciseness of a representative sample that has been obtained using tiny fractions of a population. Although it is proper to talk about a census as being a survey, it is normally not the custom to refer to the respondents in a census as a sample. A sample denotes a group of respondents that comprises much less than 100% of the population.

Considerations in Choosing Representative versus Nonrepresentative Samples

Samples are often chosen with the specific aim of their being representative, although this goal is sometimes unrealistic or is not central to the objective of a study. The main advantage of a representative sample is that it allows a researcher to generalize with substantial confidence from the sample to the population once a study is completed. A nonrepresentative sample is often less time-consuming and less expensive to obtain than a representative sample.

The above paragraph makes an important point, so let us illustrate it with a hypothetical example. Say you were interested in conducting an in-depth study of school children with epilepsy. Given that the prevalence of this neurological disease in school-age children is somewhere between 4 and 8 per 1000 (Cavazzuti, 1980; Stedman, van Heyningen, & Lindsay, 1982:66), few would fault you for basing a sample of affected children on every case that comes to your attention (such as through a large city clinic over a year's time). This somewhat haphazard sampling method (to be described in more detail later) should not be relied on as being representative of children with epilepsy. Nevertheless, because it would be almost impossible to obtain a representative sample, the alternative to using this sample would be to simply not conduct a study at all. In other words, barring the existence of some comprehensive national registry of children with epilepsy (a sampling frame) from which a random sample could be chosen, it would be virtually impossible for you or anyone else to obtain a representative sample of epileptic children.

Of course, in the above hypothetical example, you would be obliged to describe your sampling method so that readers are not misled into assuming that your findings are necessarily typical of a larger population of epileptic children. Over the course of time, other researchers interested in childhood epilepsy, using other sampling locations and techniques, will be able to check your results. In this way, any gross inaccuracies in your findings should eventually become apparent (more on this point in Chapter 14).

This hypothetical example is intended to show that, even though it is preferable to base all surveys on representative samples, there are legitimate reasons for not doing so. Another reason to conduct a survey even without a representative sample has to do with the purpose of your study. If your main reason for conducting a study is to determine how two or more variables are related to one another, the need for a representative sample is not nearly as crucial as when your main interest is to describe the prevalence and distribution of variables within a particular population.

Probability versus Nonprobability Sampling Methods

Sampling methods that can be relied on to approximate representative samples are called **probability sampling methods,** and sampling methods which should not be trusted to be representative (although they *may* be so) are called **nonprobability sampling methods.** These two methods are described below.

Main Probability Sampling Methods

Probability sampling can be accomplished in two ways; one is through random sampling, and the other is through various forms of cluster sampling. Random sampling methods can be divided into three forms: pure, systematic, and stratified. Cluster sampling can be described in two forms, although their distinction is not always perfectly apparent: simple and multistage. All of these are outlined below.

Random Sampling Methods

Pure random sampling must precisely conform to the definition that was stated earlier (i.e., random sampling requires that every member of the universe be given an equal chance of being selected). Some statistical "purists" also note that this includes the possibility that each member of the universe could be picked more than once, thus requiring replacement (i.e., putting a sampling unit back into the selection pool after it has been picked). However, few social science surveys based on random sampling practice replacement.

For a long time, the two most common techniques for obtaining a pure random sample involved (a) literally throwing the names of every member of the population into a hat (or some other container) and drawing out names one at a time, or (b) using what is called a "table of random numbers" (which is found in the back of most statistics texts). Today computers can be programmed to generate random lists of names from sampling frames. Say you wanted to get a random sample of students at your university, for instance. The registrar obviously holds the sampling frame, and could generate multiple random lists of names within a very short time.

A special type of random sampling method used only in telephone surveys is called **random digit dialing** (e.g., Wyatt & Notgrass, 1990; King & Schafer, 1992; Strunin & Hingson, 1992). Once the first three digits (the prefixes) used in an area to be sampled have been entered into a computer (which has been connected to a telephone via a modem), the computer can be programmed to dial the last four digits at random. This ensures that every household with a telephone—even those not listed in the phone directory—will have an equal chance of being called. Only homeless and institutionalized persons and those of very low income will be underrepresented from random digit dialing sampling methods (DeKeseredy & MacLean, 1991:148).

Systematic (or **interval**) **sampling** is a type of random sampling that does not perfectly meet the conditions specified in the definition of pure random sampling. However, for all practical purposes, systematic sampling is considered equivalent to random sampling. Systematic sampling takes sampling units from a sampling frame at designated intervals (such as every tenth name in a directory) or at designated positions (such as the third name from the top of each page).

The reason systematic sampling methods cannot be considered random sampling in the strictest sense is because once the interval (or the position on the page) has been designated, most members of the universe no longer have any chance of being chosen. Nevertheless, no one seriously questions that systematic sampling methods are as representative as pure random sampling methods.

Stratified random sampling is a special type of random sampling that is undertaken to allow groups with low representation in a population to be more highly represented. Users of this sampling method take a sampling frame and divide its constituents up according to one or more characteristics, and then randomly sample subjects from the resulting separate lists.

Here's an example of when to use stratified random sampling. Say you were interested in comparing the attitudes of older-than-average students and "regular" students on various issues at your college. Assume that older-than-average students (however defined) constituted only 10% of the students at your college. If you drew a random sample of 200 students, you would probably only get about 20 older-than-average students, a very small number from which to try to generalize (more will be said about sample size later in this chapter). However, if you separated the older-than-average and the regular-aged students, and then took 100 subjects from each of the two sampling frames, you would end up with two random samples of sufficient size to warrant generalizing about each.

Cluster Sampling Methods

Cluster sampling methods contain elements of random sampling, but they are distinguishable from random sampling in significant ways. Whereas random sampling is based on a complete sampling frame, cluster sampling is not. The word *cluster* in this context refers to what might be called "naturally occurring groups" of subjects. Examples of naturally occurring groups of subjects would be the members of a church congregation, students in a university, or members of each local chapter of a civic club. In cluster sampling, sampling frames come in two or more "layers." To get an idea of what this means, first consider the simplest form of cluster sampling.

In **simple cluster sampling,** a researcher picks a few clusters, and then collects data from many of the subjects comprising each of those clusters. Say, for example, a researcher was interested in studying the views of a particular religious group about whether homosexuals should be admitted as church members. If the researcher wanted to collect the data via personal interviews rather than by mailing out questionnaires, he or she would likely use simple cluster sampling. This is done by picking four or five specific church congregations geographically dispersed throughout the country and then visiting each one. At each location, the researcher obtains a list of current members, and contacts a random sample of these members for an interview. Note that even though the congregational members are randomly picked, the congregations to be sampled are not. Nevertheless, this sampling procedure will normally approximate a representative sample.

Multistage cluster sampling has become a popular sampling method for nationwide surveys, especially when subjects are personally interviewed. The techniques involved in multi-stage cluster sampling were developed in the mid-1950s by private polling agencies such as Gallup International, Roper Surveys, and Harris Polls. Here is a basic sketch of how multistage cluster sampling is commonly carried out.

1. Approximately two dozen major sampling clusters—such as counties or provinces—are picked in a way that ensures geographical diversity and roughly mirrors the mix of demographic features of the population as a whole. In other words, if the population as a whole contains 6% of persons over the age of 70, then the counties/provinces that are picked will collectively contain about the same percent. Picking these main sampling clusters is done most efficiently by computer, based upon countywide (or provincewide) census figures.

2. City and rural maps are obtained for some or all of the cities and rural areas in each of these two or three dozen counties/provinces. Depending on the urban-rural mix of the county or province involved, 20 or so city blocks and rural square miles are selected for canvassing by the interviewers.

3. Starting at a random point on each block or square mile and proceeding clockwise, the interviewers conduct a designated number of interviews (usually four to six, depending on the final sample size desired). If an interviewer cannot obtain the designated number of interviews in the chosen block/square mile, he or she usually goes to an adjacent block or square mile to complete the interviews.

By following these steps, a researcher would obtain 2,000 to 2,800 subjects, depending on the number of interviews conducted in each block or square mile sampled. The sample obtained with this set of procedures will closely approximate a representative sample.

In many surveys using multistage cluster sampling, interviewers are given guidelines to use in choosing respondents. For example, to avoid over-sampling females (which may happen if sampling is done during the day), interviewers might be required to conduct their interviews in the evening and/or to interview the same number of each sex.

There are two major advantages that either form of cluster sampling has over random sampling. First, cluster sampling allows a researcher to confine his or her interviewing to a few manageable geographical areas. Second, cluster sampling does not require a sampling frame for the entire population.

How to Assess a Sample's Representativeness

Even if you used a probability sampling method, it is possible that your sample will not end up being representative of the population you chose to study. Fortunately, there is a simple way to determine how representative your final sample is, no matter what sampling method you used.

The simplest way to assess a sample's representativeness is to compare its demographics with those of the population targeted for study. For example, if your sample includes 50% of each sex, but the targeted population contains 40% female and 60% male, according to the latest census, you would have to conclude that your sample underrepresents males.

How to Adjust for a Sample's Unrepresentativeness

Survey researchers sometimes impose representativeness on their samples after the data have been collected (Rust & Johnson, 1992). Although this may sound like ''cooking the books,'' it is not, so long as the researcher is forthright in noting that such adjustments were made. The technique is called **weighting,** and should only be used in surveys with large samples (i.e., over a thousand).

Weighting procedures can be illustrated as follows: Say census figures show that 12% of the subjects in a population targeted for study are Hispanic males between the ages of 35 and 50, but the sample you collected (by whatever means) contained only 10%. If the sample is large, computerized statistical procedures can be used to adjust all results from your survey to show what the results would have been had the sample perfectly resembled the target population. Weighting procedures are technically very complicated, and are only feasible using properly programmed computers.

Main Nonprobability Sampling Methods

If it is important that a research study be based on a representative sample, then a probability sampling method is strongly advised. For instance, if a researcher is interested in knowing what proportion of a state's voters are currently favoring a particular political candidate, a representative sample should be obtained (either in fact or via weighting). However, if a researcher is interested in identifying campaign ads that significantly increase voters' opinions of that candidate, the answer could probably be found without obtaining a representative sample. In the first instance, the representativeness of the sample is more central to the purpose of the research project than in the second case.

Another way to look at the representativeness issue is this: No research project is going to be criticized for being based on a representative sample, but many are considered weak if they are *not*. Nevertheless, most social science studies are not based on representative samples. Such studies still provide valuable information, especially when considered in the context of other studies of the same topic. If the question being asked pertains more to why people behave (or think) a particular way than to identifying how many actually do so in a particular population, the representativeness of a sample is not nearly as important.

The following section describes the main types of sampling methods that are unlikely to yield representative samples. The result of these sampling methods are often called **nonprobability samples.**

Grab Sampling

One of the crudest methods for obtaining a sample for a research study is to stand in one location such as a shopping mall or a convention booth and try to interview (or observe) whoever happens along. This is known as **grab sampling** (or sometimes **incidental sampling** or **straw polling**). Although this method is not worthless (especially for exploratory investigations), grab samples would never be used in a study where representativeness was a major goal.

Examples of grab sampling would include a quick smattering of opinion obtained by news reporters for an evening news broadcast, and all case studies conducted by social scientists (see pp. 123–124). Useful information is obtained with this sampling method, but researchers should be leery of any claim that the information can be generalized to a real population.

Quota Sampling

Quota sampling methods (as mentioned earlier in connection with multistage cluster sampling) are sometimes incorporated into probability sampling procedures to help ensure representativeness. However, as a sampling method by itself, **quota sampling** is little more than grab sampling with the added stipulation that a certain proportion of persons with certain characteristics (e.g., males versus females) are chosen. For instance, if you are interested in the opinions of students at a university where two-thirds of the student population is female, when you conduct your interviews you could make sure that you interview two females for every male. There are more sophisticated forms of quota sampling methods, but they are difficult to apply in real situations (see Babbie, 1973:107).

Self-Selected Sampling

To some extent, all samples are self-selected because no one is ever forced to participate in a social science research project. However, in **self-selected sampling methods,** subjects themselves actually take the initiative to be in a study. Good examples of surveys based on self-selected samples are questionnaires inserted into magazines, or programs that invite viewers to call a telephone number to register their opinions on some topic (e.g., Wysocki & Gilbert, 1989).

Although the results of surveys based on self-selected samples can be informative in studying relationships among variables, rarely can such surveys be considered representative of any naturally existing population, including the population of magazine subscribers or television viewers. The main problem with this sampling method is that such small proportions (i.e., usually less than 10%) of those invited to respond will actually do so. Self-selected samples, incidentally, figured prominently in the surveys used to guess who was going to win the 1948 Truman-Dewey presidential election.

Snowball Sampling

In **snowball sampling,** research subjects are recruited and then asked to help to recruit additional subjects. The advantage of this sampling method is that it can build up sample sizes quickly and/or it can recruit subjects who are otherwise hard to locate.

For example, if you are interested in the behavior of members of some secretive gang or religious cult, snowball sampling might be the only feasible way of obtaining a sizable sample. This sampling method was used in a study of homosexuality among American priests (Wolf, 1989), and in a study of criminal behavior among drug users in Scotland (Hammersley, Forsyth, & Lavelle, 1990). The likelihood is low that this sampling method will yield a representative sample.

Convenience Sampling

Convenience sampling involves obtaining subjects in large groups all at once, such as asking all the students in a sociology class to fill out a questionnaire. Convenience sampling is probably the most widely used sampling method in social science. Without intending any offense, a long-standing joke among social scientists (especially psychologists) is that their two favorite groups of subjects are rats and sophomores. In fact, some social scientists have specifically criticized colleagues for relying too heavily on college students as research subjects.

It is now common for many introductory social science courses to require participation in at least one research study, especially at large, research-oriented universities. In this way, professors are able to conduct many useful studies, and students have an opportunity to see how social science research is conducted. Nevertheless, the mix of students cannot be relied on to be representative of the university's student body as a whole. In required introductory courses, however, convenience samples may come close to being representative of college students as a whole.

Another example of convenience sampling comes from the field of ethnography (see Chapter 9). Often an ethnographer will generalize about the cultural practices of an entire culture after studying inhabitants of just one village. Most ethnographic work is based on the assumption that although convenience samples cannot be considered representative, they do provide the only real opportunity that social scientists have to collect detailed information about cultures. Also, if one ethnographic report reflects sampling bias, additional reports from other villages linked to the same culture should eventually bring researchers close to unbiased generalizations.

Event Sampling

Obtaining a sample by taking every single instance of a rare event (or rare condition) is called **event sampling.** Since this form of sampling is most often carried out in settings where people are seeking treatment, it is sometimes also called **clinical sampling.**

For example, a study of child abuse was conducted a few years ago among children with cerebral palsy (Diamond & Jaudes, 1983). The sample came from all children diagnosed with cerebral palsy who entered a Chicago children's hospital between September 1979 and August 1980. Such a sampling method is obviously not ideal for obtaining a representative sample, but given the rarity of the disease in a general population, it would be unrealistic to ever expect random or cluster samples of children with cerebral palsy to be obtained for study.

One particularly unusual example of event sampling comes from a recent study of more than 1.36 million emergency (911) calls made to the Kansas City, Kansas, police department between 1986 and 1989 (Walters, 1991). Your initial temptation might be to consider this a self-selected sample, but this categorization would imply that the number was being called for research purposes. Rather, calls made to an emergency number are best considered a type of universe, and the researcher who conducted the study simply took an event sample, i.e., all the calls in one city that came in between 1986 and 1989, from the universe.

Final Comments on Nonprobability Samples

Overall, the difference between a probability sample and a nonprobability sample is that the former has a greater chance of being representative of an identifiable population than the latter. Thus, if a researcher has a choice between conducting a study based on either a probability sample or a nonprobability sample of equal size—and there are no differences in time and expense—the probability sample should be used. However, many circumstances make probability sampling almost impossible to obtain.

Over the years, social scientists have been at odds about employing nonprobability sampling methods. Some have argued that researchers should never attempt to generalize to any ''real'' population based on a nonprobability sample (Morrison & Henkel, 1969; Berk, 1983; Grichting, 1989). Others have asserted that while probability samples are certainly preferable, when the choice is between using a nonprobability sampling method and not conducting a study at all, it is preferable to use the nonprobability sampling method (Winch & Campbell, 1969; Eysenck, 1975).

Controversy even surrounds whether what are usually called probability samples should, in fact, be given this name (compare Bailar, 1988:1058 and Fowler, 1988:56). Obviously, if the experts still cannot agree, these issues will not be settled in an introductory text. The effort here is to acquaint you with basic terminology and options.

Sample Size

As noted in Chapter 5, the larger the sample size in a survey, the more likely it is that the results will accurately reflect the universe from which the sample was obtained (all else being equal). Nevertheless, there are trade-offs when sample sizes are increased. In particular, larger sample sizes usually add time and expense to data collection, coding, and data entry.

Just for fun, how many subjects do you think were in the largest nongovernment probability sample survey ever conducted? The answer is 113,000! The study was a nationwide survey dealing with religious beliefs and practices in the United States (see Moss, 1991). Even though 113,000 represents less than 0.05% of all U.S. citizens, this sample size made it possible for the researchers to generalize about people's religious views and practices, even at the state level, with little margin for error.

The largest nonprobability sample survey appears to have been a survey conducted by the *National Geographic*. Inside all 10.5 million copies of its September 1986 issue was a questionnaire about people's sense of smell (complete with scratch-and-sniff samples of various odors). The number of readers who completed and returned this questionnaire was 1.42 million (Wysocki & Gilbert, 1989:13). A close second in nonprobability sample size was the study of the 1.36 million calls made to the 911 emergency number in Kansas City, Kansas discussed earlier in this chapter (Walters, 1991).

In attempting to balance the increased accuracy of a survey against the additional time and expense that accompanies larger sample sizes, you need to keep in mind the law of diminishing returns. As mentioned in Chapter 5, this basic law of probability means that the larger your sample size already is, the less your accuracy is increased by adding subjects. Adding 100 subjects to a sample size of 100, for example, would increase the accuracy of a survey much more than would adding 100 more subjects to a sample size of 10,000.

Incidentally, contrary to common sense, the size of the universe basically has no bearing on the size of the sample needed to achieve accuracy at a given level. Explaining why this is true would take this discussion into areas of probability theory that are of no concern to us here.

Over the years, statisticians have tried to work out precise guidelines on the size samples needed for a given level of accuracy. Although there is some value to such estimates in planning surveys, no sampling formulas or guidelines should ever replace the following common sense rule: Attempt to get as large a sample as possible within your time and expense constraints. As a rough rule of thumb, however, the following figures indicate the sample sizes needed to achieve accuracy within various sampling error limits.

Sample Size	Accuracy Within % of the Actual Figure (Degree of Sampling Error)
100	10%
400	5%
1500	2.5%
2500	2.0%
7000	1%

What these figures indicate is that if you were to obtain responses from a probability sample of 100 individuals, any percentages derived from their answers would be accurate to within ten percentage points of the real figure. In other words, if you found that 32% of your sample responded affirmatively to a particular question, the real percentage (i.e., the percentage for the entire population) would be somewhere between 22% and 42%.[2] The sample size needed for results that are within two percentage points of the real percentages would be around 2500.

Keep in mind that the figures in this table are approximations, and that they only pertain to how accuracy is affected by sample size. Any inaccuracy due to invalid, unreliable, and imprecise questions (see Chapter 7), inappropriate questions and response options (see Chapter 8), or poor sampling procedures (as discussed earlier in this chapter) would be in addition to inaccuracies due to sampling error. (Sampling error will be described in greater detail in Chapter 13).

Surveying Over Time

It is common for surveyors to want to determine not only how things are at a single point in time, but also how things are changing over time. Accordingly, a researcher would conduct what is called a **longitudinal survey** instead of a **cross-sectional survey.** Cross-sectional surveys are undertaken only once, whereas longitudinal surveys are those in which samples are obtained (from the same population) in two or more time frames. It is useful to distinguish between three different types of sampling procedures in longitudinal surveys: panel, nonpanel, and partial panel.

Panel longitudinal surveys are ones in which the same sample is used each time the survey is conducted. Panel surveys allow a researcher to follow specific individuals over time to see how they are changing. Panel surveys by economists, for example, have found that people's annual earnings often vary substantially from one

"Sure I know what the break-up of the Soviet Union
means...15 new countries on the geography test."

Copyright © by Martha Campbell.

year to the next (Schiller 1977; Lillard & Willis, 1978). **Nonpanel longitudinal surveys** involve picking an entirely new sample (within the same population, of course) each time the survey is run. The advantage to this form of longitudinal survey is that a researcher is able to estimate how the population is changing without having to locate the same subjects time after time.

Partial panel longitudinal surveys represent a compromise between the panel and nonpanel surveys. An example is the National Crime Survey, which is conducted each year among a representative sample of United States citizens to determine if they have been recent crime victims, regardless of any calls they may have made to police (Blumstein, Cohen, & Rosenfeld, 1991). Researchers make efforts to keep respondents in the survey for three consecutive years (although some will be lost due to change of residence or death). One-third of the respondents are automatically replaced every three years, so that roughly one-third of the respondents are new each year, one-third were part of the panel the previous year, and one-third were in the panel for the preceding two years.

Summary

In this chapter, surveys and sampling procedures were described. The two main categories of samples were identified as probability and nonprobability samples. Probability samples are more likely than nonprobability samples to be representative (i.e., a mirror image) of an existing population chosen for study.

There are two ways of obtaining representative samples. The first is by using a probability sampling method (one that is likely to yield a representative sample). Probability sampling methods include random sampling and cluster sampling. All but one form of random sampling require selecting sampling units (subjects) from a list of all members of the population targeted for study. These lists are referred to as sampling frames. The exception, called random digit dialing, is used in some telephone surveys. In cluster sampling, the sampling frames are in two or more "layers." The first layer may consist of clusters of subjects (e.g., all universities in some country). Within the first sampling layer, a researcher then chooses the actual subjects to be studied.

The second way to obtain a representative sample involves what is called weighting. This set of statistical procedures adjusts results after the data have been collected so that the sample's distribution of demographic characteristics is identical to the demographic characteristics of the population from which the subjects were drawn. Weighting is primarily reserved for large surveys in which researchers have access to sophisticated computer programs.

Six nonprobability sampling methods were identified: grab samples, quota samples, self-selected samples, snowball samples, convenience samples, and event samples. None of these sampling methods are to be trusted to yield representative samples, but this does not preclude their use in scientific research, especially when it is not feasible to obtain a probability sample.

Guidelines were given for deciding on the size of a sample. In general, the larger the sample the better (everything else being equal), but remember that the law of diminishing returns means that the larger your sample happens to be, the less you reduce sampling error from adding each new subject. Ultimately, researchers must always balance the accuracy needed in a survey against the additional time and expense of adding new subjects. More will be said about sampling issues and attempts to generalize about populations on the basis of samples in the next two chapters.

A distinction was made between cross-sectional and longitudinal surveys. Longitudinal surveys are subdivided into panel, nonpanel, and partial panel according to whether the same subjects are being used each time the survey is conducted.

Notes

[1] Technically, a distinction can be made between a *population* and a *universe,* with the latter being a more inclusive term. Specifically, a population refers to a collection of humans (or other living things), whereas a universe includes populations, but also refers to collections of characteristics (or numbers representing those characteristics) exhibited by members of a population.

[2] In precise statistical terms, you would say that for a sample size of 100, if you were to observe 32%, the actual figures would be ±10% approximately 95% of the time. The 95% figure is derived from the second standard error of the mean, which is the standard deviation divided by the square root of the sample size.

References

Babbie, E. R. (1973). *Survey research methods.* Belmont, CA: Wadsworth.

Babbie, E. R. (1983). *The practice of social research* (5th ed.). Belmont, CA: Wadsworth.

Bailar, B. (1988). An enterprise of social science. *Science, 240,* 1057–1059.

Berk, R. A. (1983). An introduction to sample selection bias in sociological data. *American Sociological Review, 48,* 386–398.

Blumstein, A., Cohen, J., & Rosenfeld, R. (1991). Trend and deviation in crime rates: A comparison of VCR and NCS data for burglary and robbery. *Criminology, 29,* 237–263.

Cavazzuti, G. B. (1980). Epidemiology of different types of epilepsy in school-age children of Modena, Italy. *Epilepsia, 21,* 57–62.

DeKeseredy, W. S., & MacLean, B. D. (1991). Exploring the gender, race, and class dimensions of victimization: A left realist critique of the Canadian Urban Victimization Survey. *International Journal of Offender Therapy and Comparative Criminology, 35,* 143–161.

Diamond, L. J., & Jaudes, P. K. (1983). Child abuse in a cerebral-palsied population. *Developmental Medicine and Child Neurology, 25,* 169–174.

Eysenck, H. J. (1975). Who needs random samples? *Bulletin of the British Psychological Society, 28,* 195–198.

Fowler, F. J., Jr. (1988). Survey research methods (rev. ed.). Newbury Park, CA: Sage.

Grichting, W. L. (1989). Psychology and sociology in Australia: The published evidence. *Australian Psychologist, 24,* 115–126.

Hammersley, R., Forsyth, A., & Lavelle, T. (1990). The criminality of new drug users in Glasgow. *British Journal of Addiction, 85,* 1583–1594.

King, M., & Schafer, W. E. (1992). Religiosity and perceived stress: A community survey. *Sociological Analysis, 53,* 37–47.

Lillard, L., & Willis, R. (1978). Dynamic aspects of earning mobility. *Econometrica, 46,* 985–1012.

Morrison, D. E., & Henkel, R. E. (1969). Significance tests reconsidered. *American Sociologist, 4,* 131–140.

Moss, D. (1991, April 11). Practicing or not, many identify with religion. *USA Today,* 7A.

Rust, K. F., & Johnson, E. J. (1992). Sampling and weighting in the national assessment. *Journal of Educational Statistics, 17,* 111–129.

Schiller, B. (1977). Relative earnings mobility in the United States. *Economic Review, 67,* 926–941.

Stedman, J., van Heyningen, R., & Lindsay, J. (1982). Educational underachievement and epilepsy: A study of children from normal schools, admitted to a special hospital for epilepsy. *Early Child Development and Care, 9,* 65–82.

Strunin, L., & Hingson, R. (1992). Alcohol, drugs, and adolescent sexual behavior. *International Journal of the Addictions, 27,* 129–146.

Walters, G. D. (1991). Examining the relationship between airborne pollen levels and 911 calls for assistance. *International Journal of Offender Therapy and Comparative Criminology, 35,* 162–166.

Winch, R. F., & Campbell, D. T. (1969). Proof? No. Evidence? Yes. The significance of tests of significance. *American Sociologist, 4,* 140–143.

Wolf, J. G. (Ed.). (1989). *Gay priests.* New York: Harper & Row.

Wyatt, G. E., & Notgrass, C. M. (1990). Internal and external mediators of women's rape experiences. *Psychology of Women Quarterly, 14,* 153–176.

Wysocki, C. J., & Gilbert, A. N. (1989). National Geographic smell survey: Effects of age are heterogenous. *Annals of the New York Academy of Sciences, 561,* 12–28.

Suggested Reading

Converse, J. M. (1987). *Survey research in the United States: Roots and emergence, 1890–1960.* Berkeley: University of California Press. (A well-written book on the history of survey research. Highly recommended.)

Groves, R. M., Biemer, P. M., Lyberg, L. E., Massey, J. T., Nicholls, W. L., & Waksberg, J. (1988). *Telephone survey methodology.* New York: Wiley. (A useful book if you are interested in undertaking a research project in which subjects will be interviewed via telephone.)

Kraemer, H. C., & Thiemann, S. (1987). *How many subjects? Statistical power analysis in research.* Beverly Hills, CA: Sage. (Provides a basic introduction to questions concerning sample size and how to provide reliable findings within the constraints imposed by time and expense.)

Lavrakas, P. J. (1987). *Telephone survey methods: Sampling, selection, and supervision.* Beverly Hills, CA: Sage. (Helpful information to those interested in conducting surveys via the telephone.)

Parten, M. B. (1950). *Surveys, polls and samples: Practical procedures.* (Regarded as a classic in the field of social science surveying.)

Walden, G. R. S. (1990). *Public opinion polls and surveys.* Beverly Hills, CA: Sage. (Provides an extensive annotated bibliography of studies of United States public opinion throughout the 1980s.)

Journals that specialize in survey research and sampling issues are:

Gallup Reports
Public Opinion Quarterly

CHAPTER 13

The Human Side of Sampling and the Reliability of Self-Reports

For understandable reasons, most social scientists are more interested in studying the behavior of human beings than that of any other animal. As noted in the chapter on questionnaire construction (Chapter 8), the most efficient way to obtain information about human behavior is to ask them questions. However, social scientists need to have a special awareness of techniques that have been developed for evaluating and improving the accuracy of self-reported data.

In this chapter, two major issues regarding self-reported data will be given attention. The first has to do with maximizing the chances that people who are chosen as research subjects will consent to being a part of the study. The second issue is concerned with ways of increasing the accuracies of self-reported information. Several topics to be discussed in this chapter have been touched on in previous chapters. However, now that you have a basic understanding of sampling issues (addressed in Chapter 12), it is possible to cover in greater detail topics having to do with sample retention and the accuracy of self-reported information.

People's Unwillingness to Serve as Research Subjects as a Source of Sampling Bias

Everything said in the preceding chapter about sampling and sampling error was based on the assumption that everyone who is asked to take part in a study will comply with that request. Of course, this is not an entirely warranted assumption, and any decisions that people make about participating in a social science study must be respected (a point to be reiterated in Chapter 18 when research ethics are discussed). The focus here is on practical ways of increasing the likelihood that those who are asked to be subjects will acquiesce.

Under some circumstances, virtually all subjects who are asked to be part of a survey will comply. For example, in many introductory college courses in the social sciences, students are expected to serve as subjects in at least one research project. In these cases, there is no need to distinguish between what is called a **chosen sample** and an **obtained** (or **final**) **sample.** However, in studies where subjects are under no obligation to be subjects, the distinction between these two types of samples is important.

In surveys conducted by mail, telephone, and door-to-door household contacts, the chosen sample refers to persons who were asked to participate in a study, and the obtained sample refers to those asked to participate who actually do so. The difference between these two types of samples is referred to as **sample attrition.**

As you would suspect, researchers try to minimize sample attrition. In formal terms, it is desirable to keep sample attrition at a minimum because this attrition is the source of one of two types of sampling error: **random sampling bias** (or **error**) and **systematic sampling bias** (or **error**). Random sampling bias refers to bias that can be reduced by increasing the sample size. Systematic sampling bias is sampling bias that an increased sample size will not reduce.

To illustrate these distinctions, assume that census data (based on a virtual 100% sample) indicated that the average years of education for adult citizens of some country is 12.8 years. Then assume that you drew a random sample of 4,000 persons from this population, but that only half completed your questionnaire. Say that one of your questions had to do with years of education, and that the 2,000 who completed your questionnaire reported an average of 13.8 years of education. Assuming the respondents had answered accurately, you would have to attribute the discrepancy between 12.8 and 13.8 to sampling bias. But which type?

Because 2,000 is a large sample, it is difficult to believe that a discrepancy of one year in average education would be due to chance, i.e., random sampling bias. The more reasonable explanation is that persons with the lowest amount of education were less likely to complete and return their questionnaires. If so, the discrepancy between 12.8 and 13.8 would be attributed to systematic, rather than random, sampling bias.

Studies have indicated that as long as sampling attrition in a survey is fairly small (e.g., under 15%), essentially all of the attrition can be safely attributed to random error (e.g., people being in a bad mood, too busy, etc., when the request happened to come to them) (Lansing & Kish, 1957; Stephan & McCarthy, 1963:268). When attrition exceeds 15%, however, you should be open to the possibility that some type of systematic error is confounding your findings to a significant degree.

Does a significant degree of systematic sampling bias mean that a study is worthless? Certainly not. If serious efforts are made to keep attrition low, and the degree of attrition is honestly stated, a study can still provide valuable information. After all, if someone is interested in trends and decides to replicate your study, this new study will probably contain the same degree of systematic sampling bias. Thus any change between the first and the second time the study was conducted would still be meaningful.

Keep the following basic points in mind: (a) do all that you can to minimize both types of sampling error, and (b) forthrightly report all sample attrition (advice that most, but not all, researchers follow), but (c) do not consider findings worthless even if sample attrition is extensive (e.g., in excess of 50%). The results could still be considered informative, especially for comparison with similar surveys.

The following two subsections contain techniques for minimizing sample attrition. These techniques will first be applied to mail surveys, and then to household and telephone surveys.

Minimizing Attrition in Mail Surveys

Many studies have been conducted on attrition rates in mail surveys (see Dickinson, 1990). Return rates for mailed-out questionnaires have varied from lows of about 20% to highs of more than 90% (reviewed by Linsky, 1975; Heberlein & Baumgartner, 1978). One review of 183 mail surveys revealed that the average return rate was 48% (Heberlein & Baumgartner, 1978), although one writer contended that the average is closer to 30% (Arnett, 1991:1308).

Research has indicated that the types of questions asked can greatly affect response rates. Studies that people consider interesting, important, and relevant to their lives are more likely to be completed and returned. Consequently, public health surveys have generally yielded the highest response rate (Heberlein & Baumgartner, 1978:451).

Based on current research, here are suggestions for increasing return rates of mail questionnaires:

1. *Prenotify the prospective respondent.* Numerous studies have shown that notifying prospective subjects either by letter (or postcard) or by telephone that they have been selected to take part in a survey before sending them the actual questionnaire will increase response rates in nearly all types of surveys (reviewed by Faria, Dickinson, & Filipic, 1990:553; Yammarino, Skinner, & Childers, 1991). The increase in the response rate for the average mail survey, for example, has been shown to be about 10% to 15% (Schlegelmilch & Diamantopoulos, 1991). Prenotification by telephone appears to be the most effective (Martin et al., 1989:69). However, this form of prenotification is also the most time-consuming and is more expensive than post card notification.

2. *Attach a polite and clearly written cover letter.* People's decisions about taking part in a mail survey often hinge on whether they have confidence in the competence of those who are conducting the study. Sending out a poorly planned cover letter will adversely affect the return rate. Helpful lists have been prepared containing information to include in a cover letter (Monette, Sullivan, & DeJong, 1986:146), but it comes down to using common sense and being able to put yourself in the place of a potential respondent.

Some experimentation has been conducted with personalized, or personalized-appearing, cover letters. Especially in marketing surveys, computer-generated cover letters specifying a person's name (rather than being simply addressed to occupant) yield higher response rates (Dillman & Frey, 1974; Carpenter, 1975). Other types of personalized letters (such as when the respondent's name is hand-written) also were shown to elicit somewhat higher response rates (Trice, 1986), although there have been exceptions (Ellis & Curless, 1987).

3. *Have a credible sponsor.* Studies have shown that people are more likely to complete a questionnaire that has been endorsed by a respected sponsoring organization (or individual) than one without sponsorship (Goyder, 1982; Nachmias & Nachmias, 1987:234; Fox, Crask, & Kim, 1988; Yammarino, Skinner, & Childers, 1991). One study even found that response rates were higher for questionnaires mailed from state universities than from either religious or nonreligious private universities (Richardson et al., 1971:145).

4. *Enclose a stamped self-addressed return envelope.* Higher returns are achieved if the subjects do not have to pay their own postage (Yammarino, Skinner, & Childers, 1991). However, even the type of postage appears to matter. In a review of 20 studies, return envelopes with regular first class stamps yielded an average of 9% higher returns than envelopes with business reply postage (Armstrong & Lusk, 1987).

5. *Enclose some token compensation.* Studies have shown that enclosing as little as a penny(!) can increase the completion and return rate of mail questionnaires (reviewed by Armstrong, 1975; Gajraj, Faria, & Dickinson, 1990:143). Inclusion of a one dollar bill has increased the percentage of returns for the average survey by 20% to 25% (Heberlein & Baumgartner, 1978; James & Bolstein, 1990:351).

Several experiments have been conducted in which compensation was promised to be returned when a completed questionnaire was received. The results may surprise you. Promising to send compensation on receipt of a completed form is less effective in increasing return rates for mail questionnaires than actually enclosing the compensation with the questionnaire in advance (reviewed by Gajraj, Faria, & Dickinson, 1990:143).

Studies using both monetary compensations and "tangible" compensation of roughly equivalent value (e.g., key rings and ballpoint pens) have found monetary compensations more effective in increasing return rates (Goodstadt et al., 1977; Hansen, 1980), although one study found no difference (Nederhof, 1983). One study even experimented with compensating subjects with lottery tickets for completing questionnaires. In this case, return rates were comparable to using an equivalent amount of monetary compensation (Gajraj, Faria, & Dickinson, 1990). Of course, the option of enclosing compensation for completing questionnaires is only possible for those whose research budgets can afford it.

6. *Use follow-ups.* Studies have found that one follow-up will usually increase response rates by 10% to 20%, two follow-ups by 5% to 10% more; and three follow-ups by 3% to 5% more (Heberlein & Baumgartner, 1978; James & Bolstein, 1990:351). A good policy is to include a new copy of the questionnaire in at least one of the follow-up mailings (Babbie, 1983:241). Some also recommend the use of follow-up telephone calls in order to maximize return rates (Bailey, 1978:153).

Of course, it is only possible to incorporate follow-ups into mail research designs when the names of the subjects are known (Moser & Kalton, 1971:266). Follow-ups are impossible in an anonymous survey unless they are sent to everyone who was surveyed, regardless of whether they returned their questionnaires.

7. *Keep the questionnaire short.* Researchers must recognize that, everything else being equal, as the amount of information sought increases, the likelihood that a subject will complete a questionnaire decreases (Roszkowski & Bean, 1990). One review calculated that for every two questions added to a mail questionnaire, the return rate is reduced by roughly 1% (Heberlein & Baumgartner, 1978:453). The brevity of a questionnaire appears to be more critical in mail questionnaires than in surveys conducted by interviewers or administered in a classroom setting.

8. *Make sure the questionnaire is well organized and neatly laid out.* Questionnaires that are hurriedly constructed and poorly organized frustrate respondents and cause them to doubt the value of what they are being asked to do. This lowers the chances that they will answer the questions carefully and return the questionnaire (Sanchez, 1992).

9. *Make the importance and the relevance of the survey clear to the prospective respondent.* It is not surprising that people who consider a particular study trivial or irrelevant to their own interests will be less likely to complete and return a questionnaire than their counterparts (Martin et al., 1989:70).

Each of these nine points can make a significant difference in the quality and quantity of survey responses, especially in terms of minimizing attrition. Combining several of these suggestions can make an even greater difference. To illustrate, consider a longitudinal study of drug use among college students, first conducted in 1977, then in 1983, and again in 1987 (Meilman et al., 1990). The return rate in the 1977 survey was 76.7%, and six years later it dropped to 70.5% (Meilman et al., 1990:1027). In the third phase, the researchers made a concerted effort to obtain the greatest possible return rate. They reduced the number of questions on the questionnaire and sent up to two follow-ups, one containing a dollar bill incentive. The final response rate was an impressive 87.25%. The researchers noted that, to the best of their knowledge, this was "a higher return rate than any previously reported" in a mail survey (Meilman et al., 1990:1027).

Later the same year, however, a brief marketing study was published in which a mail survey actually had a return rate exceeding 90% (James & Bolstein, 1990:351). Figure 13.1 shows some results of the study. The researchers used four follow-up mailings and the compensation enclosed in the first mailing varied from nothing to $2. For the segment of the sample in which $2 was enclosed and up to three follow-ups were run, the survey almost obtained a 100% return rate.

The higher the return rate, the better, but for most mail surveys (especially those with no follow-up mailings or compensation enclosed), return rates are less than half. Mail surveys with rates above 50% are considered adequate, and rates exceeding 70% are usually seen as very good (Babbie, 1983:242; Monette, Sullivan, & DeJong, 1986:149).

■ **FIGURE 13.1**

Cumulative response rates after each of four mailings of a survey in which five levels of compensation were used. In each mailing, a new questionnaire form was sent. (Data from James & Bolstein, 1990:351.)

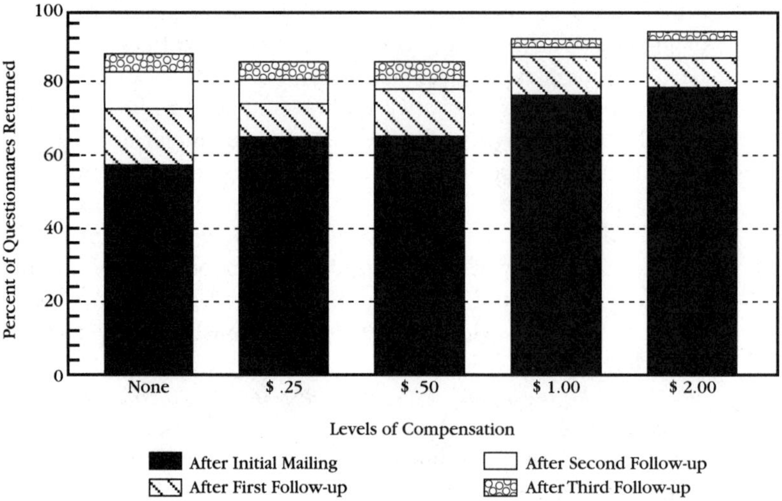

Minimizing Sample Attrition in Household and Telephone Surveys

In household and telephone surveys, attrition is largely the result of people not being at home or refusing to be interviewed. The rate of attrition in most professionally run household and telephone surveys ranges between 10% and 20%; rarely does it exceed 25% (Benson, Booman, & Clark, 1951:116; Stephan & McCarthy, 1963:266; Grimm & Wozniak, 1990:243). A good example of a well-designed household survey with low attrition is one conducted recently in Canada; the refusal rate was 3.9% and the attrition rate due to other factors (mainly not-at-homes) was 5.0% (Boyle et al., 1987).

As noted earlier, attrition rates of up to 15% should not be considered a source of significant bias (see Lansing & Kish, 1957; Stephan & McCarthy, 1963:268). Of the two main sources of attrition, refusals are more likely to be a source of systematic error than not-at-homes.

A limited amount of research has been conducted on ways to minimize refusals in household and telephone surveys. The results can be summarized as follows:

1. Experienced interviewers have lower refusal rates than those with little experience (Durbin & Stuart, 1951:184; Stephan & McCarthy, 1963:314). This difference could be due to a selection factor rather than to interviewing experience per se. In other words, interviewers who have the highest refusal rates probably tend to quit interviewing more readily than those with the lowest rates.

2. In household interviews, female interviewers experience lower refusal rates than male interviewers (Benson, Booman, & Clark, 1951).

3. Few generalizations can be made about the time of day or day of the week that refusals (or even not-at-homes) are most likely (Stephan & McCarthy, 1963:296; Ellis, 1969).

How to Check and Adjust for Systematic Sampling Bias

In some studies, it is possible to estimate how much systematic error exists in an obtained sample relative to either the chosen sample or the universe from which it was selected. Estimates can be obtained by listing the breakdown of various demographic characteristics for the obtained sample, and comparing these to either (1) the chosen sample or (2) the population as a whole (see Stephan & McCarthy, 1963:268). With large samples, it is even possible to statistically adjust responses for any degree of under- or over representation of particular demographic groups (see the discussion on **weighting** in the preceding chapter, p. 170).

Inaccuracies in Self-Reports

Who do you think are more likely to engage in drunk driving, non Hispanic whites, blacks, or Hispanics? In fact, the evidence is inconsistent. In the United States, official police statistics clearly indicate that the latter two groups have higher rates of drunk driving than the first group (reviewed by Ross et al., 1991). Police records on both alcohol-related accidents (Hyman, 1968; Waller et al., 1969; Zylman, 1972; Alcocer, 1979) and arrests for driving while intoxicated (Caetano, 1984; Barnes & Welte, 1988) suggest that blacks and Hispanics are more prone toward drunk driving than non Hispanic whites.

On the other hand, at least three studies based on self-reports have concluded the opposite, i.e., non Hispanic whites are more likely to engage in drunk driving than are blacks or Hispanics (Barnes & Welte, 1988; Herd, 1989; Smith & Remington, 1989).

Several factors may explain the inconsistencies between self-reports and official statistics on race and ethnic differences in drunk driving. These include (a) possible ethnic biases by police in arresting or checking for intoxication after an accident, (b) group differences in how drunkenness is defined and (c) intentional under- or overreporting by some groups (see Ross et al., 1991:9). These puzzling discrepancies help to illustrate why social scientists look for ways of verifying the data that they collect. The need to verify self-report data is especially great because it is so heavily used by social scientists.

There are four main sources of invalid and unreliable self-reported information: (1) subjects' failure to understand a question, (2) subjects' failure to accurately recall the answer, (3) subjects' indecision, and (4) subjects' dishonesty. Each is discussed next.

1. *Subjects' failure to understand a question.* The extent to which respondents fail to understand the questions that they are asked is unknown, but it is safe to assume that this is a significant problem. As pointed out in Chapter 8, several guidelines can be followed to minimize this source of difficulty. The most important guideline is to carefully pretest any questionnaire (or any other research instrument) before it is used with actual subjects (see pp. 107–108).

2. *Subjects' failure to accurately recall answers to questions.* Studies have been undertaken to determine how well people remember items of information about themselves and others. As you might guess, the accuracy of people's memories varies greatly from one individual to another, and from one topic to another.

Two factors have major effects on the accuracy of a subject's recall. One is the time since the event, and the other is the novelty or the importance of the event. When a long time has elapsed, and the novelty or the subjective importance of the event is minimal, the recall probability is low (Linton, 1979).

There are many events that people will accurately remember even decades later. For example, mothers recall such things as the birth weight of their children with high accuracy even decades later (Ekouevi & Morgan, 1991). Nevertheless, even such important events as the birth of a child are not recalled with complete accuracy by everyone. A recent study of mothers' reports of the *number* of children they bore found small discrepancies between what some mothers stated in an interview and what was indicated for them in hospital records (Brittain, 1992). Some of the discrepancies were because mothers failed to report all instances of stillbirths. Other causes were traced to failures to report all children born in previous marriages or prior to marriage.

To help reduce the inaccuracy resulting from memory lapses, researchers often "bound" (or limit) their questions to recent events. For example, in national crime victimization surveys (which are based on door-to-door surveys rather than calls made to police), subjects are asked to recall any crime victimizations they may have experienced just in the past six months. Studies have shown that asking subjects to remember a victimization event further back in time than six months (and especially more than a year) results in numerous errors in memory (Skogan, 1976:114). Not only do subjects forget instances of victimization as time goes by, but many also draw in events that occurred prior to the time frame specified. Researchers call this tendency to report events that occurred prior to the time specified by a question as **telescoping** (Skogan, 1976:114; Ellis et al., 1988:155).

3. *Subjects' indecision.* Research has shown that people sometimes change their minds on topics during the course of completing a questionnaire (or an interview). This is particularly common in **thematic surveys,** i.e., surveys in which lengthy and in-depth coverage is given to a single topic.

For example, a thematic survey was conducted in the 1980s in Australia regarding opinions about legalized gambling. Subjects were asked the same general question at the beginning and at the end of the interview: Whether they approved or disapproved of legalized gambling in their town. Within the span of about an hour, roughly one out of every six subjects had changed his or her opinion (Grichting & Caltabiano, 1986). This change did not appear to be due to leading questions by the interviewers, for two reasons: First, there were as many subjects who changed their opinions in a positive direction as in a negative direction. Second, before being hired, each interviewer was asked his or her opinions about legalized gambling, and there was no significant tendency for the subjects to change their opinions to match the interviewer. As odd as it seems, the study concluded that once people are asked a large number of probing questions about an issue, especially if they have not dwelled on it before the interview, subjects substantially refine and sometimes even alter their views during the time data are being collected. There is nothing you can do about these opinion changes, but it is important to be aware that they occur.

4. *Subjects' dishonesty.* If subjects agree to take part in a study, a researcher can generally assume that they will try to provide honest responses to the questions they are asked. If they do not answer honestly, it is probably because the questions are more personal or intimidating than was anticipated, or involve possible legal risks to the subjects.

Sometimes a subject may have mixed feelings on a particular issue and thus answer according to what he or she believes the researcher wants. Here is a case in point: A recent survey in Virginia, where a black was running for governor, found that the race of the interviewer significantly affected the percentage of persons who said they planned to vote for the black candidate. Specifically, more white respondents said they planned to vote for the black candidate when the interviewer was black than when the interviewer was white (Finkel, Guterbock, & Borg, 1991).

Similarly, when asked personal and emotionally sensitive questions, many subjects will lean toward responses considered most "desirable" or least embarrassing. For example, one study found that nearly 20% of teenagers who reported having had sexual intercourse in an initial survey indicated in a similar survey one year later that they had not done so. This tendency to avoid reporting intimate information was especially high among females (Rodgers, Billy & Udry, 1982:292; also see Kahn, Kalsbeek & Hofferth, 1988). Similarly, both men and women who have been divorced more than once tend to underreport the total number of divorces they have had (Preston & McDonald, 1979; Thornton & Rodgers, 1987).

Likewise, a study of sexual assault victimization employing both male and female interviewers found that the number of assaults reported to one sex was about 25% higher than to the other sex (Sorenson et al., 1987:1161). To whom do you think victims (mainly women) were more likely to report sexual assaults, male interviewers or female interviewers? The answer is that significantly more instances were reported to female interviewers than to male interviewers (also see Hall, 1985).

The Science of Polling

The order and wording of questions can skew results.
And, oh yes—people lie.

Clinton leads by 16 percentage points. No, it's Clinton by only 6. Scratch that; make it Clinton by 10.

Bad enough that press, pundits and pollsters are obsessed with the horse-race aspect of the presidential campaign. But this one seems like it's being called by track announcers who aren't watching the same race. George Bush gets a postconvention "bump" in some polls but hardly a dimple in others, including NEWSWEEK'S. Polls taken at the same time are just barely consistent given their margins of error, the "plus or minus 3 percentage points" that gives them the aura of scientificness. Political consultants blame the gyrating results on "the volatility of the electorate," and while lots of voters indeed keep changing their mind, that doesn't explain it all. Is "polling science" an oxymoron?

To be fair, polls that at first blush look contradictory may not be. A Miami Herald poll last week had George Bush ahead of Bill Clinton by 7 points (48–41) in Florida; in a New York Times/CBS News poll, Bush trailed (42–48). But since the polls had margins of error of about 4 points, they overlapped (add and subtract 4 from each number to get the possible range). The margin of error, calculated according to a textbook statistical formula, varies inversely with the sample size. In general, about 500 responses gives a possible error of 5 percent either way; 2,500 responses decreases it to 1 percent.

Besides getting enough people, the polltaker must get enough of the right kind of people—those representative of November's voters. Calling more in Philadelphia than in Anchorage is just the beginning. Polltakers also "look at the demographic distribution of the sample to make sure it conforms to what the Census tells us about the [voting age] population," says Andrew Kohut of Princeton Survey Research Associates, which polls for Times Mirror and U.S. News & World Report. This is where the black magic comes in. If the polltakers don't have enough, say, young white males among those willing to answer, they give extra weight to the ones they do have. Each polltaker does this differently. All the methods inflate the statistical heft of a few respondents, and might explain divergent results.

Registered voters: Some polls track registered voters, others "likely" voters. Neither approach is foolproof. People lie, says sociologist Seymour Martin Lipset of George Mason University: some three quarters of adults say they are registered, but only two thirds really are. The lies matter because the young, the poor, the less educated and minorities are less likely to register; these groups are more likely to vote Democratic. So surveys of "registered" voters include many who aren't, and therefore may exaggerate Clinton's strength. Of the major polls, only the Time-CNN and Louis Harris surveys screen for "likely" voters, by asking questions such as whether the respondent voted in the last presidential election. People can lie about that, too, but Time-CNN and Harris have consistently shown a smaller Clinton lead: those likely to vote tend to be older, whiter, better off and Republican. No poll can fully compensate, though, for the almost 40 percent of those phoned who refuse to be questioned or happen to be out of the house. Whose side are they on? Will the hang-ups split like the rest of the voters? The answers will come in November.

Ensuring a random sample also requires something beyond statistics. During Ronald Reagan's 1984 re-election campaign, his internal "tracking" polls showed him well ahead of Walter Mondale—except on Friday nights. "They went into a panic every week until they figured it out," says Frank Luntz, a political-science professor at the University of Pennsylvania who polled for Pat Buchanan and Ross Perot this year. The explanation: registered Republicans, on average more flush than their Democratic counterparts, were more likely to go out on the town Friday nights and not be home to answer the pollster's phone call.

Although polltakers take steps to avoid such selection effects, slips happen. CBS-New York Times, seeking the widely expected "bump" Bush would get from the GOP convention, polled on the last night of the Houston gala. Result: CBS-NYT had Bush within 3 points of Clinton. NEWSWEEK, phoning the day after, found virtually no postconvention boost: the candidates were 14 points apart. Obviously, people who answered their phones when CBS-NYT called were home; many were home to watch the Houston speeches; many watched because they are Republicans.

Even subtle differences in how questions are worded, and in which questions precede the "Bush or Clinton?" query, can skew results. Some organizations identify the candidates by name only; most give party affiliation. If Clinton is identified as the Democrat, he might fare better in the cities of the Northeast and in union strongholds, some of the last bastions of party loyalty. And if the horse-race question comes after a series on, say, the economy—asking whether the voter is better or worse off than he was four years ago, for instance—Bush fares worse. Since the ballot doesn't have an "Are you better off?" preface, such polls underestimate Bush's strength.

Three-way race: When Ross Perot still had his hat in the ring, polltakers were surprised at how his strength varied depending on how they arranged their questions. Some polls asked respondents only to choose between Bush, Clinton and Perot; others asked "Bush or Clinton?" first and only then added Perot. "When the three-way question was asked *after* the two-way question," says Larry Hugick, managing editor of The Gallup Organization (which conducts NEWSWEEK'S Polls), "Perot got more support than when the three-way question was asked alone." He speculates that asking Bush-or-Clinton first made people focus on their dissatisfaction with the choice, and made them more likely to pick Perot when his name was added. Lumping all three together made people evaluate each on his merits. All these effects are subtle, but since voters are so fickle in their affections this year the tiny influences matter. "Very small puffs of wind can move an unanchored ship," says Everett Ladd, director of the Roper Center for Public Opinion Research at the University of Connecticut.

That's why campaigns have grown more wary of tracking polls. But what may be bad for the employment prospects of polltakers may be good for democracy. "It's gotten so bad that you can see the candidates staring at the polling numbers beneath the pages of their speeches," says longtime GOP consultant Doug Bailey. Maybe, if pols believe a little less in polls, their speeches and positions will reflect the numbers a little less and their convictions a little more.

Sharon Begley with Howard Fineman in Washington and Vernon Church in New York. From NEWSWEEK, Sept. 28, 1992. © 1992, Newsweek, Inc. All rights reserved. Reprinted by permission.

Techniques for Dealing with Subject Dishonesty

Seven techniques have been developed to increase subject honesty and frankness in responding to questionnaires, or to at least estimate the degree of error attributable to dishonest or incomplete disclosure. Although these techniques pertain to the issues first raised in Chapter 7, they can now be discussed in more detail. The seven techniques are: assuring anonymity or confidentiality, the bogus pipeline technique, having subjects rate their honesty at the end of the questionnaire, checking for internal consistency, polygraph testing, independent verification, and obtaining responses to a follow-up questionnaire. Each of these techniques is discussed below.

Assuring Anonymity/Confidentiality

Probably the simplest thing a researcher can do to increase the honesty and frankness of those being surveyed is to assure them of anonymity, or at least of confidentiality (Hill, Dill, & Davenport, 1988:599). **Anonymity** suggests that the researcher never knows the identity of those who completed a questionnaire. **Confidentiality,** on the other hand, refers to the promise not to disclose any information revealed by the subjects that would cause them to be personally identified. More will be said about these concepts when discussing research ethics in Chapter 18.

Assurances of anonymity can affect the honesty and frankness of subjects answering questions about behavior that is very personal and/or illegal. For instance, in a delinquent behavior study that took place under both anonymous and nonanonymous conditions, the overall level of delinquency correlated almost perfectly (r = +.98), although the total number of offenses reported under the anonymous condition was about 10% higher than the total number of offenses reported under the nonanonymous condition (Kulik, Stein, & Sarbin, 1968).

In an interview situation, paroled child molesters admitted to more prior sex offenses and to more continuing urges to reoffend when they were assured that their responses would be kept strictly confidential than when they were not given this assurance (Kaplan et al., 1990). Similarly, drug offenders were less likely to disclose the full extent of their drug use to interviewers directly affiliated with the criminal justice system than to interviewers with no such affiliation (Joe & Gorsuch, 1977).

Sometimes, responses made on a questionnaire are more honest than responses made directly to an interviewer. For example, a study found that women who had had an abortion were more likely to disclose this information if they were allowed to do so in a sealed envelope rather than doing so directly to an interviewer (Jones & Forrest, 1992:119).

Under some circumstances, assurances of anonymity or confidentiality appear to have no effect on how people respond to questions. For example, two studies looked at how college students rated their instructors under two conditions: (1) students gave completely anonymous ratings, and (2) students were asked to sign their evaluation forms (for administrative purposes). Neither study found any significant differences in the average ratings under these two conditions (Abrami et al., 1976; Ellis, 1984).

Using the Bogus Pipeline Technique

A method called the **bogus pipeline,** first discussed in Chapter 10, was developed to increase the honesty and frankness of questionnaire respondents. This is ironic because the technique itself is an exercise in deception. As explained earlier (p. 138), the bogus pipeline methodology uses elaborate and complicated-appearing devices to make subjects believe that any dishonesty on their part will be detected (Jones & Sigall, 1971).

Studies have shown that subjects who are hooked up to these intimidating gadgets do answer certain sensitive questions in ways that are significantly ''less polite'' or more ''unorthodox'' than subjects who have no reason to think that any distortion of their views would ever be detected (Evans, Hansen, & Mittelmark, 1977; Quigley-Fernandez & Tedeschi, 1978; Bray, Hill, & Henderson, 1979). The findings from these studies suggest that our true feelings about sensitive issues are often glossed over by a ''civil veneer'' that the bogus pipeline methodology helps to remove.

Even though the bogus pipeline technique appears to significantly improve the honesty and frankness of persons responding in personal interviews, one study that compared results using the technique to results from an anonymous questionnaire containing the same questions found no significant differences in responses (Hill, Dill, & Davenport, 1988). This finding suggests that you can accomplish the same level of honesty with an anonymous questionnaire as with the bogus pipeline. Findings like this plus growing pressure on social scientists to curtail their use of deception in research probably means that studies using the bogus pipeline are not in the future of social science.

Having Subjects Self-Report Their Level of Accuracy

Another method to detect dishonesty (as well as carelessness) in responding is to ask subjects at the end of the questionnaire or the interview to rate their degree of honesty and frankness. When asked this straightforward question, a significant minority of respondents will indicate that they were less than completely honest.

For example, in a recent study of sexual aggression among New Zealand university students, males were asked to self-report whether they had ever forced a female to have sex without her consent. Because the questionnaires were all completed at one time in a large auditorium, the researchers were concerned that some respondents might not be entirely honest for fear that someone seated close to them might see their answers. Thus, at the end of the questionnaire, respondents were asked how accurately they had responded. Five percent of the male respondents indicated that their responses had not been entirely accurate (Gavey, 1991:465).

Of course, this technique for detecting dishonesty still leave researchers wondering which items were inaccurately reported. One method for finding out is to run two separate analyses, one with the suspect questionnaires included, and the other with them excluded. It can usually be assumed that any significant discrepancies were the result of dishonesty by those admitting to it at the end of the questionnaire.

Checking for Internal Consistency

Detecting errors in self-reports by asking a question more than once in the same questionnaire is called internal consistency (Farrington, 1973:101). It is not often used in the social sciences for detecting dishonesty, perhaps because inconsistent responses are as likely to reflect carelessness or unclear reasoning as being indicative of deception (see Goldsmith, 1987). Nevertheless, patterns of inconsistency have been used to indicate general tendencies toward deceptive responding (Pearson & Francis, 1989).

Testing with a Polygraph

Another method (or set of methods) that social scientists use to assess the honesty of subjects involves electronically monitoring physiological processes linked to human emotions, such as pulse, heart rate, and palm sweating. Generally, when people experience intense emotions or nervousness, these bodily indicators become elevated. Most people respond emotionally to telling lies, especially when important issues are involved and when they fear that the examiner may detect inconsistencies in their answers.

After subjects are asked a series of neutral questions to help get baseline measures of pulse, heart rate, and palm sweat, the **polygraph** (or lie detector) is used to look for subtle variations in stress levels. An offshoot of the polygraph test that has also been used for lie detection is a **voice analyzer.** It records subtle "microtremors" in the vocal cords, which also tend to accompany high emotional states (Rice, 1978).

Polygraph methods have become widely used in private business for detecting employee theft (Rice, 1978; Holden, 1986). They are also used in conducting criminal investigations. Occasionally, polygraphs have been used strictly for research purposes. For example, one study attempted to assess the accuracy of self-reported criminal behavior by comparing normal (unmonitored) self-reports to later responses made under the scrutiny of a polygraph (e.g., Clark & Tifft, 1966). The results indicated that under conditions of anonymity, most people give honest responses to questions about their involvement in criminal behavior.

Using polygraph data to verify self-reports, of course, can only be justified if it is assumed that the polygraph itself is accurate. Polygraph examiners are sometimes misled into believing that a lie has been told when it has not, or that the truth has been told when it has not (see Patrick & Iacono, 1989:353). Although it appears that polygraphs are accurate much more often than not (Patrick & Iacono, 1989), this is no consolation to anyone wrongly suspected of something because of the fallibility of a machine or its operator (see Holden, 1986).

Using Independent Verification

To independently verify a self-reported item, a second source for that information must be obtained. Some examples of these secondary sources were discussed in Chapter 10. Recall that biochemical and physiological methods were employed to measure drug use and sexual arousal apart from self-reports (pp. 136–137).

Another example of independent verification self-reports has come from studies of people's weight. As mentioned in Chapter 7 (pp. 90–91), one study found a very high correlation (r = .96) between people's self-reported weight on a questionnaire and their actual weight as indicated a few weeks later in a medical clinic (Charney et al., 1976; also see Coates, Jeffrey & Wing, 1978).

Still another example comes from comparing voter registration records against people's statements in an interview about whether they voted in the last election. What percentage of people do you think indicated that they voted in the last election but did not do so according to official tallies? Studies in the United States put the figure at about 15% (Parry & Crossley, 1950; Traugott & Katosh, 1979).

Obtaining Responses to a Follow-Up Questionnaire (Retest Stability)

A very useful way to verify questionnaire data is to have subjects complete the form a second time. This method can be especially informative if the subjects are unaware at the time they complete the initial questionnaire that they will be asked to complete it a second time. Unfortunately, social scientists do not have many opportunities to use this type of verification. For those who have used this technique, the amount of time allowed to lapse between the first and the second administration of a questionnaire varies from a few weeks (Dentler & Monroe, 1961) to a year or more. An example of the latter is the study mentioned earlier that found that roughly 20% of the teenagers who reported having had sexual intercourse on their first questionnaire said they were virgins a year later (Rodgers, Billy & Udry, 1982:292). This would be hard to attribute to anything but dishonesty, although given the extremely personal nature of the question, it is certainly understandable.

Summary

This chapter has taken an in-depth look at the special problems associated with sampling human subjects and obtaining accurate self-reported information from them. In the first part of this chapter, a distinction was made between a chosen sample, the sample a researcher initially picks, and an obtained sample, the subjects a researcher ends up with. Subtracting the obtained sample from the chosen sample yields what is referred to as sample attrition, and it is obviously something that researchers try to minimize.

A distinction was also made between two types of sampling error (or bias). Random sampling error can be reduced by increasing the sample size; systematic sampling error is the result of sample attrition, and cannot be reduced by increasing sample size. In general, sample attrition rates less than 15% do not introduce significant systematic error into a sample. High sample attrition (e.g., 50% to 60%) is sometimes unavoidable, and a study based on an obtained sample with high attrition is nonetheless nearly always preferable to no study at all.

Ways of minimizing sample attrition were discussed separately for mail surveys, and then for household and telephone surveys. Nine techniques useful in mail surveys were mentioned: (1) sending out prenotifications, (2) attaching a clearly written cover letter, (3) having a credible sponsor, (4) enclosing a stamped self-addressed return envelope, (5) enclosing token compensation, (6) sending out follow-up questionnaires, (7) keeping the questionnaires short, (8) making sure the questionnaire is neat and well organized, and (9) making the significance of the study clear to the prospective respondents.

Most sample attrition in household and telephone surveys is due to people not being at home and to refusals. In general, the latter is considered more of a source of potential systematic sampling error than are not-at-homes. There is little research yet on how to minimize not-at-homes and refusals.

The second part of this chapter dealt with inaccuracies in self-reported information. Four sources of inaccuracies were identified and discussed: (1) failure to understand a question, (2) failure to accurately recall the answer, (3) indecision, and (4) dishonesty.

This last point was given special attention with the discussion of seven techniques developed to increase subject honesty and/or detect dishonesty.

These methods are: (1) assuring anonymity and confidentiality, (2) using the bogus pipeline technique, (3) having subjects self-report their degree of honesty (or level of accuracy), (4) checking for internal consistency within a questionnaire, (5) testing with a polygraph, (6) using independent verification from a second source, and (7) comparing responses from a follow-up questionnaire to responses from an initial questionnaire.

References

Abrami, P. C., Leventhal, L., Perry, R. P., & Breen, L. J. (1976). Course evaluation: How? *Journal of Educational Psychology, 68,* 300–304.

Alcocer, A. (1979). Literature review. In Technical Systems Institute, *Drinking practices and alcohol-related problems of Spanish-speaking persons in three California locales.* Sacramento, CA: California Department of Alcohol and Drug Programs.

Armstrong, J. S. (1975). Monetary incentives in mail surveys. *Public Opinion Quarterly, 39,* 112–116.

Armstrong, J. S., & Lusk, E. J. (1987). Return postage in mail surveys. *Public Opinion Quarterly, 51,* 233–248.

Arnett, J. (1991). Still crazy after all these years: Reckless behavior among young adults aged 23–27. *Personality and Individual Differences, 12,* 1305–1313.

Babbie, E. R. (1983). The practice of social research (5th ed.). Belmont, CA: Wadsworth.

Bailey, K. D. (1978). *Methods of social research.* New York: Free Press.

Barnes, G., & Welte, J. (1988). Predictors of driving while intoxicated among teenagers. *Journal of Drug Issues, 18,* 367–384.

Benson, S., Booman, W. P., & Clark, K. E. (1951). A study of interview refusals. *Journal of Applied Psychology, 35,* 116–119.

Boyle, M. H., Offord, D. R., Hofmann, H. G., Catlin, G. P., Byles, J. A., Cadman, D. T., Crawford, J. W., Links, P. S., Rae-Grant, N. I., Szatmari, P. (1987). Ontario child health study. *Archives of General Psychiatry, 44,* 826–831.

Bray, J. H., Hill, P. C., & Henderson, A. H. (1979, April). *Increasing the validity of self-reports of drug use: Generalizability of a bogus pipeline procedure used to study cigarette smoking.* Paper presented at the annual meeting of the Southeastern Psychological Association, San Antonio, Texas.

Brittain, A. W. (1992). Can women remember how many children they have borne? Data from the East Caribbean. *Social Biology, 38,* 219–232.

Caetano, R. (1984). A note on arrest statistics for alcohol-related offenses. *Drinking and Drug Practices Surveyor, 19,* 12–17.

Carpenter, E. H., (1975). Personalizing mail surveys: A replication and reassessment. *Public Opinion Quarterly, 38,* 614–620.

Charney, E., Goodman, H., McBride, M., Lyon, B., & Pratt, R. (1976). Childhood antecedents of adult obesity. Do chubby infants become obese adults? *New England Journal of Medicine, 295,* 6–9.

Clark, J. P., & Tifft, L. L. (1966). Polygraph and interview validation of self-reported deviant behavior. *American Sociological Review, 31,* 516–523.

Coates, T., Jeffrey, R., & Wing. R. (1978). The relationship between persons' relative body weights and the quality and quantity of food stored in their homes. *Addictive Behaviors, 3,* 179–185.

Dentler, R. A., & Monroe, L. J. (1961). Social correlates of early adolescent theft. *American Sociological Review, 26,* 733–743.

Dickinson, J. R. (1990). *The bibliography of marketing research methods* (3rd ed.). Lexington, MA: Lexington Books.

Dillman, D. A., & Frey, J. H. (1974). Contributions of personalization to mail questionnaire response as an element of a previously tested method. *Journal of Applied Psychology, 59,* 297–301.

Durbin, J., & Stuart, A. (1951). Differences in response rates of experienced and inexperienced interviewers. *Journal of the Royal Statistical Society, 144,* 163–206.

Ekouevi, K., & Morgan, S. P. (1991). Note on the reliability and validity of mothers' retrospective reports of their children's birthweight. *Social Biology, 38,* 140–145.

Ellis, L. (1969). Time variations in interview quality. Unpublished master's thesis, Pittsburg State University, Pittsburg, Kansas.

Ellis, L. (1984). The effects of anonymity on student ratings of college teaching and course quality. *Journal of Instructional Psychology, 11,* 182–186.

Ellis, L., Ames, M. A., Peckham, W., & Burke, D. (1988). Sexual orientation of human offspring may be altered by severe maternal stress during pregnancy. *Journal of Sex Research, 25,* 152–157.

Ellis, L., & Curless, I. (1987). Experimentally altering compliance with reprint requests. *Journal of Social Behavior and Personality, 2,* 161–164.

Evans, R. I., Hansen, W. B., & Mittelmark, M. B. (1977). Increasing the validity of self-reports of smoking behavior in children. *Journal of Applied Social Psychology, 62,* 521–523.

Faria, A. J., Dickinson, J. R., & Filipic, T. V. (1990). The effect of telephone versus letter prenotification on mail survey response rate, speed, quality and cost. *Journal of the Marketing Research Society, 32,* 551–568.

Farrington, D. P. (1973). Self-reports of deviant behavior: Predictive and stable? *Journal of Criminal Law and Criminology, 64,* 99–110.

Finkel, S. E., Guterbock, T. M., & Borg, M. J. (1991). Race-of-interviewer effects in a pre-election pool. *Public Opinion Quarterly, 55,* 313–330.

Fox, R. J., Crask, M. R., & Kim, J. (1988). Mail survey response rate: A meta-analysis of selected techniques for inducing response. *Public Opinion Quarterly, 52,* 467–491.

Gajraj, A. M., Faria, A. J., & Dickinson, J. R. (1990). A comparison of the effect of promised and provided lotteries, monetary and gift incentives on mail survey response rate, speed and cost. *Journal of the Marketing Research Society, 32,* 141–162.

Gavey, N. (1991). Sexual victimization prevalence among New Zealand university students. *Journal of Consulting and Clinical Psychology, 59,* 464–466.

Goldsmith, R. E. (1987). Two studies of yeasaying. *Psychological Reports, 60,* 239–244.

Goodstadt, M. S., Chung, L., Kronitz, R., & Cook, G. (1977). Mail survey response rates: Their manipulation and impact. *Journal of Marketing Research, 14,* 391–395.

Goyder, J. C. (1982). Further evidence on factors affecting response rates to mailed questionnaires. *American Sociological Review, 47,* 550–553.

Grichting, W. L., & Caltabiano, M. L. (1986). Amount and direction of bias in survey interviewing. *Australian Psychologist, 21,* 69–78.

Grimm, J. W., & Wozniak, P. R. (1990). *Basic social statistics and quantitative research methods.* Belmont, CA: Wadsworth.

Hall, R. (1985). *Ask any woman: A London inquiry into rape and sexual assault.* London: Falling Wall Press.

Hansen, R. A. (1980). A self-perception interpretation of the effect of monetary and nonmonetary incentives on mail survey respondent behavior. *Journal of Marketing Research, 17,* 77–83.

Heberlein, T. A., & Baumgartner, R. (1978). Factors affecting response rates to mailed questionnaires: A quantitative analysis of the published literature. *American Sociological Review, 43,* 447–471.

Herd, D. (1989). The epidemiology of drinking patterns and alcohol-related problems among U.S. blacks. In National Institute on Alcohol Abuse and Alcoholism, *Research monograph 18: Alcohol use among U.S. ethnic minorities* (pp. 3–50). Rockville, MD: U.S. Department of Health and Human Services.

Hill, P. C., Dill, C. A., Davenport, E. C., Jr. (1988). A reexamination of the bogus pipeline. *Educational and Psychological Measurement, 48,* 587–601.

Holden, C. (1986). Days may be numbered for polygraphs in the private sector. *Science, 232,* 705.

Hyman, M. (1968). Accident vulnerability and blood alcohol concentrations of drivers by demographic characteristics. *Quarterly Journal of Studies of Alcohol,* Supplement 4, 34–57.

James, J. M., & Bolstein, R. (1990). The effect of monetary incentives and follow-up mailings on the response quality in mail surveys. *Public Opinion Quarterly, 54,* 346–361.

Joe, G., & Gorsuch, R. (1977). Issues in evaluation of drug abuse treatment. *Professional Psychology, 8,* 609–640.

Jones, E. E., & Sigall, H. (1971). The bogus pipeline: A new paradigm for measuring affect and attitude. *Psychological Bulletin, 76,* 349–364.

Jones, E. F., & Forrest, J. D. (1992). Underreporting of abortion in surveys of U.S. women: 1976 to 1988. *Demography, 29,* 113–126.

Kahn, J. R., Kalsbeek, W. D., & Hofferth, S. L. (1988). National estimates of teenage sexual activity: Evaluating the comparability of three national surveys. *Demography, 25,* 189–204.

Kaplan, M. S., Abel, G. G., Cunningham-Rathner, J., Mittleman, M. S. (1990). The impact of parolees' perception of confidentiality of their self-reported sex crimes. *Annals of Sex Research, 3,* 293–303.

Kulik, J. A., Stein, K. B., & Sarbin, T. R. (1968). Disclosure of delinquent behavior under conditions of anonymity and nonanonymity. *Journal of Consulting and Clinical Psychology, 32,* 506–509.

Lansing, J. B., & Kish, L. (1957). Family life cycle as an independent variable. *American Sociological Review, 22,* 512–516.

Linsky, A. S. (1975). Stimulating responses to mailed questionnaires: A review. *Public Opinion Quarterly, 38,* 82–101.

Linton, M. (1979, July). I remember it well. *Psychology Today,* pp. 81–86.

Martin, W. S., Duncan, W. J., Powers, T. L., & Sawyer, J. C. (1989). Costs and benefits of selected response inducement techniques in mail survey research. *Journal of Business Research, 19,* 67–79.

Meilman, P. W., Gaylor, M. S., Turco, J. H., & Stone, J. E. (1990). Drug use among college undergraduates: Current use and 10–year trends. *International Journal of the Addictions, 25,* 1025–1036.

Monette, D. R., Sullivan, T. J., & DeJong, C. R. (1986). *Applied social research: Tool for the human services.* New York: Holt, Rinehart & Winston.

Moser, C. A., & Kalton, G. (1971). *Survey methods in social investigation.* London: Heinemann.

Nachmias, D., & Nachmias, C. (1987). *Research methods in the social sciences* (3rd ed.). New York: St. Martin's Press.

Nederhof, A. J. (1983). The effects of material incentives in mail surveys: two studies. *Public Opinion Quarterly, 47,* 103–111.

Parry, H., & Crossley, H. (1950). Validity of responses to survey questions. *Public Opinion Quarterly, 14,* 61–80.

Patrick, C. J., & Iacono, W. G. (1989). Psychopathy, threat, and polygraph test accuracy. *Journal of Applied Psychology, 74,* 347–355.

Pearson, P. R., & Francis, L. J. (1989). The dual nature of the Eysenckian lie scales: Are religious adolescents more truthful. *Personality and Individual Differences, 10,* 1041–1048.

Preston, S. H., & McDonald, J. (1979). The incidence of divorce within cohorts of American marriage contacted since the Civil War. *Demography, 16,* 1–26.

Quigley-Fernandez, B., & Tedeschi, J. T. (1978). The bogus pipeline as lie detector: Two validity studies. *Journal of Personality and Social Psychology, 76,* 247–256.

Rice, B. (1978 June). The new truth machines. *Psychology Today,* 61–78.

Richardson, J. T., Frankel, R. S., Rankin, W. L., & Gaustad, G. R. (1971). Computers in the social and behavioral sciences. *American Sociologist, 6,* 143–152.

Rodgers, J. L., Billy, J. O. G., & Udry, J. R. (1982). The rescission of behaviors: Inconsistent responses in adolescent sexuality data. *Social Science Research, 11,* 280–296.

Ross, H. L., Howard, J. M., Ganikos, M. L., & Taylor, E. D. (1991). Drunk driving among American blacks and Hispanics. *Accident Analysis and Prevention, 23,* 1–11.

Roszkowski, M. J., & Bean, A. G. (1990). Believe it or not! Longer questionnaires have lower response rates. *Journal of Business and Psychology, 4,* 495–509.

Sanchez, M. E. (1992). Effects of questionnaire design on the quality of survey data. *Public Opinion Quarterly, 56,* 206–217.

Schlegelmilch, B. B., & Diamantopoulos, A. (1991). Prenotification and mail survey response rates: A quantitative integration of the literature. *Journal of the Market Research Society, 33,* 243–255.

Skogan, W. G. (1976). *Sample surveys of the victims of crime.* Cambridge, MA: Ballinger.

Smith, P., & Remington, P. (1989). The epidemiology of drinking and driving: Results of the Behavioral Risk Factor Surveillance System. *Health Education Quarterly, 16,* 345–358.

Sorenson, S. B., Stein, J. A., Siegel, J. M., Golding, J. M., & Burnam, M. A. (1987). The prevalence of adult sexual assault: The Los Angeles Epidemiologic Catchment Area Project. *American Journal of Epidemiology, 126,* 1154–1164.

Stephan, F. J., & McCarthy, P. J. (1963). *Sampling opinions.* New York: Wiley.

Thornton, A., & Rogers, W. L. (1987). The influence of individual and historical time on marital dissolution. *Demography, 24,* 1–22.

Traugott, M. W., & Katosh, J. P. (1979). Response validity in surveys of voting behavior. *Public Opinion Quarterly, 43,* 359–377.

Trice, A. D. (1986). Elements of personalization in cover letters may affect response rates in mail surveys: A further analysis of Worthen and Valcarce (1985). *Psychological Reports, 58,* 82.

Waller, J., King, E., Nielson, G., & Turkel, H. (1969). Alcohol and other factors in California highway fatalities. *Journal of Forensic Science, 14,* 429–444.

Yammarino, F. J., Skinner, S. J., & Childers, T. L. (1991). Understanding mail survey response behavior: A meta-analysis. *Public Opinion Quarterly, 55,* 613–639.

Zylman, R. (1972). Race and social status discrimination and police action in alcohol-affected collisions. *Journal of Safety Research, 4,* 75–84.

Suggested Reading

Stephan, F. J., & McCarthy, P. J. (1963). *Sampling opinions: An analysis of survey procedure.* New York: Wiley. (A well written book that covers many of the subtleties in sampling opinions.)

Summers, G. F., (Ed.). (1970). *Attitude measurement.* Chicago: Rand McNally. (An informative book of readings covering many of the difficulties in trying to measure human attitudes and behavior.)

CHAPTER 14

Theories, Models, Hypotheses, and Empirical Reality

Now that you are familiar with several important aspects of the research process, it is time to reflect on why social scientists conduct research, and what they do with what they have learned after data have been collected and analyzed. Much of the inspiration for scientific research comes from theories (Schofield & Coleman 1986:1). This chapter will discuss how theories (and related concepts) play a vital role in the research process.

The Role of Theory in Science

As the word is used in ordinary language, **theory** often denotes something that is the complete opposite of empirical reality (Maris, 1970:1070). Statements such as "Oh, that's nothing but a theory" imply that theories and empirical reality ("facts") are the exact opposite. However, as this chapter will show, theories and empirical reality can be interrelated in ways that make advancements in scientific understanding possible. Although nearly all scientific theories are eventually abandoned, you will see that theories that have certain qualities often become the crowning achievement of science.

Scientific research can be conducted without any theories to guide it, but the results of such research are often difficult to organize and interpret. Ultimately, theories make it possible for scientists to integrate and comprehend the results of massive amounts of scientific research.

The Nature of Scientific Theorizing

To begin this exploration of the role of theories in social science research, let us consider the following question: If a theory is not a fact (which it is not), why do scientists take the time to propose and test theories? To answer this question, we need to begin with a few basic definitions. A theory is defined as a set of logically related statements from which a number of hypotheses may be derived (Taylor & Frideres, 1972:465). A **hypothesis** is a statement about empirical reality that may or may not be true. Unfortunately, these two terms are sometimes used interchangeably (e.g., McBroom, 1980:181; Laughlin, 1991:148), a practice that has been justifiably criticized (e.g., Birdsell, 1981:8).

For example, the statement "Drinking coffee is dangerous to health" should be considered a hypothesis, not a theory (Kraemer & Thiemann, 1987:22). A theory would offer an explanation for why such a hypothesis might (or might not) be true, and would lead to additional testable hypotheses.

The concept of "truth" is a slippery one in science, and many scientists avoid using the term except in casual discourse. To the degree it has meaning in science, "truth" should only be applied at the level of hypotheses, not at the level of theories. For example, if you hypothesized that Variable A and Variable B are negatively related, and conducted ten massive studies in diverse regions of the world and found basically the same $-.60$ correlation in each one of these studies, you have a strong basis for considering your hypothesis true. Nevertheless, a careful scientist simply says that "a great deal of evidence has now been found to support the hypothesis" rather than declaring it true. The difference between these two pronouncements, although subtle, marks the difference between someone who is open-minded and willing to consider additional evidence, even if inconsistent with what has already been found, and someone who knows "the truth."

Now say that you are aware of a theory that predicts the hypothesized negative relationship between Variables A and B. Are you justified in declaring the theory true because the hypothesis has been repeatedly confirmed? There are three reasons for answering no. One is that, as just explained, even though ten studies have all confirmed the relationship, the next study to be conducted might not. Second, the theory probably leads to a number of other hypotheses that need to be thoroughly tested. Third, other theories may lead to the same hypothesis.

Let us consider five criteria used in assessing "good" scientific theories. Since the concept of "truth" cannot be applied to theories (although it may be applied in casual scientific discussions), "good" theories are said to have merit, or to be **elegant.**

Criteria for Assessing the Merit (or Elegance) of a Theory

Theoretical elegance is judged on the basis of five criteria. These criteria are presented roughly in the order of importance.

■ **FIGURE 14.1**

A diagrammatic scheme of two competing theories.

Levels of Scientific Inquiry	Two Imaginary Theories
Theoretical	Theory A Theory B
Hypothetical	H_1 H_2 H_3 H_1 H_2 H_3 H_4
Empirical	(Assume that all hypotheses are confirmed)

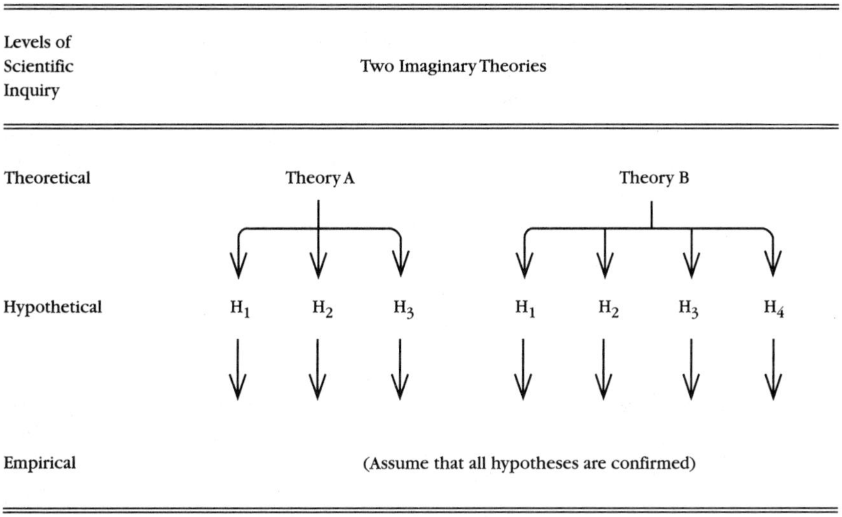

Predictive Accuracy

By any measure, the most important basis for assessing the elegance of a theory is how accurately it predicts what is observed. If a theory poorly predicts empirical reality, then it is said to have little merit. In general, answers about predictive accuracy come slowly. This is partly because few scientists may be interested in testing a new theory, and partly because observations may be difficult to make. Also, if erroneous results are obtained by the first study or two (due to invalid measurement of one of the key variables, for example), the assumption may be that the theory lacks merit, when, in fact, this is not the case.

Predictive Scope

Predictive scope refers to how many hypotheses can be accurately predicted by a theory. Thus, if two competing theories accurately predict the same number of hypotheses, their predictive scope would be equivalent. This concept of predictive scope is illustrated in Figure 14.1. To conceptualize this diagram, let us stipulate that there are three levels at which scientists may inquire about some phenomenon. The basic level consists of the empirical observations that are made. Directly ''above'' the level of empirical observations are the expectations (or hypotheses) that scientists have about what will be found when the observations are compiled and analyzed. Finally, ''overseeing'' these expectations is a level of inquiry which includes theoretical ideas about why things are as the observations suggest.

Figure 14.1 shows two imaginary theories (Theory A and Theory B) effectively competing with one another. As the diagram shows, both theories accurately predict Hypotheses 1, 2, and 3. However, unlike Theory A, Theory B also accurately predicts Hypothesis 4. Thus, Theory B would be considered more elegant (everything else being equal). The main reason for using these hypothetical examples of competing theories instead of actual instances is that in the "real world," the process of testing competing theories is often exceedingly complicated.

Let's add one more feature to the imaginary example in Figure 14.1. Say that a fifth hypothesis is derived from Theory B, but that empirical research consistently disconfirms this hypothesis. At this point, the two theories might be fairly evenly matched, and they might eventually open the way for someone to propose a third theory that could accurately predict all five hypotheses.

Simplicity

Should there be two theories that are essentially equal in predictive accuracy and scope, but one is simpler to understand than the other, it would be considered more elegant. This criterion of simplicity is also called **parsimony** and **Occam's razor** (sometimes also spelled **Ockham**). This latter term credits an 18th century scientist, named William of Occam, who devoted much of his professional career to trying to pare down scientific theories proposed by others to their bare essence (Dewsbury, 1984:187).

Falsifiability (or Absence of Ambiguity)

As noted earlier, theories can never be proven true in a strict empirical sense (if they could, once they were proven, they would be facts, not theories). Nevertheless, theories vary in how easily they can be disproven. Disproof is achieved by deriving from a theory one or more hypotheses that persistently fails to match with empirical observations.

Obviously, you can state a theory with enough ambiguity to make it essentially impossible to disprove (Shearing, 1973). An ambiguous theory, however, is not considered elegant relative to a very explicit theory. Theories that are very precise in terms of their predictions are said to have the quality of *falsifiability* (Popper, 1935; Ember & Ember, 1988:197).

Aesthetic Appeal

Many of the world's famous scientists have reported that one criteria they use in developing confidence in their theories involves a sense of beauty (see e.g., Clark, 1971:87; Forward, 1980; Chandrasekhar, 1988). Although a sense of beauty by itself

■ **FIGURE 14.2**

A simplified diagram illustrating the idealized interrelationship between scientific theories, hypotheses, empirical observations, and generalizations.

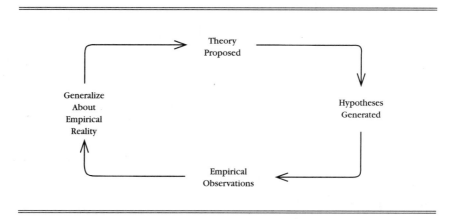

may not be very helpful in scientifically explaining the empirical world, when it is combined with a great deal of knowledge about empirical reality, aesthetics may be among the most powerful tools we possess.

Encouraging all scientists to be imaginative and creative in their theorizing, a famous biologist once expressed the view that "the universe is not only queerer than we suppose, but queerer than we *can* suppose" (Haldane, 1927). Ultimately, theory construction—if not its actual testing—provides an arena in which science and artistic creativity often mesh (Judson, 1980).

How Theories Fit into the Research Process

Because scientific theories exist at a level of abstraction that is beyond empirical reality (refer back to Figure 14.1), the only way a theory can be tested is by deriving hypotheses from it and then testing the hypotheses. Figure 14.2 provides an idealized sketch of how theories and hypotheses fit into the scientific research process. Starting at the top, and proceeding clockwise, hypotheses are derived from a particular theory. The hypotheses are then empirically tested, and on the basis of those tests, generalizations are made about the nature of reality. From these generalizations, it is sometimes necessary to modify (or even replace) the theory which began the process, thereby setting into motion another extended round of hypothesis testing. In reality, things are much more complex and chaotic than Figure 14.2 implies, and the process of testing a single theory sometimes proceeds over the course of several decades.

■ **FIGURE 14.3**

Proposed model for how drug use by peers and self interrelate. (*Genetic, Social, and General Psychology Monographs*, Vol. 116, page 159, 1990. Reprinted with permission of the Helen Dwight Reid Educational Foundation. Published by Heldref Publications, 1319 Eighteenth St., N.W., Washington, D.C. 20036–1802. Copyright © 1990.)

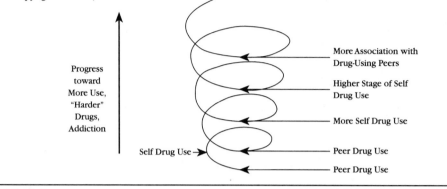

Scientific Models

The term **model** has come to be used frequently in the social sciences in recent years. Typically, the term refers to some type of simplified representation of a phenomenon. Like the concepts of theory and hypothesis (discussed in the preceding section), the terms model and theory have sometimes been used interchangeably (Coleman, 1964:518; Phillips, 1966:59; Simon, 1969:37; Hall & Hirschman, 1991), a practice that I do not encourage.

The distinction between a model and a theory is as follows: Whereas a theory puts forth an explanation in linguistic form, a model puts forth an explanation in some other (usually more tangible) form. In addition, a model is often used to illustrate and clarify some special *aspect* of a scientific theory, rather than the entire theory (Sienko & Plane, 1976:132).

There are three types of models used in the social sciences: diagrammatic (or structural) models, equational models, and animal models. Each one is described and illustrated below.

Diagrammatic (*or* Structural) Models

A diagrammatic (or structural) model is one in which a geometric sketch (or actual physical object) is used to help explain a phenomenon. Sometimes diagrammatic models are conceptually derived without using a theory, sometimes they are derived from a broader theory, and other times they are generated by a computer, based on the analysis of empirical data.

Figure 14.3 provides an example of a diagrammatic model on how the use of various recreational (as opposed to therapeutic) drugs among teenagers may escalate to additional recreational drug use and sometimes even to drug addiction (Brook et al., 1990:159). This model can be understood apart from any specific theory of drug use, although it may certainly be incorporated into a theory as well.

■ FIGURE 14.4

A basic diagrammatic model of arousal theory. (Adapted from Ellis, 1987:221.)

The Basic Model for Arousal Theory	Three Hypothetical Persons with Different Responses to Normal Environmental Conditions
Extreme Superoptimal Arousal Level ‖ ‖ ‖ ‖	} Person A
Preferred Arousal Level ‖ ‖ ‖	} Person B } Person C
Extreme Suboptimal Arousal Level	

Figure 14.4 is a theoretically derived diagrammatic model. This model illustrates what is called arousal theory (Ellis, 1987:221). Arousal theory contends that much human behavior orients toward maintaining a preferred (or optimal) level of arousal, and that people's brains differ as to how much environmental stimulation they need to maintain this optimal level of arousal. According to this theory, such behavior patterns as hyperactivity in childhood and sensation-seeking behavior during adolescence and adulthood may be reflecting attempts by people who are not getting enough stimulation under normal environmental conditions to increase their stimulus input.

Figure 14.4 is a model showing three hypothetical persons. Under normal environmental conditions, Person A is shown as feeling "overaroused," and thus would find comfort in withdrawing to a more secluded place in his or her environment (such as a quiet church service or the security of home). Person B represents where the majority of people would be situated. They generally feel comfortable with a typical level of environmental stimulation. Finally, according to the theory, Person C would be constantly seeking stimulation, even to the point of irritating and sometimes endangering him- or herself and others. In childhood, they are likely to be diagnosed as hyperactive, and in adolescence and adulthood, they may be constantly experimenting with new and dangerous things, including risk-taking, drug use, and even delinquency and crime.

Arousal theory, of course, is just that, a theory, and it remains to be firmly established. Figure 14.4 is a model used to illustrate the theory, but not in the sense that anyone would ever expect to find something physically resembling it out in the real world. Rather, such a model may be useful for illustrating a theory that can partially explain some otherwise baffling features of human behavior.

Sometimes diagrammatic models are produced by computer. The most common example is called **path analysis.** This type of complex statistical analysis will be described more in Chapter 17, but a brief sketch can be presented here.

Especially when dealing with a data set consisting of numerous interrelated variables and a large sample size, path analysis is able to generate statistically based "scenarios" of how the variables best fit together in a causal sense, based on various mathematical assumptions. The end result of path analysis is a computer-generated diagram that suggests how a number of variables *may* impinge on, and be affected by, one another. If you want to see an example, turn to page 269.

Equational (*or* Mathematical) Models

Equational forms of scientific models are more commonly found in such sciences as physics, chemistry, and astronomy than in the social sciences. Most equational models developed to explain social and behavioral phenomena are either too complex or too esoteric to warrant being outlined here.

One exception is a potentially far-reaching equation first proposed in the 1960s to explain altruism (Hamilton, 1964). Altruism refers to self-sacrificing behavior by one individual on behalf of another, and there is now evidence that this behavior is found not only in humans, but to some degree in all social animals (especially by parents on behalf of offspring) (see Wittenberger, 1981:75).

A formula to help explain altruism was initially inspired by observations of honey bees. Workers (who are sterile females) were seen subjecting themselves to certain death in defense of the hive. The theory behind the formula is an updated version of Darwin's theory of evolution, and it leads to the suspicion that somehow these workers are more likely to leave their genes in subsequent generations than are workers who do nothing to protect their hive. But how is it possible for a sterile female bee to leave genes in subsequent generations? The answer is that they may do so by proxy because they are closely related to the queen. This led a scientist named William D. Hamilton (1963, 1964) to propose that the more closely related two organisms are to one another, the more altruism they will display toward one another.

Hamilton's formula has been expressed several different ways, but its basic structure is as follows:

$$P(\text{Altruism}) = b_t (r) > c$$

where

P(Altruism)—the probability of altruism
b_t—the potential reproductive benefit of a particular altruistic act
r—the degree of genetic relatedness between an altruist and a recipient
c—the probable reproductive cost (or risk) to the prospective altruist

The model predicts that any given altruistic act is most likely to be exhibited when the altruist and the potential recipient are closely related to one another. This deduction has been supported by observations of many species, including our own (Peck & Feldman, 1988).

Social science equational models have been used most in the fields of economics and demography. Various equational models have been developed for predicting national upswings and downturns in an economy (e.g., Bradley, Gerald, & Kearney, 1993), and fluctuations in societal birth rates and death rates (e.g., Hapke, 1972; Ahlburg, 1986; de Beer, 1991). Most of these models are derived from empirical information that certain variables tend to rise and fall in a specific pattern, and/or that they tend to follow increases and decreases in other variables.

For example, it is almost without exception that the unemployment rate will rise significantly in June (due to large numbers of high school and college graduates entering the job market). Another example was the rise in the crime rate in most Western countries beginning in the 1960s (Fox, 1978; Sagi & Wellford, 1968; Wellford, 1973). This rise was predictable simply by combining two well-established facts: (1) Criminal behavior is highly concentrated in the second and third decades of life (reviewed by Ellis, 1988:534). (2) A 15-year increase in the birth rate (known as the ''baby boom'') began in the mid-1940s throughout the Western hemisphere (Rice, 1974; Westoff, 1976).

Another example of an equational model is one developed for predicting the onset of cigarette smoking, alcohol drinking, and even sexual activity among adolescents of various racial and ethnic groups (Rowe & Rodgers, 1990, 1991). The model asserted that these behaviors often spread like epidemics: the more that adolescents in a particular population were ''infected'' at any given age, the more likely others will be ''infected'' at subsequent ages.

Animal Models

The most distinctive scientific models are **animal models.** This refers to the substitution of nonhuman animals for humans with respect to some specific trait.

Increasingly, nonhuman animal models have been used in the social sciences, especially psychology. There are at least three reasons for this trend. First, while scientists are not (and should not be) free to do anything they might want to nonhuman animals simply for the sake of curiosity (see Chapter 18), there are certainly fewer ethical constraints placed on scientific research with nonhumans than with humans. Second, it has become increasingly apparent that humans and other animals share a common biological heritage (including a similar brain), suggesting that much can be learned about human behavior by studying the behavior of other species (see Rajecki, 1983; Strum, 1987; Relethford, 1990). Third, although this assumption may not be true in all cases, in general, the causes of human behavior are probably more complex than the causes of nonhuman animal behavior. If so, scientists may ultimately achieve a better understanding of human behavior by first studying similar behavior in other animals (Alonso et al., 1991:69).

Nonhuman animal models have been tentatively identified for a wide range of human behavioral and emotional/mental traits. These include:

Aggression (Blanchard & Blanchard, 1984)
Alcoholism and drug abuse/addiction (Wilson et al., 1984; Wise & Bozarth, 1987:478; Barnes, 1988; Brady, 1991; Berta & Wilson, 1992)
Anxiety (Green & Hodges, 1991)
Depression (Alonso et al., 1991)
Emotional depression and learned helplessness (Dess & Chapman, 1990; Martin, Soubrie, & Puech, 1990)
Epilepsy (King et al., 1988:1477)
Mental illness (Bond, 1984; Ellenbroek, & Cools, 1990)
Self-destructive behavior (Crawley, Sutton, & Pickar, 1985)
Sexual orientation (homosexuality/heterosexuality) (Ellis & Ames, 1987:240; Price et al., 1988; Brand & Slob, 1991)

For a clear idea of how animal models have been used in the social sciences, let us consider the last two examples in greater detail. Special strains of mice, called alcohol-preferring strains, have been artificially selected in recent years (Badaway et al., 1989). Studies have shown that these genetic strains resemble human alcoholics not only in their unusual tendencies to voluntarily consume alcohol, but also in certain aspects of their brain biochemistry (Comings et al., 1991:306). Researchers who are using this animal model for alcoholism are hopeful that by identifying the factors that cause the unusual neurochemistry in alcohol-preferring rats, they may be able to shed light on human alcoholism. Of course, no one believes that alcohol-preferring strains of rats are *exactly* like human alcoholics in all respects. Nevertheless, they may be sufficiently similar that some important knowledge will be gained that can eventually be transferred to our species.

It may sound absurd to talk about other animals having a sexual orientation, but in fact they do. Like humans, most members of all known animal species are heterosexual, at least in terms of whom they choose as sex partners. Presumably, this preference for opposite-sex members is because heterosexuals are much more likely than bisexuals, and especially than homosexuals, to have offspring. In the 1970s, researchers discovered various ways of manipulating the prenatal environment of rat fetuses to produce large proportions of males who, once they reached puberty, consistently presented to other males rather than attempting to mount females (reviewed by Ellis & Ames, 1987). These studies have provided a basis for arguing that an animal model for human sexual orientation may have been discovered. From research

"Personally, I think he's trying to cover up a shaky theory."

inspired by this model, much progress has been made in recent years in understanding the causes of variations in sexual orientation (e.g., LeVay, 1992; Burr, 1993).

It should be emphasized that the use of animal models in the social sciences remains controversial, but these models have provided many new ways of developing and testing social science hypotheses and theories. Researchers should always be on guard, however, against overgeneralizing, or equating humans and other animals (Abelson, 1992). Also, just because an animal model is useful for at least partial understanding of some aspect of human behavior does not mean that animal models will eventually be found for all, or even most, human behavior. Finally, not all social scientists who study nonhumans are doing so simply to better understand ourselves. Many contend that studying the behavior of nonhuman animals can be fascinating in its own right.

To summarize, there are three diverse types of models in social science: diagrammatic, equational, and animal models. The differences between these types are not always clear-cut, and distinguishing models from theories is sometimes impossible (mainly because a number of social scientists use the terms almost interchangeably). Nevertheless, both models and theories represent related methods that scientists use to make sense of the world.

Strictly speaking, models resemble theories in the sense that both are used to present an organized conceptual picture of some phenomenon. However, whereas theories are typically expressed linguistically, models appear in a variety of more tangible forms.

Scientific Laws

One concept that needs to be distinguished from a scientific theory is that of a **scientific law.** A scientific law is a statement about what should always happen under ideal conditions. The best known scientific law comes from the physical sciences, and is known as the law of gravity. This law states that the speed of an object in free fall (i.e., that is devoid of air resistance) will accelerate at a very specific rate the further it falls.

The difference between a scientific law and a scientific theory is that a law offers no explanation for what it is designed to predict; it is merely a statement about what will be observed under a specific set of conditions. Many laws are similar to hypotheses, except that hypotheses tend to be much less emphatic than laws, and are often derived from theories, whereas most scientific laws are not.

There are probably two reasons why scientific laws have been infrequently proposed in the social sciences, particularly in recent decades: First, few behavior patterns are sufficiently predictable (at our current level of understanding) that the word law is appropriately applied to them (Coleman, 1964:26). The second reason is that scientific laws of behavior, especially of human behavior, may be confused with civil and criminal laws which obviously apply to human behavior and are themselves the object of scientific study (particularly in the field of criminology) (see Ellis, 1990).

Scientific Paradigms

In the early 1960s, Thomas Kuhn (1962) published a widely read book in which he argued that scientists in each major discipline usually work for decades without agreeing on a common paradigm. A **paradigm** refers to a set of assumptions about the nature of the phenomenon to be explained and the basic approach that will be taken to obtain those explanations (Simberloff, 1976:572). Paradigms are best thought of as more general and encompassing than theories; in fact, they are the broad perspective within which all theories are thought to emanate.

Kuhn contended that at some point during the pre-paradigm stage, a discipline will acquire enough basic knowledge, and will have entertained sufficient numbers of theories of the phenomenon it has chosen to study, that someone within the discipline will propose a broad perspective that will spark a "paradigmatic revolution." This revolution may last for decades, but will sooner or later transform the discipline into what Kuhn called **normal science.** By this, Kuhn meant that the vast majority of scientists working in the discipline would be in agreement about a basic approach.

Scientists in most of the physical sciences seem to have had their paradigmatic revolution, and are now settled into normal science (see McCann, 1978). This means that the major disputes are no longer about how to approach the discipline, but about substantive issues over details.

What about the social sciences? Most students only need to take courses from more than one instructor to know that the social sciences are all still in the pre-paradigm stage of development (Jeffery, 1977:10; Wilson, 1980:4; Weingart, 1986; Bauer, 1992:133).

Hypothesis Testing and Attempts to Generalize

Now that we have discussed the derivation of hypotheses from theories, we should turn our attention to testing hypotheses and attempting to generalize about phenomena on the basis of evidence. The issue of hypothesis testing was discussed in Chapter 5, but it is now time to cover it in more detail. In particular, you should become familiar with additional issues surrounding decisions to accept or reject a particular hypothesis. This will help you understand how researchers sometimes go beyond hypothesis testing to the point of making sweeping generalizations about the nature of reality.

Universes as a Whole, Local Universes, and Samples

Chapter 5 contained a brief discussion of how increasing sample size can usually increase the confidence a scientist has in correlation coefficients. For example, a researcher would have more confidence in $r_{(1000)} = .30$ than in $r_{(5)} = .80$. Why? Even though .80 is a higher correlation coefficient than .30, the tremendous difference in sample size (1000 vs. 5) makes it absurd to have as much confidence in the second coefficient as in the first. Also, Chapter 9 mentioned that increases in sample size, especially for samples drawn randomly from a population, allows one to generalize with greater confidence (i.e., with a lower margin of error).

Let us now consider sample sizes in concert with the notion of hypothesis testing. In doing so, think of universes not simply as populations of living things (e.g., humans living in a particular society), but also as various physical and behavioral characteristics exhibited by members of a population. For example, if you are making a hypothesis about the correlation between the height of basketball players and the number of points they will score, the universe could be all persons who have ever attempted to make a basket. Obviously, universes of this magnitude are so large that they can be considered infinite.

It is impossible to study random samples of most infinite universes because they tend to be very widely dispersed over both time and space. For this reason, researchers generally seek random samples of what are called **local universes.** Local universes are restricted in time and space to what is reasonably accessible to a researcher (or to a team of researchers).

In our example of speculating about how height and basket-making ability may be related, a local universe might consist of all basketball players at a particular high school during two or three consecutive seasons. A researcher is not studying this

■ **FIGURE 14.5**

A diagrammatic representation of the concepts of a universe as a whole, a local universe, and a sample.

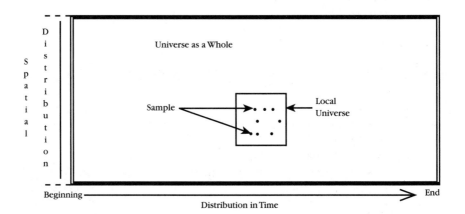

local universe because he or she is specifically interested in this school for the few seasons involved. Rather, the researcher picks this local universe assuming that what is found in it will most likely be true of the universe as a whole.

The basic distinction between a universe as a whole, a local universe, and a sample is represented in Figure 14.5: Even though a researcher can only sample a small local universe, doing so can still be helpful in coming to an accurate generalization about the universe as a whole. This is because other researchers can supplement the first researcher's sample with other samples from other local universes until a stable picture of the universe as a whole eventually emerges.

Put another way, even though most scientific hypotheses (and theories) are about universes as a whole, and most studies rely on samples of local universes, these studies are still valuable for testing scientific hypotheses. Scientists, however, must be very guarded when generalizing from just one or two studies of local universes. But after a half a dozen or so studies of various local universes have been conducted, some confident generalizations are usually possible, especially if all the studies have come to the same conclusion.

The Null Hypothesis and Type I and Type II Errors

It is now useful to elaborate on the concept of a **null hypothesis** (discussed in Chapter 5). You may recall that a null hypothesis is one asserting that no differences or relationships exist, and that the opposite of a null hypothesis is called an **alternative** or **research hypothesis.** A null hypothesis is often symbolized as H_0, and asserting that the height of basketball players has no relationship to their probability of making baskets would be an example of an H_0.

■ **FIGURE 14.6**

A diagrammatic representation of a researcher's options concerning the null hypothesis (H_0) and the possible outcome of each decision. (Adapted from Arney, 1990:207.)

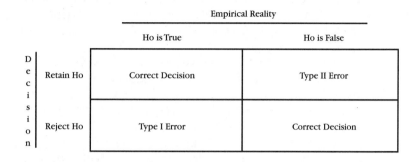

The concept of a null hypothesis is important in science because, whereas alternative hypotheses can be extremely varied, null hypotheses are always the same. In the case of height and basket-making probability, for example, you could hypothesize a positive correlation, a negative correlation, or any number of curvilinear relationships.

Therefore, even though researchers rarely test the null hypothesis, it is considered a useful standard for describing hypothesis testing. Researchers use the null hypothesis to characterize what can happen each time hypotheses are tested. Figure 14.6 shows these possibilities.

Figure 14.6 illustrates the four logical options of how empirical reality relates to null hypotheses. Note that two types of error are represented: Type I error and Type II error. A **Type I** error is defined as rejecting the null hypothesis when it is in fact true, and a **Type II** error is defined as accepting the null hypothesis when it is in fact false. (To keep them straight, students may memorize the nonsense rhyme ''Type I reject, Type II accept'' and note that there are two ''c''s in the word accept, but only one in the word reject.)

Now that you understand how Type I and Type II errors are defined, recall the discussion in Chapter 5 about levels of statistical significance. Normally, if the chance of a Type I error is 5% or less, scientists will reject the null hypothesis and, by so doing, necessarily accept some alternative (or research) hypothesis. Sometimes scientists decide to set the risk of a Type I error at an even lower level, such as the .01 level.

A major point to keep in mind is this: when studying samples with the hope of generalizing to a universe (even a local universe), the only way the probability of error can ever equal zero is when your sample and your universe are the same.

Deciding When to Accept and When to Reject a Hypothesis

Resuming our earlier example of the possible relationship between height and basket-making success, say that a researcher decided to conduct a study of 100 persons who had each been observed making ten attempts at a basket during a series of basketball games. The researcher then determined the success rates (i.e., percentage of baskets divided by attempts) for each of the 100 players, and then correlated these ratios with the height of each player.

Assume that the resulting correlation was r = .14. The researcher must now decide whether the hypothesis was confirmed. In doing so, he or she would note that the direction of the relationship was as expected, i.e., the taller players tended to have higher success rates than the shorter players. The relationship, however, is obviously very weak. It is so weak, in fact, that it is reasonable to wonder whether the correlation coefficient is significantly different from r = .00. In other words, if we reject the null hypothesis by declaring r = .14 significant, what is the probability that we are doing so erroneously?

Based on laws of probability (see Chapter 5 for a basic discussion), it has been determined that there is about a 7% chance that a correlation of r = .14 from a sample of 100 would occur by chance (Fisher & Yates, 1963:Table C). As a result, scientists would declare the hypothesis "not confirmed," since the normal convention is to risk no more than a 5% probability of error when declaring a research hypothesis confirmed. In other words, in this case, the null hypothesis would be retained. Had the correlation coefficient been somewhat larger—i.e., above .18—the relationship would have been statistically significant beyond the 5% level, thus warranting the rejection of the null hypothesis.

Summary

This chapter focused on scientific theorizing and hypothesis testing. It was noted that scientific theories are usually formulated to cover such a massive number of events that it is unrealistic to ever try to completely test theories. Nevertheless, if several tests based on samples all point toward confirming the hypotheses derived from a particular theory, this can be considered evidence in favor of a theory.

The chapter pointed out distinctions between such terms as empirical observations, hypotheses, and theories. If there are such things as "facts" in science, they refer to the empirical observations described in research reports. But, unlike facts in ordinary discourse, scientific facts are tentative, awaiting additional confirmation (or refutation) by observers of other samples.

Hypotheses are statements about empirical reality, which may or may not be true. Sometimes hypotheses come to a researcher "out of the blue," but generally they are derived from some theory. As suggested by Figure 14.1, a theory exists "above" empirical reality. Theories become connected to empirical reality when numerous hypotheses derived from them are confirmed by empirical observation.

Scientific theories are judged most importantly on their predictive accuracy and their predictive scope. Other criteria are simplicity, falsifiability, and aesthetic appeal.

Scientific models refers to a host of special "tools" used by scientists to help conceptualize reality. Although the terms theories and models are sometimes used interchangeably, the most common difference is that theories are usually presented in linguistic form, whereas models are presented in some nonlinguistic form. Three categories of scientific models were identified: diagrammatic models, equational models, and animal models. Diagrammatic (or structural) models appear in two or three dimensional space, and include computer-generated models, such as in path analysis. Equational models use a mathematical equation to express a way of understanding some phenomenon or forecasting future events. Animal models have been increasingly used in the social sciences in recent years, partly because of growing evidence of the close genetic and neurological similarities between humans and other species (especially other mammals).

Scientific laws are statements that specify the conditions under which some outcome will occur. It was noted that scientific laws are rare in the social sciences relative to the physical sciences.

When discussing the testing of hypotheses, remember that most hypotheses are stated in terms of large, almost infinite universes, and that most research studies (by necessity) are based on tiny fractions of those universes, called samples. Trying to generalize from samples to universes entails risks of error. Among the terms used to describe such risks are Type I and Type II errors, and these errors are defined in terms of the null hypothesis. The null hypothesis is a hypothesis that states that there is no difference or no relationship with respect to two or more variables. Type I errors occur when a true null hypothesis is erroneously rejected, and Type II errors occur when a false null hypothesis is erroneously accepted.

Finally, it should be reiterated that although this chapter has focused on hypotheses derived from theories, many hypotheses in the social sciences are still derived from little more than hunches. In any case, because hypotheses are tested and retested, and because findings are shared, science slowly inches its way toward a more complete comprehension of nature, including human nature.

References

Abelson, P. H. (1992). Diet and cancer in humans and rodents. *Science, 255,* 141.

Ahlburg, D. A. (1986). A relative cohort size forecasting model of Canadian total live births. *Social Biology, 33,* 51–56.

Alonso, S. J., Castellano, M. A., Afonso, D., & Rodriguez, M. (1991). Sex differences in behavioral despair: relationships between behavioral despair and open field activity. *Physiology & Behavior, 49,* 69–72.

Arney, W. R. (1990). *Understanding statistics in the social sciences.* New York: Freeman.

Badaway, A. B., Morgan, C. J., Lane, J., Dhaliwal, K., & Bradley, D. M. (1989). Liver tryptophan pyrrolase: A major determinant of the low brain 5-hydroxytryptamine concentration in alcohol-preferring C57BL mice. *Biochemistry Journal, 264,* 597–599.

Barnes, D. M. (1988). The biological tangle of drug addiction. *Science, 241,* 415–417.

Bauer, H. H. (1992). *Scientific literacy and the myth of the scientific method.* Urbana: University of Illinois Press.

Berta, J., & Wilson, J. R. (1992). Seven generations of genetic selection for ethanol dependence in mice. *Behavior Genetics, 22,* 345–359.

Birdsell, J. B. (1981). *Human evolution: An introduction to the new physical anthropology.* Boston: Houghton Mifflin.

Blanchard, D. C., & Blanchard, R. J. (1984). Affect and aggression: An animal model applied to human behavior. *Advanced Studies in Aggression, 1,* 1–62.

Bond, N. W. (Ed.). (1984). *Animal models in pyschopathology.* New York: Academic Press.

Bradley, J., Gerald, J. F., & Kearney, I. (1993). Modelling supply in an open economy using a restricted cost function. *Economic Modelling, 10,* 11–21.

Brady, J. V. (1991). Animal models for assessing drugs of abuse. *Neuroscience & Biobehavioral Reviews, 15,* 35–43.

Brand, T., & Slob, A. K. (1991). Neonatal organization of adult partner preference behavior in male rats. *Physiology and Behavior, 49,* 107–111.

Brook, J. S., Brook, D. W., Gordon, A. S., Whiteman, M., & Cohen, P. (1990). The psychosocial etiology of adolescent drug use: A family interaction approach. *Genetic, Social, and General Psychology Monographs, 116,* 111–267.

Burr, C. (1993, March). Homosexuality and biology. *Atlantic Monthly,* pp. 47–65.

Chandrasekhar, S. (1988). *Truth and beauty.* Chicago: University of Chicago Press.

Clark, R. (1971). *Einstein: The life and times.* New York: Times Mirror World.

Coleman, J. S. (1964). *Introduction to mathematical sociology.* Glencoe, NY: Free Press.

Comings, D. E., Muhleman, D., Dietz, G. W., Jr., Donlon, T. (1991). Human tryptophan oxygenase localized to 4q31: Possible implications for alcoholism and other behavioral disorders. *Genomics, 9,* 301–309.

Crawley, J. N., Sutton, M. E., & Pickar, D. (1985). Animal models of self-destructive behavior and suicide. *Psychiatric Clinics of North America, 8,* 299–310.

de Beer, J. (1991). Births and cohort size. *Social Biology, 38,* 146–153.

Dess, N. K., & Chapman, C. D. (1990). Individual differences in taste, body, weight, and depression in the ''helplessness'' rat model and in humans. *Brain Research Bulletin, 24,* 669–676.

Dewsbury, D. A. (1984). *Comparative psychology in the twentieth century.* Stroudsburg, PA: Hutchinson Ross.

Eichelman, B. (1992). Aggressive behavior: From laboratory to clinic. *Archives of General Psychiatry, 49,* 488–492.

Ellenbroek, B. A., & Cools, A. R. (1990). Animal models with construct validity for schizophrenia. *Behavioral Pharmacology, 1,* 469–490.

Ellis, L. (1987). Religiosity and criminality from the perspective of arousal theory. *Journal of Research in Crime and Delinquency, 24,* 215–232.

Ellis, L. (1988). The victimful-victimless crime distinction and seven universal correlates of victimful criminal behavior. *Personality and Individual Differences, 9,* 525– 548.

Ellis, L. (1990). The evolution of collective counterstrategies to crime: From the primate control role to the criminal justice system. In L. Ellis and H. Hoffman (Eds.), *Crime in biological, social, and moral contexts* (pp. 81–99). New York: Praeger.

Ellis, L., & Ames, M. A. (1987). Neurohormonal functioning and sexual orientation: A theory of homosexuality-heterosexuality. *Psychological Bulletin, 101,* 233–258.

Ember, C. R., & Ember, M. (1988). *Anthropology* (5th ed.). Englewood Cliffs, NJ: Prentice-Hall.

Fisher, R. A., & Yates, F. (1963). *Statistical Tables for Biological, Agricultural, and Medical Research* (6th ed.). London: Longman.

Forward, R. L. (1980, December). Spinning new realities. *Science 80* (1), 40–49.

Fox, J. A. (1978). *Forecasting crime data.* Lexington, MA: Heath.

Green, S., & Hodges, H. (1991). Animal models of anxiety. In P. Willner (Ed.), *Behavioural models in psychopharmacology: Theoretical, industrial and clinical perspectives* (pp. 21–49). Cambridge: Cambridge University Press.

Haldane, J. B. S. (1927). *Possible worlds and other essays.* London: Chatto & Windus.

Hall, G. C. N., & Hirschman, R. (1991). Toward a theory of sexual aggression: A quadripartite model. *Journal of Consulting and Clinical Psychology, 59,* 662–669.

Hamilton, W. D. (1963). The evolution of altruistic behavior. *American Naturalist, 97,* 354–356.

Hamilton, W. D. (1964). The genetical evolution of social behaviour. *Journal of Theoretical Biology, 7,* 1–52.

Hapke, R. (1972, May). The limits to growth: Implications for the United States. *Zero Population Growth National Reporter, 4,* 8–9.

Jeffery, C. R. (1977). *Crime prevention through environmental design.* Beverly Hills, CA: Sage.

Judson, H. F. (1980, November 17). Where Einstein and Picasso meet. *Newsweek,* p. 23.

King, F. A., Yarbrough, C. J., Anderson, D. C., Gordon, T. P., & Kenneth, G. G. (1988). Primates. *Science, 240,* 1475–1482.

Kraemer, H. C., & Thiemann, S. (1987). *How many subjects?* Newbury Park, CA: Sage.

Kuhn, T. S. (1962). *The structure of scientific revolutions.* Chicago: University of Chicago Press.

Laughlin, C. D. (1991). Womb = woman = world: Gender and transcendence in Tibetan Tantric Buddhism. *Pre- and Peri-Natal Psychology Journal, 5,* 147–165.

LeVay, S. (1992). *The sexual brain.* New York: Bradford.

Maris, R. (1970). The logical adequacy of Homans' social theory. *American Sociological Review, 35,* 1069–1081.

Martin, P., Soubrie, P., & Puech, A. J. (1990). Reversal of helpless behavior by serotonin uptake blockers in rats. *Psychopharmacology, 101,* 403–407.

McBroom, P. (1980). *Behavioral genetics.* Washington, DC: U.S. Government Printing Office (NIMH Monograph).

McCann, H. G. (1978). *Chemistry transformed: The paradigmatic shift from phlogiston on oxygen.* Norwood, NJ: Ablex.

Peck J. R., & Feldman, M. W. (1988). Kin selection and the evolution of monogamy. *Science, 240,* 1672–1674.

Phillips, B. S. (1966). *Social research: Strategy and tactics.* New York: Macmillan.

Popper, K. (1935). *Logik der furschung.* Wien: Springer.

Price, E. O., Katz, L. S., Wallach, S. J. R., & Zenchak, J. J. (1988). The relationship of male-male mounting to the sexual preferences of young rams. *Applied Animal Behaviour Science, 21,* 347–355.

Rajecki, D. W. (Ed.). (1983). *Comparing Behavior: Studying man studying animals.* New York: Erlbaum.

Relethford, J. (1990). *The human species.* London: Mayfield.

Rice, B. (1974). The baby boom comes of age. *Psychology Today, 8,* 33–34.

Rowe, D. C., & Rodgers, J. L. (1990). Adolescent smoking and drinking: Are they 'epidemics'? *Journal of Studies of Alcohol, 52,* 110–117.

Rowe, D. C., & Rodgers, J. L. (1991). An 'epidemic' model of adolescent sexual intercourse: Applications to national survey data. *Journal of Biosocial Science, 23,* 211–219.

Sagi, P. C., & Wellford, C. F. (1968). Age composition and patterns of change in criminal statistics. *Journal of Criminal Law, Criminology, and Police Science, 59,* 29–36.

Schofield, R. S., & Coleman, D. (1986). Introduction. In D. Coleman & R. S. Schofield (Eds.), *The state of population theory*: *Forward from Malthus* (pp. 1–13). London: Basil Blackwell.

Shearing, C. D. (1973). How to make theories untestable: A guide to theorists. *American Sociologist, 8,* 33–37.

Sienko, M. J., & Plane, R. A. (1976). *Chemistry* (5th ed.). New York: McGraw-Hill.

Simberloff, D. (1976). Species turnover and equilibrium island biogeography. *Science, 194,* 572–578.

Simon, J. L. (1969). *Basic research methods in the social sciences.* New York: Random House.

Strum, S. C. (1987). *Almost human: A journey into the world of baboons.* New York: Random House.

Taylor, K. W., & Frideres, J. (1972). Issues versus controversies: Substantive and statistical significance. *American Sociological Review, 37,* 464–472.

Weingart, P. (1986). T. S. Kuhn: Revolutionary or agent provocateur? In K. W. Deutsch, A. S. Markovits, and J. Platt (Eds.), *Advances in social sciences, 1900–1980* (pp. 265–277). Lanham, MD: University Press of America.

Wellford, C. F. (1973). Age composition and the increase in recorded crime. *Criminology, 2,* 61–70.

Westoff, C. F. (1976). The decline of unplanned births in the United States. *Science, 191,* 38–41.

Wilson, E. O. (1980). *Sociobiology* (abridged). Cambridge, MA: Harvard University Press.

Wilson, J. R., Erwin, V. G., DeFries, J. C., Petersen, D. R., & Cole-Harding, S. (1984). Ethanol dependence in mice: Direct and correlated responses to ten generations of selective breeding. *Behavioral Genetics, 14,* 235–256.

Wise, R. A., & Bozarth, M. A. (1987). A psychomotor stimulant theory of addiction. *Psychological Review, 94,* 469–492.

Wittenberger, J. F. (1981). *Animal social behavior.* Boston: Duxbury.

Suggested Reading

Kuhn, T. S. (1962). *The structure of scientific revolutions.* Chicago: University of Chicago Press. (This is a widely cited book about how new scientific paradigms replace old ones through the maturation of science in various areas.)

Lastrucci, C. L. (1963). *The scientific approach*: *Basic principles of the scientific method.* Cambridge, MA: Schenkman. (A classic in the basic description of the scientific method, especially as it pertains to the integration of research and theory.)

Skinner, Q. (Ed.). (1985). *The return of grand theory in the human sciences.* New York: Cambridge University Press.

Willner, P. (Ed.). (1991). *Behavioural models in psychopharmacology: Theoretical, industrial and clinical perspectives.* Cambridge: Cambridge University Press. (This book provides numerous examples of animal models for various human behavior patterns and mental health conditions.)

Some social science journals that specialize in theory formulation are *Sociological Theory, Psychological Review,* and *Contemporary Anthropology.*

Professional social science journals that are especially relevant to topics discussed in this chapter include *Economic Modelling,* and *Theory & Psychology.*

CHAPTER 15

Experimentation

When you were a child, did it seem like you were always getting in trouble, being a nuisance to your parents and teachers? Or was there anyone in your school or neighborhood who fit this description? When this type of behavior is extreme, it is given a clinical diagnosis of attentional-deficit hyperactivity disorder (ADHD), or simple hyperactivity. One topic to be discussed in this chapter is the outcome of research on how to treat ADHD.

An important type of research not yet discussed is **experimental research.** The distinguishing feature of experimental research is that it involves directly manipulating one or more variables that are being studied. In all other research designs, researchers merely *observe* variations in variables. It will be shown in this chapter that experimentation often provides powerful evidence about the underlying causes of events.

You may recall that near the end of Chapter 4, the adage "Correlation does not equal causation" was discussed (p. 56). What this adage means is that simply observing a relationship between two variables does not warrant concluding that one variable caused the other (although this is certainly one possible explanation of a relationship). In experimental research, a scientist systematically manipulates a suspected causal variable, and then documents whether predicted changes actually occur in some other variable (Stroebe & Diehl, 1991). Before describing specific types of experimental designs, some terminology needs to be presented.

Basic Experimental Terminology

Among the terms that are fundamental to experimental research are independent variable and dependent variable. An **independent variable** is one that is under the control of a researcher in the sense that the researcher can manipulate the level at which subjects are exposed to the variable. An independent variable is also called a **treatment variable,** especially in experiments conducted in clinical settings.

A **dependent variable** is one that may be altered as a result of changes made in the independent variable (Howell, 1989:10). A helpful way to remember the distinction between these two terms is to say that the independent variable is considered a possible cause, and the dependent variable is considered a possible effect.

In most (but not all) experiments, there are at least two groups of subjects. One group, called the **experimental group** (or **experimentals**), is exposed to the independent variable to an unusual degree. The other group, called the **control group** (or **controls**), is exposed to the independent variable to a "normal" degree (or, in some cases, not at all).

Distinguishing between a control group and an experimental group is sometimes arbitrary, but usually it is obvious. To give an example, in recent years several experimental studies have been undertaken to determine what possible effect exposing males to various forms of sexually explicit mass media might have on subsequent aggression toward women (including the commission of rape) (for reviews see Zillmann, 1984; Check & Malamuth, 1986; Donnerstein, Linz, & Penrod, 1987). In most of these experiments, the independent variable would be exposure to sexually explicit material, and the dependent variable(s) would involve levels of aggression exhibited toward women. Experimental subjects would be shown sexually explicit material, and control subjects would see some "neutral" material such as a nature film, or perhaps see no film at all.

In some studies, the dependent variables have consisted of answers to questionnaire items about how subjects *think* they would respond under various hypothetical situations in which they might have an opportunity to aggress toward women (including opportunities to commit rape) (e.g., Malamuth, Haber, & Fesbach, 1980). In other studies, the dependent variable has involved asking male subjects about how severely males should be punished for committing various aggressive acts toward women (e.g., Donnerstein, Linz, & Penrod, 1984). The dependent variable in other studies involved confronting male subjects with a female lab assistant who hurled insults at the males after they had viewed either a sexually explicit video or some control video (such as a nature film) to see if exposure to the sexual material increased the likelihood that the male would respond aggressively to the affront (e.g., Malamuth & Ceniti, 1986).

In these experiments, researchers walk a thin line between making their studies as realistic as possible, but causing no significant harm to subjects. Issues regarding the protection of human subjects will be discussed in more detail in Chapter 18.

The concept of **experimental control** is important in most scientific experiments. It refers to a process of assigning subjects to the experimental and control groups at random. For example, if 100 subjects are considered eligible for exposure to an independent variable, experimental control can be achieved by randomly picking 50 of them to be in the experimental group, leaving the remaining 50 for the control group. Experimental control helps to ensure that the groups to be compared are equivalent with respect to all variables except the one being manipulated. Of course, the more subjects you have in each randomly selected group, the more confidence you can have that the groups are equivalent.

Another term that is important in experimental research is that of a **time frame.** This refers to the length of time that the dependent variable is monitored for evidence of any effects of exposure to the independent variable. In most of the experiments with sexually explicit videos, for example, the time frame would be the length of time between exposure to the sexually explicit material (or some control material), and when aggressive acts toward women would be expected to occur.

The length of the time frame must be relevant to the dependent variable being investigated. Thus, if a particular experiment involves the use of a fast-acting medication on some aspect of alertness, the time frame might be in minutes. But if the independent variable is a prison rehabilitation program designed to reduce recidivism, the time frame might be months or even years.

Main Types of Experimental Designs

Although there is a wide variety of experimental designs, most can be categorized as follows: the **classical design,** the **after-only design,** the **before-after no control group design,** the **cross-over design,** the **Solomon four-group design,** and the **factorial design.** Simple diagrams are used to illustrate the essential features of each design. In describing each design, the focus will be on the simplest form of each, although more elaborate versions of each design are often utilized.

Classical Experimental Design

In its simplest form, the classical design involves subjects being randomly assigned to two groups, the experimental group and the control group. To ensure that subjects are randomly assigned, a coin flip might be used for each pair of subjects. For an experiment to fit the minimum requirements of a classical design, there must also be at least two time frames.

Figure 15.1 offers a graphic representation of a classical experimental design. For the moment, pay attention only to the four squares outlined with the solid lines. Along the top of Figure 15.1, two time frames—T_1 and T_2—are represented. Along the side, an experimental group (G_E) and a control group (G_C) are represented. Within each of the four cells, observations on the dependent variable (DV) are

■ FIGURE 15.1

A representation of a classical experimental design. Additional cells, shown in dashed lines, can make the classical design more elaborate.

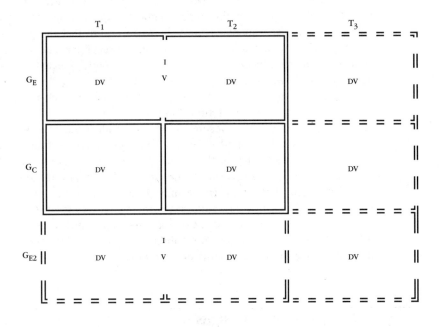

represented. For the experimental group, the imposition of the independent variable (IV) is represented between T_1 and T_2. T_1 may be referred to as the **pre-exposure time frame** (the time frame prior to either group receiving exposure to the independent variable), and T_2 may be called the **post-exposure time frame** (the time frame following unusual exposure to the IV by the G_E). One other time frame should be mentioned: the **interim-exposure time frame.** This is the time frame during which the IV is actually being administered to the G_E. Interim-exposure time frames are sometimes relevant to IVs that take considerable time to have effects (as opposed to those that have almost immediate effects).

Now let's turn our attention to the dashed outlines at the bottom and side of Figure 15.1. These squares represent the fact that the classical design can be made more elaborate by adding time frames and/or groups of subjects beyond those that are minimally required. A second experimental group could be added to a classical experimental design by having two degrees of experimental exposure to the independent variable. For example, if the independent variable were a particular drug, one experimental group might get the drug once a day, whereas the second experimental group might receive it twice a day (the control group, of course, would not receive the drug at all).

■ **FIGURE 15.2**

A classical experimental design of an experiment undertaken to reduce the number of women smoking during pregnancy. (Burling et al., 1991.)

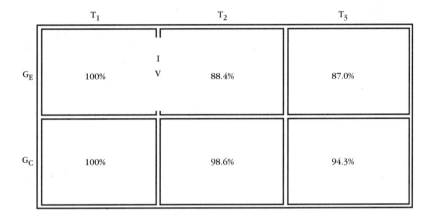

Figure 15.2 illustrates a classical experimental design that involved one more time frame than the two that are minimally required. The study comes from a recent program designed to reduce the number of women who smoked during pregnancy (Burling et al., 1991). The time frames in this study are the three times that a group of pregnant smoking women visited a prenatal health clinic. Between the first and the second visit, half the mothers (chosen at random) were sent a one-page letter that briefly informed them of the possible health risks of smoking, particularly to the fetus they were carrying (e.g., low birth weight).

As you can see from viewing Figure 15.2, receipt of this letter slightly lowered the number of women who continued to smoke during pregnancy. However, it is also worth noting that even some of the mothers who were not sent the letter stopped smoking later on in pregnancy. Statistically, only the difference between the two groups of expectant mothers in the second time frame were significantly different.

After-Only Experimental Design

As in a classical design, an after-only experimental design must have at least two groups of subjects. However, in the after-only design, no observations occur prior to the time the independent variable is imposed on the experimental group. This is illustrated in Figure 15.3. Again as in a classical design, subjects are almost always assigned to the experimental and control groups at random. There are various reasons why researchers choose not to include pretest observations of the dependent variable in an experiment. One is that repeated measurement of the dependent

■ **FIGURE 15.3**

A representation of a basic after-only experimental design with the minimum number of cells.

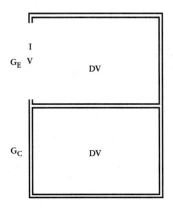

variable sometimes alters this variable's subsequent levels in some unacceptable ways. Another reason might pertain to how urgently the researcher wants the results; an after-only design often requires half the time to conduct as a classical design.

For an example of an after-only experimental design, recall that in Chapter 2 one of the methods mentioned for getting copies of scientific reports was to write directly to the author (p. 28). Using postcards, compliance rates are usually about 60%. A series of experiments was recently undertaken to identify ways to increase compliance rates (Ellis & Curless, 1987). These experiments demonstrated that compliance could be substantially increased by using letters instead of postcards, and by enclosing a self-adhesive return address label along with the letter.

The results from one of the experiments is shown in Figure 15.4. It compared the use of two form letters, one with a return address label enclosed with the letter (G_E) and the other without a return address label enclosed (G_C). (The sample sizes are uneven because very soon after this experiment began, the researchers sensed that the compliance rate was higher for the experimental group, so they switched from sending out every other request using the experimental method to a two-to-one ratio.)

Another example of an after-only experimental design comes from several clinical studies of the effects of methylphenidate (Ritalin) on boys with attention-deficit hyperactivity disorder (ADHD). According to a recent survey in the United States, this drug is now being administered to more than 6% of the nation's elementary school children (predominantly boys) (Safer & Krager, 1988).

One cause of childhood hyperactivity and consequent inattention to teachers and parents appears to be sub-optimal arousal of the brain, as discussed in Chapter 14 (pp. 207–208). In the same general class of drugs as caffeine and the amphetamines, methylphenidate is a stimulant drug that elevates brain activity (Julien,

■ **FIGURE 15.4**

A representation of an actual after-only experiment.

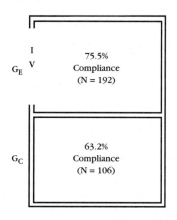

1978:18; Uelmen & Haddox, 1974:55). When administered to someone who is suboptimally aroused, theoretically, stimulant drugs raise the arousal level to within preferred ranges (Ellis, 1987:502; Russo et al., 1991:400).

For children with significant ADHD symptoms, several studies have indicated that methylphenidate improves classroom behavior (reviewed by Pelham et al., 1985 and Whalen et al., 1987; see also Gadow et al., 1992) and promotes congenial relationships with peers and family members (Barkley et al., 1984; Cunningham, Siegel, & Offord, 1985). In these and similar experiments, researchers have divided ADHD children into at least one experimental group and one control group and used ratings by teachers, parents, or peers of the children's subsequent behavior as the dependent variable. Experiments involving the treatment of ADHD children with methylphenidate have consistently found that about 80% of the experimentals exhibit significantly diminished ADHD symptoms compared to controls (Whalen et al., 1987; Carlson et al., 1992).

Before-After No Control Group Design

Although the term before-after no control group design is cumbersome, it precisely characterizes the nature of a widely used experimental design in the social sciences. It is the only experimental design in which there is only one group of subjects, all of whom will be exposed to the independent variable at some point in the experiment. This design is also unique in that it can even be used with a single subject (although it is certainly preferable to use more than one subject).

■ FIGURE 15.5

A representation of a basic before-after no control group experimental design with the minimum number of cells.

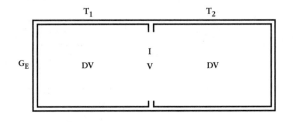

Figure 15.5 provides a basic diagram representing the minimal features of the before-after no control group design. Because all subjects in experiments following this design are exposed to the independent variable (usually after at least one pre-treatment time frame), they are all assigned to an experimental group.

Because it has no control group, you may consider this design to be poorly equipped to provide evidence regarding the effect of varying the independent variable on the dependent variable. This is true when you consider only the basic form of the design—as shown in Figure 15.5—but by adding more than the minimum two time frames, the design can be strengthened. This strength is illustrated in Figure 15.6, which represents an imaginary experiment of a new treatment for alleviating Symptom X. As you can see, each time the independent variable is imposed (represented by the shaded cell), the symptom level drops by half.

If this experiment had been stopped after the second week, the researcher could not be confident that the drop in symptoms from the first to the second week was really attributable to the treatment. There is a widely known phenomenon in clinical research called **spontaneous recovery,** which refers to the tendency for people to seek treatment when the symptoms are the worst. Because symptoms for most diseases fluctuate in severity, there is a significant probability that soon after a patient comes to a clinician, the symptoms of the disease will be less severe than at the point of first appearance.

Because the before-after no control group experiment shown in Figure 15.6 was continued on through several more time frames following the initial treatment, the treatment/no treatment regimen allowed the researcher to demonstrate that each time treatment was withheld, the symptoms reappeared at high levels. This design could be further strengthened by adding more subjects with the same symptoms, and putting them on a different schedule of treatment/no-treatment.

The term **reversal design** is sometimes applied to the type of before-after no control group experiment represented by Figure 15.6. When this term is used, the design is specified with the letter "A" when the treatment is withheld, and the letter "B" when it is imposed. Thus, Figure 15.6 would represent an ABABBA reversal design. The most widely used reversal design is the **ABAB design** (see Eichelman, 1992:491).

■ FIGURE 15.6

A representation of a hypothetical before-after no control group experimental design. (Shading represents exposure to the IV.)

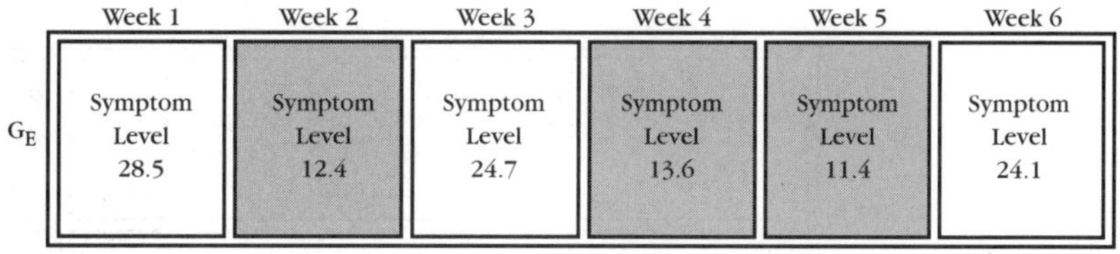

	Week 1	Week 2	Week 3	Week 4	Week 5	Week 6
G_E	Symptom Level 28.5	Symptom Level 12.4	Symptom Level 24.7	Symptom Level 13.6	Symptom Level 11.4	Symptom Level 24.1

Reversal experimental designs are especially common in clinical research. This is because they are the only experimental designs that can be carried out with single subjects (Benjamin, Mazzarins, & Kupfersmid, 1983; Monette, Sullivan, & DeJong, 1986:265). More will be said about clinical research in Chapter 20.

Cross-Over Design

Another type of experimental design that social science students should be familiar with is called a cross-over design. Its key feature is that, at some point in time, all participants serve as both experimental subjects and control subjects.

One study that used a cross-over design was undertaken to determine if social interactions, especially with an attractive, flirtatious female, would result in elevated testosterone levels among male subjects (Dabbs, Ruback, and Besch, 1987). Testosterone levels were measured in small samples of saliva, which subjects "donated" by spitting into a vile. Three measures of the dependent variable were taken. One was a baseline measure obtained at the time subjects entered the laboratory. The second measure was taken after half the subjects had been isolated in a room with another male subject, and the other half of the subjects had been isolated in a room with an attractive and friendly female confederate. The third measure of the dependent variable was secured about 15 minutes following the time that the males who had been with another male subject were switched to the female confederate, and those with the female confederate were switched to interacting with another male subject.

In this study, as in most cross-over designs, each subject served under both experimental conditions. In case you are curious about the findings, the experiment revealed that testosterone levels significantly rose after both forms of social interaction, but especially after interacting with the female confederate.

Another study using a cross-over design was conducted a few years ago to determine whether college students in an introductory sociology course learned as well from watching videotaped lectures as they did from watching the same lectures in-person (Ellis & Mathis, 1985). In this study, students were randomly selected to watch half the lectures in-person and the other half of the lectures live on a television monitor in an

■ **FIGURE 15.7**

A representation of the basic design and results from a cross-over experiment. (Adapted from Ellis & Mathis, 1985.) (Shading represents exposure to televised lectures.)

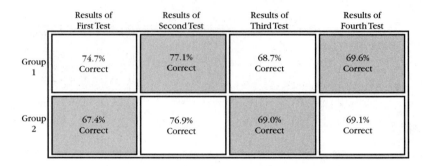

	Results of First Test	Results of Second Test	Results of Third Test	Results of Fourth Test
Group 1	74.7% Correct	77.1% Correct	68.7% Correct	69.6% Correct
Group 2	67.4% Correct	76.9% Correct	69.0% Correct	69.1% Correct

adjoining room. After each exam (of which there were four) the group of students who had watched the in-person lectures were switched to the live televised lectures until the next exam, and then they were switched back.

The basic results of this experiment are shown in Figure 15.7. It revealed that there were no significant differences in overall test scores with the exception of the first test. Here, the students assigned to the televised lectures averaged about eight percentage points lower than those exposed to the in-person lectures. This difference was attributed to technical sound problems in the video equipment, which were repaired after the first week of class.

Notice that in Figure 15.7, the groups are simply identified as "Group 1" and "Group 2" instead of "experimentals" and "controls." The reason is that in this and other cross-over experimental designs, all groups of subjects are exposed to the independent variable, although not in the same temporal sequence.

Solomon Four-Group Design

The Solomon four-group design is a specialized and rarely used design (for an example, see Fonow, Richardson, & Wemmerus, 1992). Its presentation to students in social science research methods is primarily to illustrate the extent to which a researcher can go to achieve experimental control over variables.

As shown in Figure 15.8, the Solomon four-group design consists of an after-only experimental design attached to a classical design. It requires assigning subjects to a minimum of four groups, two experimental groups and two control groups. Both experimental groups receive the same level of exposure to the independent variable, and both control groups are denied anything beyond the normal level of exposure to the independent variable. The difference, however, is that one experimental group

■ **FIGURE 15.8**

A representation of a basic Solomon four-group experimental design with the minimum number of cells.

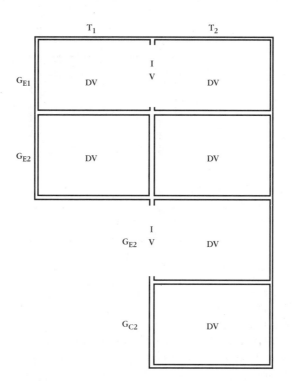

and one control group are pretested, and the other two groups are not. The purpose of this elaborate set of procedures is to see if repeated measurement of the dependent variable interacts in some way with exposure to the independent variable.

Factorial Experimental Design

Most factorial designs only involve a single time frame. In these designs, there must be at least four groups of subjects exposed to at least two levels of at least two variables. This minimum set of conditions constitutes what is called a **two-by-two factorial design.** This design is represented by Figure 15.9. A factorial experiment in which subjects are exposed to two levels of one variable and three levels of a second variable is called a **two-by-three factorial design.**

If you add a third variable with two levels of exposure, the design becomes a **two-by-two-by-three factorial design.** To visualize this design, imagine Figure 15.9 (including the add-on segment) extending into a third dimension with two cells. This means that a total of twelve cells are ''filled'' with groups of experimental subjects.

■ **FIGURE 15.9**

A representation of a two-by-two factorial experimental design.

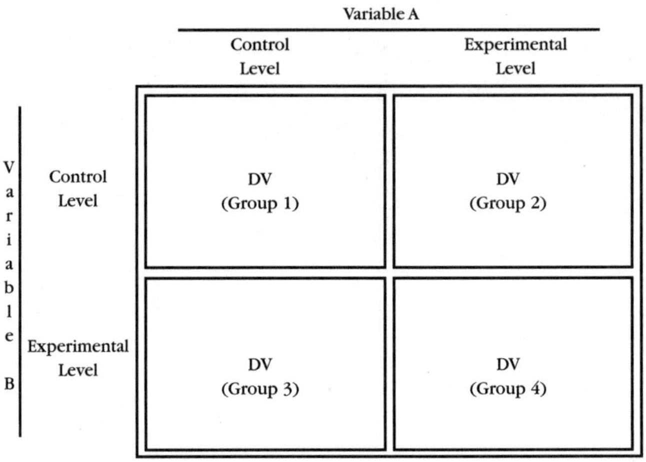

Variable A

	Control Level	Experimental Level
Variable B Control Level	DV (Group 1)	DV (Group 2)
Experimental Level	DV (Group 3)	DV (Group 4)

An example of a factorial design is a study undertaken to determine if two variables affected judgments about the appropriate sentence for persons found guilty in mock trials (Sigall & Ostrove, 1975). Each subject in the study was given one of six portfolios containing a description of two different crimes and a photograph of four different defendants. Three independent variables were manipulated in the portfolios: the physical attractiveness of the defendant (attractive or unattractive), the type of crime (burglary or swindling), and the gender of the defendant (male or female). Results were assessed separately according to the sex of the subjects, effectively adding a fourth independent variable. Thus, the design can be thought of as a two-by-two-by-two-by-two factorial design.

The main finding from the study was that regardless of the sex of the subject, attractive female defendants were sentenced less harshly than other defendants in burglary cases, but not in swindling cases. A recent replication of this study found that for both types of offenses, attractive female defendants were less harshly sentenced (Wuensch, Castellow, & Moore, 1991).

Factorial designs are employed to check not only for the effects of two (or more) independent variables acting alone, but also for **interactive effects.** Interactive effects refer to the effects that two or more independent variables may have on a dependent variable that neither independent variable has by itself. Interactive effects are often important to establish because in the "real world," it is common for many variables to be acting in concert rather than one at a time.

Interactive effects can be of two types. One type is an **augmenting effect,** where the effects of one variable enhance the effects of the other. The other type is a **counteracting effect,** where the increases in one variable tends to neutralize or diminish the effects of the other variable.

One last note: factorial experimental designs can be combined with other basic designs already discussed. No attempt will be made here to describe these elaborate combined designs, but you should be aware that they are possible.

The Importance of Experimental Research

Experiments are conducted with one overriding objective: to identify cause-effect relationships between variables. The value of this objective would be hard to exaggerate. As briefly mentioned in Chapter 4, when nonexperimental research is all that a researcher has for understanding how variables are related, he or she can be misled into believing causal connections exist when they do not (p. 56).

There are two phrases that scientists often use, which refer to the fact that experimentation is very helpful in separating cause-effect relationships between variables from simple "coincidental" relationships. One phrase is *correlation ≠ causation.* It means that just because two variables happen to be significantly associated with each other (based on, say, dozens of studies) does not prove that one is a cause, and the other is the effect (although this is certainly one possibility).

The other phrase is the *third variable problem.* This phrase refers to the possibility that whenever there is a relationship between two variables, one or more third variables may be responsible for the relationship. Through experimentation, researchers have the best chance of determining the true nature of how variables are interrelated in terms of cause and effect.

Shortcomings of Experimental Research

Now that the value of experimental research has been illustrated, some of the problems and shortcomings need to be mentioned. Most problems fall into the following four interrelated categories: ethics, time and expense, lack of realism, and the fact that many questions are simply beyond the reach of experimentation.

Ethical considerations are not confined to experimental research, but there are some unique and perplexing ethical dilemmas that must be confronted before conducting experiments, especially on human subjects. These will be spelled out in more detail in Chapter 18, but they include issues surrounding the deception and informed consent of experimental subjects, and legal and moral responsibility for harm suffered by subjects. Another ethical dilemma often accompanying human experimentation involves the fact that subjects must be randomly denied treatment in order to demonstrate the treatment's effectiveness on other subjects.

Experimental research is more time-consuming and expensive than nonexperimental research. Imagine how much time and money would be required to follow subjects over the course of most experiments when compared to the time and expense associated with administering a questionnaire.

Many experiments lack essential elements of realism. For example, say that you wanted to find out for sure whether certain forms of mass media teach children to be violent. Experiments designed to find out have had to confine their scope to short-term effects, usually in artificial laboratory settings, rather than the possible long-term effects in the "real world" (Parke, 1974:499).

Finally, many questions are simply beyond the reach of experimental research. Even if all considerations of ethics, time, and expense were set aside, there are still many studies that would be too massive to ever conduct. Examples can be found in such disciplines as economics, geography, political science, and sociology, where some of the central theories have to do with the collective behavior of millions of people. Although it is sometimes possible to "simulate" such behavioral processes in a laboratory on a small scale, researchers are often left wondering how pertinent these small scale simulations really are to the collective behavior itself.

Options for Selecting Controls in Scientific Experiments

Meaningful experiments always contain some type of experimental control. As explained earlier in this chapter, experimental control refers to some type of empirical method for determining how things would have been had there been no unusual degree of exposure to an independent variable. Sometimes experimental control is achieved by comparing scores on an independent variable for the same group of subjects at two or more time frames (one with the independent variable in place, and one when it is not in place).

The most common method of selecting control subjects is by random assignment. Sometimes subjects will be stratified according to one or more characteristics (e.g., sex) before being randomly assigned. This ensures that an equal number of individuals with these characteristics is assigned to each group.

Overcoming Special Pitfalls With Human Experimentation

Experimentation, especially with human subjects, entails a couple of special problems that need to be addressed before concluding this chapter. These problems have both procedural and ethical ramifications.

Expectancy (Placebo) Effect

Any human subject who agrees to take part in an experiment has expectations about what will happen. Subtle and often unintentional clues may affect those expectations, which in turn can have major effects on the results of the experiment.

Some of the best evidence for the expectancy effect has come from experiments involving drugs that are, in fact, inert substances (called placebos). For this reason, the expectancy effect is also referred to as the placebo effect, especially in experiments with drugs.

One special experimental procedure used with human subjects to control for any placebo effect is called a **double-blind experiment.** After subjects agree to take part in a double-blind experiment, they are randomly assigned to the experimental and control groups. Neither the subjects nor the experimenters who have contact with them ever know which subjects are in which groups. Only a "third party" connected with the experiment will have this knowledge.

Double-blind procedures are used most in studies that involve the testing of drugs that may influence behavior, such as drugs used in the treatment of various forms of mental illness or behavior problems (e.g., Marini et al., 1976; Taylor et al., 1990). For example, most of the studies discussed earlier (p. 226) regarding the effects of methylphenidate on ADHD symptoms have used double-blind procedures.

To give another example, an experiment was carried out recently to determine whether giving young children vitamin and mineral supplements might improve their scores on intelligence tests (Benton & Cook, 1991). Forty-four subjects were randomly assigned to experimental and control groups. Neither they, their parents, nor their teachers knew which students were being given capsules containing the vitamins and minerals, and which were being given placebos. After six weeks, the children who had taken the capsules containing the vitamin and mineral supplements registered a 7.6 point gain on the test, compared to a 1.7 point loss by those who had taken the placebos. Although this difference was statistically significant, a similar experiment reported in the same year failed to find a significant effect (Todman, Crombie, & Elder, 1991).

Before leaving this topic, it should be said that in at least some clinical double-blind experiments, the precautions fail. For example, in a recent study of patients with persistent panic attacks, the majority of physicians and patients were able to correctly guess the group which patients had been assigned to the experimental and control groups, mainly because of the drug's obvious effectiveness (Margraf et al., 1991).

Hawthorne Effect

In the late 1920s, industrial consultants were asked to recommend ways to improve work productivity in an electronics assembly plant in a district of Chicago known as Hawthorne. The consultants explored various possibilities, and, through a series of experiments (of a before-after no control group design), they eventually concluded that improved lighting in the plant promoted worker productivity. Months later they

"Find out who set up this experiment. It seems that half of the patients
were given a placebo, and the other half were given a different placebo."

recommended a further increase in luminescence, and found additional productivity
improvements. However, they eventually lowered the luminescence and found that
productivity further improved.

What could explain their findings? Operators of the plant finally came to the
conclusion that the extra attention and concern given to workers during the experiment were more crucial to increasing worker productivity than was the lighting.
As a result, whenever extraneous factors such as extra attention and reinforcement in an experiment with people have effects on behavior, it is referred to as the
Hawthorne effect (Jones, 1990).

Writers have embellished the Hawthorne experiments over the years, in part because careful analyses of the findings were never published (Diaper, 1990). Because it was poorly documented, some have even called the Hawthorne effect a "phantom phenomenon" (Granberg & Holmberg, 1992:241; see also Jones, 1992). Nevertheless, the concept of a Hawthorne effect is useful for illustrating how unforeseen variables may inadvertently confound even a carefully designed experiment with human subjects (Gillespie, 1991).

Summary

This chapter has focused attention on the concept of experimentation in the social sciences. The overriding feature which distinguishes experimental research from non-experimental research is that the researcher actually manipulates a variable suspected of being a cause in order to see if a second variable is altered as a result. The manipulated variable is called the independent variable, and the variable that may change as a result is called the dependent variable (whether it changes or not).

Six major types of experimental designs were identified and discussed: the classical design, the after-only design, the before-after no control group design, the cross-over design, the Solomon four-group design, and the factorial design. A brief description of each design follows.

In the classical design, subjects are divided into at least two groups; an experimental group and a control group. There is also a minimum of two time frames in a classical experiment, one time frame before the experimental group receives exposure to an unusual level of the independent variable, and the other after it has received this exposure. Assuming that subjects were assigned at random, there should be no significant difference between the two groups in the initial time frame. In the second time frame, any significant differences between the experimental group and the control group should be the result of exposing the experimental group to the unusual levels of the independent variable.

To construct an after-only design, the classical design is cut in half by removing the initial time frame. Provided that a researcher has a large group of subjects randomly assigned to each of the experimental and control conditions, this removal makes the after-only design only slightly weaker than its classical counterpart. The only purpose served by the initial time frame in the classical design is to give assurance that the experimental and control groups are indeed statistically equivalent before the experimental group is manipulated by the independent variable. In an after-only design, no such assurance is obtained.

The before-after no control group design can also be considered a truncated version of the classical design; in this case, the control group has been removed. With this design, a researcher can strengthen the experiment by adding more than the minimum two time frames. Within these additional time frames, the independent variable can be imposed, withheld, and then reimposed several times to confirm that it is the independent variable that is responsible for significant increases or decreases in the dependent variable.

The cross-over experimental design is unique in that each group of subjects in the experiment is exposed to the independent variable, although not all at the same time or in the same sequence.

The Solomon four-group design essentially affixes an after-only design onto a classical design. This is a rarely used design, but it illustrates the lengths to which a researcher can go to verify the effects an independent variable has on a dependent variable apart from any effects caused by repeated measurement of the independent variable.

Finally, in the factorial experimental design two or more independent variables are manipulated at a time. In this way it is possible to discover not only their separate effects on one or more dependent variables, but also whether there are interactive effects.

Both the value and the drawbacks of scientific experimentation were discussed and illustrated near the end of this chapter. Lastly, the concepts of the expectancy effect and the Hawthorne effect were introduced. The expectancy (or placebo) effect refers to the tendency for subjects to anticipate results from experimentation, often based on subtle clues that the researcher may neither intend nor be aware of. If these clues are in any way associated with the independent variable(s) being manipulated, they can confound an experiment in ways very misleading to a researcher. One experimental procedure that has been specially designed to reduce the expectancy effect is called double-blind experimentation. The Hawthorne effect refers to the unintended effects that researchers may have on the results of an experiment because of the extra attention and reinforcement given to subjects.

Although there are a number of pitfalls that scientists need to look out for, the potential benefits from experimental research would be difficult to exaggerate. Whenever a researcher's primary interest is causal relationships between variables, he or she should give serious thought to experimental research. In the next chapter, we look at research designs that are designed to simulate experimental research.

References

Barkley, R. A., Karlsson, J., Strzelecki, E., & Murphy, J. V. (1984). Effects of age and Ritalin dosage on mother-child interactions of hyperactive children. *Journal of Consulting and Clinical Psychology, 52,* 739–749.

Benjamin, R., Mazzarins, H., & Kupfersmid, J. (1983). The effect of time-out (TO) duration on assaultiveness in psychiatrically hospitalized children. *Aggressive Behavior, 9,* 21–27.

Benton, D., & Cook, R. (1991). Vitamin and mineral supplements improve the intelligence scores and concentration of six-year-old children. *Personality and Individual Differences, 12,* 1151–1158.

Burling, T. A., Bigelow, G. E., Robinson, J. C., & Mead, A. M. (1991). Smoking during pregnancy: Reduction via objective assessment and directive advice. *Behavior Therapy, 22,* 31–40.

Carlson, C. L., Pelham, W. E., Milich, R., & Dixon, J. (1992). Single and combined effects of methylphenidate and behavior therapy on the classroom performance of children with attention-deficit hyperactive disorder. *Journal of Abnormal Child Psychology, 20,* 213–232.

Check, J. V. P., & Malamuth, N. M. (1986). Pornography and sexual aggression: A social learning theory analysis. *Communication Yearbook, 9,* 181–213.

Cunningham, C. E., Siegel, L. S., & Offord, D. R. (1985). A developmental dose-response analysis of the effects of methylphenidate on the peer interactions of attention deficit disordered boys. *Journal of Child Psychology and Psychiatry, 26,* 955–972.

Dabbs, J. M., Jr., Ruback, R. B., & Besch, N. F. (1987, August 30). Males' saliva testosterone following conversations with male and female partners. American Psychological Association Poster Session, New York.

Diaper, G. (1990). The Hawthorne effect: A fresh examination. *Educational Studies, 16,* 261–267.

Donnerstein, E., Linz, D., & Penrod, S. (1984). The effects of multiple exposures to filmed violence against women. *Journal of Communications, 34,* 130–147.

Donnerstein, E., Linz, D., & Penrod, S. (1987). *The question of pornography.* New York: Free Press.

Eichelman, B. (1992). Aggressive behavior: From laboratory to clinic. *Archives of General Psychiatry, 49,* 488–492.

Ellis, L. (1987). Neurohormonal bases of varying tendencies to learn delinquent and criminal behavior. In E. K. Morris & C. J. Braukmann (Eds.), *Behavioral approaches to crime and delinquency.* New York: Plenum.

Ellis, L., & Curless, I. (1987). Experimentally altering compliance with reprint requests. *Journal of Social Behavior and Personality, 2,* 161–164.

Ellis, L., & Mathis, D. (1985). College student learning from televised versus conventional classroom lectures: A controlled experiment. *Higher Education, 14,* 165–173.

Fonow, M. M., Richardson, L., & Wemmerus, V. A. (1992). Feminist rape education: Does it work? *Gender and Society, 6,* 108–121.

Gadow, K. D., Paolicelli, L. M., Nolan, E. E., Schwartz, J., Sprafkin, J., & Sverd, J. (1992). Methylphenidate in aggressive hyperactive boys: II. Indirect effects of medication treatment on peer behavior. *Journal of Child and Adolescent Psychopharmacology, 2,* 49–61.

Gillespie, R. (1991). *Manufacturing knowledge*: A history of the Hawthorne experiments. New York: Cambridge University Press.

Granberg, D., & Holmberg, S. (1992). The Hawthorne effect in election studies: The impact of survey participation on voting. *British Journal of Political Science, 22,* 240–247.

Howell, D. C. (1989). *Fundamental statistics for the behavioral sciences* (2nd ed.). Boston: PWS-Kent.

Jones, S. R. G. (1990). Worker interdependence and output: The Hawthorne studies reevaluated. *American Sociological Review, 55,* 176–190.

Jones, S. R. G. (1992). Was there a Hawthorne effect? *American Journal of Sociology, 98,* 451–468.

Julien, R. M. (1978). *A primer of drug action* (2nd ed.). San Francisco: Freeman.

Malamuth, N., & Ceniti, J. (1986). Repeated exposure to violent and nonviolent pornography: Likelihood of raping ratings and laboratory aggression against women. *Aggressive Behavior, 12,* 129–137.

Malamuth, N., Haber, S., & Fesbach, S. (1980). Testing hypotheses regarding rape: Exposure to sexual violence, sex differences and the normality of rapists. *Journal of Research in Personality, 14,* 121–137.

Margraf, J., Ehlers, A., Roth, W. T., Clark, D. B., Sheikh, J. Agras, W. S., & Taylor, C. B. (1991). How ''blind'' are double-blind studies? *Journal of Consulting and Clinical Psychology, 59,* 184–187.

Marini, J. L., Sheard, M., Bridges, C., & Wagner, E. (1976). An evaluation of the double-blind design in a study comparing lithium carbonate with placebo. *Acta Psychiatrica Scandinavia, 53,* 343–349.

Monette, D. R., Sullivan, T. J., & DeJong, C. R. (1986). *Applied social research: Tool for the human services.* New York: Holt, Rinehart, & Winston.

Parke, R. D. (1974). A field experimental approach to children's aggression: Some methodological problems and some future trends. In J. deWit and W. W. Hartup (Eds.), *Determinants and origins of aggressive behavior* (pp. 499–508). The Hague: Mouton.

Pelham, W. E., Bender, M. E., Caddell, J., Booth, S., & Moores, S. (1985). The dose-response effects of methylphenidate on classroom academic and social behavior in children with attention deficit disorder. *Archives of General Psychiatry, 42,* 948–952.

Russo, M. F., Lahey, B. B., Christ, M. A., Frick, P. J., McBurnett, K., Walker, J. L., Loeber, R., Stouthamer-Loeber, M., & Green, S. (1991). Preliminary development of a sensation seeking scale for children. *Personality and Individual Differences, 12,* 399–405.

Safer, D. J., & Krager, J. M. (1988). A survey of medication treatment for hyperactive/inattentive students. *Journal of the American Medical Association, 260,* 2256–2258.

Sigall, H., & Ostrove, N. (1975). Beautiful but dangerous: Effects of offender attractiveness and nature of the crime on juridic judgement. *Journal of Personality and Social Psychology, 31,* 410–414.

Stroebe, W., & Diehl, M. (1991). You can't beat good experiments with correlational evidence: Mullen, Johnson, and Salas's meta-analytic misinterpretations. *Basic and Applied Social Psychology, 12,* 25–32.

Taylor, C. B., Hayward, C., King, R., Ehlers, A., Margraf, J., Maddock, R., Roth, W. T., & Argras, W. S. (1990). Cardiovascular and symptomatic reduction effects of alprazolam and impipramine in patients with panic disorder: Results of a double-blind placebo controlled trial. *Journal of Clinical Psychopharmacology, 10,* 112–118.

Todman, J., Crombie, I., & Elder, L. (1991). An individual difference test of the effect of vitamin supplementation on non-verbal IQ. *Personality and Individual Differences, 12,* 1333–1337.

Uelmen, G. F., & Haddox, V. G. (1974). *Drug abuse and the law.* St. Paul, MN: West.

Whalen, C. K., Henker, B., Swanson, J. M., Granger, D., & Kliewer, W. (1987). Natural social behaviors in hyperactive children: Dose effects of methylphenidate. *Journal of Consulting and Clinical Psychology, 55,* 187–193.

Wuensch, K. L., Castellow, W. A., & Moore, C. H. (1991). Effects of defendant attractiveness and type of crime on juridic judgment. *Journal of Social Behavior and Personality, 6,* 713–724.

Zillmann, D. (1984). *Connections between sex and aggression.* Hillsdale, NJ: Erlbaum.

Suggested Reading

Leavitt, F. (1991). *Research methods for behavioral scientists.* Dubuque, IA: Wm. C. Brown. (This text provides a useful overview of behavioral and social science research, with particularly insightful coverage devoted to experimental designs in Chapters 14 through 16.)

Solso, R. L., & Johnson, H. H. (1989). *An introduction to experimental design in psychology: A case approach* (4th ed.). New York: Harper & Row. (This text contains numerous examples of different experimental designs in research using both humans and non-human animals.)

CHAPTER 16

Quasi-Experimentation

Do genetic factors have a significant impact on human personality or academic performance, or on tendencies to become alcoholic or even criminal? Among the research designs to be discussed in this chapter are ones that have addressed such questions. You will see that even without strict experimental manipulation of variables, it is sometimes possible to glean inferences about causal relationships with substantial confidence.

The prefix *quasi* means "sort of." As implied by this prefix, **quasi-experimental designs** are closely related to experiments even though they fall short of being experiments in some significant way. All quasi-experiments are similar to experiments in that their main purpose is to answer questions about causation. For this reason, the terms **independent variables** and **dependent variables** are used in describing quasi-experimentation even though the designation is sometimes less certain than in true experiments. In this chapter, the nature of quasi-experimental research is explored.

Quasi-Experimental Designs

The term quasi-experimental was first used in the 1960s to refer to studies that were not true experiments, although they had important features in common with experiments (see Campbell & Stanley, 1966). It is important to note that there is both a narrow and a broad sense in which the term quasi-experiment has come to be used (Rossi & Freeman, 1989:312). In a broad sense, quasi-experiments include all studies, other than true experiments, that are designed to answer causal questions. In a narrower sense, studies that rely primarily on multivariate statistics are excluded. It is in this narrower sense that the term quasi-experiment will be used in this text. Studies which rely on multivariate statistics as an alternative to experimentation will be discussed in Chapter 17.

Quasi-experiments take advantage of "natural" changes in the intensity of independent variables, and may be divided into three main categories. In addition, a fourth category of quasi-experimental designs has been specially developed for addressing so-called nature-nurture questions (questions having to do with the relative influence of genetic and environmental factors on human behavior). The three general categories are called **retrospective** (or **ex post facto**) **designs, prospective designs,** and **time series designs.** Each is discussed separately below.

Retrospective (Ex Post Facto) Designs

Ex post facto means "after the fact." Studies that fall under the category of retrospective (or ex post facto) quasi-experiments simulate after-only experimental designs, except they do not use randomized assignment. As described in the preceding chapter, after-only experiments involve two or more randomly assigned groups of subjects. In ex post facto designs, there is no random assignment of subjects before one of the groups receives an unusual degree of exposure to an independent variable.

Although the terms "experimental group" and "control group" are sometimes used in reference to quasi-experimental designs, the preferable terminology is **exposure group** and **comparison group** (Rossi & Freeman, 1989:277). In this way, a clearer distinction is maintained between experimental and quasi-experimental research.

Let's look at an example of a retrospective (or ex post facto) design. On a dark night in 1984, the Union Carbide plant in Bhopal (pronounced Bo′ paul), India, accidentally released a large quantity of very poisonous gas (methyl isocyanate or MIC). The gas spread over several miles of residential area, killing several thousand people.

About six years after the disaster, a researcher looked for evidence of increased risk of miscarriages among women who were in the affected area at the time of the MIC release (Kapoor, 1991). This study provides a clear example of a quasi-experiment which simulates an after-only experiment.

The women in the exposed area, of course, became the exposure group. The women comprising the comparison group were chosen from an unexposed neighborhood of Bhopal of roughly the same socioeconomic status as the exposure group. In addition, the researcher made sure that all the subjects in both groups were between the ages of 20 and 44 and had at least one pregnancy in the preceding five years. Finally, both samples consisted of equal proportions of Hindus and Muslims, the two main religious/ethnic groups in Bhopal.

Such a process of "constructing" comparable exposure and comparison groups is called **matching.** Specifically, it was **group matching,** because no attempt was made to ensure that each individual in the exposure group had a comparable individual in the comparison group. Only the entire two groups were matched by a number of characteristics. Had the subjects comprising the comparison group been chosen to match each member of the exposure group individually, the procedure would be called **individual matching.** Which type of matching do you think is more difficult and, for this reason, less commonly used? The answer is individual matching, even though it is considered better for ensuring that the subjects in both groups are equivalent except for their degree of exposure to the independent variable.

The results from the Bhopal study showed that whereas the rate of known miscarriages among 139 women in the comparison area was 7.8% (which is very close to India's national rate of registered miscarriages), among 136 women in the exposure area, the miscarriage rate was 26.3%.

Such a quasi-experiment can always be criticized on grounds that the two groups may not have been equivalent in some important ways *other* than their degree of exposure to MIC (no matter how much care was taken in matching them demographically and otherwise) (Rossi & Freeman, 1989:322). Nevertheless, the study provides scientific information, because no true experiment with humans will ever be carried out. Especially in light of the more than three-fold difference in miscarriage rates between the exposure and comparison groups, and the number of deaths caused by the chemical, it seems obvious that exposure to nonlethal dosages of MIC has adverse effects on the ability of human mothers to carry fetuses to term.

Another example of a retrospective (or ex post facto) study using group matching was a project undertaken in Australia to evaluate the effectiveness of an Alcoholics Anonymous (AA) program for women (Smith, 1985). Treatment outcome for 43 AA participants was compared to 35 similarly diagnosed Australian women. The two groups of women were found not to be significantly different on the basis of place of birth, years of residency in Australia, age of first intoxication, and age of first seeking treatment. There was, however, a significant difference between the two groups in age of first beginning to drink: 18.8 for the exposure (or treatment) group as opposed to 22.2 for the comparison group.

The treatment group fared significantly better than the comparison group on a number of outcome measures, particularly length of abstinence from alcohol. Because this was not a true experiment, any conclusions should be extremely guarded. Nevertheless, this quasi-experimental research project, especially if considered with other studies of alcoholism treatment programs (see Sobell & Sobell, 1980), provides support for the view that AA-type approaches to alcoholism can be effective, at least for women.

Ideally, matching is performed with as many characteristics as possible, although it is typically confined to a half dozen traits at most. Among the most common traits used for matching are age, sex, race, and years of education. Obviously, the more characteristics that are used to match exposure and comparison group members, the more confidence there is that the two groups are indeed equivalent except with respect to the independent variable. Were it possible to match two groups of subjects on every characteristic imaginable, an ex post facto quasi-experiment would provide just as convincing a case for a causal relationship (or lack of one) as would an actual controlled experiment (Rossi & Freeman, 1989:322).

Prospective Quasi-Experimental Designs

A prospective quasi-experimental design is similar to a retrospective design except that in a prospective design, variations in the independent variable are measured as they occur, rather than retrospectively. Among examples of prospective quasi-experiments are studies of the effects of exposing human fetuses to various drugs (including alcohol) during pregnancy (see Ernhart et al., 1987; Fried & Watkinson, 1988; Richardson, Day, & Taylor, 1989; Streissguth, Barr, & Sampson, 1990; Neuspiel & Hamel, 1991). With laboratory animals, it is possible to perform carefully controlled experiments to assess the effects of such drugs on offspring (McGivern et al., 1984; Shah & Weat, 1984; Abel, 1989). However, with humans this would obviously be unethical, because most of the effects tend to be detrimental.

Prospective quasi-experimental designs for assessing the effects of prenatal drug exposure typically have the following basic structure: Substantial numbers of women who have recently confirmed their pregnancies at a health clinic will be invited to participate in a study. If they agree to take part, they will be asked to keep a record of various activities, including their use of various drugs. Some time after their children are born, the mothers will be asked to bring their children to the clinic for testing, and the results of these tests are then correlated with the mother's drug use history.

To give a specific example, 650 women were interviewed during each trimester about alcohol consumption during pregnancy. The study found that women who gave birth to infants with the lowest birth weights and head circumferences reported drinking significantly more than mothers of normal and high birth weight infants, particularly during the first two months of pregnancy (Day et al., 1989). Such evidence was particularly disturbing to the researchers because during much of this time, most of the women did not yet know for sure that they had conceived.

Researchers must be equally cautious in interpreting prospective quasi-experiments and retrospective quasi-experiments. In neither case are subjects randomly assigned to the exposure and comparison groups. In the above example, because the drinking mothers and the nondrinking mothers were not randomly assigned, there could be numerous nondrinking variables that were actually responsible for the difference in birth weight and head circumference.

Generally, prospective designs are considered more persuasive than retrospective designs, especially when the independent variable occurred long ago. The main drawback to a prospective design, however, is that a researcher must wait until the dependent variable manifests itself. Since this sometimes takes several years, it may be difficult to track down all the subjects in order to measure the dependent variable.

Time Series Designs

Most time series quasi-experiments have a structure that closely resembles before-after no control group experiments. These quasi-experiments involve following a dependent variable over time in a single group of subjects (or in a population) and observing whether the values of the dependent variable change in apparent response to changes in an independent variable.

■ FIGURE 16.1

Yearly proportion of peace abstracts to all abstracts. (Ellis, 1973.)

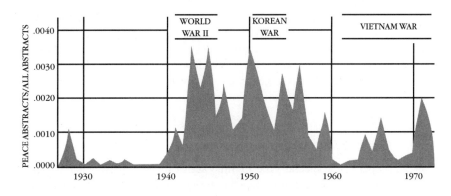

Here is an example of a time series quasi-experiment: In 1972, one of the few good things that was said to have come out of the Vietnam War was a major increase in "peace research" by social scientists (Anonymous, 1972). I decided to conduct a time series quasi-experiment to test this hypothesis (Ellis, 1973). The methodology involved consulting the index to every volume of the *Psychological Abstracts,* beginning with the first volume published in 1927 and extending through 1972. All citations to terms such as *peace, war,* and *international relations* were counted and then divided by the total number of abstracts referenced each year.

Figure 16.1 presents the findings. It shows that the proportion of social science research devoted to peace and international relations increased during wartime (albeit unevenly), and for a few years thereafter. However, an increase in peace research was actually somewhat *less* true of the Vietnam War than for the wars preceding it, especially World War II.

Reflect for a moment on how closely this study approximates a before-after no control group experiment. The only difference is that there was no control actually imposed over the independent variable. Of course, had there only been one war throughout the study period, attributing increases in peace research to the outbreak of war would have been more uncertain. However, with three wars (of varying durations), and all three associated with increases in the proportion of social science research devoted to peace, one can be fairly confident in concluding that a significant causal relationship has been identified.

A time series design can be strengthened if one or more reversals occur in the independent variable. A **reversal** in a time series design refers to time frames during which the independent variable reverts back to its initial pretreatment level. In the peace research example, each period of peace following the initial outbreak of war would be considered a reversal.

Occasionally, two different populations may be monitored over extended periods of time during which both populations will experience different degrees of change in the dependent variable. In this case, the time series design would take on characteristics more similar to a classical experiment than to a before-after no control group experiment.

The basic design of a time series study is as follows: A researcher identifies some independent variable that is suspected of causing a dependent variable. Subjects (or populations) exhibiting the dependent variable are monitored over time until substantial changes occur in the independent variable. Then the researcher determines whether or not changes occur in the dependent variable that may be reasonably attributed to changes in the independent variable.

Event-Specific Alignment Design

There is a special type of time series quasi-experimental design that deserves attention because it can be especially powerful in addressing causal questions. This design may be called an **event-specific alignment study.** Like other time series quasi-experiments, it most closely resembles a before-after no control group experiment, and may be either retrospective or prospective.

An interesting example of the event-specific alignment design is a study conducted to shed light on a long-standing controversy over whether the death penalty deters murder. Without going into detail on the history of the controversy, many studies have been conducted since the turn of the century to find out whether executing persons for serious crimes deterred others from committing those offenses in subsequent years (Knorr, 1979; Sellin, 1980; Eysenck & Gudjonsson, 1989:177). Since it is not possible to conduct a controlled experiment to answer this question, researchers have used various types of correlative research designs. These correlative designs have largely consisted of comparing geographical regions (e.g., states or countries) with different legal statutes pertaining to the death penalty to see if those in which the greatest numbers are executed tend to have the lowest murder (or other serious crime) rates (e.g., Ehrlich, 1975, 1977). While they attempt to statistically control for numerous extraneous variables (using procedures to be discussed in Chapter 17), these studies have been inconclusive to most social scientists because states and countries do not pass or impose death penalty statutes at random. As a rule, it has been found that states that use the death penalty the most tend to be those with the *highest* murder rates! Few would argue that this is because the death penalty causes murder (by setting a bad example, perhaps) (for an exception see Bowers & Pierce, 1975). Rather, increased legislative authorization for the use of the death penalty probably reflects responses to citizen demands that more be done to deal with the "crime problem."

To circumvent weaknesses in past death penalty research designs, one researcher employed an event-specific alignment design on data pertaining to murders in London, England, between 1858 and 1921 (Phillips, 1980). The results provided evidence both for and against the hypothesis that there is a deterrent effect. The researcher showed this by determining when every murder in England took place between 1858

■ **FIGURE 16.2**

Number of murders during the four weeks preceding through the six weeks following 22 executions in London, England, between 1851 and 1921. (Adapted from Phillips, 1980:145.)

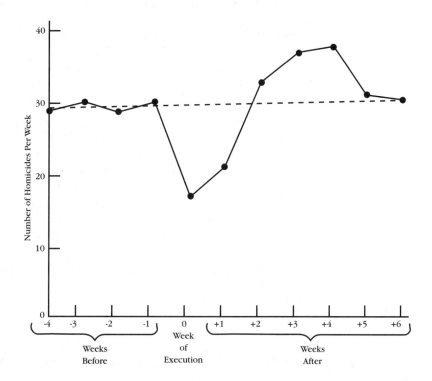

and 1921, years during which 22 persons were publicly executed for murder in London. Each time during these years that a murder occurred between four weeks ahead of and six weeks following an execution, its precise week of occurrence was noted.

The main findings are shown in Figure 16.2. Notice that the number of murders was average in the four weeks preceding the 22 executions. Then in the week that the executions took place, the number of murders dropped by almost half, and the number remained low for the following week. This suggests that the executions did have a deterrent effect. However, notice that by the third and fourth weeks following these 22 executions, the number of murders rose well above average, almost completely cancelling out the apparent earlier deterring effects of the executions.

This interesting study obviously needs to be replicated, and leaves open questions about what might have happened if executions had occurred regularly every couple of weeks. Nevertheless, it provides an illustration of how social scientists can sometimes work around obstacles to controlled experimentation.

Another example of an event-specific alignment study is the one reproduced on page 79, which deals with suicide and the full moon (Lester, Brockopp, & Priebe, 1969).

Notice that the timing of 399 suicides spanning a four-year period were aligned according to which of the four phases of the moon they occurred in. Since almost equal numbers of suicides occurred in each of the four phases, the researchers could only conclude that suicides and the phases of the moon were unrelated phenomena.

Basically, the event-specific alignment design is similar to other time series quasi-experimental designs except that all the instances in which the independent variable is imposed are aligned at a common point. Then observations of the dependent variable are made during specified units of time leading up to and following the imposition of the independent variable. There are at least two reasons this type of design is less commonly employed than the general time series design:

1. The independent variable can not be imposed so often that the control conditions do not have time to be expressed. In other words, if publicized executions had all occurred in London during the study period once every few days, this study would not have been possible.
2. The length of time during which the independent variable is imposed must be uniform. For this reason, the event-specific alignment design would not be appropriate for the peace research study mentioned earlier (because the length of each war varied greatly).

Despite the limited conditions for using an event-specific alignment design, it can be a powerful design option in a social scientist's research arsenal for assessing 'cause-and-effect relationships.

Special Quasi-Experimental Designs for Addressing Nature-Nurture Issues

Special quasi-experimental designs have been developed for addressing some of the most basic questions that social scientists face: so-called **nature-nurture questions** (Pastore, 1949; Turkheimer, 1991:392). Such questions have to do with the degree to which human behavior is genetically programmed as opposed to being acquired through learning. Using laboratory animals, nature-nurture questions have been addressed with rigorously controlled experimental breeding studies that would be unethical if performed on humans.

Such experiments have shown that selective breeding can alter many behavior patterns, including basic learning ability, sociability, aggression, nest building, courtship and copulation patterns, and preferences for consumption of alcohol (Wilson et al., 1984; Wimer & Wimer, 1985). Such evidence has encouraged many social scientists to look for similar evidence in humans.

Simply studying regular family members for similarities in behavior has not been very helpful in answering nature-nurture questions because family members normally share both genes and environments. However, there are two quasi-experimental designs that can be very helpful in separating the influence of genetics and the rearing environment on human behavior patterns. Conclusions from these studies in recent years have been fascinating.

Twin Studies

Twin studies take advantage of the fact that there are two types of twins, both with a known degree of genetic relatedness to one another. Identical twins (also called monozygotic or MZ twins) are, for all intents and purposes, genetic clones of one another. Except for rare mutations occurring after conception, they share 100% of their genes in common. Therefore, any differences they exhibit in either physical appearance or behavior would almost certainly be attributed to environmental factors. Fraternal twins (also called dizygotic or DZ twins), on the other hand, are no more similar to one another than are ordinary siblings. Since all siblings receive half their genes from each parent, on average they will share 50% of their genes in common, particularly if they are of the same sex.

The precise two-to-one ratio in the number of genes shared by sets of identical and fraternal twins makes it possible to examine behavioral traits for evidence of genetic and environmental influence. To the degree genetic factors influence a trait, identical twins should be twice as similar (or **concordant**) as are fraternal twins. If this rate of concordance fails to be empirically confirmed, the influence of environmental factors must be substantial, especially if identical twins are no more concordant than fraternal twins are for the trait. A variety of twin study designs have been developed over the years (Segal, 1990:613), although they are all rooted in the fundamental logic just outlined. Human behavior traits that twin studies have suggested are significantly influenced by genetic factors include intelligence and educational achievement (Tambs et al., 1989; Lykken et al., 1990), occupational status (Fulker, 1978; Tambs & Sundet, 1985), lifetime earnings (Taubman, 1976), and even homosexuality (Bailey & Pillard, 1991; Bailey et al., 1993).

Some critics of the twin study method have argued that identical twins are found to be twice as concordant on so many traits not because of the influence of genetics on those traits, but because identical twins are treated more similarly by their parents and others than are fraternal twins. However, this may be because identical twins elicit more similar treatment (Rowe, 1990:608). Studies have generally failed to confirm that ''similar treatment'' is responsible for identical twins being roughly twice as concordant in numerous behavioral traits as are fraternal twins (reviewed by Segal, 1990:614).

Adoption Studies

Most people have one set of parents. However, approximately 1% of infants born in western countries every year are adopted at or near birth by persons unrelated to them (Cadoret, 1986:45). Such children have two sets of parents: The parents who rear them (their rearing parents), and those who gave them their genes (their genetic parents). Social scientists have used this to help determine, with fascinating results, how much influence genetic factors and family environment have over behavior.

Adoption studies, in fact, are very similar to a type of experimental design used to address nature-nurture issues with laboratory animals, a design called a **cross-fostering experiment** (Carter-Saltzman, 1980:1263; Roubertoux & Carlier, 1988:175). In these experiments, offspring are removed from their genetic mother immediately after birth and given to a foster mother for rearing. To the degree that the offspring end up more closely resembling their genetic mother than their rearing mother for a given behavior pattern, genetic factors are deemed important for the expression of the pattern (see for example Huck & Banks, 1980; Roubertoux & Carlier, 1988).

Like twin studies, adoption studies have suggested that many human behavior traits are genetically influenced. For example, adoptees reared by nongenetic relatives have been found to more closely resemble one or both of their genetic parents than either of their rearing parents for all of the following traits: alcoholism, various forms of mental illness, and hyperactivity (reviewed by Cadoret, 1986). Adoption studies have also suggested that genes contribute significantly to variations in such traits as scholastic achievement (Teasdale & Sorensen, 1983; Thompson, Detterman, & Plomin, 1991) and criminality (reviewed by Ellis, 1982; Mednick, Gabrielli, & Hutchings, 1987; Raine & Dunkin, 1990). One adoption study even suggested that handedness was substantially influenced by genetic factors (Carter-Saltzman, 1980).

Although there are important qualifications that are too complex to delineate here, the adoption studies alluded to above have indicated that researchers can often better predict behavior patterns of adoptees by knowing the degree to which these patterns were present in their genetic parents than in their rearing parents. Nevertheless, the fact that behavior patterns of adopted offspring are not fully explained by behavior of *either* set of parents makes it very likely that influences from environmental factors outside the family are often very important.

Those interested in nature-nurture questions should be aware of an especially innovative and powerful quasi-experimental design which uses twins who have been reared apart by two sets of adoptive parents. Twins separated from birth and reared most of their childhood by separate families are rare. Thus far, only two research projects employing a combined adoption/twin design have been reported (Holden, 1980; Lichtenstein, Pedersen, & McClearn, 1992; Waldman, DeFries, & Fulker, 1992).[1] Based on data from these two combined adoption/twin studies, genetic factors have been implicated as playing a significant role in affecting shyness/extraversion, dominance/submissiveness, intellectual ability (Holden, 1980; Bouchard et al., 1990; Waldman, DeFries, & Fulker, 1992), and even in occupational interests (Moloney, Bouchard, & Segal, 1991) and occupational status attainment (Lichtenstein, Pedersen, & McClearn, 1992).

In closing, it should be noted that nature-nurture studies of human behavior continue to be controversial. Some of the controversy has to do with details in methodology and interpretations of the findings (Fulker, Wilcock, & Broadhurst, 1972;

"Dr. Farnsworth is attempting to isolate the gene that makes people do this sort of thing for a living."

Loehlin, 1989). Considerable controversy, however, has also swirled around the moral and legal implications of some of the findings from this research (e.g., Pastore, 1949; Montagu, 1980; also see Snyderman & Rothman, 1988). More attention will be given to these issues in Chapter 19.

Summary

If a scientist is interested in whether Variable A causes Variable B, the best way to come to a confident conclusion is by conducting experiments in which Variable A is systematically manipulated and Variable B is observed for evidence of consistent changes. When such experiments are impractical or unethical, it is sometimes possible to conduct quasi-experiments. In the narrow sense of the word, quasi-experiments refer to studies which take advantage of "natural" manipulations of independent variables as though they were being carried out by a researcher. In the broader sense of the term (which is not the usage in this text), quasi-experimental studies also include designs which rely primarily upon multivariate statistics to achieve "control" over independent variables (to be discussed in the following chapter).

There are two general types of quasi-experimental designs: ex post facto and time series studies. Most ex post facto designs resemble after-only experiments. However, instead of having true experimental groups and control groups whose members have been chosen at random, ex post facto studies have comparison groups and exposure groups. A comparison group is "constructed," using some type of matching procedure, sometime after the exposure group has received an unusual degree of exposure to an independent variable.

Time series quasi-experimental designs typically simulate before-after no control group experiments. However, in true experiments of this type the researcher dictates when the independent variable will be imposed and withheld, but in time series studies, this decision is not within the researcher's control. A special type of time series design was mentioned that can be especially powerful in simulating before-after no control group experiments. It is the event-specific alignment study. This design involves aligning the temporal occurrence of events at a specific point (0) and then counting those same temporal events both backward (−1, −2, etc.) and forward (+1, +2, etc.) in sequence leading up to and following the initial temporal event.

In addition to general quasi-experimental designs, there are special types of quasi-experimental designs that are used for answering nature-nurture questions. The two most widely used are twin studies and adoption studies. Twin studies take advantage of the fact that humans have two types of twins, identical and fraternal, with known genetic relationships to one another. This makes it possible to estimate the relative influence of genetic and familial environmental factors on behavior patterns.

Adoption studies take advantage of the fact that many infants are adopted each year by nonrelatives, effectively giving them two sets of parents: their genetic parents and their rearing parents. This makes it possible to estimate the degree to which genetics and familial environmental factors influence the behavior of adoptees.

There are, in fact, several types of both twin study designs and adoption study designs, and recently a combined twin/adoption study design has been utilized. The latter involves studying twins who were reared apart in order to assess the influence of both genetic and environmental factors on behavior.

Notes

[1] This is one type of quasi-experimental research in which multivariate statistics are frequently used. These statistical methods are explored in Chapter 17.

References

Abel, E. L. (1989). Parental and maternal alcohol consumption: Effects on offspring in two strains of rats. *Alcoholism: Clinical and Experimental Research, 13,* 533–541.

Anonymous. (1972). Peace research. *Behavior Today, 3* (21), 2.

Bailey, J. M., & Pillard, R. C. (1991). A genetic study of male sexual orientation. *Archives of General Psychiatry, 48,* 1089–1096.

Bailey, J. M., Pillard, R. C., Neale, M. C., and Agyei, Y. (1993). Heritable factors influence sexual orientation in women. *Archives of General Psychiatry, 50,* 217–223.

Bouchard, T. J., Jr., Lykken, D. T., McGue, M., Segal, N. L., and Tellegan, A. (1990). Sources of human psychological differences: The Minnesota study of twins reared apart. *Science, 250,* 223–228.

Bowers, W. J., & Pierce, G. L. (1975). The illusion of deterrence in Isaac Ehrlich's research on capital punishment. *Yale Law Journal, 85,* 187–208.

Cadoret, R. J. (1986). Adoption studies: Historical and methodological critique. *Psychiatric Developments, 1,* 45–64.

Campbell, D. T., & Stanley, J. C. (1966). *Experimental and quasi-experimental designs for research.* Skokie, IL: Rand McNally.

Carter-Saltzman, L. (1980). Biological and sociocultural effects on handedness: Comparison between biological and adoptive families. *Science, 209,* 1263–1265.

Day, N. L., Jasperse, D., Richardson, G., Robles, N., Sambamoorthi, U., Taylor, P., Scher, M., Stoffer, D., & Cornelius, M. (1989). Prenatal exposure to alcohol: Effect on infant growth and morphologic characteristics. *Pediatrics, 84,* 536–541.

Ehrlich, I. (1975). The deterrent effects of capital punishment: A question of life and death. *American Economic Review, 65,* 397–417.

Ehrlich, I. (1977). Capital punishment and deterrence: Some further thoughts and additional evidence. *Journal of Political Economics, 85,* 741–788.

Ellis, L. (1973). Contributions to the history of psychology: XIV. Trends in peace research. *Psychological Reports, 33,* 349–350.

Ellis, L. (1982). Genetics and criminal behavior: Evidence through the end of the 1970s. *Criminology, 20,* 43–66.

Ernhart, C. B., Sokol, R. M., & Martier, S. (1987). Alcohol teratogenicity in the human: A detailed assessment of specificity, critical period, and threshold. *American Journal of Obstetrics and Gynecology, 156,* 33–39.

Eysenck, H. J., & Gudjonsson, G. H. (1989). *The causes and cures of criminality.* New York: Plenum.

Fried, P. A., & Walkinson, B. (1988). 12- and 24-month neurobehavioural follow-up of children prenatally exposed to marijuana, cigarettes, and alcohol. *Neurotoxicology and Teratology, 10,* 305–313.

Fulker, D. W. (1978). Multivariate extensions of a biometrical model of twin data. In W. E. Nancy (Ed.), *Progress in clinical and biological research.* New York: A. R. Liss.

Fulker, D. W., Wilcock, J., & Broadhurst, P. L. (1972). Studies in geneotype-environment interaction. I. Methodology and preliminary multivariate analysis of a diallel cross of eight strains of rats. *Behavior Genetics, 2,* 261–287.

Holden, C. (1980). Twins reunited. *Science, 80* (1), 55–59.

Huck, W., & Banks, E. M. (1980). The effects of cross-fostering on the behaviour of two species of north American lemmings, *Dicrostonyx Groenlandicus* and *Lemmus Trimucronatus*: II. Sexual behaviour. *Animal Behaviour, 28,* 1953–1062.

Kapoor, R. (1991). Fetal loss and contraceptive acceptance among the Bhopal gas victims. *Social Biology, 38,* 242–248.

Knorr, S. J. (1979). Deterrence and the death penalty—a temporal, cross-sectional approach. *Journal of Criminal Law and Criminology, 70,* 235–254.

Lester, D., Brockopp, G. W., & Priebe, K. (1969). Association between a full moon and completed suicide. *Psychological Reports, 25,* 598.

Lichtenstein, P., Pedersen, N. L., and McClearn, G. E. (1992). The origins of individual differences in occupational status and educational level. *Acta Sociologica, 35,* 13–31.

Loehlin, J. C. (1989). Partitioning environmental and genetic contributions to behavioral development. *American Psychologist, 44,* 1285–1292.

Lykken, D. T., Bouchard, T. J., Jr., McGue, M., & Tellegen, A. (1990). The Minnesota twin family registry: Some initial findings. *Acta Genetic and Medical Gemellology, 39,* 35–70.

McGivern, R. F., Clancy, A. N., Hill, M. A., & Noble, E. P. (1984). Prenatal alcohol exposure alters adult expression of sexually dimorphic behavior in the rat. *Science, 224,* 896–898.

Mednick, S. A., Gabrielli, W. F., & Hutchings, B. (1987). Genetic factors in the etiology of criminal behavior. In S. A. Mednick, T. E. Moffitt, & S. A. Stock (Eds.), *The causes of crime* (pp. 74–91). Cambridge: Cambridge University Press.

Moloney, D. P., Bouchard, T. J., & Segal, N. L. (1991). A genetic and environmental analysis of the vocational interests of monozygotic and dizygotic twins reared apart. *Journal of Vocational Behavior, 39,* 76–109.

Montagu, A. (1980). *Sociobiology examined.* New York: Oxford University Press.

Neuspiel, D. R., & Hamel, S. C. (1991). Cocaine and infant behavior. *Developmental and Behavioral Pediatrics, 12,* 55–64.

Pastore, N. (1949). *The nature-nurture controversy.* New York: King's Crown Press.

Phillips, D. P. (1980). The deterrent effect of capital punishment: New evidence on an old controversy. *American Journal of Sociology, 86,* 139–148.

Raine, A., & Dinkin, J. J. (1990). The genetic and psychophysiological basis of antisocial behavior: Implications for counseling and therapy. *Journal of Counseling and Development, 68,* 637–644.

Richardson, G. A., Day, N. L., & Taylor, P. M. (1989). The effect of prenatal alcohol, marijuana, and tobacco exposure on neonatal behavior. *Infant Behavior and Development, 12,* 199–209.

Rossi, P. H., & Freeman, H. E. (1989). Evaluation: A systematic approach. Newbury Park, CA: Sage.

Roubertoux, P. L., & Carlier, M. (1988). Differences between CBA/H and NZB mice on intermale aggression. II. Maternal effects. *Behavior Genetics, 18,* 175-184.

Rowe, D. C. (1990). As the twig is bent? The myth of child-rearing influences on personality development. *Journal of Counseling & Development, 68,* 606–611.

Segal, N. L. (1990). The importance of twin studies for individual differences research. *Journal of Counseling & Development, 68,* 612–622.

Sellin, T. (1980). *Penalty of death.* Beverly Hills: Sage.

Shah, K. R., & Weat, M. (1984). Behavioral changes in rats following perinatal exposure to ethanol. *Neuroscience Letters, 47,* 145–148.

Smith, D. I. (1985). Evaluation of a residential AA programme for women. *Alcohol & Alcoholism, 20,* 315–327.

Snyderman, M., & Rothman, S. (1988). *The IQ controversy, the media and public policy.* New Brunswick: Transaction.

Sobell, L. C., & Sobell, M. B. (1980). *Alcohol treatment outcome evaluation* (Substudy No. 1132). Toronto: Addiction Research Foundation.

Streissguth, A. P., Barr, H. M., & Sampson, P. D. (1990). Moderate prenatal alcohol exposure: Effects on child IQ and learning problems at age 7 1/2 years. *Alcoholism: Clinical and Experimental Research, 14*, 662–669.

Tambs, K., & Sundet, J. M. (1985). Heredity and environmental influence in educational attainment: The effect of genes and environmental factors on differences in educational attainment, intelligence, professional status, and need achievement estimated in a twin study. *Tidsskr. Samfunnsforsk, 26*, 437–456.

Tambs, K., Sundet, J. M., Magnus, P., & Berg, K. (1989). Genetic and environmental contributions to the covariance between occupation status, educational attainment, and IQ: A study of twins. *Behavior Genetics, 19*, 209–222.

Taubman, P. (1976). The determinants of earnings: Genetics, family and other environments: A study of white male twins. *American Economic Review, 66*, 858–870.

Teasdale, T. W., & Sorensen, T. I. A. (1983). Educational attainment and social class in adoptees: Genetic and environmental contributions. *Journal of Biosocial Science, 15*, 509–518.

Thompson, L. A., Detterman, D. K., & Plomin, R. (1991). Associations between cognitive abilities and scholastic achievement: Genetic overlap but environmental differences. *Psychological Science, 2*, 158–164.

Turkheimer, E. (1991). Individual and group differences in adoption studies of IQ. *Psychological Bulletin, 110*, 392–405.

Waldman, I. D., DeFries, J. C., & Fulker, D. W. (1992). Quantitative genetic analysis of IQ development in young children: Multivariate multiple regression with orthogonal polynomials. *Behavior Genetics, 22*, 229–238.

Wilson, J. R., Erwin, V. G., DeFries, J. C., Petersen, D. R., & Cole-Harding, S. (1984). Ethanol dependence in mice: Direct and correlated responses to ten generations of selected breeding. *Behavioral Genetics, 14*, 235–256.

Wimer, R. E., & Wimer, C. C. (1985). Animal behavior genetics: A search for the biological foundations of behavior. *Annual Review in Psychology, 36*, 171–218.

Suggested Reading

Campbell, D. T., & Stanley, J. C. (1966). *Experimental and quasi-experimental designs for research.* Chicago: Rand McNally.

Cook, T. D., & Campbell, D. T. (1979). *Quasi-experimentation: Design and analysis issues for field studies.* Chicago: Rand McNally.

Snyderman, M., & Rothman, S. (1988). *The IQ controversy, the media and public policy.* New Brunswick: Transaction. (This book provides an informative overview of the controversy surrounding evidence that genetic factors are important in influencing intelligence and even account for race differences in intelligence scores.)

Among the social science journals that are most active in publishing research on the nature-nurture issue are *Behavioral and Brain Sciences, Behavior Genetics,* and *Personality and Individual Differences.* No journals currently specialize in publishing quasi-experimental research.

CHAPTER 17

Multivariate Statistical Studies

W hich foster greater academic achievement, public or parochial schools? Although this question is steeped in controversy, social scientists have given it considerable research attention in recent years. We can use these studies as a vehicle for illustrating some of the research methods to be discussed in this chapter.

Say you are a social scientist attempting to determine if a difference exists between public schools and parochial schools in promoting academic achievement. What kind of a research design would you use? Of course, as an initial step, it would be wise to compare large samples of students who had attended each of these two types of schools to find out if there is a difference in academic performance on some standardized tests. Such studies have been conducted in the United States and Australia, and they consistently show that students graduating from parochial schools attain higher scores on most academic performance measures than students graduating from public schools in the same geographical area (Coleman, Hoffer, & Kilgore, 1981, 1982a, 1982c; Heyne & Hilton, 1982; Alexander & Pallas, 1983:174; Young & Fraser, 1990:18).

Of course, such comparative studies do not tell you what caused the average differences. Because children are not randomly assigned to the schools they attend, there are numerous ways that those attending public schools could differ from those attending parochial schools. Cultural and family background factors could be the real cause of the average difference in student scores. Also, some parochial schools have admissions standards; public schools do not (see Goldberger & Cain, 1982; Hollifield, 1983).

Because the question being addressed is one of causation, the best research design would be some type of rigorous experiment. Perhaps you could take a large group of children who are just entering grade school, and randomly send half of them to a dozen public schools and send the other half to a dozen parochial schools. The students could then be given standardized tests periodically to see if significant differences appear in their academic achievement. How many experiments of this type do you think have been conducted? If you suspect none and that it is unlikely that any ever will be, you are correct. Imagine the difficulties in locating parents who would be willing to relinquish all control over the type of school their children attended for the sake of an experiment.

Because a large scale experiment would be virtually impossible, maybe a quasi-experiment could be devised. Perhaps you could find several hundred children who were going to attend parochial schools, and then locate matched comparison children with the same aptitude test scores and background characteristics who were going to attend public schools in the same geographical area. Periodic testing could determine if these two matched groups of students eventually diverge in their academic achievement. This quasi-experimental design also has never been carried out, although it is somewhat more feasible than a true experiment.

This chapter will show that there is yet another way that scientists address causal questions, one that is neither experimental nor quasi-experimental. This alternative method uses **multivariate statistics.** After describing and illustrating the nature of studies based on these statistics, we will return to the studies of how public and parochial schools may differ in their effects on student achievement.

The Nature of Multivariate Statistics

Multivariate statistics help determine how three or more variables are interrelated. Most multivariate statistics have been developed by combining two types of statistical concepts: correlations (as described in Chapter 4) and analysis of variance (as briefly described in Chapter 5, p. 70). Over the years, mathematicians and statisticians have devised ingenious ways of extending and elaborating on these fundamental statistical concepts. As we will see, these methods are often used by scientists to better understand and depict the complexities of their empirical observations.

Although some multivariate statistics can be traced back to the early 20th century (Spearman, 1927), their scientific applications were meager until the 1950s. This was when high speed computers were first programmed to perform the tedious mathematical calculations required to apply multivariate statistics to large data sets (Kerlinger, 1964:659; Jolly & Plog, 1976:296). The purpose of this chapter is not to teach you the mathematics underlying multivariate statistics, but to acquaint you with the logic and the most important terminology surrounding their use.

To understand the principles behind multivariate statistics, recall three basic points made in Chapter 4 regarding correlations: First, scattergrams can show how two variables are correlated (p. 46). Second, scattergrams can be represented with **correlation coefficients,** which range from −1.00 to +1.00 (p. 48). Third, the so-called **variance** in a correlation coefficient (shared variance) can be estimated by squaring the coefficient (see p. 56).

■ **FIGURE 17.1**

The probability of delinquency in relation to the probability of obtaining college certification and attitudes toward the fairness of the certification process. (Adapted from Engel & Hurrelmann, 1989:172 of *Delinquent behavior in adolescence: Potential and constraints of preventive strategies in school settings* in P. A. Albrecht and O. Backes [Eds.], *Crime prevention and Intervention: Legal and ethical issues.* Hawthorne, NY: Walter de Gruyter.)

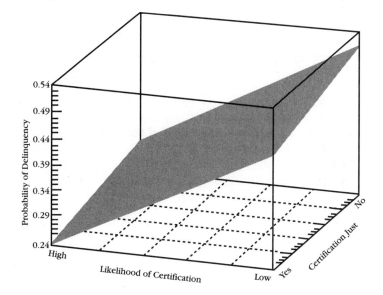

Now, say a study was conducted in which a researcher was interested not simply in how two variables were related, but in how three variables were related. The relationships between three variables can be represented with a three-dimensional (or cubical) scattergram. All the points representing the subjects' scores would be suspended within the cube (instead of on a flat surface, as when only two variables are being correlated). If relationships exist between any two (or all three) of the variables represented within the cube, the points will be clustered around a **regression plane** (as opposed to a regression line) inside the cube. The tilt of the plane depends on whether the correlations are positive or negative.

An example of a three-variable relationship is shown in Figure 17.1. This graph is based on a study of how the following three variables were related among a sample of female German teenagers: probability of delinquency, the subjects' estimates of their probability of being eligible to attend college when they graduate from high school, and their estimates of the fairness of the school process that determine their eligibility (Engel & Hurrelmann, 1989). Although each subject's position within the cube is not shown, Figure 17.1 shows the regression plane, i.e., the plane which comes closest to running through all the points in the cube.

As you can see, the female students who feel they had the best chance of being eligible to attend college and who felt that the certification process was fair have the lowest rate of delinquent behavior.

In extending the concept of correlation beyond two dimensions, mathematicians have developed formulas that make it possible to calculate correlation coefficients for three, four, or even dozens of variables all at once. These statistical formulas go beyond three dimensions, though it is impossible for us to visualize such relationships.

The Main Types of Multivariate Statistics

Multivariate statistics serve two purposes: One purpose is to classify and categorize, and the other is to help identify cause-and-effect relationships. The main multivariate statistic used in classifying is called **factor analysis.** The three most used multivariate statistics for helping to identify cause-and-effect relationships are **partial regression** (or **partially**), **multiple regression,** and **path analysis** (Games, 1990:239). Each of these four types of multivariate statistics is discussed separately below.

Factor Analysis

Say you administered a 100-item questionnaire to a group of subjects for the purpose of probing their beliefs about a wide range of topics. As you attempted to make sense of the results, it occurred to you that some items might actually be asking subjects about essentially the same thing, only with slightly different words. But how could you be sure other than simply using your own intuition? Factor analysis is a powerful statistical method that can help scientists investigate this possibility.

In formal terms, factor analysis refers to a set of procedures that can be applied to a set of data for the purpose of identifying variables that all reflect some common underlying factor or dimension (Cerezo, 1991:410). Factor analysis is able to detect common patterns in the way subjects respond to questions. However, because factor analysis is nothing but a set of mathematical rules for analyzing data, it offers no cognitive interpretation of the subjective meaning of the questions or of the responses to those questions.

The mathematical principles of factor analysis were initially developed in the early part of the 20th century (Porter, 1986:314; Cerezo, 1991:410). Over the years, several specialized subroutines have been developed for researchers wishing to explore a variety of possible interpretations.

The concept of **factor loading** (or simply **loading**) is central to factor analysis. An individual variable (usually comprised of a particular question) is said to **load** heavily on a particular factor to the degree that the variable correlates with all other variables comprising that particular factor. Factor loadings are expressed by coefficients ranging from +1.00 to −1.00.

To give an example, think back to the discussion in Chapter 7 (p. 88) of how handedness has come to be measured using responses to several items, rather than

Table 17.1 Results of Factor Analysis of Hand Preference Items With All Items Having Factor Loadings of .60 or Higher Shown

	Factor 1	*Factor 2*	*Factor 3*	*Factor 4*
Write	.88			
Throw Ball	.87			
Cut Bread	.85			
Brush Teeth	.85			
Throw Spear	.84			
Sew	.82			
Use Pencil Eraser	.72			
Use Tweezers	.72			
Strike Match	.71			
Manipulate Tool	.70			
Flip Coin	.68			
Pick Up Pen	.60			
Pick Up Piece of Paper		.77		
Pick Up Small Object		.70		
Pick Up Penny		.68		
Pick Up Baseball		.65		
Pick Up a Nut or Washer		.62		
Pet Dog or Cat		.61		
Pick Up Jar		.61		
Pick Up Comb		.60		
Pick Up Briefcase			.69	
Pick Up Heavy Object			.68	
Rest Bat on Shoulder				.73
Rest Axe on Shoulder				.62

Adapted from Steenhuis & Bryden, 1989:297. Reprinted by permission from CORTEX.

simply asking people if they are right- or left-handed. In a recent Canadian study, subjects were asked how often they used either their right or left hand to perform 32 different tasks (Steenhuis & Bryden, 1989). When the results were factor analyzed, they revealed that handedness may be comprised of as many as four distinct factors. Table 17.1 presents the main findings.

The researchers who conducted this study used a stringent arbitrary cutoff point of .60 to separate coefficients that loaded heavily on a particular factor from those that did not. Consequently, 7 of the 32 handedness items are not included in Table 17.1 because they failed to load on any of the four factors at or above the .60 cutoff point. Of the 25 handedness items that loaded on one of these four factors, 12 loaded heavily on the first factor. Take a look at these 12 items, and notice how intuitively they seem to have something in common, especially when compared to the items comprising any of the other three factors.

An important step in factor analysis is for researchers to decide on the most appropriate name to give each factor (something no computer can yet do!). In the case of

Table 17.1, the researchers assigned names to each factor by thinking of words that seemed to epitomize the content of the items loading most strongly on each of the four factors. Here is what the researchers proposed calling the four factors identified in Table 17.1:

Factor 1—The skilled handedness factor
Factor 2—The less skilled handedness factor
Factor 3—The heavy lifting handedness factor
Factor 4—The bimanual activity factor

The fourth factor merits a special comment. The two items comprising this factor were unique in that, unlike their responses to items in the first three factors, subjects reported no hand preferences when performing these two tasks. For this reason, the name "bimanual activity factor" was chosen.

Incidentally, the research team that conducted this study subsequently conducted another study using another Canadian sample to see how stable the factors were. Factor stability is always an important issue in factor analysis. The new study revealed that the same four factors emerged. Although the loadings of each item onto the four factors were not *exactly* the same, they were impressively close, and the same items loaded on each of the four factors (Bryden, MacRae, & Steenhuis, 1991).

It is interesting to compare this study with a handedness study conducted in Brazil, which was also factor analyzed (Brito, et al., 1992). In the Brazilian study, only 10 items were presented to subjects: writing, drawing, throwing, using a scissors, using a toothbrush, using a knife, using a spoon, using a broom, striking a match, and opening a box. Subjects reported on a 5-point scale how often they used their right or left hand in performing each task. Factor analysis revealed that 8 of these items loaded heavily on a single factor, while 2 items failed to load heavily on any factor.

To give you practice in interpreting factor analysis, look back to Table 17.1 and see if you can find the items that are similar to items in the Brazilian study. Now see if you can answer two questions:

(1) Assuming that handedness is essentially the same phenomenon in Brazil that it is in Canada, which of the four factors in the Canadian study do you think turned up as the only factor in the Brazilian study?
(2) Of the 10 items in the Brazilian study, which 2 do you think failed to load onto the single handedness factor that emerged out of that study?

The best way to answer these two questions is to look for items that are the same, or virtually the same, in both the Canadian and Brazilian questionnaires. You should find that (1) most of the items included in the Brazilian study were identical to those which loaded heavily on Factor 1 (the skilled handedness factor), and (2) the two items in the Brazilian study that are most dissimilar to those comprising Factor 1 in the Canadian study are use of the broom and opening a box (Brito et al., 1992:64).

Having a basic understanding of factor analysis is important for two reasons. First, factor analysis has become a widely used statistical tool for helping to develop valid and reliable methods of measuring all types of multi-item scales. Second, in a more general vein, comprehending factor analysis gives you an appreciation of the complexity and tentativeness of scientific efforts to improve the measurement of variables, especially hard-to-measure variables (of which social scientists have more than their fair share!).

One of the most ambitious uses of factor analysis has involved efforts to identify all factors (or dimensions) comprising the human personality. In recent years, several studies have converged on the conclusion that, perhaps worldwide, human personalities may come down to five basic dimensions (Zuckerman et al., 1991; Costa & McCrae, 1992; Hofstee, 1992; McCrae, 1992; Paunonen et al., 1992), although there is still dissension on this point (Eysenck, 1992; McAdams, 1992).

Factor analysis is not just used to classify patterns in the way humans respond to questionnaires. Ethologists in India have used it to identify the number of distinct castes within species of social wasps (Gadagkar & Joshi, 1983, 1984). Over a two-month period, these researchers marked each member of four different wasp colonies with a distinctive harmless paint. Then the researchers painstakingly observed and recorded the frequency with which each wasp exhibited a wide variety of different behavior patterns.

The results from these observations were factor analyzed to look for evidence of task specialization. The factor analysis revealed that the wasps fell neatly into three distinct clusters, or castes (not counting the queen). One caste was called "fighters," because they specialized in patrolling and defending the nest, another was named "sitters," because they devoted an unusual amount of time caring for larvae in the nest, and the third was called "foragers" because their behavior was oriented toward scouting for food or building material and bringing it back to the nest. During the observation period, the researchers were able to document that whenever an old queen died or disappeared, new queens (egg-layers) usually arose from the most dominant members of the fighter caste.

Factor analysis has become a widely used method in the social sciences for helping identify items of information that all measure the same underlying factor. This is not to say that human judgments are eliminated in these classification tasks. Factor analysis programs are incapable of naming the factors, and there are various options within most factor analysis programs that make it possible to expand or reduce the number of factors identified (Tremblay, 1992:196).

Basic Concepts in the Use of Multivariate Statistics for Causal Analysis

Before turning attention to the use of multivariate statistics for identifying cause-and-effect relationships, we need to discuss some additional terminology common to all multivariate statistics. One basic concept is that of a **zero-order** (or **simple**) **correlation matrix.** This matrix consists of an array of correlation coefficients showing how each variable in a data set is associated with all the other variables. Such a matrix is shown in Table 17.2.

Table 17.2 A Zero-Order Correlation Matrix

	A	B	C	D	E	F	G
				Variables			
A	1.00	.07	.43	−.11	−.22	.02	.20
B	.07	1.00	.06	−.04	.06	.24	.32
C	.43	.06	1.00	−.58	.12	.12	.07
D	−.11	−.04	−.58	1.00	.16	.10	−.15
E	−.22	.06	.12	.16	1.00	.30	−.05
F	.02	.24	.12	.10	.30	1.00	.08
G	.20	.32	.07	−.15	−.05	.08	1.00

Without considering what Variables A through G specifically represent, there are two features of Table 17.2 worth noting. First, notice the series of perfect positive (r = 1.00) correlations running diagonally through the matrix. These represent the effect of correlating each variable with itself. (Sometimes these perfect correlations are merely left blank or represented by dashed lines.) Second, notice that these perfect correlations cut the correlation matrix in half, and that the coefficients on the upper right half of the matrix duplicate the coefficients in the lower left half of the matrix. (Because these two halves of a correlation matrix duplicate one another, sometimes only the top right half will be printed.)

From a zero-order correlation matrix, researchers can get a bird's-eye view, so to speak, of which variables are most and least related to one another. Interesting patterns may be detected. For example, the strongest correlation shown in Table 17.2 is between Variables C and D (r = −.58), although the relationship between Variables A and C is also fairly strong (r = .43). If you knew what each of these variables identified, it might be possible to speculate about how they may be causally connected (based on some theory or on their temporal ordering). This often marks the beginning of how researchers go beyond simple comparative correlative studies, and enter the world of multivariate analysis.[1]

Other concepts important in using multivariate statistics for making causal inferences are **statistical control** and **spuriousness.** Statistical control refers to mathematical manipulations which effectively convert a variable into a constant. Although the mathematics involved in statistically controlling variables is fairly complex (and not a matter to be pursued here), the basic principle can be easily illustrated. Let's look at a hypothetical example.

Assume that a researcher working with Table 17.2 suspects that one of the reasons Variables C and D are inversely correlated is that increases in Variable A cause Variable C to rise and Variable D to fall. If this hypothesis is true, holding Variable A constant should cause the inverse correlation between Variables C and D to disappear. Say that Variable A is statistically controlled and the correlation between Variables C and D falls from r = −.58 to r = −.31. This .27 drop in the correlation coefficient means that about 7% of the variance in the correlation between Variables

C and D is explainable in terms of the effects of Variable A on both of these variables (i.e., the square of .27 equals .0729). Some concrete examples of controlling for variables will be cited shortly.

Reflect for a moment on how the concept of statistical control compares with the notion of **experimental control** (as discussed in Chapter 15). Experimental control is usually achieved by randomly assigning subjects to experimental and control groups. Statistical control, on the other hand, is achieved by manipulating numbers after data have been collected. Statistical control should never be thought of as a complete substitute for experimental control when trying to identify cause-and-effect relationships. Nevertheless, statistical control can be helpful when experimental control is not possible.

The term spuriousness refers to correlations that are only coincidental to a more fundamental relationship. Thus, if about half the correlation between Variables C and D are the result of Variable A affecting both of them, researchers would say that much of the relationship between Variables C and D is spurious.

It should be noted that although the term spurious is often used by researchers in an either/or sense, it actually varies along a continuum. Thus the careful researcher will identify degrees of spuriousness, rather than simply saying that a relationship is or is not spurious. Also, just as studies based on multivariate statistics do not prove causation to the degree that experiments do, neither do multivariate statistics prove spuriousness; they merely provide evidence of such.

Two other terms that play a central role in the use of multivariate statistics for causal analysis are **predictor** (or **independent**) **variables** and **criterion** (or **dependent**) **variables.** In this text, the terms predictor and criterion will be used consistently instead of independent and dependent to underscore the nonexperimental nature of studies based on multivariate statistics (for a similar perspective, see Sobel, 1992:665). A predictor variable is a variable that the researcher chooses to treat as a possible cause, and a criterion variable is one that the researcher chooses to treat as a possible effect.

There are a couple of self-evident rules that researchers follow in designating predictor and criterion variables. One is that the criterion variable must always have occurred at a later time than any of the predictor variables. The other rule is that there should be some reasonable explanation for how a predictor variable *could* have caused a criterion variable. Usually, these explanations will be based on a theory that a researcher decides to test.

Let us now consider each of the three main types of multivariate statistics used to help identify cause-and-effect relationships.

Partial Regression

The multivariate statistic called partial regression, partial correlation, or simply partialling attempts to identify cause-and-effect relationships by statistically removing spurious relationships from relationships that are thought to be of a direct causal nature. Computer programs for calculating partial regression usually offer different options for researchers to choose. For example, one option allows a researcher to pick specific control variables that are to be held constant, while other options may automatically hold constant only control variables that correlate with a criterion variable to the greatest degree in the zero-order matrix.

To illustrate partial regression, recall the discussion of arousal theory in Chapter 14 (pp. 207–208). In a nutshell, the theory argues that a lot of behavior can be explained as attempts to maintain a preferred level of arousal. The theory asserts that some people have brains that are suboptimally aroused under "normal" environmental conditions. Such people will prefer levels of environmental stimulation that exceed what most others prefer. These persons, according to the theory, will exhibit behavior patterns that increase the level of stimulation they are receiving, and, in the process, they may irritate others (who prefer lower levels of stimulation). Arousal theory leads to the suspicion that persons who are suboptimally aroused will be drawn to delinquent and criminal behavior to a greater degree than persons in general (Ellis, 1987).

For many years, studies have found a significant inverse relationship between religiosity and the probability of engaging in delinquent and criminal behavior (reviewed by Ellis, 1985:506; Gartner, Larson, & Allen, 1991). These observations, considered in the light of arousal theory, led to a study designed to determine how much of the inverse correlation could be eliminated by partialling out the influence of suboptimal arousal (Ellis & Thompson, 1989). In the study, three types of variables were measured: extent of delinquency and criminality, degree of religiosity, and a measure of boredom susceptibility (operationalized in terms of how boring versus how comforting subjects considered church services).

At the zero-order level, the study confirmed all the previous findings of inverse relationships between most types of criminality and religiosity. However, once the measure of boredom susceptibility was statistically partialled out of the relationships between criminality and religiosity, these relationships dropped substantially. In most cases, they dropped to a point where they were no longer statistically significant (Ellis & Thompson, 1989; also see Cochran, Wood, & Arneklev, 1991). To give an example, the zero-order relationship between illegal drug use and the number of church services attended among males was $r = -.33$ ($p. < .001$). This relationship dropped to $r = -.11$ (no longer statistically significant) once boredom susceptibility was partialled out (Ellis & Thompson, 1989:137).

Overall, this research project suggests (but does not prove) that there may be a neurological explanation for the well-established tendency for persons who are more religious to commit fewer delinquent and criminal acts than persons who are less religious. Specifically, persons who are suboptimally aroused under most normal environmental conditions are more likely to become delinquent and criminal, and are less inclined to attend church services than people in general.

Another example of partial regression comes from a recent analysis of more than one million emergency calls made to the police department in Kansas City, Kansas, between 1986 and 1989 (Walters, 1991). This study found a substantial positive correlation between the daily pollen count (as assessed by an environmental quality agency) and the number of calls that the police department received each day.

However, the daily pollen count was found to be strongly correlated with the daily high temperature. So which of these two variables was actually more responsible for the number of daily calls received by the police?

The researcher discovered that partialling out temperature depressed the pollen count/emergency call relationship more than partialling out pollen count depressed the temperature/emergency call relationship. This supports the view that daily pollen count is largely spurious, and that temperature is probably a more important causal variable.

Is it possible that other variables not measured in the study, such as humidity and amount of daylight, may have been even more influential on calls to police than daily temperature? Of course. In fact, you could conjecture about hundreds of possible variables that were *really* responsible for a correlation. If variables are not measured, there is obviously no way for them to be statistically controlled.

Multiple Regression

Multiple regression refers to statistical procedures in which two or more predictor variables are regressed (or fitted) onto a single criterion variable. Conceptualizing the mathematics that makes this procedure possible requires accepting the idea that scattergrams can be mathematically configured in three, four, or more dimensions (as briefly outlined earlier).

The mathematical principles behind multiple regression are similar to those underlying partial regression. In fact, the same data set can sometimes be analyzed with either of these statistical procedures to arrive at essentially the same conclusions.

The main difference between multiple regression and partial regression is in how they are used. Partial regression is used to eliminate presumed spurious influences of third variables from causal connection between variables of interest. Multiple regression is used to help identify combinations of two or more predictor variables for some specific criterion variable. Often, in the process of identifying the best combination of predictor variables, the confounding effects of spurious relationships are eliminated by controlling certain variables. Another difference is that multiple regression is usually applied to data sets with greater numbers and more diverse types of variables than is the case with partial regression.

An example of multiple regression comes from a series of studies in the United States that have attempted to determine if rape rates can be linked to the sale of sexually-oriented men's magazines (Baron & Straus, 1984, 1989; Scott & Schwalm, 1988). These studies have shown that a substantial positive correlation exists between a state's per capita sales of such magazines and its rape rate. This evidence supports arguments by many feminists that access to pornography is a cause of rape (e.g., Morgan, 1980; Ratterman, 1982; Dworkin, 1985).

Researchers involved in these studies have considered a number of other variables to see if they can explain a state's rape rates separate from per capita purchases of sexually-oriented men's magazines. For example, statistical controls have been introduced for each state's per capita alcohol sales, degree of urbanization, average socioeconomic status and racial composition, and even rates of other types of crime.

Table 17.3 Zero-Order Correlations Among Five Variables

	Sons' First Job Status	Sons' Educ.	Fathers' Occup. St.	Fathers' Educ.
Sons' Current Occup. Status	.54	.60	.41	.32
Sons' First Job Status	—	.54	.42	.33
Sons' Education		—	.44	.45
Fathers' Occup. Status			—	.52
Fathers' Education				—

Adapted from Blau & Duncan, 1967:169.

Per capita sales of "macho" magazines such as *American Rifleman* and *Guns and Ammo,* and even popular magazines such as *National Geographic* and *Newsweek* have also been entered into regression formulas (Scott & Schwalm, 1988; Baron & Straus, 1989:95).

Overall, these studies have concluded that much of the zero-order correlations between rape rates and per capita sales of sexually-explicit men's magazines can be eliminated by controlling for these "extraneous variables," although a significant proportion of the correlation remains. Therefore, much of the zero-order positive correlation between a state's per capita sales of these magazines and its rape rates is probably spurious. Is it possible that the relationship between state rape rates and the availability of sexually-explicit men's magazines can eventually be accounted for entirely by extraneous factors? Time will tell.

Path Analysis

A third major type of multivariate statistics used for detecting cause-and-effect relationships is path analysis. This type of statistical procedure provides a visual model of how variables may be related in a causal chain.

An example of path analysis comes from a classical study undertaken in the 1960s to help identify causes of intergenerational occupational mobility among American males (i.e., upward or downward movement in sons' occupational status compared to their fathers) (Blau & Duncan, 1967). The analysis began with a zero-order correlation matrix showing how "current" occupational status of sons (when the data were collected in 1962) was correlated with such things as the sons' educational levels and occupational status of the sons' first jobs, and with their fathers' occupational status and educational level. This zero-order correlation matrix is shown in Table 17.3.

Notice that all the correlations in Table 17.3 are positive, and that several are of substantial magnitude. Using the sons' current occupational status as the criterion variable, the researchers attempted to determine what predictor variables were most influential. If a judgment were made simply on the basis of which of the four possible predictor variables was most strongly correlated with the sons'

Path coefficients among five variables. (Adapted from Blau & Duncan, 1967:107. Reprinted with the permission of The Free Press, A Division of MacMillan, Inc. from THE AMERICAN OCCUPATIONAL STRUCTURE by Peter M. Blau and Otis Dudley Duncan. Copyright © 1967 by Peter M. Blau and Otis Dudley Duncan.)

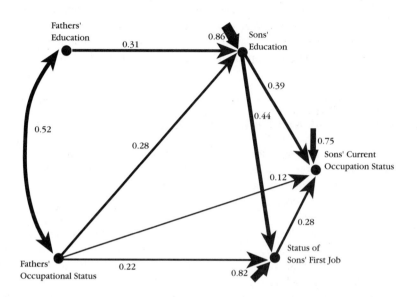

current occupational status, the sons' education would be considered the most important causal factor. Notice that the sons' current occupational status and the sons' years of education correlate quite strongly (r = .60).

The main result of the path analysis is shown in Figure 17.2. Based strictly on the statistical configuration of how these variables were interrelated for each son-father pair, this diagram estimates how the other four variables may impinge on the sons' current job status.

Noteworthy features of the diagram are as follows: Coinciding with the width of each arrow is a path coefficient; the wider the arrow, the larger the path coefficient. Squaring each coefficient provides an estimate of the variance that is explained by the predictor variable labeled at the back of each arrow. The three short arrows represent path coefficients that no variable in the diagram could explain, and squaring these coefficients provides an estimate of what is called the **unexplained variance.**

Overall, this diagram (or model) suggests that, of the predictor variables used in the path regression, the most important influence on current occupational status of males is their own levels of education. Some educational influences appear to be direct, but others seem to be indirect, i.e., mediated via the positive influence that the status of the sons' first jobs had on the status of their current jobs.

Figure 17.2 also suggests that fathers' education and fathers' occupational status influence their sons' current occupational status, mainly via the influence that both these paternal variables have on the sons' education. Nevertheless, it should be emphasized that most of the variance in sons' education and sons' first job status is unexplained, leaving plenty of room for subsequent research attempts to account for more variance in status attainment (e.g., Jencks et al., 1972; Psacharopoulos & Velez, 1992).

This example illustrates the main thrust of path analysis presentation and interpretation. It is important to emphasize that, like all multivariate statistics, path analysis is nonexperimental research and, therefore, cannot be interpreted with the same confidence that is placed in a well-designed experiment involving the same basic variables and a comparable sample size (Gilbert & Kahl, 1987:173).

The Effects of Public versus Parochial Schools on Student Academic Achievement

Having now considered the main types of multivariate statistics used in addressing cause-and-effect questions, let us return to the question posed at the beginning of this chapter: Which type of school promotes greater academic achievement in students, public or parochial schools?

Research undertaken to address this question first appeared in the early 1980s (Coleman, Hoffer, & Kilgore, 1981) and ignited a great deal of controversy (reviewed by Jencks, 1985). The controversy involved not only the nature of the evidence, but also the policy implications (i.e., whether or not government should finance parochial schools).

Recall points made earlier in this chapter: Simple comparative studies have shown that students graduating from parochial schools score higher on standardized tests of academic performance than do students graduating from public schools. Although this is consistent with the idea that parochial schools do a better job of teaching academic skills, there are certainly other explanations. Because rigorous experimental studies are unlikely to ever be undertaken, social scientists have used multiple regression studies instead.

The multiple regression studies have measured numerous potential predictor variables for academic performance of students attending both public and parochial schools. Included are many demographic and family background variables (e.g., parental education and income). Then, researchers have tried various combinations of predictor and control variables to identify which variables account for the greatest variation in academic performance.

Most of the initial studies were conducted by sociologist James C. Coleman and his associates. Their studies indicated that the average difference in academic achievement between students attending public and parochial schools was almost an entire grade level. Although some of the difference was eliminated by controlling for demographic and background variables, about half a grade level remained unexplained (Coleman, Hoffer, & Kilgore, 1981, 1982b, 1982c; Hoffer, Greeley, & Coleman, 1985). Consequently, Coleman and his associates have suggested that parochial schools enhance academic achievement of their students to a greater degree than do public schools.

Several researchers have reanalyzed the same data set that Coleman and his associates used. In doing so, they have identified control variables, not included in Coleman's analyses, that seem to almost completely eliminate the average differences in academic achievement between public and parochial school students (Goldberger & Cain, 1982; McPartland & McDill, 1982; Alexander & Pallas, 1983). An analysis of a completely different data set also suggested that combinations of control variables can explain nearly all the variation in academic performance without concluding that parochial schools provide a more conducive academic learning environment than public schools (Morgan, 1983). Coleman and his supporters have argued that, for various reasons, some of the control variables used in these other studies were inappropriate (Coleman & Hoffer, 1983).

So which conclusion is correct? Unfortunately, the answer still depends on whom you ask. Claims and counterclaims have frequently appeared in the social science literature. Basically, all the studies agree that standardized test scores of students attending parochial schools are higher than those of students attending public schools (for review see Jencks, 1985). But why? Coleman and his associates have argued that significant differences remain in favor of parochial schools even after controlling for all reasonable differences between the types of students attending both types of schools. They attribute most of these differences to the additional discipline and stricter enforcement of attendance policies by parochial schools (Coleman, Hoffer, & Kilgore, 1982a). Additional analyses have led them to attribute beneficial effects to the tendency of parochial schools to direct more students toward academic rather than vocational tracks, and to their tendency to require more homework than most public schools (Hoffer, Greeley, & Coleman, 1985; also see Jensen, 1986). Critics have asserted that, once all the appropriate statistical controls are imposed, the difference in achievement of students attending public and parochial schools is too small to be of any practical significance (Alexander & Pallas, 1985; Willms, 1985).

Of course, this issue is not of interest only to social scientists. As you may know, there is considerable debate in the United States over governmental financing of private education, and much of the debate is being fueled by these very studies (Morgan, 1983:200; Allis, 1991; Edwards & Whitty, 1992). Chapter 20 will examine many other ways that social science research is influencing public policies.

Some Final Comments on Multivariate Statistics Used in Making Causal Inferences

Multivariate statistics are widely utilized in the social sciences for making inferences about cause-and-effect relationships. This is especially true in the disciplines of sociology, political science, and economics, where many theories and hypotheses are difficult to address experimentally.

Despite their widespread use, multivariate statistics remain a source of suspicion and reservation in the minds of many researchers (e.g. see Gordon, 1967; Coser,

1975; Wilson & Herrnstein, 1985:156). The main problem with using multivariate statistics for making causal inferences involves the way extraneous variables are controlled. It is impossible to statistically control for all the variables that might be confounding a relationship of interest simply because not all variables can be measured (Frankfort-Nachmias & Nachmias, 1992:417). Although it is true that experimental research can also be misleading, trying to find causes based on even the best multivariate statistics is problematic. Nevertheless, multivariate statistical studies of causal relationship are certainly better than merely guessing about causation, and have definite advantages over interpreting correlations between two variables without any statistical controls.

The focus of this chapter has been on the logical reasoning and basic terminology underlying the use of multivariate statistics in social science research. If you are interested in the mathematical formulas and resulting output, consult some of the suggested readings at the end of this chapter.

Finally, it needs to be mentioned that, despite the fact that studies involving multivariate statistics are normally considered a substitute for experimental research, at times multivariate statistics are actually employed in the analysis of experimental data. This, however, is not common, and is beyond the scope of this text.

Summary

This chapter has focused on the use of multivariate statistics in social science research. These statistics are used to investigate how three or more variables are all interrelated, rather than to simply consider two variables at a time. Despite their mathematical complexity, the basic principles underlying multivariate statistics are fairly easy to understand.

Most multivariate statistics can be classified into one of four categories: factor analysis, partial regression, multiple regression, and path analysis. Factor analysis is a type of statistic used to reduce large numbers of variables (such as items on a questionnaire) down to smaller numbers of factors. This reduction made possible by the development of mathematical formulas and procedures that detect patterns in the way subjects respond to various items and assign a coefficient to each item on the basis of how closely it epitomizes an underlying factor.

The other three multivariate statistics are used to identify possible causal relationships between variables in the absence of experimental evidence. Terms common to these three statistics are zero-order (or simple) correlation matrix, control variables and spuriousness, predictor (independent) variables, and criterion (dependent) variables.

A zero-order correlation matrix arrays all the correlation coefficients derived from a data set into a table in order to give researchers a bird's-eye view of all possible two-variable combinations. Control variables are ones that are mathematically converted into constants (i.e., are held constant) in a multivariate statistical calculation. Spuriousness refers to zero-order correlations between two variables that are at least partly "explained away" by holding one or more third variables constant.

Predictor (or independent) variables in studies involving multivariate statistics are ones that are treated as causal variables by a researcher, and criterion (or dependent) variables are those that a researcher treats as effect variables.

Partial regression involves refining zero-order correlations by eliminating variables thought to be confounding a causal relationship. With multiple regression, researchers identify two or more predictor variables that can be regressed onto a criterion variable, often while holding other variables constant. Path analysis has been developed to help researchers construct models that show how variables within a data set may be mathematically woven into a series of cause-and-effect relationships.

Even though studies based on multiple regression tend to be more complex from a mathematical standpoint than studies utilizing experimental designs, you should not interpret the greater mathematical complexity as suggesting that the findings warrant greater confidence than much simpler experimental designs. Nevertheless, multiple regression studies have become an extremely valuable addition to the arsenal of statistical tools used in social science research.

Notes

[1] It should be noted that variables comprising a correlation matrix may not have been measured appropriately for the application of Pearson correlation (the most common method used to derive a zero-order correlation matrix). Many computer programs with multivariate statistical capabilities are programmed to adjust for variables with restricted value ranges (called **dummy variables**), and still compute fairly meaningful correlation coefficients. For an example of a recent study that utilized dummy variables in its analysis, see Tang & Tzeng (1992:166).

References

Alexander, K. L., & Pallas, A. M. (1983). Private schools and public policy: New evidence on cognitive achievement in public and private schools. *Sociology of Education, 56,* 170–182.

Alexander, K. L., & Pallas, A. M. (1985). School sector and cognitive performance: When is a little a little? *Sociology of Education, 58,* 115–128.

Allis, S. (1991, May 27). Can Catholic schools do it better? *Time,* pp. 48–49.

Baron, R. A., & Straus, M. A. (1984). Sexual stratification, pornography, and rape in the United States. In N. M. Malamuth & E. Donnerstein (Eds.), *Pornography and sexual aggression* (pp. 185–209). New York: Academic Press.

Baron, R. A., & Straus, M. A. (1989). *Four theories of rape.* New Haven, CT: Yale University Press.

Blau, P. M., & Duncan, O. D. (1967). *The American occupational structure.* New York: Wiley.

Brito, G. N. O., Lins, M. F. C., Paumgartten, F. J. R., & Brito, L. S. O. (1992). Hand preference in 4- and 7-year-old children: An analysis with the Edinburgh inventory in Brazil. *Developmental Neuropsychology, 8,* 59–68.

Bryden, M. P., MacRae, L., & Steenhuis, R. E. (1991). Hand preference in school children. *Developmental Neuropsychology, 7,* 477–486.

Cerezo, J. A. L. (1991). Human nature as social order: A hundred years of psychometrics. *Journal of Social and Biological Structures, 14,* 409–434.

Cochran, J., Wood, P. B., & Arneklev, B. J. (1991, November). Is the religiosity-delinquency relationship spurious?: A test of arousal and social control theories. Paper presented at the convention of the American Society of Criminology, San Francisco.

Coleman, J. S., & Hoffer, T. (1983). Response to Taeuber-James, Cain-Goldberger and Morgan. *Sociology of Education, 56,* 219–234.

Coleman, J. S., Hoffer, T., & Kilgore, S. (1981). *Public and private schools.* Chicago: National Opinion Research Center.

Coleman, J. S., Hoffer, T., & Kilgore, S. (1982a). Cognitive outcomes in public and private schools. *Sociology of Education, 55,* 65–76.

Coleman, J. S., Hoffer, T., & Kilgore, S. (1982b). Achievement and segregation in secondary schools: A further look at public and private school differences. *Sociology of Education, 55,* 162–182.

Coleman, J. S., Hoffer, T., & Kilgore, S. (1982c). *High school achievement.* New York: Basic.

Coser, L. (1975). Two methods in search of a substance. *American Sociological Review, 40,* 691–700.

Costa, P. T., Jr., & McCrae, R. R. (1992). Four ways five factors are basic. *Personality and Individual Differences, 13,* 653–665.

Dworkin, A. (1985). Against the male flood: Censorship, pornography, and equality. *Harvard Women's Law Journal, 8,* 1–29.

Edwards, T., & Whitty, G. (1992). Parental choice and educational reform in Britain and the United States. *British Journal of Educational Studies, 40,* 101–117.

Ellis, L. (1985). Religiosity and criminality: Evidence and explanations surrounding complex relationships. *Sociological Perspective, 28,* 501–520.

Ellis, L. (1987). Religiosity and criminality from the perspective of arousal theory. *Journal of Research on Crime and Delinquency, 24,* 215–232.

Ellis, L., & Thompson, R. (1989). Relating religion, crime, arousal, and boredom. *Sociology and Social Research, 73,* 132–139.

Engel, U., & Hurrelmann, K. (1989). Delinquent behavior in adolescence: Potential and constraints of preventive strategies in school settings. In P. A. Albrecht and O. Backes (Eds.), *Crime prevention and intervention: Legal and ethical issues* (pp. 167–184). Berlin: Walter de Gruyter.

Eysenck, H. J. (1992). A reply to Costa and McCrae: P or A and C—the role of theory. *Personality and Individual Differences, 13,* 867–868.

Frankfort-Nachmias, C., & Nachmias, D. (1992). *Research methods in the social sciences,* (4th ed.). New York: St. Martin's Press.

Gadagkar, R., & Joshi, N. V. (1983). Quantitative ethology of social wasps: Time-activity budgets and caste differentiation in *Ropalidia Marginata* (Hymenoptera: Vespidae). *Animal Behavior, 31,* 26–31.

Gadagkar, R., & Joshi, N. V. (1984). Social organization in the Indian wasp *Ropalidia cyathiformis* (Hymenoptera: Vespidae). *Zeitschrift fur Tierpsychologie, 64,* 15–32.

Games, P. A. (1990). Correlation and causation: A logical snafu. *Journal of Experimental Education, 58,* 239–246.

Gartner, J., Larson, D. B., & Allen, G. D. (1991). Religious commitment and mental health: A review of the empirical literature. *Journal of Psychology and Theology, 19,* 6–25.

Gilbert, D., & Kahl, J. A. (1987). *The American class structure,* (3rd ed.). Chicago: Dorsey Press.

Goldberger, A. S., & Cain, G. G. (1982). The causal analysis of cognitive outcomes in the Coleman, Hoffer and Kilgore report. *Sociology of Education, 55,* 103–122.

Gordon, R. A. (1967). Values in the ecological study of delinquency. *American Sociological Review, 32,* 927–944.

Heyne, B., & Hilton, T. L. (1982). The cognitive tests for high school and beyond: An assessment. *Sociology of Education, 55,* 89–102.

Hoffer, T., Greeley, A. M., & Coleman, J. S. (1985). Achievement growth in public and Catholic schools. *Sociology of Education, 58,* 74–97.

Hofstee, W. K. B. (1992). Integration of the big-5 and circumplex approaches to trait structure. *Journal of Personality and Social Psychology, 63,* 146–163.

Hollifield, J. (1983, December). Private lessons. *Psychology Today,* p. 18.

Jencks, C. (1985). How much do high school students learn? *Sociology of Education, 58,* 128–135.

Jencks, C., Smith, M., Acland, H., Bane, D. C., Gintis, H., Heyns, B., & Michelson, S. (1972). *Inequality: A reassessment of family and schooling in America.* New York: Basic Books.

Jensen, G. F. (1986). Explaining differences in academic behavior between public-school and Catholic-school students: A quantitative case study. *Sociology of Education, 59,* 32–41.

Jolly, C. J., & Plog, F. (1976). *Physical anthropology and archaeology.* New York: Alfred A. Knopf.

Kerlinger, F. N. (1964). *Foundations of behavioral research.* New York: Holt, Rinehart & Winston.

McAdams, D. P. (1992). The 5-factor model in personality—A critical appraisal. *Journal of Personality, 60,* 329–361.

McCrae, R. R. (1992). An introduction to the 5-factor model and its applications. *Journal of Personality, 60,* 175–215.

McPartland, J. M., & McDill, E. L. (1982). Control and differentiation in the structure of American education. *Sociology of Education, 55,* 77–88.

Morgan, R. (1980). Theory and practice: Pornography and rape. In L. Lederer (Ed.), *Take back the night: Women on pornography* (pp. 134–140). New York: William Morrow.

Morgan, W. R. (1983). Learning and student life quality of public and private school youth. *Sociology of Education, 56,* 187–202.

Paunonen, S. V., Jackson, D. N., Trzebinski, J., & Forsterling, F. (1992). Personality structure across cultures: A multimethod evaluation. *Journal of Personality and Social Psychology, 62,* 447–456.

Porter, T. M. (1986). *The rise of statistical thinking, 1820–1900.* Princeton, NJ: Princeton University Press.

Psacharopoulos, G., & Velez, E. (1992). Schooling, ability, and earnings in Columbia, 1988. *Economic Development and Cultural Change, 40,* 629–643.

Ratterman, D. (1982, August). Pornography: The spectrum of harm. *Aegis,* pp. 42–52.

Scott, J. E., & Schwalm, L. A. (1988). Rape rates and the circulation rates of adult magazines. *Journal of Sex Research, 24,* 241–250.

Sobel, M. E. (1992). The American occupational structure and structural equation modeling in sociology. *Contemporary Sociology, 21,* 662–666.

Spearman, C. E. (1927). *The ability of man.* New York: Macmillan.

Steenhuis, R. E., & Bryden, M. P. (1989). Different dimensions of hand preference that relate to skilled and unskilled activities. *Cortex, 25,* 289–304.

Tang, T. L., & Tzeng, J. Y. (1992). Demographic correlates of the Protestant work ethic. *Journal of Psychology, 126,* 163–170.

Tremblay, R. E. (1992). The prediction of delinquent behavior from childhood behavior: Personality theory revisited. In J. McCord (Ed.), *Facts, frameworks and forecasts* (pp. 193–230). Brunswick, NJ: Transactions.

Walters, G. D. (1991). Examining the relationship between airborne pollen levels and 911 calls for assistance. *International Journal of Offender Therapy and Comparative Criminology, 35,* 162–166.

Willms, J. D. (1985). Catholic-school effects on academic achievement: New evidence from the high school and beyond follow-up study. *Sociology of Education, 58,* 98–114.

Wilson, J. Q., & Herrnstein, R. J. (1985). *Crime and human nature.* New York: Simon & Schuster.

Young, D. J., & Fraser, B. J. (1990). Science achievement of girls in single-sex and co-educational schools. *Research in Science & Technological Education, 8,* 5–20.

Zuckerman, M., Kuhlman, D. M., Thornquist, M., & Kiers, H. (1991). Five (or three) robust questionnaire scale factors of personality without culture. *Personality and Individual Differences, 12,* 929–941.

Suggested Reading

Aiken, L. S., & West, S. G. (1991). *Testing and interpreting interactions in multiple regression.* Beverly Hills, CA: Sage.

Bennett, S., & Bowers, D. (1976). *An introduction to multivariate techniques for social and behavioral sciences.* New York: Wiley.

Cohen, J., & Cohen, P. (1975). *Applied multiple regression/correlation analysis for behavioral sciences.* New York: Wiley.

Harman, H. H. (1976). *Modern factor analysis* (3rd. ed. rev.). Chicago: University of Chicago Press. (A well written book on how to conduct factor analysis and interpret statistical output from computerized factor analysis programs.)

Namboodiri, N. K., Carter, L. E., & Blalock, H. M., Jr. (1975). *Applied multivariate analysis and experimental designs.* New York: McGraw-Hill.

Pedhazur, E. J. (1982). *Multiple regression in behavioral research.* New York: Holt, Reinhart, & Winston.

CHAPTER 18

Ethical Issues in the Social Sciences, I: Responsibilities to Subjects and to Fellow Social Scientists

If someone revealed in the course of an interview that he or she had committed a crime, is the researcher ethically obliged to keep that information confidential or legally bound to report it? Can social scientists ever justify deceiving subjects or causing them to become emotionally upset in order to advance scientific knowledge? If so, who makes that decision? Do social scientists ever lie about their research findings? What happens if they do?

The above questions reflect issues that this chapter will address. You will see that they are difficult questions in that many of the "answers" are only guidelines rather than ironclad rules. Nevertheless, it is important for students interested in social science research to be aware of the issues, and know what precedents have been set.

The topics to be discussed have been organized under two major headings. The first has to do with how subjects in a study are to be treated. The second pertains to how researchers should relate to one another professionally.

Social Scientists' Ethical Responsibilities to Their Subjects

There are certain long-standing ethical principles to which social scientists have always been bound regarding how they should treat human subjects. Other ethical and even legal responsibilities have only recently been instituted.

In this section, the following topics will be considered: (a) confidentiality of data, (b) informed consent, (c) deception and harm to human subjects, (d) how decisions are made about what is and is not permissible in research with human subjects, and (e) humane treatment of nonhuman animal subjects.

Confidentiality of Social Science Data

Confidentiality refers to the assurance given by a researcher to not reveal the identity of persons who provide research information. Such assurances are generally considered morally equivalent to the assurances that newspaper and television reporters make to not disclose the identity of their sources without permission. It is also similar to the confidentiality to which physicians, ministers, and professional counselors are bound in their relationships with clients.

As discussed earlier (p. 192), a special type of confidentiality is called anonymity. It refers to the practice of not asking for any information that would reveal the identity of specific subjects. Anonymity is most easily assured with questionnaires completed by subjects, as opposed to information obtained by direct observation or an interview. Assurances of both confidentiality and anonymity should not be made by a researcher unless he or she intends to abide by those commitments.

In spite of the clear moral commitment researchers have to abide by assurances of confidentiality, in fact, the legality of such assurances has never been fully tested in court. Therefore, if subjects are being asked to report information that could be used in a court of law, they should be so informed of that risk (Frankfort-Nachmias & Nachmias, 1992:87).

Despite the above caveat, there appears to have never been an instance in which a social scientist's data has been successfully subpoenaed for the purpose of criminal prosecution of a research subject. There was, however, a recent subpoena issued on behalf of a cigarette manufacturer for data from a social science study of children's responses to cigarette billboard advertisements (DiFranza et al., 1991). This investigation had to do with charges of fraud against the researchers, not charges of illegality against the subjects in the study (Barinaga, 1992). (Scientific fraud will be discussed as a separate issue later in this chapter.)

In order to maintain the confidentiality of data, the following procedures should be followed: First, keep all data under lock and key, and restrict access to original data to a minimum number of trusted research associates. Second, although it is sometimes necessary to know the names of subjects while data are being collected, afterward it is often no longer necessary. Therefore, as soon as possible, permanently detach the names of all subjects from the data records, destroy the names, and use arbitrary numbers for identifying each record (Riecken & Boruch, 1979:258).

Some types of marketing research present special problems from the standpoint of confidentiality. For example, in focus group research (see p. 125), subjects are often videotaped, and it is common to play back segments of those tapes for clients interested in the results. Detailed ethical codes are still being worked out to accommodate these and related ethical issues (Robson, 1991).

Informed Consent

In most countries, **informed consent** is now legally required of all research projects involving human subjects. It entails letting prospective subjects know the basic purpose of a study, and then obtaining their permission to be involved (with the understanding that they are free to withdraw at any time). The only exception to this requirement would be persons who are unwitting subjects in direct observations (e.g., observing seat belt usage by passing motorists).

Informed consent is either explicit (i.e., in written form), or implicit (i.e., by subjects' taking and returning a completed questionnaire). Implicit informed consent is mainly acceptable when persons are asked to complete and return an anonymous questionnaire.

As will be discussed more in the following section, informed consent does not mean that subjects must be told everything that they will experience in a study. Rather, they must be given sufficient information about the study so as to make an intelligent decision about whether to become involved.

The concept of informed consent clearly implies that participation in a study is not coerced. However, such an implication is difficult to avoid in some cases, especially in captive populations such as prisons. Imagine that you needed a pool of subjects to test the effectiveness of a new treatment program. You would be implicitly coercing prisoners to be subjects in the study if there was even a possibility that they could be released earlier than those who chose not to participate in the study (see Greenland, 1988).

Deceiving or Causing Harm to Human Subjects

The concepts of deceiving and causing harm to subjects are often closely related, especially in the social sciences. The first refers to any misinformation that is intentionally given to subjects about the study in which they will be involved. The second concept covers any physical or emotional discomfort that subjects may experience as a result of their taking part in a study. Most harm experienced by subjects in social science research is of an emotional rather than of a physical nature.

To give a clear example, experiments undertaken by Stanley Milgram in the late 1960s involved both deception and harm (see p. 138). Subjects were led to believe that they controlled an apparatus for inflicting electric shock onto other ''subjects'' (actually confederates of the study). Then, the subjects were instructed to inflict increasing levels of shock, ostensibly to punish subjects for inaccurate recall of a list of nonsense words. Since these experiments were really undertaken to determine the conditions under which people would follow orders to hurt others, the research was very deceptive. Most of the subjects experienced considerable emotional distress, especially when they were instructed to inflict shock at levels that were in the ''danger'' zone of the gages they controlled (Milgram, 1963:375).

There are many other examples of deception and/or the induction of emotional harm. These include studies which have exposed subjects to gruesome photographs, pressured them to lie or cheat, falsely told them that they possessed undesirable personality traits or that they failed a basic competency test, or led them to believe that an emergency had just occurred (e.g., someone collapsed or a fight broke out in front of them) (Neuman, 1991:442).

Examples of deception and induced harm in social science research are most common in experimental research (discussed in Chapter 15). Few survey-type studies involve deception or the risk of emotional harm to subjects. The only exception are surveys in which subjects are asked to reveal information about their own sexual and/or illegal behavior. In these surveys, subjects must be clearly forewarned of the nature of the questions and of their right to not answer any questions they choose. More will be said about studies of intimate sexual behavior in Chapter 19.

Much of the deception used in social science research only lasts as long as the subject's participation in the study. At the end of their participation, the subjects are **debriefed,** i.e., informed of the true nature of the study. Debriefing sessions are considered important in research to remove any long-term adverse effects caused by the involvement in certain studies. For example, a number of experiments were carried out in the 1980s to look for evidence of males becoming more sexually aggressive after viewing various types of pornographic films (e.g., Malamuth & Check, 1981, 1983, 1985; Donnerstein, Linz, & Penrod, 1987; Zillman & Bryant, 1984). Consequently, most researchers who conduct experiments in which these films are shown make sure that all subjects are carefully debriefed afterward. Follow-up evaluations of these sessions have indicated that they are effective in eliminating possible long-term adverse effects of certain pornographic film exposure (reviewed by Malamuth & Check, 1984; Ellis, 1989:34).

Two extreme positions have been taken on the issue of whether social scientists should be allowed to deceive (and, in the process, sometimes emotionally harm) subjects. One position has been that deceptive research should be banned (Baumrind, 1964, 1971; Warwick, 1974, 1975:105). Those who advocate this view defend it by noting that subjects who agree to participate in a social science study have a fundamental right to assume that they will not be tricked, humiliated, or emotionally traumatized.

The second position is that deception and at least small risks of emotional harm to subjects can be justified if the knowledge to be gained is sufficient, and there is no other way to obtain the knowledge (Milgram, 1964; Schlenker & Forsyth, 1977; Forsyth, 1991). For example, if by causing some emotional discomfort to people, you could discover a way to prevent certain types of crime, most would probably regard the trade-off justified. This position has been adopted by most committees who have drafted guidelines for social science research (e.g., Report of the APA, 1990).

Oftentimes, the deception only involves withholding details regarding the purpose of a study and not actually telling subjects anything that is untrue. For example, in one of the cross-over experiments described in Chapter 15 (p. 229), male subjects were told that the purpose was to study how the act of talking produced ''chemical changes in saliva.'' What they were not told was that researchers were specifically interested in knowing whether or not talking to an attractive, flirtatious female (a confederate of the experiment) caused an elevation in male testosterone levels in saliva (Dabbs, Ruback, & Besch, 1987). While the subjects could have been more precisely informed about the purpose of the study, doing so may have altered the outcome (since subjects would then be aware that the flirtatious behavior was not genuine). Usually, if subjects are given only general, but still accurate, information about the purpose of a study and there is no significant risk of emotional or physical harm, the study would not be considered unethical, especially if subjects are debriefed at the end of their participation.

Most social science codes of ethics do not close the door on the use of deception and harm to subjects, but more restrictions are placed on researchers now than, say, thirty years ago. The main reason is that researchers no longer make decisions on their own about whether studies are ethical. As discussed in the following section, most countries have established committees that oversee scientific research involving human subjects.

Decision-Making Process Regarding the Ethical Acceptability of a Proposed Research Project

For most of the time that social science research has been conducted, all ethical decisions were at the discretion of the researchers involved. During the 1960s, however, leading associations of social scientists began formalizing basic guidelines for professional ethics. Included were ethics surrounding informed consent and deception and risking harm to research subjects.

By the 1970s, public attention in several Western countries was drawn to various ethically questionable research practices, and pressure mounted for governmental intervention, especially in the United States. This prompted most professional social science organizations to formalize ethical guidelines and to establish enforcement procedures (Green, 1971).

Also in the 1970s, the United States government issued regulations concerning ethical treatment of subjects in scientific research. Most far-reaching were federal regulations requiring that all institutions receiving federal research funds (primarily universities and hospitals) maintain a committee to oversee all research involving human subjects. These committees are called **Institutional Review Boards for the Protection of Human Subjects** (IRBs). In Britain and its commonwealths, they are called Research Ethics Committees (RECs) (McNeill, Berglund, & Webster, 1992:317). These committees must review and approve most research involving human subjects before the projects can be undertaken, especially if any federal funding is involved.

The regulations surrounding the functioning of IRBs are too complex to describe in any detail here. However, you should be familiar with a few of the most basic procedures. Before a researcher can conduct a study, a written proposal must be submitted to the IRB at the institution where the researcher works. IRBs usually have five members and meet periodically to consider applications. Their major focus is not on the technical or theoretical merits of each proposed study, but on the ethical and legal issues surrounding it.

IRBs seek assurance that any deception or risk of physical or emotional harm to human subjects can be explicitly justified. IRBs also assess the adequacies of the research procedures and facilities for keeping data confidential.

It is unlikely that much of the research conducted prior to the 1970s would be permitted today. In particular, Milgram's (1963, 1974) studies probably would not be given IRB approval. Not only would the deception of subjects be of concern to the committee members, but the stress placed on subjects would have been considered excessive for the amount of knowledge gained.

Another example of studies that are not routinely approved today are the bogus pipeline experiments. Recall that these studies tricked subjects into believing that a new brain-wave method to detect lying had been developed. Thus, subjects were intimidated into answering truthfully about their feelings on a variety of very sensitive issues, e.g., their attitudes toward various minority groups (pp. 192–193).

Humane Treatment of Animals

Should our sense of morality be extended to the way we treat other animals or be limited only to human beings? This is a question with a long philosophical history (Rollin, 1981; Lansdell, 1988; Rowan, 1991:284) that certainly cannot be fully explored here. It is relevant to note that other animals (especially mammals) appear to be just as sensitive to pain and even emotional distress as are humans (Pollock, 1961; Averill, 1968; Maple, 1979:41; Gould, 1982:484; Dewsbury, 1984:39). If so, can we humans morally justify doing things that cause other creatures to suffer in order to advance our own scientific knowledge?

Numerous instances of cruelty to laboratory animals have been documented in recent years (Rollin, 1981; Jasper & Nelkin, 1991). In one series of experiments, the nerves to both arms of two rhesus monkeys were severed. This caused them to bite and scratch their useless appendages, and resulted in chronic infections for years until the animals were finally killed (Anonymous, 1991b).

Obviously, it is not possible to take all the same steps to ensure ethical treatment of nonhuman subjects as are now being taken with human subjects (e.g., assuring confidentiality, informed consent). Nevertheless, many in the scientific community believe that more measures are needed to prevent emotional and physical trauma to laboratory animals.

Consider the following experiment: Four rhesus monkeys were strapped into a chair and physically restrained to assess their responses to stress (Norman & Smith, 1992:406). The researchers reported that ''Except for a period of disorientation lasting about 10–15 min[utes] while emerging from the anesthetic, the animals struggled only occasionally against the confinement during the 6-hour period of restraint.'' Despite the minimal struggle, the release of various hormones by these monkeys suggested that they experienced dramatic emotional stress due to the prolonged restraint. Can the knowledge gained from this type of research justify putting the animals through such an ordeal? Scientists are not of one mind on this question.

In the United States, universities and hospitals where studies of laboratory animals are conducted now must obtain approval for their research from committees that are similar to IRBs. The committees that oversee animal research are commonly called **Institutional Animal Care and Use Committees** (IACUCs). Members of these committees are required to scrutinize each proposed study to ensure that the animals are subjected to minimal pain and injury. If significant pain or injury is involved, it must be justified in terms of the knowledge to be gained. These are obviously rather loose guidelines, but the alternative is to either allow any type of animal experimentation that individual researchers decide to perform or to ban it altogether.

Social Scientists' Ethical Responsibilities to One Another

This section is about ethical issues pertaining to how social scientists relate to one another (rather than to their subjects). Specifically, the following topics will be addressed: (a) types of scientific fraud, (b) some examples of known or suspected cases of fraud in the social sciences, (c) ways of keeping scientific fraud at a minimum, and (d) obtaining, for the purpose of verification, data that someone else has collected.

Types of Scientific Fraud

In science, fraud refers to intentional misrepresentation of scientific ideas or findings. Scientific fraud can be subsumed under two categories: (a) plagiarism, and (b) intentional misrepresentation of one's research findings.

Plagiarism

Intentionally representing someone else's writings or ideas as your own is called **plagiarism.** It comes in three forms. The most common form is copying passages from an article or book without crediting the original author. This type of plagiarism is clear-cut to document, although the dividing line between plagiarism and "liberally paraphrasing" a sentence or two is sometimes fuzzy.

The other two forms of plagiarism are **ghostwriting,** and **piggybacking.** While ghostwriting is said to be common in the authorship of popular books (such as autobiographies by celebrities), it is considered unethical in professional writings (including student papers, theses, and dissertations). Attempts have been made in the United States to shut down companies that sell their services as ghostwriters, especially those catering to academic markets. However, these efforts have been viewed as conflicting with First Amendment guarantees of free speech (Etzioni, 1976).

Piggybacking is including, as the author of a publication, someone who made no significant contribution to the document. It often happens when a subordinate is pressured by someone in authority into including his or her name on a manuscript undeservedly (e.g., see Goodyear, Crego, & Johnson, 1992). Guidelines were recently proposed about who should be listed as authors of a scientific publication (Culliton, 1988a). Although there are many ways of contributing to a scientific publication that justify being listed as an author, usually there should be some active participation in formulating the methodology, in analyzing the results, or in writing the actual report.

Plagiarism has damaged the careers of otherwise reputable social scientists (D'Antonio, 1989; Blum, 1989). Other respected public figures have also had their reputations and accomplishments forever tarnished because of plagiarism (Broad, 1980; Broad & Wade, 1982:57; Coughlin, 1991).

To avoid plagiarizing, never use the exact phrase of another writer without doing the following: In the case of a phrase or sentence or two, place quotation marks around the quoted passage. If several sentences are being quoted, the passage should be indented. Even sentences that contain close paraphrasing of someone else's words should be avoided unless that person is explicitly given credit. (To properly cite passages taken from others, see pages 82–84.)

Intentional Fabrication of Research Findings

The most difficult-to-prove type of fraud is that in which a researcher lies about what he or she found in a study. This type of fraud can be very destructive to the scientific method because it may take decades to determine that a particular finding was in error.

There appear to be two main reasons why someone would intentionally misrepresent his or her research findings (Wilson, 1991). First, most scientists are highly motivated people and would like to make an important contribution to their field. In addition, scientists who conduct and publish research are encouraged to do so by their employing institutions because the reputations of most universities and hospitals depend heavily on research excellence. Basically, the more and the better the research, the more grants an institution is likely to receive.

At some universities and hospitals, competition for grants and other indicators of "research excellence" are exceedingly intense; these have come to be known as "publish or perish" institutions (Sapp, 1990). The pressure to publish is nearly always more intense for new researchers than for those who have already established a substantial track record. It has been suggested that this is why most persons convicted of science fraud have been relatively young researchers (Smith, 1985:1292).

The second reason for scientific fraud is that the likelihood of being caught, especially for minor fraud, is probably extremely low. Although it may never be proven, some have estimated that for every serious case of scientific fraud, there may be a thousand minor instances (Broad & Wade, 1982). Minor fraud would include researchers changing a few numbers in a data set to push a "not quite significant" finding over the .05 level, or "conveniently omitting" findings that were inconsistent with one's theory (or political ideology). Ninety-two percent of readers of an English general science magazine, responding to an anonymous survey, said they were personally aware of at least one instance of cheating in science (St. James-Roberts, 1976).

"Surely you were aware when you accepted the position, Professor, that it was publish or perish."

Current Contents © 1990 by ISI®

Examples of Fraud, or Possible Fraud, in the Social Sciences

Before considering some of the most famous cases of social science fraud, three general comments are in order. First, charges of fraud can be easily made. However, they are not only not always true, but sometimes not even warranted by evidence. Consider the assertion that Gregor Mendel, the 19th century founder of modern genetics, faked some of his findings (see Bauer, 1992:105). The basis for this charge was the almost perfect correspondence between what he predicted theoretically and what he observed. Some considered the fit "just too good—a 10,000 to 1 shot" (Silberner, 1982:40; also see Broad & Wade, 1982:227). Because Mendel's basic theory has been upheld by others, and because there is no way for Mendel to ever respond to the charge, it is unfair to take seriously the suggestion that he fabricated his data.

Second, fraud does not appear to be as significant a problem in social science as in other fields. The majority of well-documented instances of scientific fraud have involved the fields of biology and medicine (e.g., Golden, 1981; Begley, 1982; Broad & Wade, 1982:225; Culliton, 1983a, 1983b; Wallis, 1983; Vaux & Schade, 1988; Dong, 1991; Elmer-DeWitt, 1991; Marshall, 1991; Roberts, 1991). Whereas this could be interpreted as meaning that fraud is comparatively uncommon in the social sciences, it could also reflect the less tangible nature of what is studied in social science compared to biology and medicine.

Third, although the serious nature of scientific fraud is hard to exaggerate, the fact that all observations are open to verification by others means that a fraudulent report will not permanently derail efforts to arrive at the truth (Silberner, 1982:41). Recall the discussion in Chapter 1 of verifiability as a key feature of the scientific method (p. 10). Erroneous information (whether intended or accidental) may slow down the accumulation of scientific knowledge, but it does not stop it.

The Piltdown Skull Hoax

The most famous example of scientific fraud ever perpetrated is on the periphery of social science because it involves physical anthropology rather than cultural anthropology. In 1911, a human-like fossil was supposedly found in an English gravel pit. The brain case was within range of modern humans, but the jaw bone was ape-like, lacking the distinctive chin crease that only modern humans have (Campbell, 1985:273). For a number of years, this specimen was believed by many anthropologists to be an important "missing link" in the line of creatures leading to contemporary humans (Feder & Park, 1989:128; Thomson, 1991:196). Today it is universally recognized as a human cranium pieced together with a jaw fragment from an orangutan, with both fragments cleverly stained to appear ancient (Stein & Rowe, 1982:317; Spencer, 1990).

Proof that the Piltdown "discovery" was a hoax came in the 1950s from two sources (Weiner, 1955; Blinderman, 1986). First, microscopic inspection revealed metal file scratches on some of the teeth. Second, a series of carbon-14 tests showed that the skeletal fragments came from individuals who died quite recently (Stein & Rowe, 1982:318; Spencer, 1990).

The Tasiday Hoax

Another example of fraud involved the purported discovery of a stone age tribe in the Philippine Islands (Anonymous, 1971; Nancy, 1975). The people supposedly had no contact with the outside world or knowledge of agriculture. Reports (complete with photographs) suggested that they still lived in shallow caves, and were perhaps the only remaining example of uncontaminated stone age people living in the 20th century.

In 1986, a skeptical Swiss journalist went to the island, and found that the caves had never been occupied by humans, certainly not in recent times (Marshall, 1989:1113). What appears to have happened is that some of the local farmers were coaxed or bribed into staging a "stone age" life-style, probably by government officials (Begley & Seward, 1986; Marshall, 1989:1114). Although social scientists were not to blame for this particular instance of fraud, many of them certainly were taken in by it.

Charges Against Cyril Burt

Thus far, the most widely publicized charges against a social scientist for fraud have been made against an early 20th century English psychologist, Cyril Burt. A few years after his death, charges began to surface that he had fabricated some of his data (Kamin, 1974; Dorfman, 1978; Hawkes, 1979; Hearnshaw, 1979). Fueling these charges was dispute over some of the conclusions of Burt's research. In particular, Burt hypothesized that genetic factors had important influences on human intelligence. Although this hypothesis remains controversial from the standpoint of its implications, both twin and adoption studies strongly support the hypothesis (Hattie, 1991:272; Thompson, Detterman, & Plomin, 1991; Eysenck, 1992:753).

Even though Burt's basic hypothesis about the importance of genetics on human intelligence appears accurate, several scientists have alleged that some of his data is bogus. In addition, suspicions have been raised that he published defenses of his work under fictitious names, and that he substantially distorted summaries of research findings by some of his former students (Fletcher, 1991:319). What is the verdict on these charges? Regarding the most serious charge—that of having fabricated data—opinions vary. Whereas some writers have concluded that the evidence against Burt is strong to overwhelming (e.g., Dorfman, 1978; Hawkes, 1979; Broad & Wade, 1982:208; Roubertoux & Capron, 1990:556; Fancher, 1991; Billings, Beckwith, & Alper, 1992), several others have pronounced him vindicated (Stigler, 1979; Joynson, 1989; Johnson, 1990; Fletcher, 1991; Holden, 1991; Jensen, 1991; Eysenck, 1992). Without being able to confront Burt directly, it seems unlikely that this controversy will ever be resolved (Hattie, 1991:272).

Other Cases of Possible Social Science Fraud

Another charge of fraud in the social sciences was made against researchers who claim that, with proper treatment, many alcoholics can resume social drinking without relapsing back to excessive drinking (Sobell & Sobell, 1978; also see Lloyd & Saltzberg, 1975; Holden, 1980; Heather & Robertson, 1981; Peele, 1983). An official investigation failed to confirm that the data supporting this conclusion had been fabricated, except for minor misrepresentations of certain follow-up procedures that the researchers did not fully undertake (Norman, 1982; Pendery, Maltzman, & West, 1982).

Fraud charges were also leveled against social scientists involved in ape language research, arguing that they fabricated much of their data (Wade, 1980:1351). Recall that ape language research has involved teaching either the American Sign Language or some computerized language to chimpanzees (see Chapter 9, p. 126). These fraud charges were never officially investigated.

Recently, a researcher was charged with having "cooked" his data in a study of detrimental effects of childhood exposure to lead on intelligence (Palca, 1991). A panel convened to investigate the charges, and concluded that although the researcher did not fabricate his data, he did fail to fully and accurately describe his statistical methodology (Palca, 1992; Knoll, 1992:178).

Finally, as alluded to near the beginning of this chapter, a cigarette manufacturing company recently subpoenaed both the raw data and notes surrounding a published study on the effects of a cartoon-like caricature ("Joe Camel") in cigarette ads on children's attraction to smoking. Instead of pursuing any litigation against the researchers, the company turned the subpoenaed notes over to a newspaper reporter, raising counter-claims of ethical violations (Barinaga, 1992).

Methods for Minimizing Scientific Fraud

In light of the fact that most documented instances of fraud (i.e., those in the fields of biology and medicine) have involved young researchers, three suggestions have been made for reducing scientific fraud: (a) As students, researchers need greater supervision by those who have more-established careers; (b) young researchers should be encouraged to present preliminary findings at review sessions and seminars to obtain feedback; (c) researchers should understand the importance of keeping careful records of all observations and maintaining them for at least five years beyond publication (Norman, 1984). The basic philosophy behind these suggestions is that if young researchers are properly trained in how to conduct research, they will be less tempted to "cut corners" and possibly even fabricate data when difficulties are encountered.

One problem with disclosing cases of possible fraud is that individuals who bring charges, and journals that publish such charges, risk being sued for libel if their charges cannot be proven (Culliton, 1988b:18). If fraud is suspected, it is advised that everyone cooperate fully in the investigation (Roberts, 1991:1344).

One lingering issue surrounding scientific fraud pertains to the responsibility for instituting, enforcing, and investigating fraud charges. Should colleges, universities, and hospitals where research is being conducted take responsibility, or should federal (or other) agencies that provide funding for the research? Under present guidelines, the institution at which the research took place holds the primary responsibility for investigating charges of fraud (Dong, 1991).

Releasing Original Data for Verification

If you collected a set of data, and, after publishing the results, researchers asked you to send them a copy of the raw data so they could verify your analysis, would you send it to them? What do you think most researchers would do in this circumstance?

Several years ago, a graduate student in psychology wrote to 37 researchers who had published articles in psychology journals asking them for their raw data. Of the 32 researchers who responded to the request, more than half (21) stated that the data had been misplaced or destroyed. Only 9 researchers expressed a willingness to comply with the request without unreasonable restrictions. Of the 7 researchers who actually did submit their data for reanalysis, 3 were judged to have committed a significant error in their statistical analyses (Wolins, 1962). More recently, a study confirmed that fewer than half of psychologists who are asked to provide their raw data for the purpose of verifying their analysis will actually do so (Craig & Reese, 1973; see Broad & Wade, 1982:78).

In the United States, a congressional law was recently passed mandating the sharing of data by researchers who receive federal grant funding for a research project (Anonymous, 1991a). The law reads that anytime within five years following the publication of results of a federally funded study, the data must be shared with any qualified professional wishing to recheck the findings. Only federally funded studies are covered by this legislation.

Summary

Social scientists have been confronted by many ethical issues since their disciplines began forming in the 1800s. Among the main ethical issues are the treatment of subjects, and how social scientists should relate to one another professionally.

The following topics were discussed about the treatment of human subjects: Confidentiality, informed consent, deception and harm, and decision-making about what is and is not ethically acceptable in social science research.

Subjects should always be assured that the information they provide will be kept confidential. This is most easily done by ensuring anonymity (i.e., making sure that the subject's identity is never revealed to those involved in the research). Other methods of keeping information confidential were also discussed.

Informed consent means that persons are aware of the basic nature of the study, and have agreed to be subjects based on that awareness. Such consent is especially important for experimental research, and usually should be obtained in writing. If subjects are completing anonymous questionnaires, informed consent is normally inferred by the fact that they completed the questionnaire, provided they are explicitly told that they are free to not answer any questions they choose.

The deception and the potential harm of subjects are closely linked, especially in social science research. Most of the harm that social science subjects risk is emotional, often due to not being fully aware of the nature of the study. While some scientists favor the complete elimination of deception (and thereby most risks of emotional harm) in social science research, most guidelines allow at least short-term deception, provided the knowledge to be gained seems sufficiently important (and there is not a nondeceptive way to acquire the same knowledge).

Final decisions about the ethics of social science studies involving human subjects are now made by committees instead of by individual researchers. During the 1970s, these committees were established at most major universities and hospitals, and are known as Institutional Review Boards (IRBs) in the United States, and Research Ethics Committees (RECs) in Britian and its Commonwealths. Similar boards overseeing the humane treatment of laboratory animals are called Institutional Animal Care and Use Committees (IACUCs).

The ethical responsibilities that social scientists have toward one another involve honest representation of a researcher's ideas and findings. Intentional misrepresentation of ideas and findings is considered scientific fraud, which has two main categories: plagiarism, and intentional faking of research findings.

Plagiarism is the representation of someone else's writing as your own. Although most forms of plagiarism involve "lifting" sentences and paragraphs from someone else's writings, other forms include the use of ghostwriters and piggybacking. Even though ghostwriting is done with the knowledge and consent of the real author, and is not unusual in the publishing of popular books, it is generally considered unethical in scientific writing.

Piggybacking is including as the author of a manuscript someone who did not make significant contributions to the manuscript. It is most likely to occur when a subordinate is pressured to include as a coauthor a person who merely supervised the writing of a paper.

Intentional faking of research findings is very difficult to prove, and for this reason is likely to be far more prevalent than will ever be known. The answer to why scientists fake their findings probably lies in the intense competition for grants and glory, both of which are among the goals motivating scientific research. Nevertheless, because faking data works contrary to the main goal of scientific research—i.e., knowledge—every effort must be made to prevent it.

For whatever reasons, there are more well-established examples of scientific fraud in the fields of biology and medicine than in the social sciences. Nevertheless, several suspected, and a few proven, cases of fraud have cast shadows over the social sciences. These include the Piltdown skull hoax, the Tasiday hoax, and charges against Cyril Burt.

A few methods were identified for helping to minimize scientific fraud. They include providing greater supervision of young researchers, because they have been involved in a disproportionate number of fraud cases. Also discussed was the need for more cooperation by all scientists to allow other scientists to reexamine their data.

References

Anonymous. (1971). First glimpse of a stone age tribe. *National Geographic, 140,* 880–882.

Anonymous. (1991a). NIH bill to mandate ROTC program for biomedicine and data sharing. *Science, 253,* 611.

Anonymous. (1991b, April 14). After justices act, lab monkeys are killed. *New York Times* (national), p. 15.

Averill, J. R. (1968). Grief. *Psychological Bulletin, 70,* 721–748.

Barinaga, M. (1992). Who controls a researcher's files? *Science, 256,* 1620–1621.

Bauer, H. H. (1992). *Scientific literacy and the myth of the scientific method.* Urbana: University of Illinois Press.

Baumrind, D. (1964). Some thought on ethics of research: After reading Milgram's 'Behavioral study of obedience'. *American Psychologist, 19,* 421–423.

Baumrind, D. (1971). Principles of ethical conduct in the treatment of subjects: Reaction to the draft report of the Committee on Ethical Standards in Psychological Research. *American Psychologist, 26,* 887–896.

Begley, S. (1982, February 5). A case of fraud at Harvard. *Newsweek,* pp. 89–91.

Begley, S., & Seward, D. (1986 May 5). Back from the stone age? *Newsweek,* p. 55.

Billings, P. R., Beckwith, J., & Alper, J. S. (1992). The genetic analysis of human behavior: A new era? *Social Science and Medicine, 35,* 227–238.

Blinderman, C. (1986). *The Piltdown inquest.* Buffalo: Prometheus.

Blum, D. E. (1989). A dean is charged with plagiarizing a dissertation for his book on Muzak. *Chronicle of Higher Education, 35,* A17.

Broad, W. (1980). Would-be academician pirates papers. *Science, 208,* 1438–1440.

Broad, W. J., & Wade, N. (1982). *Betrayers of the truth.* New York: Simon & Schuster.

Campbell, B. G. (1985). *Humankind emerging* (4th ed.). Boston: Little, Brown.

Coughlin, E. K. (1991, October 16). Plagiarism by Martin Luther King affirmed by scholars at Boston U. *Chronicle of Higher Education, 38,* A21.

Craig, J. R., & Reese, S. C. (1973). Retention of raw data: A problem revisited. *American Psychologist, 28,* 723.

Culliton, B. J. (1983a). Fraud inquiry spreads blame. *Science, 219,* 937.

Culliton, B. J. (1983b). Emory reports on Darsee's fraud. *Science, 220,* 936.

Culliton, B. J. (1988a). Authorship, data ownership examined. *Science, 242,* 658.

Culliton, B. J. (1988b). A bitter battle over error (II). *Science, 241,* 18–21.

Dabbs, J. M., Jr., Ruback, R. B., & Besch, N. F. (1987, August 30). Males' saliva testosterone following conversations with male and female partners. American Psychological Association Poster Session, New York.

D'Antonio, W. V. (1989, August). Executive office report: Sociology on the move. *ASA Footnotes, 17,* 2.

Dewsbury, D. A. (1984). *Comparative psychology in the twentieth century.* Stroudsburg, PA: Hutchinson Ross.

DiFranza, J. R., Richards, J. W., Paulman, P. M., Wolf-Gillespie, N., Fletcher, C., Jaffe, R. D., & Murray, D. (1991). RJR Nabisco's cartoon camel promotes Camel cigarettes to children. *Journal of the American Medical Association, 266,* 3149–3153.

Dong, E. (1991). Confronting scientific fraud. *Chronicle of Higher Education, 38,* A52.

Donnerstein, E., Linz, D., & Penrod, S. (1987). *The question of pornography.* New York: Free Press.

Dorfman, D. D. (1978). The Cyril Burt question: New evidence. *Science, 204,* 1177–1180.

Ellis, L. (1989). *Theories of rape: Inquiries into the causes of sexual aggression.* New York: Hemisphere.

Elmer-DeWitt, P. (1991, April 1). Thin skins and fraud at M. I. T. *Time,* p. 65.

Etzioni, A. (1976). Paper mills. *Science, 192,* 325.

Eysenck, H. J. (1992). The Cyril Burt scandal—A verdict of "not guilty." *Personality and Individual Differences, 13,* 753–754.

Fancher, R. E. (1991). The Burt case: Another foray. *Science, 253,* 1565–1566.

Feder, K. L., & Park, M. A. (1989). *Human antiquity: An introduction to physical anthropology and archaeology.* Mountain View, CA: Mayfield.

Fletcher, R. (1991). *Science, ideology, and the media: The Cyril Burt scandal.* New Brunswick, NJ: Transaction Books.

Forsyth, D. R. (1991). A psychological perspective on ethical uncertainties in research. In A. J. Kimmel, *New directions in methodology of social and behavioral science* (pp. 91–100). San Francisco: Jossey-Bass.

Frankfort-Nachmias, C., & Nachmias, D. (1992). *Research methods in the social sciences* (4th ed.). New York: St. Martin's Press.

Golden, F. (1981, December 7). Fudging data for fun and profit. *Time,* p. 83.

Goodyear, R. K., Crego, C. A., & Johnson, M. W. (1992). Ethical issues in the supervision of student research: A study of critical incidents. *Professional Psychology: Research and Practice, 23,* 203–210.

Gould, J. L. (1982). *Ethology.* New York: Norton.

Green, P. (1971, March). The obligations of American social scientists. *Annals of the American Academy of Political and Social Science, 394,* 13–27.

Greenland, C. (1988). The treatment and maltreatment of sexual offenders: Ethical issues. *Annals of the New York Academy of Sciences, 528,* 373–378.

Hattie, J. (1991). The Burt controversy: An essay review of Hearnshaw's and Joynson's biographies of Sir Cyril Burt. *Alberta Journal of Educational Research, 37,* 259–275.

Hawkes, N. (1979). Tracing Burt's descent to scientific fraud. *Science, 205,* 673–675.

Hearnshaw, L. S. (1979). *Cyril Burt: Psychologist.* London: Hodder & Stoughton.

Heather, N., & Robertson, I. (1981). *Controlled drinking.* New York: Methuen.

Holden, C. (1980). Rand issues final alcoholism report. *Science, 207,* 855–856.

Holden, C. (1991). Rehabilitation for Burt. *Science, 251,* 27.

Jasper, J. M., & Nelkin, D. (1991). *The animal rights crusade: The growth of a moral protest.* New York: Free Press.

Jensen, A. R. (1991). IQ and science: The mysterious Burt affair. *Public Interest, 105,* 93–106.

Johnson, D. (1990). Can psychology ever be the same again after the human genome is mapped? *Psychological Science, 1,* 331–332.

Joynson, R. B. (1989). *The Burt affair.* London: Routhledge.

Kamin, L. J. (1974). *The science and politics of IQ.* Hillsdale, NJ: Lawrence Erlbaum.

Knoll, E. (1992). What is scientific misconduct? *Knowledge: Creation, Diffusion, Utilization, 14,* 174–180.

Lansdell, H. (1988). Laboratory animals need only humane treatment: Animal ''rights'' may debase human rights. *International Journal of Neuroscience, 42,* 169–178.

Lloyd, R. W., & Saltzberg, H. C. (1975). Controlled social drinking: An alternative to abstinence as a treatment goal for some alcohol abusers. *Psychological Bulletin, 82,* 815–842.

Malamuth, N., & Check, J. V. P. (1981). The effects of mass media exposure on acceptance of violence against women: A field experiment. *Journal of Research in Personality, 15,* 436–446.

Malamuth, N., & Check, J. V. P. (1983). Sexual arousal to rape depictions: Individual differences. *Journal of Abnormal Psychology, 92,* 55–67.

Malamuth, N., & Check, J. V. P. (1984). Debriefing effectiveness following exposure to rape depictions. *The Journal of Sex Research, 20,* 1–13.

Malamuth, N. M., & Check, J. V. P. (1985). The effects of aggressive pornography on beliefs in rape myths: Individual difference. *Journal of Research in Personality, 19,* 299–320.

Maple, T. L. (1979). Primate psychology in historical perspective. In J. Erwin, T. L. Maple, & G. Mitchell (Eds.), *Captivity and behavior* (pp. 29–58). New York: Van Nostrand Reinhold.

Marshall, E. (1989). Anthropologists debate Tasaday hoax evidence. *Science, 246,* 1113–1114.

Marshall, E. (1991). Sullivan overrules NIH on sex survey. *Science, 253,* 502.

McNeill, P. M., Berglund, C. A., & Webster, I. W. (1992). Do Australian researchers accept committee review and conduct ethical research? *Social Science and Medicine, 35,* 317–322.

Milgram, S. (1963). Behavioral study of obedience. *Journal of Abnormal and Social Psychology, 6,* 371–378.

Milgram, S. (1964). Issues in the study of obedience: A reply to Baumrind. *American Psychologist, 19,* 848–852.

Milgram, S. (1974). *Obedience to authority.* New York: Harper & Row.

Nancy, J. (1975). *The gentle Tasaday: A stone age people in the Philippine rain forest.* New York: Harcourt Brace Jovanovich.

Neuman, W. L. (1991). *Social research methods.* Boston: Allyn & Bacon.

Norman, C. (1982). No fraud found in alcoholism study. *Science, 218,* 771.

Norman, C. (1984). Reduce fraud in seven easy steps. *Science, 224,* 581.

Norman, R. L., & Smith, C. J. (1992). Restraint inhibits lutenizing hormone and testosterone secretion in intact male rhesus macaques: Effects of concurrent naloxone administration. *Neuroendocrinology, 55,* 405–415.

Palca, J. (1991). Get-the-lead-out guru challenged. *Science, 263,* 842–844.

Palca, J. (1992). Panel clears Needleman of misconduct. *Science, 256,* 1389.

Peele, S. (1983, April). Through a glass darkly. *Psychology Today,* pp. 38–42.

Pendery, M. L., Maltzman, I. M., & West, L. J. (1982). Controlled drinking by alcoholics? New findings and a reevaluation of a major affirmative study. *Science, 217,* 169–175.

Pollock, G. H. (1961). Mourning and adaptation. *International Journal of Psychoanalysis, 42,* 341–361.

Report of the American Psychological Association. (1990). Ethical principles of psychologists (Amended June 2, 1989). *American Psychologist, 45,* 390–395.

Riecken, H. W., & Boruch, R. F. (1979). *Social experimentation.* Orlando, FL: Academic Press.

Roberts, L. (1991). Misconduct: Caltech's trial by fire. *Science, 253,* 1344–1346.

Robson, S. (1991). Ethics: Informed consent or misinformed compliance? *Journal of the Market Research Society, 33,* 19–28.

Rollin, B. E. (1981). *Animal rights and human morality.* Buffalo, NY: Prometheus Books.

Roubertoux, P. L., & Capron, C. (1990). Are intelligence differences hereditarily transmitted? *Cahiers de Psychologie Cognitive, 10,* 555–594.

Rowan, A. N. (1991). The human-animal interface: Chasm or continuum? In M. H. Robinson & L. Tiger (Eds.), *Man & beast revisited* (pp. 279–289). Washington, DC: Smithsonian.

St. James-Roberts, I. (1976). Are researchers trustworthy? *New Scientist, 72,* 466–469.

Sapp, J. (1990). *Where the truth lies.* New York: Cambridge University Press.

Schlenker, B. R., & Forsyth, D. R. (1977). On the ethics of psychological research. *Journal of Experimental Social Psychology, 13,* 369–396.

Silberner, J. (1982, August). Cheating in the labs. *Science Digest,* pp. 38–41.

Smith, R. J. (1985). Scientific fraud probed at AAAS meeting. *Science, 228,* 1292–1293.

Sobell, V., & Sobell, L. C. (1978). *Behavioral treatment of alcohol problems.* New York: Plenum.

Spencer, F. (1990). *Piltdown: A scientific forgery.* New York: Oxford University Press.

Stein, P. L., & Rowe, B. M. (1982). *Physical anthropology* (3rd ed.). New York: McGraw-Hill.

Stigler, S. M. (1979). Letter. *Science, 244,* 242–244.

Thomson, K. S. (1991). Piltdown man: The great English mystery story. *American Scientist, 79,* 194–201.

Thompson, L. A., Detterman, D. K., & Plomin, R. (1991). Associations between cognitive abilities and scholastic achievement: Genetic overlap but environmental differences. *Psychological Science, 2,* 158–165.

Vaux, K., & Schade, S. (1988). In search for universality in the ethics of human research. In S. Spicker, I. Alon, A. de Vries, H. T. Engelhart (Eds.), *The use of human beings in research.* Boston: Kluwer Academic Publishers.

Wade, N. (1980). Does man alone have language? Apes reply in riddles, and a horse says neigh. *Science, 208,* 1349–1351.

Wallis, C. (1983, February 28). Fraud in a Harvard lab. *Time,* p.49.

Warwick, D. P. (1974). Who deserves protection? *American Sociologist, 9,* 158–159.

Warwick, D. P. (1975, February). Social scientists ought to stop lying. *Psychology Today,* pp. 105–106.

Weiner, J. S. (1955). *The Piltdown forgery.* London: Oxford Press.

Wilson, G. T. (1991, November 6). Who should police fraud in research? *Chronicle of Higher Education, 38,* p. B3.

Wolins, L. (1962). Responsibility for raw data. *American Psychologist, 17,* 657–658.

Zillman, D., & Bryant, J. (1984). Effects of massive exposure to pornography. In N. M. Malamuth & E. Donnerstein (Eds.), *Pornography and sexual aggression* (pp. 115–148). New York: Academic Press.

Suggested Reading

Beauchamp, T., Faden, R., Wallace, R. J., & Walters, L., (Eds.). (1982). *Ethical issues in social science research.* Baltimore: Johns Hopkins University Press. (This collection of readings provides useful information about how social scientists have confronted complex ethical issues facing their disciplines.)

Broad, W. J., & Wade, N. (1982). *Betrayers of the truth.* New York: Simon & Schuster. (This book provides an account of most cases of science fraud documented to date.)

Jasper, J. M., & Nelkin, D. (1991). *The animal rights crusade: The growth of a moral protest.* New York: Free Press. (This book provides a history of attempts to prevent cruelty to animals, especially the cruelty that occurs in scientific laboratories. Most of the examples discussed in this book come from research in the fields of medicine and cosmetics, but some experiments performed by social and behavioral scientists are also discussed.)

Journals that publish articles on ethical issues in social science are *Environmental Ethics, Ethics,* and *Philosophy of the Social Sciences.*

CHAPTER 19

Ethical Issues in the Social Sciences, II: Responsibilities to Humanity, and the Ultimate Nature and Use of Social Science Knowledge

W hen social scientists encounter behavior that they find morally offensive, should they make an effort to change the behavior or simply learn to be more tolerant? What should social scientists do if they make a discovery that could reinforce gender or racial prejudice? Is it possible for social scientists to be completely objective in studying human behavior? Are there questions that social scientists just should not ask?

This chapter extends social science ethics beyond treatment of subjects and fellow social scientists. Attention is directed toward two broad questions: What responsibilities do social scientists have to humanity as a whole? And, what is the nature and ultimate use of the "knowledge" that social scientists are accumulating?

Social Scientists' Responsibilities to Humanity

Two issues will be explored under this heading. The first has to do with respecting unfamiliar cultures and customs while not surrendering your own sense of right and wrong. The second is how social scientists have confronted some of their most controversial topics, such as questions about human sexuality, and about sex and race differences in intellectual abilities and behavior.

Respect for Other People, Both Living and Dead

Research has shown that in most societies, people prefer having male children over female children, especially if they can have only one child (Peterson & Peterson, 1973; Coombs, Coombs, & McClelland, 1975; Hoffman, 1975; Williamson, 1976, 1978; Choe, 1987; Weisfeld, 1990:35; Muhuri & Preston, 1991; Renteln, 1992). This preference appears to be inversely associated with education levels (Gilroy & Steinbacher, 1992). In parts of the world, the preference for males is so strong that female fetuses are selectively aborted (Hull, 1990:75; Renteln, 1992:410), and female newborns are given less care (Minces, 1982:31; Ballweg & Pagtolun-An, 1992:73), more often abandoned (Warren, 1985:36), and even killed (Hoebel, 1947; de Castro, 1952:162; Renteln, 1992:411). Assuming that you find these practices morally wrong, how would you react if conducting research in a culture where such practices are fairly common?

Recall from an earlier chapter (Chapter 9) the concept of ethnocentrism, which reflects the view that your own customs and values are superior to those of another culture. Social scientists go to considerable lengths to avoid ethnocentrism when studying foreign cultures (or even subcultures). How then could you ever justify attempting to change any custom that you consider morally objectionable?

Moral Relativism-Universalism

At the heart of this issue is the concept of **moral** (or **cultural**) **relativism** (not to be confused with empirical relativism, a term that will be discussed later in this chapter). Moral relativism refers to the assumption that morality is always specific to the particular culture in which it developed (Bagish, 1990:30). From this perspective, nothing is really right or wrong except within the cultural belief system to which the person making the judgment is accustomed (Appell, 1980:354). Moral relativists object to anyone applying his or her own moral values on another culture (Friedl & Whiteford, 1988:19). Thus, from the moral relativist perspective, moral values are social customs, and social scientists have no right to impose their social customs on people living in another society.

A view that is contrary to moral relativism is a **qualified moral universalism.** This view holds that, although most moral standards are arbitrary and culturally unique, some are immutable and pan-cultural (Westermarck, 1908; Durkheim, 1933:72; Burkett & White, 1974:456; Miethe, 1982:523; Kohlberg, Levine, & Hewer, 1983:75).

The distinction between pan-cultural and culturally unique morals can be grasped by distinguishing social morals from ascetic morals (Middleton & Putney, 1962). **Social morals** pertain to how people should relate to one another without harm and pain, whereas **ascetic morals** have to do with arbitrary practices (e.g., whether it is right or wrong to eat certain foods, use various drugs, or utter certain words). Central to the concept of social morality is the recognition that no one should intentionally injure other group members, except possibly in self defense or in defense of others (Sumner, 1940:499; Glaser, 1971:5; Dickstein, 1979:40; Wolfgang, 1975:477; Poznaniak, 1980:95).

From a qualified moral universalist's perspective, people can justifiably act on social moral standards, regardless of the culture involved. For example, after the Second World War, people throughout the world condemned Nazi atrocities against Jews as "crimes against humanity." So widespread was the condemnation that the United Nations convened a judicial body to prosecute those who were most involved in orchestrating the acts. In contrast, a moral relativist would have simply encouraged greater tolerance toward Nazi social customs (Bagish, 1990).

Social scientists who have argued against extreme forms of moral (or cultural) relativism, and in favor of qualified moral universalism (e.g., Bagish, 1990), have not done so from the ethnocentric perspective that their own culture's values are superior to the values of another culture. In fact, they sometimes consider foreign cultures to have moral standards that are "better" than those prevalent in their own culture. Unfortunately, no survey is currently available that has assessed where social scientists position themselves along the moral relativist-universalist continuum.

Respect for Those No Longer Living

If you choose to study a culture that no longer exists, would you have the right to excavate its burial sites and remove objects from the sites for display in a museum? What if some of those objects included human remains? Before answering, think about how you might feel if a social scientist wanted to study your great grandparents' culture, and to do so excavated of their grave sites.

There is no dispute that archaeological research has provided social scientists with valuable insight into the past (Fagan, 1986; Feder & Park, 1989). It used to be the case that archaeologists, like all other social scientists, did their research without any formal codes of ethics. However, in the 1970s ethical guidelines for archaeological research began to be adopted. Pressure to develop these guidelines came from Native Americans in the United States and Canada who objected to the excavation of ancestral burial sites (Talmage, 1982). In some cases, tribal groups have won lawsuits against indefinite museum storage, and sometimes even excavation, of Native American remains (Talmage, 1982:47). With all in agreement that much still remains to be discovered about Native American culture, both before and since European settlement, many archaeologists are expressing concern over these legal actions (see Roe, 1992).

Addressing Extremely Controversial and Potentially Prejudicial Topics

Much of what social scientists study is controversial. However, there are certain topics that are especially so. Conspicuous among these are investigations that link behavior either to sex or to race, especially within a nature-nurture context (Scarr, 1988; Levin, 1990; Eysenck, 1991:244). Studies of human sexuality can also be extremely controversial from an ethical standpoint (Davis & Whitten, 1987:71). Severe repercussions have sometimes befallen social scientists working in these areas, including shunning by colleagues (Gordon, 1980; Gross, 1990:43), termination of financial support and denial of academic tenure (Marshall, 1991; Holden, 1992), getting unsatisfactory work ratings (Pearson, 1991:238), being shouted down in public forums (Pearson, 1991:32 & 166), and even receiving threats of bodily harm (Sewall & Lee, 1980; Scarr, 1988:57; Tiger, 1991:332). Following are some examples that even today continue to be of concern to the social science community.

Research on Human Sex Differences in Behavior

Average sex differences may exist in a wide array of human behavior patterns (Maccoby & Jacklin, 1974; Ellis, 1986). However, there is no consensus among social scientists about the universality of these sex differences or what causes them. Although considerable research has suggested that biological factors play a major role (Hagen, 1979; Durden-Smith & deSimone, 1983; Rossi, 1985; Ellis, 1986; Masters, 1989; Kemper, 1990; Moir & Jessel, 1990), some of the research has been discounted (Gagnon & Simon, 1973; Rose, Kamin, & Lewontin, 1984; O'Kelly & Carney, 1986:285; Nielsen, 1990:147). Social scientists who view the evidence for biological causes as unconvincing have proposed that sex differences in behavior are most likely the result of social learning (e.g., Henley & Freeman, 1975:393; Fox, Tobin, & Brody, 1979; Rosaldo, 1980:400; O'Kelly & Carney, 1986; Eagly, 1987; Crapo, 1990:245; Eagly & Johnson, 1990).

A number of social scientists have expressed concern that any evidence that biological factors contribute to sex differences in behavior will serve to justify continued male domination of economic and political affairs (Lowe, 1986:17; O'Kelly & Carney, 1986:162). Thus, there is an undercurrent of emotions and ideology that is interspersed with the strictly empirical questions surrounding sex differences in behavior (Archer, 1986:51). Consequently, social scientists conducting research on sex differences in behavior often tend to slant their interpretations in accordance with their ideology. (The broader issue of whether objectivity is even possible in the social sciences will be addressed in the second half of this chapter.)

Research on Human Sexuality

Two studies of sexual behavior were recently denied funding by the U.S. Secretary of Health and Human Services. In both cases, the studies had been reviewed and approved for funding on their scientific merit by a panel of scientists commissioned by the National Institutes of Health (NIH).

One study would have surveyed approximately 25,000 junior high and high school students about their sexual behavior. Funding for the study was stopped two months after it had begun. The reason given by the Secretary of Health and Human Services was that the study "could inadvertently convey a message undermining warnings about the dangers of promiscuous sex" (Marshall, 1991).

The second study to have its funding withdrawn by the Secretary of Health and Human Services was designed to update and extend pioneering research by the Kinsey Institute of Indiana University (Kinsey et al., 1948, 1953). The Kinsey studies of sexual behavior were conducted in the 1940s (with private, not public, funds) (Moffat, 1991). Critics of the administrative decisions not to fund these in-depth studies of human sexual behavior fear that social science research will become increasingly politicized (Anonymous, 1991:12; Burd, 1991).

In 1991, a bill was passed by the U.S. Congress to overturn the ban on funding these two projects (Anonymous, 1991). This was followed by the introduction of a counter bill that would disallow funding of all social science research dealing with "perverse types of conduct" (Marshall, 1991). The second amendment was defeated. Finally, a substitute amendment was passed, which permitted government funding of research dealing with human sexuality, but stipulated that several extra layers of review processes would be required. In the meantime, concern over the spread of the AIDS virus has prompted large-scale surveys in France and England concerning explicit sexual behavior (Aldhous, 1992).

Research on Race and Intelligence

Tests for measuring intellectual ability and performance were first developed and utilized around the turn of the 20th century (Schneider, 1992). Since then, IQ and academic performance tests have come to be widely used, especially in industrialized countries. In the United States alone, an estimated 100 million such tests are administered each year (Anonymous, 1980:97). These tests are used to place secondary students in curricula that will maximally challenge them, to help determine how schools and school districts are doing in educating their students, and to help decide which students should be admitted to selective colleges and universities.

Since the 1920s, numerous studies have been published on how racial groups vary in their average scores. In the late 1960s, an article was published by Arthur Jensen (1969) that reviewed these studies, and in which it was concluded that genetic factors were probably responsible for much of the average difference in scores between whites and blacks. This conclusion outraged many scientists (and citizens in general) because it seemed to be an affront to social efforts at achieving racial equality (e.g., Rose, Kamin, & Lewontin, 1984).

In the intervening years, additional studies have shown that blacks score below whites, and that whites in turn score below most oriental groups, especially in nonverbal test items (e.g., those dealing with mathematics) (Loehlin, Lindzey, & Spuhler, 1975; Lynn, 1978, 1991a; Scarr, 1981; Jensen, 1985). Four important qualifications need to be emphasized: (a) the variability within each racial group is great (Snyderman & Rothman, 1988:107), (b) ethnic variations (within each racial category) in average scores have also been noted (Dunn, 1987), (c) persons of mixed racial or ethnic composition (which is very common in contemporary societies such as the United States and Canada) tend to receive scores that are intermediate to those of largely unmixed racial or ethnic groups (Lynn, 1991a), and (d) racial and ethnic variables are closely tied to social status variables so that the causal significance of race-intelligence relationships are exceedingly complex (Stanovich, 1985).

Risqué Relics

What's an editor to do? Hershel Shanks, editor of *Biblical Archaeology Review,* was about to publish an article by Harvard archeologist Lawrence Stager on the people of the ancient seaport of Askelon, in present-day Israel. The trouble was the illustrations: 1800-year-old oil lamps depicting sex scenes that would easily garner an X rating today. The pictures illustrated important points in the article. But if Shanks published them, how would his readers—who include an unusual number of devout Christians and Jews—react? His solution: Ask the readers.

These were no demure nudes. The lamps showed couplings between various gender combinations, all working parts in plain view. The dirty digs came from an ancient bathhouse, says Joe Greene, an archeologist colleague of Stager. "It's not clear what sort of a bathhouse it was," he adds. Though Christian and Jewish families lived in the area, Stager blames the X-rated artwork on the pagan Romans, who he says were more accepting of casual sex and male homosexuality than the other groups.

Shanks published the results of his reader poll and the accompanying comments in the July issue. A solid majority—80%—voted for publication, though 30% thought the pictures should appear on a perforated page to keep them from the eyes of children. Many of the 20% who said no also worried about their kids, who, they said, often read the semipopular journal. "Some people even use this in Sunday school," says Steve Feldman, who works for the journal.

The majority ruled: The pictures appear in the same issue, in full detail, There are no little black rectangles hiding anything, though the illustrations are printed opposite an ad, so readers can tear them out without losing any of the article. Chances are, many readers will leave their copy intact. Wrote one respondent: "Don't underestimate the value of the added excitement of sex in interesting a child in any subject, including archeology."

From *Science,* 253 (July 12, 1991), p. 143. Copyright © 1991 by the AAAS.

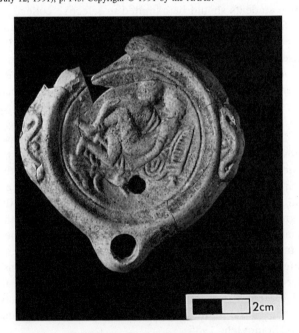

2cm

Oil lamp with erotic scene.   Photograph by Carl Andrews, courtesy of Leon Levy Excavation.

As in the case of sex differences in behavior, there is little dispute among social scientists about the existence of the racial differences in test scores. However, in explaining those differences, especially within a nature-nurture context, disagreements abound. On the one hand, numerous social scientists have contended that biological factors appear to be important (Shuey, 1976; Willerman, 1979; Lynn, 1991b; Gottfredson, 1986; Dunn, 1987; Rushton, 1989; Levin, 1990). Many others have argued that racial variations in scores on tests of intellectual ability and performance are the result of either social environmental factors or of invalid tests (Lazarus & Monat, 1979:48; Bock & Moore, 1986; Schusky & Culbert, 1987:51; Murphy, 1989:20; Mercer, 1988; Barnouw, 1989:388; Sue & Okazaki, 1990:919).

Where do most social scientists stand on this extremely controversial issue? A recent survey of psychologists indicates that most accept the view that some biological factors are involved (Snyderman & Rothman, 1988:129). However, a survey among sociologists showed that the vast majority believe that social environmental factors are overwhelmingly responsible for average race differences in intellectual performance (Sanderson & Ellis, 1992:37).

How should social scientists deal with these issues in the future? At one extreme are those who argue that some issues are so emotionally sensitive and potentially destructive to the social fabric of a pluralistic society that the issues should only be considered in ways that bring people together, not drive them apart. Others have contended that the foremost responsibility of science is to answer empirical questions as objectively as possible, no matter what may be the result (Scarr, 1988:59; Eysenck, 1991:247).

A middle position might be that while no scientific inquiry should be suppressed even if it is potentially destructive to human civility and social order, social scientists should not be oblivious to such possibilities (Loehlin, 1992). One social science code of ethics addressed this issue by stating that researchers should not only be sensitive to the scientific significance of what is being observed, but also to the ethical and political implications (American Psychological Association Ad Hoc Committee, 1982:74).

Underlying the debate about how social scientists should deal with controversial topics is a fundamental question: Can social scientists really be objective in what they do, or are their observations little more than reflections of their own cultural and political biases? It is to this important question that we now turn.

Objectivism versus Relativism in the Social Sciences

Albert Einstein (1949:50) declared that science was "international," meaning that objective reality transcended national and political boundaries. Around the same time, another German offered another view: "Science is a social phenomenon. The idea of free and unfettered science," according to Adolf Hitler, "is absurd" (Rauschning, 1939:220; also see McKee, 1969:495; Bauer, 1992:62).

Controversy over the degree to which an objective reality is knowable has been frequently debated. Several social scientists have argued that cultural and political biases are bound to shade social scientists' perceptions of reality (Gouldner, 1970; Murphy, 1971; Shields, 1975; Haraway, 1989; Collins, 1981). Such a point of view may be referred to as **empirical relativism** (Goldenberg, 1989; Sanderson, 1991:472). (Note that empirical relativism should not be confused with moral relativism, a concept discussed earlier in this chapter.)

According to empirical relativists, people's perceptions of social reality are always distorted by their cultural upbringing and political ideology (Fairchild, 1991:112). In other words, "truths" in social science are little more than reflections of the cultural backgrounds and ideological biases of those who perceive those "truths" (Rose, Kamin, & Lewontin, 1984).

Empirical relativism is in direct opposition to **empirical objectivism** (or **realism**), the belief that an objective knowable reality exists quite apart from those perceiving it (Merton, 1957:551; Arnhart, 1992; Hammersley, 1992:43). If objectivism is in fact true, it should be possible for scientists to set aside their cultural backgrounds and ideological beliefs when making empirical observations (McKee, 1969:495; Blalock, 1991:xiii).

An intermediate position on the empirical relativist-objectivist controversy recognizes that although bias-free observations should always be a goal, no scientist is justified in *assuming* that he or she is being completely objective (Mahoney, 1985, 1987). Instead, increasing confidence in the objective reality of some observations only comes after several scientists have verified one another's accounts. The more diverse the cultural and ideological background of those who conduct the verifications, the better. This intermediate position means that objectivity in the social sciences can be at least approximated provided that social scientists of diverse cultural and ideological backgrounds cooperate in exchanging information on what they observe (Rapp, 1992:864).

What do social scientists think of the empirical relativist-objectivist issue? According to a recent survey conducted in Canada and the United States, most social scientists were intermediate regarding empirical relativism-objectivism although they were more relativistic than were physicists and chemists (Goldenberg, 1989:473). The differences between the views of social and natural scientists probably reflect a feeling among social scientists that their objectivity is more difficult to maintain than is the objectivity of natural scientists (Beeghley, 1989:12; Sanderson, 1991:462; for a contrary view see Harding, 1991).

The possibility of anyone's empirical observations being biased by his or her cultural and ideological backgrounds underscores the need for **replication studies.** The purpose of these studies is to verify the results of some prior study. Replication studies have not been a high priority in the social sciences (Bornstein, 1990; also see Abelson & Karlik, 1977). This is probably because they are less "glamorous" than original research, and because most journal editors prefer to publish research that breaks new ground rather than that which simply rechecks what has already been reported.

"What's most depressing is the realization that everything
we believe will be disproved in a few years."

Copyright © by Sidney Harris.

The main point regarding the empirical relativist-objectivist controversy may be summarized as follows: It is naive for social scientists to assume that they can be totally objective in the observations they make (Rapoport, 1991:99). Given the nature of what social scientists are attempting to understand, the possibility of cultural and ideological biases are ever-present. The most certain way to detect and correct such biases is to make sure that (a) no important empirical findings go unverified, and (b) there is cultural and ideological diversity among those contributing to the social science literature.

Consider the following example: A recent study by Simon LeVay (1991) found that a small, obscure portion of the brain in male homosexuals was less than one-half the size of the same region in the average male heterosexual. Soon after his research report appeared, it was noted that the researcher was himself a homosexual and a staunch supporter of gay rights (Gelman, 1992:49; Marshall, 1992:620). Is it possible that the researcher was therefore biased in his observations? According to one critic, LeVay is "definitely on a political crusade" (see Marshall, 1992:621).

Even though other lines of evidence have implicated biological factors in human sexual orientation (see Ellis & Ames, 1987; Small, 1993), LeVay's was the first study to report the discovery of an actual brain difference between homosexuals and heterosexuals. Obviously, replication studies are needed.

Finally, assuming that social scientists are able to accumulate objective knowledge, what should be done with it? Most people hope that, besides the value of knowledge for its own sake, scientific knowledge will eventually help to improve the human condition. Chapter 20 will cover social science research that is aimed explicitly toward helping solve practical human problems.

Summary

In this, the second of two chapters dealing with ethical issues in the social sciences, two broad questions were addressed: What responsibilities do social scientists have to humanity? And, ultimately, what can be done with the accumulation of objective social science knowledge?

The first question led to discussions of two major topics: Respecting unfamiliar customs without betraying personal moral standards, and confronting emotional and politically controversial topics in social science.

Social scientists vary in their opinions regarding unfamiliar customs to which they may have moral objections. At one extreme are the moral relativists. They believe that all moral standards are relative to the culture in which the standards exist, and that persons socialized in one culture should not pass judgment on any actions of people socialized in another culture. Near the other extreme is a qualified moral universalism. It holds that certain moral universals exist, and that social scientists have a right to make judgments about the morality of people's actions in all cultures when the behavior is relevant to these moral universals.

Extreme moral relativism has been criticized because it does not allow social scientists to condemn such cultural practices as slavery or genocide. Critics of qualified moral universalism have suggested that this perspective opens the door to ethnocentric beliefs about the superiority of one's own social customs. There is currently no survey evidence documenting where most social scientists stand on this issue.

Social scientists are currently in substantial disarray over what should be done about extremely controversial topics such as those linking behavior with sex and race. Because the causes of sex and race differences in behavior are still poorly understood, some contend that social scientists should avoid research that is potentially destructive to the delicate social fabric within which we all live. Others have asserted that scientific research should only be concerned with objectively seeking the truth, no matter where it leads. Most of the opposition to research on human sexual behavior has come, not from within the ranks of social science itself, but from those outside of social science who oppose public funding of such research.

The second major question addressed in this chapter was whether social scientists can ever make unbiased observations. Views on this question can be conceptualized along an empirical relativism-objectivism continuum. The former asserts that all "knowledge" is embedded within an observer's cultural and ideological perspective and is therefore never completely objective. The latter view is that, no matter what culture human beings live in, they all share the same sensory apparatuses, and therefore see things the same way. An intermediate position is that no scientist can (or should) be confident that his or her observations are completely objective. However, if scientific knowledge is shared across diverse cultures and among people of varying political persuasions, a picture of objective reality will gradually emerge.

References

Abelson, P. H., & Karlik, C. (1977). Letter. *Science, 195,* 9.

Aldhous, P. (1992). French venture where U.S. fears to tread. *Science, 257,* 25.

American Psychological Association Ad Hoc Committee on Ethical Standards in Psychological Research. (1982). *Ethical principles in the conduct of research with human participants.* Washington, DC: American Psychological Association.

Anonymous. (1980, February 18). Tests: How good? How fair? *Newsweek,* pp. 97–101.

Anonymous. (1991, September). Social science triumphs in Congress after setback on American teenage study. *Footnotes* (published by the American Sociological Association), *19,* 1, 12.

Appell, G. N. (1980). Talking ethics: The uses of moral rhetoric and the function of ethical principles. *Social Problems, 27,* 350–357.

Archer, J. (1986). Animal sociobiology and comparative psychology: A review. *Current Psychological Research and Reviews, 5,* 48–61.

Arnhart, L. (1992). Feminism, primatology, and ethical naturalism. *Politics and the Life Sciences, 11,* 157–170.

Bagish, H. H. (1990). Confessions of a former cultural relativist. In Annual Editions, *Anthropology 90/91.* Guilford, CT: Dushkin.

Ballweg, J. A., & Pagtolun-An, I. G. (1992). Parental underinvestment: A link in the fertility-mortality continuum. *Population Research and Policy Review, 11,* 73–89.

Barnouw, V. (1989). *Physical anthropology and archaeology* (5th ed.). Chicago: Dorsey.

Bauer, H. H. (1992). *Scientific literacy and the myth of the scientific method.* Urbana: University of Illinois Press.

Beeghley, L. (1989). *The structure of social stratification in the United States.* Boston: Allyn & Bacon.

Blalock, H. M., Jr. (1991). *Understanding social inequality.* Newbury Park, CA: Sage.

Bock, R. D., & Moore, E. G. J. (1986). *Advantage and disadvantage.* Hillsdale, NJ: Erlbaum.

Bornstein, R. F. (1990). Publication politics, experimenter bias and the replication process in social science research. *Journal of Social Behavior and Personality, 5,* 71–81.

Burd, S. (1991, October 2). Scientists fear rise of intrusion in work supported by NIH. *Chronicle of Higher Education, 38,* A2 & A30.

Burkett, S. R., & White, W. (1974). Hellfire and delinquency: Another look. *Journal for the Scientific Study of Religion, 13,* 455–462.

Choe, M. K. (1987). Sex differentials in infant and child mortality in Korea. *Social Biology, 34,* 12–25.

Collins, H. M. (1981). Son of seven sexes: The social destruction of a physical phenomenon. *Social Studies of Science, 11,* 33–62.

Coombs, C. H., Coombs, L. C., & McClelland, G. H. (1975). Preference scale for number and sex of children. *Population Studies, 29,* 273–298.

Crapo, R. H. (1990). *Cultural anthropology* (2nd ed.). Guilford, CT: Dushkin.

Davis, D. L., & Whitten, R. G. (1987). The cross-cultural study of human sexuality. *Annual Review in Anthropology, 16,* 69–98.

de Castro, J. (1952). *The geography of hunger.* Boston: Little, Brown.

Dickstein, E. B. (1979). Biological and cognitive bases of moral functioning. *Human Development, 22,* 37–59.

Dunn, L. M. (1987). *Bilingual Hispanic children on the U.S. mainland: A review of research on their cognitive, linguistic, and scholastic development.* Circle Pine, MN:American Guidance Service.

Durden-Smith, J., & deSimone, D. (1983). *Sex and the brain.* New York: Warner.

Durkheim, E. (1933). *The division of labor.* New York: Free Press.

Eagly, A. H. (1987). *Sex differences in social behavior: A social-role interpretation.* Hillsdale, NJ: Erlbaum.

Eagly, A. H., & Johnson, B. T. (1990). Gender and leadership styles: A meta-analysis. *Psychological Bulletin, 198,* 233–256.

Einstein, A. (1949). *The world as I see it.* New York: Wisdom Library.

Ellis, L. (1986). Evidence of neuroandrogenic etiology of sex roles from a combined analysis of human, nonhuman primate, and nonprimate mammalian studies. *Personality and Individual Differences, 7,* 519–552.

Ellis, L., & Ames, M. A. (1987). Neurohormonal functioning and sexual orientation: A theory of homosexuality-heterosexuality. *Psychological Bulletin, 101,* 233–258.

Eysenck, H. J. (1991). Science, racism, and sexism. *Journal of Social, Political, and Economic Studies, 16,* 217–250.

Fagan, B. M. (1986). *People of the earth: An introduction to world prehistory* (5th ed.). Boston: Little, Brown.

Fairchild, H. H. (1991). Scientific racism: The cloak of objectivity. *Journal of Social Issues, 47,* 101–115.

Feder, K. L., & Park, M. A. (1989). *Human antiquity: An introduction to physical anthropology and archaeology.* Mountain View, CA: Mayfield.

Fox, L. H., Tobin, D., & Brody, L. (1979). Sex role socialization and achievement in mathematics. In M. A. Wittig & A. C. Petersen (Eds.), *Sex-related differences in cognitive functioning* (pp. 303–319). New York: Academic Press.

Friedl, J., & Whiteford, M. B. (1988). *The human portrait: Introduction to cultural anthropology* (2nd ed.). Englewood Cliffs, NJ: Prentice Hall.

Gagnon, J., & Simon, W. (1973). *Sexual conduct.* Chicago: Aldine.

Gelman, D. (1992, February 24). Born or bred? *Newsweek,* pp. 46– 53.

Gilroy, F. D., & Steinbacher, R. (1992). Sex selection technology utilization: Further implications for sex ratio imbalance. *Social Biology, 38,* 285–288.

Glaser, D. (1971). *Social deviance.* Chicago: Markham.

Goldenberg, S. (1989). What scientists think of science. *Social Science Information, 28,* 467–481.

Gordon, R. A. (1980). Robert A. Gordon replies. In E. Sargarin (Ed.), *Taboos in criminology* (pp. 136–147). Beverly Hills, CA: Sage.

Gottfredson, L. A. (1986). Societal consequences of the g factor in employment. *Journal of Vocational Behavior, 29,* 379–410.

Gouldner, A. (1970). *The coming crisis in Western sociology.* New York: Basic Books.

Gross, B. R. (1990). The case of Philippe Rushton. *Academic Questions, 3,* 35–46.

Hagen, R. (1979). *The bio-sexual factor.* Garden City, NY: Doubleday.

Hammersley, M. (1992). *What's wrong with ethnography?* London: Routhledge.

Haraway, D. (1989). *Primate visions: Gender, race, and nature in the world of modern science.* New York: Routhledge.

Harding, S. (1991). *Whose science? Whose knowledge?* Ithaca, NY: Cornell University Press.

Henley, N., & Freeman, J. (1975). The sexual politics of interpersonal behavior. In J. Freeman (Ed.), *Women: A feminist perspective.* Palo Alto, CA: Mayfield.

Hoebel, E. A. (1947). Eskimo infanticide and polyandry. *Scientific Monthly, 64,* 535–538.

Hoffman, L. N. (1975). The value of children to parents and the decrease in family size. *Proceedings of the American Philosophical Society, 119,* 430–438.

Holden, C. (1992). Settlement at U. of Delaware. *Science, 256,* 962.

Hull, T. H. (1990). Recent trends in sex ratios at birth in China. *Population and Development Review, 16,* 63–83.

Jensen, A. R. (1969). How much can we boost IQ and educational achievement? *Harvard Educational Review, 39,* 1–123.

Jensen, A. R. (1985). The nature of the black-white difference on various psychometric tests: Spearman's hypothesis. *Brain and Behavioral Sciences, 8,* 193–219.

Kemper, T. D. (1990). *Social structure and testosterone.* New Brunswick: Rutgers University Press.

Kinsey, A. C., Pomeroy, W. B., Martin, C. E., & Gebhard, P. H. (1948). *Sexual behavior in the human male.* New York: Saunders.

Kinsey, A. C., Pomeroy, W. B., Martin, C. E., & Gebhard, P. H. (1953). *Sexual behavior in the human female.* New York: Saunders.

Kohlberg, L., Levine, C., & Hewer, A. (1983). *Moral stages: A current formulation and a response to critics.* Basel: S. Karger.

Lazarus, R. S., & Monat, A. (1979). *Personality* (3rd ed.). Englewood Cliffs, NJ: Prentice-Hall.

LeVay, S. (1991). A difference in hypothalamic structure between heterosexual and homosexual men. *Science, 253,* 1034–1037.

Levin, M. (1990). Implications of race and sex differences for compensatory affirmative action and the concept of discrimination. *Journal of Social, Political, and Economic Studies, 15,* 175–212.

Loehlin, J. C. (1992). Should we do research on race differences in intelligence? *Intelligence, 16,* 1–4.

Loehlin, J. C., Lindzey, G., & Spuhler, J. N. (1975). *Race differences in intelligence.* San Francisco: Freeman.

Lowe, M. (1986). Science and gender as political science. *Contemporary Sociology, 15,* 15–17.

Lynn, R. (1978). Ethnic and racial differences in intelligence: International comparisons. In R. T. Osborne, C. E. Noble, & N. Weyl (Eds.), *Human variation: The biopsychology of age, race, and sex* (pp. 261–286). New York: Academic Press.

Lynn, R. (1991a). Race differences in intelligence: A global perspective. *Mankind Quarterly, 31,* 254–296.

Lynn, R. (1991b). The evolution of racial differences in intelligence. *Mankind Quarterly, 32,* 99–173.

Maccoby, E., & Jacklin, C. (1974). *The psychology of sex differences.* Stanford: Stanford University Press.

Mahoney, M. J. (1985). Open exchange and the epistemic process. *American Psychologist, 40,* 20–39.

Mahoney, M. J. (1987). Scientific publications and knowledge politics. *Journal of Social Behavior and Personality, 2,* 165–176.

Marshall, E. (1991). Sullivan overrules NIH on sex survey. *Science, 253,* 502.

Marshall, E. (1992). Sex on the brain. *Science, 257,* 620–621.

Masters, R. D. (1989). Gender and political cognition: Integrating evolutionary biology and political science. *Politics and the Life Sciences, 8,* 3–47.

McKee, J. B. (1969). *Introduction to sociology.* New York: Holt, Rinehart, & Winston.

Mercer, J. R. (1988). Ethnic differences in IQ scores: What do they mean? (A response to Lloyd Dunn). *Hispanic Journal of Behavioral Sciences, 10,* 199–218.

Merton, R. K. (1957). *Social theory and social structure.* New York: Free Press.

Middleton, R., & Putney, S. (1962). Religion, normative standards, and behavior. *Sociometry, 25,* 141–152.

Miethe, T. D. (1982). Public consensus on crime seriousness. *Criminology, 20,* 515–526.

Minces, J. (1982). *The house of obedience: Women in Arab society.* London: Zed Press.

Moffat, A. S. (1991). Another sex survey bites the dust. *Science, 253,* 1483.

Moir, A., & Jessel, D. (1990). *Brain sex.* New York: Dell.

Muhuri, P. K., & Preston, S. H. (1991). Effects of family composition on mortality differentials by sex among children in Matlab, Bangladesh. *Population and Development Review, 17,* 415–434.

Murphy, R. F. (1971). *The dialectics of social life.* New York: Basic Books.

Murphy, R. F. (1989). *Cultural and social anthropology: An overview* (3rd ed.). Englewood Cliffs, NJ: Prentice-Hall.

Nielsen, J. M. (1990). *Sex and gender in society* (2nd ed.). Prospect Heights, IL: Waveland.

O'Kelly, C. G., & Carney, L. S. (1986). *Women and men in society* (2nd ed.). Belmont, CA: Wadsworth.

Pearson, R. (1991). *Race, intelligence and bias in academe.* Washington, DC: Scott-Townsend.

Peterson, C. C., & Peterson, J. L. (1973). Preference for sex of offspring as a measure of change in sex attitudes. *Psychology, 10,* 3–5.

Poznaniak, W. (1980). Attitudes of criminals and noncriminals toward moral norms and moral rigorism. *Polish Psychological Bulletin, 11,* 87–97.

Rapoport, A. (1991). Ideological commitments in evolutionary theories. *Journal of Social Issues, 47,* 83–99.

Rapp, R. (1992). A standpoint on science. *Science, 256,* 863–864.

Rauschning, H. (1939). *Hitler speaks: A series of political conversations with Adolf Hitler on his real aims.* London: T. Butterworth.

Renteln, A. D. (1992). Sex selection and reproductive freedom. *Women's Studies International Forum, 15,* 405–426.

Roe, E. M. (1992). Intertextual evaluation, conflicting evaluative criteria, and the controversy over Native American burial remains. *Evaluation and Program Planning, 15,* 369–381.

Rosaldo, M. Z. (1980). The use and abuse of anthropology: reflections on feminism and cross-cultural understanding. *Signs, 5,* 389–417.

Rose, S., Kamin, L. J., & Lewontin, R. C. (1984). *Not in our genes: Biology, ideology and human nature.* London: Penguin.

Rossi, A. (1985). Gender and parenthood. In A. Rossi (Ed.), *Gender and the life course.* Hawthorne, NY: Aldine.

Rushton, J. P. (1989). Japanese inbreeding depression scores: Predictors of cognitive differences between blacks and whites. *Intelligence, 13,* 43–51.

Sanderson, S. K. (1991). *Macrosociology: An introduction to human societies* (2nd ed.). New York: HarperCollins.

Sanderson, S. K., & Ellis, L. (1992). Theoretical and political perspectives of American sociologists in the 1990s. *American Sociologist, 23,* 26–42.

Scarr, S. (1981). *Race, social class and individual differences in IQ.* Hillsdale, NJ: Erlbaum.

Scarr, S. (1988). Race and gender as psychological variables. *American Psychologist, 43,* 56–59.

Schneider, W. H. (1992). After Binet-French intelligence testing, 1900–1950. *Journal of the History of the Behavioral Sciences, 28,* 111–132.

Schusky, E. L., & Culbert, T. P. (1987). *Introducing culture* (4th ed.). Englewood Cliffs, NJ: Prentice-Hall.

Sewall, G., & Lee, D. E. (1980, January 14). Jensen's rebuttal. *Newsweek,* p. 59.

Shields, S. A. (1975). Functionalism, Darwinism and the psychology of women. *American Psychologist, 30,* 739–754.

Shuey, A. M. (1976). *The testing of Negro intelligence.* New York: Social Science Press.

Small, M. F. (1993, March). The gay debate: Is homosexuality a matter of choice or chance? *American Health, 12,* 70–76.

Snyderman, M., & Rothman, S. (1988). *The IQ controversy, the media and public policy.* New Brunswick: Transaction Publishers.

Stanovich, K. E. (1985). The black-white differences are real: Where do we go from here? *Behavioral and Brain Sciences, 8,* 242–243.

Sue, S., & Okazaki, S. (1990). Asian-American educational achievement. *American Psychologist, 45,* 913–920.

Sumner, W. G. (1940). *Folkways.* Boston: Ginn.

Talmage, V. A. (1982, November/December). The violation of sepulture: Is it legal to excavate human burials? *Archaeology, 35,* 44–49.

Tiger, L. (1991). Human nature and the psycho-industrial complex. In M. H. Robinson & L. Tiger (Eds.), *Man & beast revisited* (pp. 331–340). Washington, DC: Smithsonian Institution Press.

Warren, M. A. (1985). *Gendercide: The implications of sex selection.* Totowa, NJ: Rowman & Allanheld.

Weisfeld, G. E. (1990). Sociobiological patterns of Arab society. *Ethology and Sociobiology, 11,* 23–49.

Westermarck, E. (1908). *The origin and development of the moral ideas.* London: Macmillan.

Willerman, L. (1979). *The psychology of individual and group differences.* San Francisco: Freeman.

Williamson, N. E. (1976). *Sons or daughters: A cross-cultural survey of parental preferences.* Beverly Hills, CA: Sage.

Williamson, N. E. (1978). Boys or girls? *Population Bulletin, 33,* 1–35.

Wolfgang, M. E. (1975). Delinquency and violence from the viewpoint of criminology. In W. S. Fields & W. H. Sweet (Eds.), *Neural bases of violence and aggression* (pp. 456–489). St. Louis: Warren H. Green.

Suggested Reading

Einstein, A. (1949). *The world as I see it.* New York: Wisdom Library. (A readable collection of essays and letters about science and the human condition by one of the giants in 20th century science.)

Lynd, R. S. (1939). *Knowledge for what? The place of social science in American culture.* Princeton, NJ: Princeton University Press. (A classic liberal statement of how social science knowledge should be used for the betterment of humankind.)

Skinner, B. F. (1971). *Beyond freedom & dignity.* New York: Bantam. (This book formulates a famous behavioral psychologist's proposals for how science can contribute to improvements in human behavior.)

CHAPTER 20

Evaluation and Other Forms of Applied Research in the Social (and Health) Sciences

In the early 1970s, a program for curbing juvenile delinquency was initiated in New Jersey. It received much publicity and since its development, similar programs have been instituted in several other states as well as in other countries (Homant & Osowski, 1982:55; Lewis, 1983:210). The program, called *Scared Straight,*[1] was targeted for first-time nonviolent offenders in their early- to mid-teens (Finckenauer, 1982). The program's rationale was that many delinquents fail to understand the severe legal consequences of their continued delinquent and criminal activities. If they were to visit an adult prison, and be given a realistic picture of what a convict's life is like, maybe they could be turned away from future delinquency and crime.

In the typical Scared Straight program, a dozen or so young offenders are boarded onto a bus and taken to a maximum security prison. For an hour or so in the morning, they get a fairly standard tour of the prison. After lunch, the youths are taken to a room where they are confronted by five or six shouting, cursing prison inmates (often "lifers") chosen for their no-nonsense attitudes and for their skills in describing in brutal detail what prison life is like (Lundman, 1984:136; Waters & Wilson, 1979). A typical session with the prisoners will last two to three hours, and is drawn to a close with stern warnings from the inmates that the youngsters themselves can expect to be behind bars in a few more years unless they change their ways. It is common for the youngsters, normally jovial in the morning, to be sobbing before the session with the inmates is over.

Does the Scared Straight program work? An American television documentary starring a well-known actor (Peter Falk) hailed it as "90% successful," and showed that most of the participating youngsters believed that the experience made a difference in their lives (Waters & Wilson, 1979; Rice, 1980; Finckenauer, 1982:211). This type of evidence is known as anecdotal evidence, i.e., evidence based on impressionistic testimonials about the effects of some program or treatment.

Although certainly not worthless, especially in the initial stages of a program's evaluation, anecdotal evidence can be unreliable and sometimes very misleading (Dewsbury, 1984:184). Not only are there usually no control subjects in anecdotal evidence, but it is very common for participants in treatment programs to give favorable opinions, even when the programs are scientifically shown to be ineffective (Peele, 1983:41). In addition, for programs designed to reform delinquents and criminals, enthusiasm about the treatment is often a major criterion used by corrections officials to decide who is ready for release. Sensing that this is part of the game that must be played, and having no other treatments to compare it to, many recipients of Scared Straight treatment could be misleading officials about its effectiveness.

Before describing the scientific research on Scared Straight, stop for a moment and think about how to objectively answer the following question: Does Scared Straight work? First, you have to define ''work'' in a way that can be objectively measured. In this regard, most people would agree that the main objective of corrections programs is to reduce subsequent arrests (Minnesota Governor's Commission, 1973; Petersilia & Turner, 1986). Therefore, rearrest rates could be used to operationalize your dependent variable.

Your next major step might be to find a sizable number of delinquents, and assign half at random to the Scared Straight program. If random assignment is not possible, you might use a quasi-experimental design involving two carefully matched groups of delinquents.

Thus far, six studies of Scared Straight have been conducted. Four of these studies were ex post facto quasi-experiments. One of these four found that the exposure group had a significantly lower rearrest rate than the comparison group (Langer, 1981). Another found no difference between the exposure and comparison groups (Vreeland, 1981). A third reported significantly higher rearrest rates among the youths with the Scared Straight experience compared to those without it (Finckenauer, 1982:134). In the fourth study, results were presented separately by sex. For females, no significant effects were detected, while males with the Scared Straight experience had significantly higher rearrest rates than those without the experience (Buckner & Chesney-Lind, 1983).

The remaining two studies of Scared Straight involved after-only experimental designs. One study made its assessment after a six month follow-up (Yarborough, 1979), and the other after twelve months (Lewis, 1983). Both studies found no significant differences in overall recidivism rates between the experimentals and the controls. In summary, only one of the six studies of the effects of Scared Straight found the program effective in reducing recidivism rates. Additional research is in order (especially experimental studies), but at this point most scientific evidence does not support the view that Scared Straight reduces the probability of subsequent rearrest. Notice that this conclusion stands in stark contrast to the anecdotal evidence.

Scientific literature contains numerous examples of empirical research confirming anecdotal impressions, but it also contains many examples of empirical evidence contradicting anecdotal impressions. Despite all the logical arguments about why

Scared Straight programs are intended to give young offenders a realistic picture of what a convict's life is like. © James L. Shaffer.

Scared Straight *should* work, by and large the research suggests that it does not. With this example as a backdrop, let us now explore an important category of research in the social (and health) sciences, collectively known as applied research.

Types of Applied Research

It is important to know the difference between **basic research** and **applied research.** Basic (or pure) research is undertaken to expand scientific knowledge in some area. Applied research is for the purpose of finding solutions to practical problems (Rossi, Wright, & Wright, 1978:172; Rottenberg, 1988:390; Rossi & Freeman, 1989:420). In this context, a problem can include any social, health, or interpersonal condition that human beings want to change.

Distinguishing between applied and basic research is important, but there are two reasons why they should never be thought of as mutually exclusive. First, some studies serve both practical and pure research objectives, and thus can fit into either category (Rossi & Freeman, 1989:420). Second, much applied research is built on the foundations laid by basic research, and occasionally some basic research will spin off from applied research.

Applied research is divided into three categories: epidemiological (or diagnostic), feasibility, and evaluation. Each is described below, with an extended treatment given to the latter.

Epidemiological research assesses the prevalence of a problem. It typically consists of a survey based on a representative (or near-representative) sample that allows a researcher to estimate the proportion of a population that exhibits the problem. In clinical settings (to be discussed shortly), the equivalent of epidemiological research is called **diagnostic research.**

For example, many children born to mothers who drink substantial amounts of alcohol during pregnancy have been shown to suffer major physical and neurological damage (Abel, 1981; Fried, 1984:90). Even moderate use of alcohol during pregnancy now appears to cause more subtle damage in many cases (Able, 1984; Fried, 1984:91; Rosett & Weiner, 1984). As part of public health efforts to reduce alcohol drinking during pregnancy, epidemiological surveys have been conducted in several countries to estimate the extent to which pregnant women drink, and to identify subpopulations most in need of prevention efforts (Barrison, Waterson, & Murray-Lyon, 1985:17; Moss & Hensleigh, 1988; Rubin, Krasilnikoff, & Leventhal, 1988).

The findings from epidemiological research can be used in at least four ways. First, it can help determine the full extent to which a prevention or treatment program is needed. Second, such research can help identify subpopulations that are most in need of intervention. Third, it can help researchers identify some causes of the problem (and thereby devise more effective remedies). And, fourth, when repeated over several time frames, epidemiological research can help determine the extent to which a remedial program was successful.

Feasibility research estimates such things as the relative costs and benefits of alternative courses of action, and the public acceptability of those actions. Like epidemiological research, feasibility research often involves surveying a population. (In fact, sometimes epidemiological and feasibility surveys are conducted together.) However, feasibility research almost always goes beyond scientifically reporting survey results. Feasibility research pieces together cost estimates of various courses of action and the expected benefits. This research often includes recommendations about facilities and personnel needs.

Evaluation (or **evaluative**) **research** assesses the effectiveness of programs intended to alleviate social, health, or interpersonal problems. Evaluation research is also used in the fields of business and advertising for studying the effectiveness of marketing campaigns. Because evaluation research is an important type of applied research in the social (and health) sciences, we will explore it in considerable detail.

Evaluation Research

Evaluation research is an especially important type of applied research in the social and health sciences. It may be divided into two overlapping categories: clinical and nonclinical. They are discussed separately next.

Clinical Evaluation Research

Clinical evaluation research is concerned with individualized treatment of specifically diagnosed physical or mental illnesses or with interpersonal difficulties (e.g., marital or family discord). Clinical treatment is normally administered to persons who have sought help voluntarily or under slight social pressure. There are many examples of clinical programs being scientifically evaluated, especially in the fields of psychiatry, psychology, and social work.

One example was discussed in Chapter 15 (p. 226) regarding studies in which the stimulant drug methylphenidate (brand name Ritalin) has been used to reduce disruptive behavior of children diagnosed with attention-deficit hyperactive disorder (ADHD). These drugs do not cure the disorder, and do not eliminate all symptoms associated with hyperactivity and inattention, but they have been helpful in most cases (reviewed by Whalen et al., 1987; Carlson et al., 1992).

Another drug evaluated for its ability to curb undesirable behavior works by temporarily interfering with the body's production of the main male sex hormone, testosterone. Administering such drugs to male sex offenders seems to substantially lower their probability of re-offending (Berlin & Meinecke, 1981; Bradford, 1988; Kiersch, 1990).

History

If you were living a century and a half ago and became ill, all you could expect for care would be treatments based on "traditions" and the acquired expertise of individual physicians. It was not until the early 1800s that experimental methods (as outlined in Chapter 15) began to be used to assess the effectiveness of medical and surgical techniques (Hudson, 1983:215).

Considering the success in using experimental methods to assess the effectiveness of medicines and surgery, it may be surprising to learn that another century went by before experimentation was used to assess methods for treating mental illnesses. Two events are credited for having brought about scientific experimentation in the treatment of mental illnesses. One event was the publication of a review article in the 1950s by an English psychologist, Hans Eysenck (1952) (pron. I'sink). The article provoked a storm of controversy about the effectiveness of what was then the most widely used treatment for mental illness—psychotherapy. The impact of this article on the mental health community was characterized by one writer as a "bombshell" (Phares, 1979:457), so let us look at it in more detail.

In the article, Eysenck reached two conclusions: First, despite the widespread use of psychotherapy throughout the first half of the 20th century, very little was known from a scientific standpoint about its effects. Second, what could be gleaned from the available research was that psychotherapy had few beneficial effects, except possibly for persons with the least serious forms of mental disturbances. These issues, incidentally, still have not been settled, partly because there is such a wide variation in types of psychotherapy (Kasdin, 1989; for more recent evaluation studies on psychotherapy, see Bergin & Strupp, 1972; Sloane et al., 1976; Phares, 1979:468; Brown, 1987; Elson, 1992).

Shortly after its publication, Eysenck's article was denounced by most psychotherapists willing to comment publicly (Phares, 1979:458; Barlow & Hersen, 1984:13). Gradually, however, a number of psychotherapists conceded that rigorous research was needed to assess the effectiveness of psychotherapy (Barlow & Hersen, 1984:12). Others contended that scientific evaluation of something so complex and individualized as psychotherapy was impossible. Many believed that the unfavorable scientific results reflected inadequate research methodology rather than ineffective psychotherapy (reviewed by Barlow & Hersen, 1984:21).

The second event that helped bring about an increase in evaluation research was the behaviorist movement, which first began in psychology in the 1920s. **Behaviorism** is an approach to the study of behavior that focuses on the overt, observable aspects of behavior rather than on the subjective, cognitive aspects (Griffin, 1985:615; Cooper, Heron, & Herward, 1987:7; Sperry, 1987:37).

Most research conducted by behaviorists during the 1930s and 1940s involved recording simple behavior patterns by laboratory animals (e.g., how many times they would press a lever in order to obtain a food pellet) (Skinner, 1966:21). The emphasis that was placed on careful measurement of individual behavior became a hallmark of behaviorism (Barlow & Hersen, 1984:29). By the 1950s and 1960s behaviorists had moved much of their research out of animal laboratories and into clinical practice, with treatments for such things as phobias and childhood behavior problems (Cooper, Heron, & Herward, 1987:12). To understand how behaviorists emphasized the careful measurement of individual patient behavior in clinical research, it helps to outline the specific designs most often used.

Research Designs

The ideal research design for all forms of evaluation research is experimental (Sheldon & Parke, 1975:695; Glaser, 1978:88). Although all the experimental designs that are described in Chapter 15 can be used to evaluate the effects of various clinical treatment programs, some designs are used more often than others. Clinical studies often involve tracking single subjects over extended time frames. Thus, a special type of before-after no control group design called the **single-subject experimental design** is often utilized (Hersen & Barlow, 1976). Recall that any before-after no control group design must have at least two time frames, one before and one after imposition of an independent variable (see p. 228). With just two time frames, this design is very weak for making causal inferences, and this is especially the case when only one subject is being studied.

There are two ways to strengthen the basic before-after no control group design, and both ways have frequently been incorporated into clinical research with single subjects (Barlow & Hersen, 1984:88). The first way is to have a number of time frames both before and after imposition of the independent variable during which the dependent variable is measured. This allows the researcher to compare several measurements of the dependent variable before and after imposition of the independent variable, rather than measuring the dependent variable just once before and once after treatment.

The second way to strengthen the basic before-after no control group design is to convert it into a reversal experimental design. Recall that reversals are time frames following the initial introduction of treatment during which treatment is withheld, and sometimes is even reintroduced and again withheld. Reversals are incorporated into a "family" of experimental designs called ABA, ABAB, etc. (pp. 228–229). If each time the treatment is introduced, the symptoms diminish, and each time the treatment is withheld, the symptoms reappear, a researcher gains confidence in the effectiveness of the treatment (Levy & Olson, 1979; Barlow & Hersen, 1984:26).

Oftentimes, both ethical and practical considerations mitigate against treatment reversals in clinical research. From an ethical standpoint, if someone receiving treatment dramatically improves, a clinician would feel morally obliged to maintain the treatment. Nevertheless, from a scientific standpoint, one or more reversals can be helpful in determining whether the improvement was real or merely coincidental, or perhaps was even reflecting a placebo or Hawthorne effect.

From a practical standpoint, reversals are not possible with certain forms of treatment. For example, some treatment effects linger indefinitely beyond the time they are first administered. These effects are called **carry-over effects** (Barlow & Hersen, 1984:99). Although, clinically, carry-over effects are desirable, from a research perspective they make demonstrating the effectiveness of the treatment more difficult.

Nonclinical Evaluation Research

Nonclinical evaluation research is designed to assess the effects of programs that are applied to persons who did not individually seek help. Thus, nonclinical evaluation research is directed at groups of persons with some common problem. Sometimes entire populations will be the intended beneficiaries of a nonclinical program (e.g., most public health programs).

Before exploring how nonclinical programs are evaluated, it should be noted that clinical and nonclinical programs overlap. For example, some might consider Scared Straight a clinical program, provided that the lifers are viewed as "counselors" to the young delinquents. However, because the youngsters are dealt with in groups and did not voluntarily seek treatment, most would not regard Scared Straight as clinical treatment.

Following are discussions of some of the wide array of nonclinical programs that have been scientifically evaluated.

Considerable research has been undertaken in recent years to help teachers improve their teaching skills. These studies usually give teachers the following types of feedback: Either they receive periodic summaries of student ratings of their "teaching quality," or they are notified of the average scores their students receive on standardized tests (e.g., Anderson, Evertson, & Brophy, 1979; Millman, 1981; Feldman, 1987; Tan, 1992). Teachers in these studies are usually told to take the feedback "for whatever it's worth," and then are encouraged to experiment with different teaching methods while continuing to get feedback. Although most teachers improve with experience, these studies have shown that teachers receiving feedback improve faster than those who do not receive feedback.

The field of automobile safety provides several examples of nonclinical evaluation research. For instance, studies have been undertaken to determine the effects of raising and lowering the legal drinking age (Smith & Burvill, 1986), of varying the penalties for drunk driving (Ross, McCleary, & Epperlein, 1982; Ross, 1984; Forcier et al., 1986), and of mandating seat belt usage (Robertson, 1978; Conybeare, 1980). The dependent variable in most of these studies has been motor vehicle accident rates. These studies indicate that legal measures can significantly affect accident rates, at least during the first few years after a law is passed (especially if the laws are strictly enforced).

Another type of nonclinical evaluation research has been directed toward reform of welfare programs. In some cases, controlled experiments have been conducted involving hundreds or even thousands of welfare recipients. To give an example, one problem with most traditional welfare programs has been that if a recipient finds a job, welfare payments are automatically reduced by the amount being earned. In a few experimental programs, complete with control groups, different financial arrangements have been made to reward welfare recipients for working at jobs involving relatively low pay (Kershaw & Fair, 1976; Holden, 1987:608; Lie & Moroney, 1992).

History

With a few isolated exceptions, nonclinical evaluation research first developed in the 1950s, about the same time as its clinical counterpart (Rossi & Freeman, 1989:23). In the 1960s, a major boom in nonclinical evaluation research occurred in the United States when the Kennedy and Johnson Administrations declared "war on poverty" and on various related social problems (e.g., crime, illiteracy) (Rossi & Freeman, 1989:27; Coleman, 1990:134).

Funding for these programs was usually dispensed to local, state, and federal agencies (and sometimes to nonprofit organizations) in the form of grants. As part of the application process, applicants had to do more than just describe their program. They were also required to specify in precise measurable terms what they expected to accomplish, and to tell exactly how they would determine whether their program achieved its objectives.

Despite the above stipulations, many of the program evaluations that came out of the 1960s were little more than compilations of anecdotal comments made by program recipients. However, numerous evaluations were based on rigorous experimental designs (Dixon & Wright, 1975:58). The results of these studies have provided valuable information about the effectiveness of publicly funded efforts to confront various social problems.

Most of the programs initiated in the 1960s were disappointing in terms of their impact on America's social problems (Sheldon & Parke, 1975:694; Rossi, Wright, &

Wright, 1978). As a result, many social scientists found themselves seriously rethinking the theories on which these proposals were based (Alexander, 1972; Etzioni, 1973, 1977). This point will be returned to later in this chapter.

Research Designs

Like clinical evaluation studies, nonclinical evaluation studies ideally rely on experimental designs. Quasi-experimental designs (Campbell & Boruch, 1975; Peterson & Remington, 1989) and purely multivariate statistical designs (e.g., Coleman, 1990:140) are also employed. This brief review will focus on the use of experimental designs.

An important distinction in nonclinical evaluation research is between **summative** and **on-going** (or **process**) **research designs.** A summative research design is used for assessing programs that have a logical beginning and end for accomplishing their goals. An example would be Scared Straight.

An on-going research design is one that focuses on some aspect of organizational functioning. This type of evaluation research has no projected end point at which the evaluation will stop. For example, say that a new management style was planned to improve productivity. How could a researcher help determine whether this management style was actually better than the one it replaced? Strictly from a research design standpoint, the agency's employees could be divided into two randomly selected groups, with half assigned to work under the old management style and the rest to work under the new style. From a practical standpoint, however, maintaining these two separate groups would itself probably interfere with the organization's productivity.

An alternative would be a before-after no control group design. Such a design would require measuring the dependent variable (productivity) before the new management style went into effect, and then remeasuring it sometime after the new style was instituted. Let us assume that this was the chosen design, i.e., productivity was measured for the year prior to and for the year after the new management style went into effect. Such a simple before-after no control group design is weak, but, it can be strengthened in the same two ways mentioned in regard to single-subject clinical experiments. One involves adding several time frames for measuring productivity before or after introducing the new management style. The second would be to add reversals, or to even introduce some third management style. An agency can continue evaluating indefinitely the effects of different management styles, which is why the term on-going evaluation research design is used to describe it.

This hypothetical example can be considered an experimental design as long as the researcher has some control over the imposition of the independent variable. In this case, the control would be through cooperation between the researcher and the organization's administration.

Sometimes an evaluator has essentially no control over when the independent variable will be altered. Then a researcher simply looks retrospectively at how productivity has waxed and waned with changes in management styles. In these cases, the on-going evaluation research design should be considered quasi-experimental (an example is presented later in this chapter).

The Organizational Structure of Nonclinical Evaluation Research

Unlike clinical evaluation research, most nonclinical evaluation research is conducted in an organizational setting. Such a setting presents special problems that a researcher should be aware of. These problems are related to the following bureaucratic steps involved in organizational research: authorization, planning, implementation, day-to-day program functioning, and evaluation.

The *authorization* of a program usually comes from government or business administrators, who themselves often function under the approval of other officials (such as legislators, governors, or stockholders). Once authorizing personnel are convinced that a problem exists, they seek *planning* proposals (often in the form of a feasibility report).

After planners and administrative officials have agreed on which plan to implement, they often must seek funding and authorization for hiring the necessary personnel. After the program has been implemented, its *day-to-day functioning* must be managed and kept on track.

Even though the *evaluation* of most programs cannot take place until after they have been functioning for a significant amount of time (often years), evaluators should be involved in the project even before it is implemented. If evaluators are not involved early on in program planning, they may not be able to ensure proper evaluation of a program's impact. With the degree of organizational complexity usually required to conduct a successful nonclinical evaluation, it is not surprising that only a small fraction of new programs are ever scientifically evaluated.

Locating the Reports of Evaluation Research

Especially in the past 25 years, a number of journals have specialized in publishing the results of evaluation research (see the list at the end of this chapter). Nevertheless, many valuable studies of an evaluative nature never appear in conventional journals (or books). Instead, these studies are only "published" as in-house documents. **In-house** (or **agency-sponsored**) **documents** are published by, and only circulate within, a department or agency. Thus, in-house publications rarely come to the attention of the research community at large.

Currently, even the most sophisticated computerized literature searches contain little information about in-house documents. In the future, a central clearinghouse for such documents may be established, at least for keeping track of evaluation research reports. In the meantime, those interested in the effectiveness of agency-sponsored programs must use some ingenuity in locating relevant documents. It is often a good idea to write letters (form letters are fine) to each state, municipal, or federal agency that may have operated a program of interest, asking them for relevant documents and also asking for the names of any other contact persons.

Is it appropriate to cite an in-house document, and if so, how is this done? In reviewing past literature, you may cite in-house documents, although if a more widely circulated publication contains the same information, citing the latter is preferable. As a rule, unless authors are identified, the sponsoring agency is cited as the author, and the title of the document is treated like the title of a book (with the publisher being the agency that released the document).

The main point to keep in mind when citing an in-house document is that you want to assist your readers as much as possible in locating the document. Providing more than the usual amount of information (e.g., a publication number) can help.

Head Start: A Classical Example of Nonclinical Evaluation Research

One of the most famous social programs from the 1960s was a preschool educational enrichment program for underprivileged children called Head Start. This program is worth special attention here for two reasons. First, it has been the object of much evaluation research. Second, it highlights some of the complexities surrounding evaluation research, both from a scientific standpoint and in terms of the social and political decision making that has ensued.

Head Start was (and still is) a preschool program provided primarily to children from poor backgrounds. The program's purpose is to give these children cultural and educational experiences that middle and upper status children typically receive at home. As originally formulated, the purpose of Head Start was to prevent poor children from falling behind in academic achievement (Zigler & Muenchow, 1992).

Studies have shown that in the first three or four years of grade school, Head Start children performed as well on standardized tests as middle and upper status children, while poor children without Head Start experience did not. However, beyond primary school, Head Start children have been shown to slip in academic achievement to levels that are comparable to poor children without Head Start (Westinghouse Learning Corporation, 1969; Bentler & Woodward, 1978; Scheirer, 1978:56; Seitz, Apfel, & Rosenbaum, 1981; Becker & Gersten, 1982; Miller & Bizzell, 1984; Head Start Bureau, 1985; Stephan, 1986; Haskins, 1989; Holden, 1990:1400; Kantrowitz & McCormick, 1992). In other words, beyond the 4th or 5th grade, Head Start students do not perform significantly better academically than control students from the same neighborhoods and socioeconomic background.

Despite this evidence, Head Start programs have remained very popular among the general public and among politicians responsible for the programs' financing. Funding for America's Head Start (and related) programs have increased almost every year since these programs first began in the 1960s (Rothbart, 1975:23; Leslie, 1989).

Social scientists have been puzzled, if not dismayed, by the inconsistency between the evidence that Head Start has not accomplished its main objective, and the fact that it continues to receive both popular and political support. At least three factors can help explain this paradox, and they offer lessons to those interested in evaluation research.

First, people who are not well-trained in science often become confused by the bewildering array of claims and counterclaims surrounding scientific and anecdotal evidence. Especially when the evidence is counter-intuitive, people often trust their intuition rather than the evidence based on sound research methodology.

Second, when confronted by serious problems, people prefer to do something rather than nothing, even if the chance of success is only slight. This tendency to grasp at straws not only typifies how some people try to solve social problems, but also helps explain the vast expenditures every year on quack medical cures.

Third, even if a program does not accomplish its originally intended objective, there are sometimes other benefits that may justify its continuation (Scheirer, 1978). For instance, Head Start provides a relatively safe and well-managed day care for poor families (especially single mothers), thereby freeing them to secure employment. In addition, Head Start appears to have promoted the physical health of participants (Stephan, 1986). Also, one study of a program similar to Head Start (although quite a bit more expensive) found that, even though achievement on standardized tests was not affected, several other behavior patterns were improved. Specifically, recipients of the preschool program had significantly lower high school dropout rates, lower unemployment, fewer teenage pregnancies, and lower arrest rates (Berrueta-Clement, Schweinhart, & Barnett, 1984). However, at least one replication effort reportedly failed to confirm the findings of this latter study (Holden, 1990:1402).

An Example of a Quasi-Experimental Design Used in Evaluation Research

For another example of evaluation research, consider a quasi-experiment undertaken in Wisconsin to assess the impact of raising cigarette taxes on cigarette consumption (Peterson & Remington, 1989). The main data for the study is contained in a graph showing the annual per capita sales of cigarette packs between 1950 and 1988 (Figure 20.1).

This graph shows that per capita cigarette purchases followed an irregular increase between 1950 and 1980, but a substantial drop began in 1983. This drop came in the wake of a 9-cents-per-pack state tax increase. The drop in sales continued during a time that (a) a Wisconsin clean indoor air act went into effect, and (b) an 8-cents-per-pack federal tax was imposed.

Give some thought to the following questions: First, why would this study be categorized as a quasi-experimental design rather than an experimental design? Second, how could the design have been strengthened? Third, does this study provide persuasive evidence that increasing taxes on cigarettes caused a drop in the purchase of cigarettes? And, fourth, why would this study be considered a nonclinical, rather than a clinical, evaluation research?

In answer to the first question, the study was not an experiment because the researchers had no influence over the imposition of either tax increase or over the passage of the clean indoor air act. The researchers merely made retrospective observations of how these three factors coincided with changes in the dependent variable (cigarette sales).

■ **FIGURE 20.1**

Per capita sales of cigarettes in Wisconsin, 1950–1988 (Adapted from the *Wisconsin Medical Journal,* November 1989, p. 41).

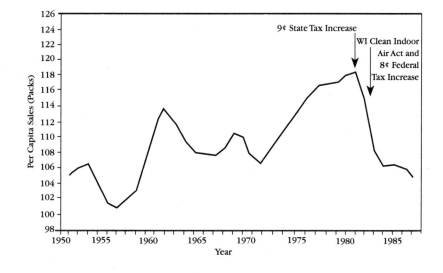

In answer to the second question, there are various methods that could be used to justify making causal inferences with greater confidence. Here are some examples: The study could be extended and converted into an actual experiment if the researchers could convince legislators to hike the cigarette tax even higher. If this were to be done at, say, three-year intervals and the cigarette purchasing rate went down more with each hike, the case for a causal linkage would be strengthened. Better still, if the researchers could convince legislators to lower the tax for a few years, and then see if the cigarette purchases rebounded, this would really build a strong case for a causal connection. Another way to strengthen the design would be to leave it as a quasi-experiment, but add one or more comparison groups. These comparison groups could be some neighboring states where cigarette taxes were not raised in the 1980s. These states should not have exhibited the slump in sales until about a year later, when the federal tax was imposed.

In answer to the third question, the study provides some evidence (although far from definitive) that increasing cigarette taxes causes a drop in cigarette purchases. (No confident conclusions can be made about the effects of the passage of the clean indoor air act.) In the full text of the article, explanations are offered for the two other main drops in cigarette purchases (i.e., those in the early 1950s and the early 1960s). However, the researchers argue that the only time taxes on cigarettes were significantly raised was in the 1980s, and this was when the greatest drop occurred in cigarette purchases.

This study was clearly nonclinical. Raising cigarette taxes is obviously a different approach to reducing cigarette consumption than numerous programs in which clients seek and obtain individualized treatment, which also have been scientifically evaluated (e.g., Lichstein & Sallis, 1981; Murray, Luepker, & Johnson, 1984; Hajek et al., 1989; Minnekerhugel, Unland, & Buchkremer, 1992).

Some Final Thoughts About Evaluation Research

Evaluation research can be both extremely rewarding and very frustrating. Reward comes from knowing that the power of the scientific method is being harnessed to help improve the human condition.

Frustration, especially in nonclinical evaluation research, can come from the difficulties experienced in securing the necessary cooperation within a large organization long enough to objectively evaluate a program. Another source of frustration is that decisions about whether to retain a program are often made without seriously considering evidence from evaluation reports (Rothbart, 1975:25; Rossi & Freeman, 1989:29). It should be kept in mind that agency heads and program managers often have little training in social research methods, and they must often make decisions on grounds having little to do with program effectiveness (Halpert, 1973:377).

When confronted with organizational obstacles, researchers need to remain calm and professional. The wheels of science grind slowly and finely, whereas administrative decisions often take place quickly and on the basis of very incomplete knowledge. Ultimately, researchers should remember that their main function is to provide honest and objective assessments. How those assessments are utilized is largely an administrative decision. Sometimes evaluation efforts do not have much impact when they first appear, but may be very influential years later.

Some programs are retained far beyond the point of being cost-effective simply because of political and bureaucratic "inertia" (Arnhoff, 1975:1277). For these programs, state and federal legislators have passed so-called **sunset laws.** These laws automatically terminate program funding after a specified number of years unless extraordinary steps are taken to maintain funding. Oftentimes, funding maintenance can only occur if evaluation research results have been favorable.

Finally, social scientists need to be cautioned against overselling the value of programs for dealing with major social problems. As noted earlier, many social scientists who proposed solutions to social problems in the 1960s lost credibility for themselves, and for social science in general, in the face of hard evidence that most of the social programs instituted during those years were ineffective (Etzioni, 1973, 1977). If there is a lesson to be learned, it is that social scientists should be cautious in claiming to have solutions to the problems they study. At the same time, social scientists should not exaggerate the power of evaluation research for assessing the effects of social programs. Although the collective efforts of evaluation research have contributed greatly toward determining the effectiveness of programs, one or two evaluation studies rarely settle questions about a program's effectiveness.

Summary

Applied research is research undertaken to help deal with "real world" problems. In the social sciences, most problems are of a social or health (both mental and public) nature. The opposite of applied research is basic (or pure) research, although these two types of research are not always mutually exclusive, and oftentimes complement one another.

Three types of applied research can be identified: epidemiological, feasibility, and evaluation. Epidemiological (or diagnostic) research is undertaken to identify the extent of a problem at one or more points in time. It is often used to determine where a problem exists to the greatest degree.

Feasibility research is used to help develop a plan for effectively dealing with a problem. Such things as the availability of resources, cost-benefit ratios, and the likelihood of client or public acceptance of a plan are all part of feasibility research.

Evaluation (or evaluative) research refers to studies undertaken to help determine the degree to which some form of treatment or other program was effective in accomplishing its intended objectives. Ideally, evaluation research is based on experimental designs, although quasi-experimental and occasionally strictly multivariate statistical designs are also used.

Evaluation research can be divided into two categories: clinical and nonclinical. Clinical evaluation research evaluates the effectiveness of individualized treatment for persons who have voluntarily sought help. The history of clinical evaluation research can be traced back to events in the 1950s.

Even though many experimental designs are used in clinical evaluations, the most frequently used designs are variations on the before-after no control group design. This choice of designs is especially common for what are called single-subject experiments. Even though the basic before-after no control group design is weak for justifying causal inferences, it can be strengthened in two ways, both of which are often found in single-subject experiments. One way is to measure the dependent variable over multiple time frames both before and after imposition of the independent variable, and the other way is to introduce one or more reversals of the independent variable while continuing to measure the dependent variable.

Nonclinical evaluation research assesses the effectiveness of programs designed to help groups (and sometimes entire populations) of people, most of whom have not individually sought help. Historically, the most significant rise in such research came in the 1960s with U.S. governmental attempts to deal with poverty and other social problems.

Methodologically, two main categories of nonclinical evaluation studies can be identified: summative and on-going (or process). Summative studies employ a wide range of experimental designs and are applied to programs that have a logical end point after which assessments of effectiveness are made. On-going studies usually involve some aspect of the continuing functioning of an organization. Most on-going evaluation studies utilize before-after no control group experimental designs. The same two methods for strengthening this design in single-subject clinical studies can also be used in on-going nonclinical evaluation studies.

Many of the difficulties in conducting evaluation research were discussed.

Notes

[1] Several programs very similar to Scared Straight have been developed. The best known of these are called *JOLT* (for *Juvenile Offenders Learn Truth*) (Yarborough, 1979; Homant & Osowski, 1982:57), *Face-to-Face* (Vreeland, 1981), and *Stay Straight* (Buckner & Chesney-Lind, 1983). For our purposes, the research on the effects of these programs are all dealt with under the name Scared Straight.

References

Abel, E. L. (1981). Behavior teratology of alcohol. *Psychological Bulletin, 90,* 564–581.

Abel, E. L. (1984). *Fetal alcohol syndrome and fetal alcohol effects.* New York: Plenum.

Alexander, T. (1972). The social engineers retreat under fire. *Fortune, 86,* 132–148.

Anderson, L., Evertson, C., & Brophy, J. (1979). An experimental study of effective teaching in first-grade reading groups. *Elementary School Journal, 79,* 193–223.

Arnhoff, F. N. (1975). Social consequences of policy toward mental illness. *Science, 188,* 1277–1281.

Barlow, D. H., & Hersen, M. (1984). *Single case experimental designs: Strategies for studying behavior change* (2nd ed.). New York: Pergamon.

Barrison, I. G., Waterson, E. J., & Murray-Lyon, I. M. (1985). Adverse effects of alcohol in pregnancy. *British Journal of Addiction, 80,* 11–22.

Becker, W. C., & Gersten, R. (1982). A follow-up of Follow Through: The later effect of the direct instruction model on children in fifth and sixth grades. *American Educational Research Journal, 19,* 75–92.

Bentler, P. M., & Woodward, J. A. (1978). A Head Start reevaluation: Positive effects are not yet demonstrable. *Evaluation Quarterly, 2,* 493–509.

Bergin, A E., & Strupp, H. H. (1972). *Changing frontiers in the science of psychotherapy.* New York: Aldine.

Berlin, F. S., & Meinecke, C. F. (1981). Treatment of sex offenders with antiandrogenic medication: Conceptualization, review and treatment modalities, and preliminary findings. *American Journal of Psychiatry, 138,* 601–607.

Berrueta-Clement, J. R., Schweinhart, L. J., & Barnett, W. S. (1984). *Changed lives: The effects of the Perry preschool program on youths through age 19.* Ypsilanti, MI.: High Scope Press.

Bradford, J. M. (1988). Organic treatment for the male sex offender. *Annals of the New York Academy of Sciences, 528,* 193–202.

Brown, J. (1987). A review of meta-analyses conducted on psychotherapy outcome research. *Clinical Psychology Review, 7,* 1–23.

Buckner, J. C., & Chesney-Lind, M. (1983). Dramatic cures for juvenile crime: An evaluation of a prisoner-run delinquency prevention program. *Criminal Justice and Behavior, 10,* 227–247.

Campbell, D. T., & Boruch, R. F. (1975). Making the case for randomized assignment to treatments by considering the alternatives: Six ways in which quasi-experimental evaluations in compensatory education tend to underestimate effects. In C. A. Bennett & A. A. Lunmsbaine (Eds.), *Evaluation and experiment.* New York: Academic Press.

Carlson, C. L., Pelham, W. E., Milich, R., & Dixon, J. (1992). Single and combined effects of metylphenidate and behavior therapy on the classroom performance of children with attention-deficit hyperactive disorder. *Journal of Abnormal Child Psychology, 20,* 213–232.

Coleman, J. S. (1990). *Equality and achievement in education.* Boulder, CO: Westview Press.

Conybeare, J. A. C. (1980). Evaluation of automobile safety regulations: The case of compulsory seat belt legislation in Australia. *Policy Sciences, 12,* 27–39.

Cooper, J. O., Heron, T. E., & Herward, W. L. (1987). *Applied behavior analysis.* Columbus, OH: Merrill.

Dixon, M., & Wright, W. C. (1975). *Juvenile delinquency prevention programs.* Nashville, TN: Peabody College for Teachers.

Dewsbury, D. A. (1984). *Comparative psychology in the twentieth century.* Stroudsburg, PA: Hutchinson Ross.

Elson, J. (1992, July 6). Is Freud finished? *Newsweek,* p. 60.

Etzioni, A. (1973). Faulty engineers or neglected experts. *Science, 181,* 13.

Etzioni, A. (1977, December). One and a half cheers for social science. *Psychology Today,* p. 168.

Eysenck, H. J. (1952). The effects of psychotherapy: An evaluation. *Journal of Consulting Psychology, 16,* 319–324.

Feldman, K. A. (1987). Research productivity and scholarly accomplishment of college teachers as related to their instructional effectiveness: A review and exploration. *Research in Higher Education, 23,* 227–298.

Finckenauer, J. O. (1982). *Scared straight! and the panacea phenomenon.* Englewood Cliffs, NJ: Prentice-Hall.

Forcier, M. W., Kurtz, N. R., Parent, D. G., & Corrigan, M. D. (1986). Deterrence of drunk driving in Massachusetts: Criminal justice system impacts. *International Journal of the Addictions, 21,* 1197–1220.

Fried, P. A. (1984). Alcohol and the newborn infant. In S. Kacew & M. J. Reasor (Eds.), *Toxicology and the newborn* (pp. 86–100). The Netherlands: Elsevier.

Glaser, D. (1978). Evaluation of sex offender treatment programs. Appendix B in E. M. Brecher, *Treatment programs for sex offenders* (pp. 85–92). Washington, DC: U.S. Government Printing Office (Stock No. 027–000–00591–8).

Griffin, D. R. (1985). Animal consciousness. *Neuroscience & Biobehavioral Reviews, 9,* 615–622.

Halpert, H. P. (1973). Research utilization, a problem in goal setting: What is the question. *American Journal of Public Health, 63,* 377–378.

Hajek, P., Jarvis, M. J., Belcher, M., Sutherland, G., & Belcher, M. (1989). Effect of smoke-free cigarettes on 24 h cigarette withdrawal: A double-blind placebo-control study. *Psychopharmacology, 97,* 99–102.

Haskins, R. (1989). Beyond metaphor: The efficacy of early childhood education. *American Psychologist, 44,* 274–282.

Head Start Bureau. (1985). *Final report: The impact of Head Start on children, families, and communities.* Washington, DC: U.S. Government Printing Office (DHHS Publication No. OHDS 85–31193).

Hersen, M., & Barlow, D. H. (1976). *Single case experimental designs.* New York: Pergamon.

Holden, C. (1987). Is the time ripe for welfare reform? *Science, 238,* 607–609.

Holden, C. (1990). Head start enters adulthood. *Science, 247,* 1400–1402.

Homant, R. J., & Osowski, G. (1982). The politics of juvenile awareness programs: A case study of JOLT. *Criminal Justice and Behavior, 9,* 55–68.

Hudson, R. P. (1983). *Disease and its control: The shaping of modern thought.* Westport, CT: Greenwood.

Kantrowitz, B. A., & McCormick, J. M. (1992, January 27). A head start does not last. *Newsweek,* pp. 44–45.

Kazdin, A. E. (1989). *Behavior modification in applied settings* (4th ed.). Pacific Grove, CA: Brooks/Cole.

Kershaw, D., & Fair, J. (1976). *The New Jersey income maintenance experience.* New York: Academic Press.

Kiersch, T. A. (1990). Treatment of sex offenders with Depo-Provera. *Bulletin of the American Academy of Psychiatry and Law, 18,* 179–187.

Langer, S. (1981). *'Scared straight'? Fear in the deterrence of delinquency.* Lanham, MD: University Press of America.

Leslie, C. (1989, February 20). Everybody likes head start. *Newsweek,* pp. 49–50.

Lewis, R. V. (1983). Scared straight—California style: Evaluation of the San Quentin Squires program. *Criminal Justice and Behavior, 10,* 209–226.

Lichstein, K. L., & Sallis, J. F. (1981). Covert sensitization for smoking: In search of efficacy. *Addictive Behavior, 6,* 83–91.

Lie, G-Y., & Moroney, R. M. (1992). A controlled evaluation of comprehensive social services provided to teenage mothers receiving AFDC. *Research on Social Work Practice, 2,* 429–447.

Lundman, R. J. (1984). *Prevention and control of juvenile delinquency.* New York: Oxford University Press.

Miller, L. B., & Bizzell, R. P. (1984). Long-term effects of four preschool programs: Ninth- and tenth-grade results. *Child Development, 55,* 1570–1587.

Millman, J. (Ed.). (1981). *Handbook of teacher evaluation.* New York: Academic Press.

Minnekerhugel, E., Unland, H., & Buchkremer, G. (1992). Behavioral relapse prevention strategies in smoking cessation. *International Journal of the Addictions, 27,* 627–634.

Minnesota Governor's Commission on Crime Prevention and Control. (1973). *Evaluation design of community-based corrections projects.* St. Paul: Minnesota Department of Corrections.

Moss, N., & Hensleigh, P. A. (1988). Substance use by Hispanic and white non-Hispanic pregnant adolescents: A preliminary survey. *Journal of Youth and Adolescence, 17,* 531–541.

Murray, D., Luepker, R., & Johnson, C. A. (1984). The prevention of cigarette smoking in children: A comparison of four strategies. *Journal of Applied Social Psychology, 14,* 274–288.

Peele, S. (1983, April). Through a glass darkly. *Psychology Today,* pp. 38–42.

Petersilia, J. E., & Turner, S. (1986). *Prison versus probation in California: Implications for crime and offender recidivism.* Washington, DC: National Institute of Justice (R–3186–NIJ).

Peterson, D. E., & Remington, P. (1989, November). Publicity, policy and trends in cigarette smoking: Wisconsin 1950-1988. *Wisconsin Medical Journal,* pp. 40–41.

Phares, E. J. (1979). *Clinical psychology: Concepts, methods, and profession.* Homewood, IL: Dorsey.

Rice, B. (1980, October). The erratic life of "scared straight." *Psychology Today,* p. 14.

Robertson, L. S. (1978). The seat belt use law in Ontario: Effects on actual use. *Canadian Journal of Public Health, 69,* 154–157.

Rosett, H. L., & Weiner, L. (1984). *Alcohol and the fetus: A clinical perspective.* New York: Oxford University Press.

Ross, H. L. (1984). *Deterring the drunk driver: Legal policy and social control* (rev. ed.). Lexington, MA: Lexington Books.

Ross, H. L., McCleary, R., & Epperlein, T. (1982). Deterrence of drinking and driving in France: An evaluation of the law of July 12, 1978. *Law and Society Review, 16,* 345–374.

Rossi, P. H., & Freeman, H. E. (1989). *Evaluation: A systematic approach* (4th ed.). Newbury Park, CA: Sage.

Rossi, P. H., Wright, J. D., & Wright, S. R. (1978). The theory and practice of applied social research. *Evaluation Quarterly, 2,* 171–191.

Rothbart, G. S. (1975). Book review. *Contemporary Sociology, 4,* 23–25.

Rottenberg, S. (1988). The economic approach applied to science polity. *International Journal on the Unity of the Sciences, 1,* 387–398.

Rubin, D. H., Krasilnikoff, P. A., & Leventhal, J. M. (1988). Cigarette smoking and alcohol consumption during pregnancy by Danish women and their spouses—A potential source of fetal morbidity. *American Journal of Drug and Alcohol Abuse, 14,* 405–417.

Scheirer, M. A. (1978). Program participants' positive perceptions: Psychological conflict of interest in social program evaluation. *Evaluation Quarterly, 2,* 53–70.

Seitz, V., Apfel, N. H., & Rosenbaum, L. K. (1981). Project Head Start and follow-through: A longitudinal evaluation of adolescents. In M. J. Begab, H. C. Haywood, & H. L. Garber (Eds.), *Psychosocial influences in retarded performance, Volume 2.* Baltimore, MD: University Park Press.

Sheldon, E. B., & Parke, R. (1975). Social indicators. *Science, 188,* 693–699.

Skinner, B. F. (1966). Operant behavior. In W. K. Honig (Ed.), *Operant behavior: Areas of research and application* (pp. 12–34). New York: Appleton-Century-Crofts.

Sloane, R. B., Staples, F. R., Cristol, A. H., Yorkston, N. J., & Whipple, K. (1976). Patient characteristics and outcome in psychotherapy and behavior therapy. *Journal of Consulting and Clinical Psychology, 44,* 330–339.

Smith, D. I., & Burvill, P. W. (1986). Effect on traffic safety of lowering the drinking age in three Australian states. *Journal of Drug Issues, 16,* 183–198.

Sperry, R. W. (1987). Structure and significance of the consciousness revolution. *Journal of Mind and Behavior, 8,* 37–66.

Stephan, S. (1986). *Funding, administration, and recent evaluations.* Washington, DC: Congressional Research Service.

Tan, C. M. (1992). An evaluation of the use of continuous assessment in the teaching of physiology. *Higher Education, 23,* 255–272.

Vreeland, A. D. (1981). *Evaluation of Face-to-Face: A juvenile aversion program.* Dallas: University of Texas Health Science Center.

Waters, H. F., & Wilson, C. H. (1979, April 23). Telling it like it is. *Newsweek,* p. 101.

Westinghouse Learning Corporation. (1969). *The Impact of Head Start: An evaluation of the effects of Head Start on children.* Washington, DC: U.S. Office of Economic Opportunity.

Whalen, C. K., Henker, B., Swanson, J. M., Granger, D., & Kliewer, W. (1987). Natural social behaviors in hyperactive children: Dose effects of methylphenidate. *Journal of Consulting and Clinical Psychology, 55,* 187–193.

Yarborough, J. C. (1979). *Evaluation of JOLT as a deterrence program.* Madison: Michigan Department of Correction.

Zigler, E., & Muenchow, S. (1992). *Head Start: The inside story of America's most successful educational experiment.* New York: Basic Books.

Suggested Reading

Caro, F. G. (1977). *Reading in evaluation research* (2nd ed.). Scranton, PA: Basic Books. (This book of readings provides helpful guidelines and examples of evaluation research, especially in the field of education.)

Epstein, I., & Tripodi, T. (1977). *Research techniques for program planning, monitoring, and evaluation.* New York: Columbia University Press. (One of the most comprehensive and clearly written general texts available on evaluation research and related topics.)

Rutman, L. (1977). *Evaluation research methods: A basic guide.* Beverly Hills, CA: Sage. (This is an excellent sourcebook for providing an overview of the fundamentals of evaluation research as well as how this research links up with program planning and implementation.)

Numerous social science journals specialize in publishing evaluation and other applied research. Below are the titles of many of these journals, with separate listings for clinical and nonclinical areas.

Specialized Journals in Clinical Applied Research

Cognitive Therapy and Research
Behavioral Psychotherapy
Behavioral Research and Therapy
Clinical Social Work Journal
Journal of Applied Behavior Analysis
Journal of Applied Psychology
Journal of Applied Social Psychology
Journal of Behavior Therapy and Experimental Psychiatry
Journal of Clinical Psychiatry
Journal of Clinical Psychology
Journal of Consulting and Clinical Psychology
Journal of Counseling Psychology
Journal of Substance Abuse Treatment

Specialized Journals in Nonclinical Applied Research

American Journal of Public Health
Education Studies
Evaluation Quarterly
Evaluation Review
Evaluation and the Health Professions
Evaluation and Program Planning
Journal of Early Intervention
Journal of Safety Research
Policy Sciences
Prevention
Prevention in the Human Services
Preventive Medicine
Public Health
Public Welfare
Social Indicators Research

CHAPTER 21

Epilogue

The primary and most immediate purpose of this book has been to give students an in-depth tour of how scientific methods are used for studying social and behavioral phenomena. This concluding chapter is addressed to students who want to further develop their understanding of research methods. Much of what you need to learn beyond the basics can be acquired not by further reading and classroom instruction, but by actually conducting scientific research. Therefore, as soon as possible, you should begin to exercise your research skills and then look for help whenever you have problems.

You should expect to learn new things and improve your research skills every time you undertake a research project. As you gain experience, however, your learning will become increasingly subtle and specific to a particular area of study.

Five suggestions can be made to help you to perfect your research skills beyond the ideas presented in this text.

First, if your goal is to become truly proficient at research, one suggestion can not be overemphasized: Start *doing* research as soon and as often as possible. There is no substitute for practice once the basics are understood. As you start, be careful not to take on bigger projects than you can successfully execute, and do not be disappointed if your early attempts fail to yield anything worth publishing.

Second, seek out and give serious attention to the advice and criticisms of fellow researchers and teachers. Take their comments as evidence of their desire to help, not as an attempt to be discouraging. If you have a "thin skin" when others criticize your ideas, your career as a researcher will be filled with frustration. On the other hand, if you can accept criticism, it can be extremely useful. This does not mean that you should automatically follow all advice that others give you; it simply means that, as much as your intellectual integrity will allow, you should seek out and try to accommodate the reactions of others to your work. The more you write, the more you will realize that no one's research efforts are beyond improvement, but the more people you have critique your work, the closer it will come to perfection.

Third, become proficient in statistics. This text was specially designed to emphasize the importance of statistics in social science research. Nevertheless, it leaves out details that researchers need to be familiar with in order to carry out empirical research. Besides taking courses in statistics, you can gain valuable insights by reading research reports with an eye toward noting which statistical methods were used and why. Becoming acquainted with at least one of the spreadsheet and statistical programs that are currently available on computer is also important for all contemporary researchers.

Fourth, familiarize yourself with the essential linkage between scientific theory and empirical research. Learn to shuttle between these two complementary realms of scientific thought. As you do so, you will sharpen your intellectual abilities to formulate empirically testable hypotheses.

Fifth, maintain a sensitivity to the ethical issues that surround your research. Whether you seek pure knowledge or practical solutions, never lose sight of the social fabric of which you and the entire scientific enterprise are a part. The threads of this fabric can be frayed by those who disregard the impact of their work on the lives of others. Rest assured that knowledge engenders social change, albeit ever so slowly. As a social scientist, you must not be irresponsible in promoting that change.

If you plan to pursue a career in which research methods are important, it may be wise to keep this text for reference. From time to time, you will want to refresh your memory about various research concepts. Those of you who become extensively involved in scientific research may find helpful information in the suggested readings at the end of each chapter.

In closing, I hope that you have gotten more out of this text than just an understanding of the process of conducting social scientific research. Perhaps my ultimate goal has been to share some of the wonder and joy that we social scientists feel when we peer beneath some tiny portion of the shroud that covers secrets of our own existence as social creatures.

Major Journals in the Various Social (and Related) Sciences

W orldwide, it has been conservatively estimated that there are more than 6,000 professional journals published in the social sciences (Brittain, 1990:106) For all the sciences combined, the estimate is more than 108,000, up nearly 60,000 in just the past two decades (Hamilton, 1990:1331)! Some social science journals are very general in the topics they cover, whereas others are very specific.

You should become acquainted with journals in your own chosen area of study. To get you started, below are brief lists of widely read journals in each of the main social sciences. In providing this list, there is no intention to suggest that these are necessarily the "best" journals. In fact, researchers are still wrangling over what criteria to use in assessing the "quality" of journals and of the articles they publish (see Boor, 1982). Also, because no clear boundaries separate the social sciences from one another, many interdisciplinary journals may be just as influential as are the leading discipline-affiliated journals (Allen, 1990). Furthermore, readers should bear in mind that some journals considered to be dominant in the United States and Canada may not be so in other countries.

With these qualifications in mind, listed below are five of the leading journals affiliated with each of the main social sciences.

Anthropology

American Anthropologist
American Journal of Physical Anthropology
Current Anthropology
Folia Primatologica
Primatology

Criminology/Criminal Justice

Criminal Justice and Behavior
Criminology
International Journal of Criminology and Penology
Journal of Criminal Law and Criminology
Law and Society Review

Economics

American Economic Review
Bell Journal of Economics
Business Economics
Economic Development and Cultural Change
Review of Economics and Statistics

Geography

Association of American Geographers Annals
Cartographic Journal
Geography
Geographical Review
Journal of Geography

History

American Historical Review
English Historical Review
Journal of American History
Western Historical Quarterly
William and Mary Quarterly

Philosophy

American Philosophical Quarterly
Analysis
British Journal of Philosophy of Science
Journal of Philosophy
Philosophical Review

Political Science

American Journal of Political Science
American Political Science Review
Politics and Society
Politics and the Life Sciences
Public Opinion Quarterly

Psychology

American Psychologist
American Journal of Psychology
Journal of Personality and Social Psychology
Psychological Bulletin
Psychological Reports

Social Work

Health and Social Work
Journal of Independent Social Work
Research on Social Work Practice
Social Work
Social Work in Education

Sociology

American Sociological Review
American Journal of Sociology
Social Forces
Social Problems
Qualitative Sociology

Social scientists share many interests and research methods, and a growing proportion of journals are of an interdisciplinary nature. Ten of the hundreds of important interdisciplinary journals are as follows:

Aggressive Behavior
Archives of Sexual Behavior
Journal for the Scientific Study of Religion
Journal of Sex Research
Journal of Marriage and the Family
Journal of Conflict Resolution
Journal of Social Issues
Journal of Studies on Alcohol
Sex Roles
Social Science Information

In addition to the numerous journals that cut across social science disciplines are many journals that link social science with the natural sciences, especially with biology. Ten of these journals are as follows:

Advances in the NeuroSciences
Behavioral Neuroscience
Behavioral Neuropsychiatry

Behavior Genetics
Cortex
Hormones and Behavior
Neuropsychobiology
Neuropsychologia
Neurobehavioral Toxicology and Teratology
Physiology and Behavior

Here are five of the major journals in each of the near social sciences:

Education

Educational and Psychological Measurement
Educational Research
Educational Studies
Journal of Higher Education
Research in Special Education

Ethology

American Journal of Primatology
Animal Behavior
Ethology
Ethology and Sociobiology
Primates

Psychiatry

American Journal of Psychiatry
Biological Psychiatry
Psychiatric Annals
Psychiatric Research
Social Psychiatry

Public Health

American Journal of Public Health
American Review of Public Health
Journal of Health and Social Behavior
Public Health Reports
Vital and Health Statistics

Sociobiology

Behavioral Ecology and Sociobiology
Brain and Behavior
Ethology and Sociobiology
Politics and the Life Sciences
Social Biology

Journals in the fields of journalism/communications and marketing/business that rely heavily on social science research methodology are as follows:

Journalism/Communications

Communication Research
Journalism Quarterly
Journal of Broadcasting and Electronic Media
Journal of Communication
Newspaper Research Review

Marketing/Business

Journal of Advertising Research
Journal of Consumer Research
Journal of Marketing
Journal of Marketing Research
Marketing Science

References

Allen, M. P. (1990, November). The "quality" of journals in sociology reconsidered: Objective measures of journal influence. *ASA Footnotes, 18,* 4–5.

Boor, M. (1982). The citation impact factor: Another dubious index of journal quality. *American Psychologist, 37,* 975–977.

Brittain, J. M. (1990). Cultural boundaries of the social sciences in the 1990s; new policies for documentation, information and knowledge creation. *International Social Science Journal, 41,* 105–117.

Hamilton, J. (1990). Publishing by—and for?—the numbers. *Science, 250,* 1331–1332.

Referencing Formats for Various Social Science Associations and Journals

T he main referencing formats used in the social sciences are illustrated in this appendix. Since referencing formats are distinctive for articles, authored books, and chapters in edited books, these are presented separately for each format.

Here are some additional general comments to note about referencing in the social sciences:

A. In order to make it easier for editorial changes and comments to be inserted, most journal and book editors ask that all references be double spaced throughout.

B. Underlining in references are translated into italics in typeset publications.

C. For government documents with no clear author, the institution sponsoring the publication is considered the author. For other articles with no author indicated, Anonymous is usually used.

D. The word ''The'' is dropped from the beginning of all journal titles.

E. In most publications, references are arranged alphabetically according to the senior author's last name (occasionally they are listed in the order in which they were cited in the body of the article).

F. For two articles by the same author(s), the one with the oldest publication date is listed first. And when there are two articles by the same author(s) published in the same year, one is assigned the letter ''a'' at the end of the year of publication, and the other is assigned the letter ''b.''

Referencing Format in Journals Published by the American Psychological Association

Articles

Fedigan, L. M. (1983). Dominance and reproductive success in primates. *Yearbook of Physical Anthropology, 26,* 91–129.

Nigro, G. N., Hill, D. E., Gelbein, M. E., & Clark, C. L. (1988). Changes in the facial prominence of women and men over the last decade. Psychology of Women Quarterly, 12, 225–235.

Kohfeld, C. W., & Spague, J. (1990). Demography, police behavior, and deterrence. *Criminology, 28,* 111–136.

Wimberly, D. W. (1990). Investment dependence and alternative explanations of third world mortality: A cross-national study. *American Sociological Review, 55,* 77–91.

Authored Books

Akers, R. L. (1985). *Deviant behavior: A social learning approach* (3rd ed.). Belmont, CA: Wadsworth.

Tirole, J. (1988). *Theory of industrial organization.* Cambridge, MA: MIT Press.

Relethford, J. (1990). *The human species: An introduction to biological anthropology.* Mountain View, CA: Mayfield.

Chapters in Edited Books

Bernstein, I. S., Gordon, T. P., & Rose, R. M. (1983). The interaction of hormones, behavior and social context in nonhuman primates. In B. B. Svare (Ed.), *Hormones and aggressive behavior* (pp. 535–561). New York: Plenum.

Ellis, L. (1987). Neurohormonal bases of varying tendencies to learn delinquent and criminal behavior. In E. K. Morris & C. J. Braukmann (Eds.), *Behavioral approaches to crime and delinquency* (pp. 499–518). New York: Plenum.

Goodkasian, G. A. (1990). Confronting domestic violence: The role of criminal court judges. In L. J. Siegel (Ed.), *American justice: Research of the National Institute of Justice* (pp. 163–172). St. Paul, MN: West.

Some Special Notes

Author(s)—only initials of first and middle names.

Date—in parentheses followed by a period.

Title of article—no caps except first word and after a colon.

Name of journal—cap each significant word and underline.

Volume of journal—underline or boldface.

Name of book—no caps except first word and after a colon.

Name of chapter in book—no caps except first word and after a colon.

Paging of chapter in book—after title of book in parentheses, followed by period.

Editor(s) of an edited book—initials placed before last name.

Referencing Format in Journals Published by the American Sociological Association

Articles

Fedigan, Linda M. 1983. "Dominance and Reproductive Success in Primates." *Yearbook of Physical Anthropology,* 26:91–129.

Nigro, Georgia N., Hill, Dina E., Gelbein, Martha E., and Clark, Catharine L. 1988. "Changes in the Facial Prominence of Women and Men Over the Last Decade." *Psychology of Women Quarterly,* 12:225–235.

Kohfeld, Carol W., and Spague, John (1990). "Demography, Police Behavior, and Deterrence." *Criminology,* 28:111–136.

Wimberly, Dale W. 1990. "Investment Dependence and Alternative Explanations of Third World Mortality: A Cross-National Study." *American Sociological Review,* 55:77–91.

Authored Books

Akers, Ronald L. 1985. Deviant Behavior: A Social Learning Approach, (3rd ed.). Belmont, CA: Wadsworth.

Tirole, Jean. 1988. *Theory of Industrial Organization.* Cambridge, MA: MIT Press.

Relethford, John. 1990. *The Human Species: An Introduction to Biological Anthropology.* Mountain View, CA: Mayfield.

Chapters in Edited Books

Bernstein, Irvin S., Gordon, Thomas P. and Rose, Richard M. 1983. "The Interaction of Hormones, Behavior and Social Context in Nonhuman Primates." Pp. 535–561 in *Hormones and Aggressive Behavior,* edited by Bruce B. Svare. New York: Plenum.

Ellis, Lee. 1987. "Neurohormonal Bases of Varying Tendencies to Learn Delinquent and Criminal Behavior." Pp. 499–518 in *Behavioral Approaches to Crime and Delinquency,* edited by Edward K. Morris and Charles J. Braukmann. New York: Plenum.

Goodkasian, Gail A. 1990. "Confronting Domestic Violence: The Role of Criminal Court Judges." Pp. 163–172 in *American Justice: Research of the National Institute of Justice,* edited by Larry J. Seigel. St. Paul, MN: West.

Some Special Notes

Author(s)—use first name plus middle initial (or first initial plus middle name, if author so indicates).

Date—is followed by a period (is not in parentheses).

Title of article—in quotation marks, cap all significant words.

Name of journal—cap each significant word and underline.

Volume and paging of journals—separated by colon.

Name of all books—cap each significant word and underline.

Name of chapter in book—cap all significant words.

Paging of chapters in an edited book—indicate just before title of the book.

Editor(s) of an edited book—names appear after the title of the book.

Referencing Format in Journals Published by the American Society of Criminology

Articles

Fedigan, Linda M.
   1983   Dominance and reproductive success in primates. Yearbook of Physical Anthropology 26:91–129.
Nigro, Georgia N., Hill, Dina E., Gelbein, Martha E., and Clark, Catharine L.
   1988   Changes in the facial prominence of women and men over the last decade. Psychology of Women Quarterly 12:225–235.
Kohfeld, Carol W., and Spague, John
   1990   Demography, police behavior, and deterrence. Criminology 28:111–136.
Wimberly, Dale W.
   1990   Investment dependence and alternative explanations of third world mortality: A cross-national study. American Sociological Review 55:77–91.

Authored Books

Akers, Ronald L.
   1985   Deviant Behavior: A Social Learning Approach, Third Edition. Belmont, Calif.: Wadsworth.
Tirole, Jean
   1988   Theory of Industrial Organization. Cambridge, Mass.: MIT Press.
Relethford, John
   1990   The Human Species: An Introduction to Biological Anthropology. Mountain View, Calif.: Mayfield.

Chapters in Edited Books

Bernstein, Irvin S., Gordon, Thomas P., and Rose, Richard M.
   1983   The interaction of hormones, behavior and social context in nonhuman primates. In Bruce B. Svare (ed.), Hormones and Aggressive Behavior. New York: Plenum.
Ellis, Lee
   1987   Neurohormonal bases of varying tendencies to learn delinquent and criminal behavior. In Edward K. Morris and Charles J. Braukmann (eds.), Behavioral Approaches to Crime and Delinquency. New York: Plenum.
Goodkasian, Gail A.
   1990   Confronting domestic violence: The role of criminal court judges. In Larry J. Seigel (ed.), American Justice: Research of the National Institute of Justice. St. Paul, Minn.: West.

Some Special Notes

No underlining or quotation marks are used anywhere.

Author(s)—use first name plus middle initial (or first initial plus middle name, if author so indicates).

Date—indent three spaces directly below author(s).

Title of article—begin two spaces directly after date and maintain all subsequent lines ten spaces in. Cap only first word and after a colon.

Name of journal—cap each significant word.

Volume and paging of journals—separated by colon.

Name of book—cap each significant word.

Name of chapter in book—no caps except first word and after a colon.

Paging of chapter in book—not reported.

Editor(s) of an edited book—names preceded by the word *In* and followed by book title.

Referencing Format in Journals Published by the American Anthropological Association

Articles

Fedigan, Linda M.
> 1983   Dominance and Reproductive Success in Primates. Yearbook of Physical Anthropology 26:91–129.

Nigro, Georgia N., Dina E. Hill, Martha E. Gelbein, and Catharine L. Clark
> 1988   Changes in the Facial Prominence of Women and Men over the Last Decade. Psychology of Women Quarterly 12:225–235.

Kohfeld, Carol W., and John Spague
> 1990   Demography, police behavior, and deterrence. Criminology 28:111–136.

Wimberly, Dale W.
> 1990   Investment Dependence and Alternative Explanations of Third World Mortality: A Cross-National Study. American Sociological Review 55:77–91.

Authored Books

Akers, Ronald L.
> 1985   Deviant Behavior: A Social Learning Approach, Third Edition. Belmont, CA: Wadsworth.

Tirole, Jean
> 1988   Theory of Industrial Organization. Cambridge, MA: MIT Press.

Relethford, John.
> 1990   The Human Species: An Introduction to Biological Anthropology. Mountain View, CA: Mayfield.

Chapters in Edited Books

Bernstein, Irvin S., Thomas P. Gordon, and Richard M. Rose
   1983   The Interaction of Hormones, Behavior and Social Context in Nonhuman Primates. In Hormones and Aggressive Behavior. Bruce B. Svare, ed. Pp. 535–561. New York: Plenum.
Ellis, Lee
   1987   Neurohormonal Bases of Varying Tendencies to Learn Delinquent and Criminal Behavior. In Behavioral Approaches to Crime and Delinquency. Edward K. Morris and Charles J. Braukmann, eds. Pp. 499–518. New York: Plenum.
Goodkasian, Gail A.
   1990   Confronting Domestic Violence: The Role of Criminal Court Judges. In American Justice: Research of the National Institute of Justice. Larry J. Seigel, ed. Pp. 162–172. St. Paul, MN: West.

Some Special Notes

No underlining or quotation marks are used anywhere.
Author(s)—use first name plus middle initial (or first initial plus middle name, if author so indicates). After the first of more than one author, the remainder are listed with first name first.
Date—indent three spaces directly below author(s).
Title of article—begin two spaces directly after date. Indent all subsequent lines six spaces. Cap each significant word.
Name of journal—cap each significant word.
Volume and paging of journals—separated by a colon.
Name of book—cap each significant word.
Name of chapter in book—cap each significant word.
Paging of chapter in book—following editors.
Editor(s) of an edited book—names follow title of book.

Referencing Format in Journals Published by the American Political Science Association

Articles

Fedigan, Linda M. 1983. "Dominance and Reproductive Success in Primates." *Yearbook of Physical Anthropology,* 26:91–129.
Nigro, Georgia N., Dina E. Hill, Martha E. Gelbein, and Catharine L. Clark. 1988. "Changes in the Facial Prominence of Women and Men over the Last Decade." *Psychology of Women Quarterly,* 12:225–235.
Kohfeld, Carol W., and John Spague. 1990. "Demography, Police Behavior, and Deterrence." *Criminology,* 28:111–136.
Wimberly, Dale W. 1990. "Investment Dependence and Alternative Explanations of Third World Mortality: A Cross-National Study." *American Sociological Review,* 55:77–91.

Authored Books

Akers, Ronald L.   1985. *Deviant Behavior: A Social Learning Approach, Third Edition.* Belmont, CA: Wadsworth.

Tirole, Jean   1988. *Theory of Industrial Organization.* Cambridge, MA: MIT Press.

Relethford, John.   1990. *The Human Species: An Introduction to Biological Anthropology.* Mountain View, CA: Mayfield.

Chapters in Edited Books

Bernstein, Irvin S., Thomas P. Gordon, and Richard M. Rose.   1983. ''The Interaction of Hormones, Behavior and Social Context in Nonhuman Primates.'' *Hormones and Aggressive Behavior,* ed. Bruce B. Svare. New York: Plenum.

Ellis, Lee   1987. ''Neurohormonal Bases of Varying Tendencies to Learn Delinquent and Criminal Behavior.'' *Behavioral Approaches to Crime and Delinquency,* ed. Edward K. Morris and Charles J. Braukmann. New York: Plenum.

Goodkasian, Gail A.   1990. ''Confronting Domestic Violence: The Role of Criminal Court Judges.'' *American Justice: Research of the National Institute of Justice,* ed. Larry J. Seigel. St. Paul, MN: West.

Some Special Notes

Names of all authors are spelled out. Only senior author has last name
.   appearing first.

Cap first letter of all significant words in titles of articles and book chapters, and put them in quotes.

Year of publication appears between names of authors and title of article, book chapter, or book, in both cases separated by two spaces, but without parentheses. Note that a period always appears at the end of the last author listed (just ahead of the year), and at the end of the year.

Paging for book chapters is not given.

Paging for journal articles is preceded by the volume, separated by a colon.

Referencing in Journals Published by the American Psychiatric Association

Articles

Fedigan LM: Dominance and reproductive success in primates. Yrbk Phys Anthropol. 1983; 26:91–129

Nigro GN, Hill DE, Gelbein ME, and Clark CL: Changes in the facial prominence of women and men over the last decade. Psychol Women Quart 1988; 12:225–235

Kohfeld CW, and Spague J: Demography, police behavior, and deterrence. Criminology 1990; 28:111–136

Wimberly DW: Investment dependence and alternative explanations of third world mortality: A cross-national study. Am Sociol Rev 1990; 55:77–91

Authored Books

Akers RL: Deviant Behavior: A Social Learning Approach, 3rd Ed. Belmont, Calif., Wadsworth, 1985

Tirole J.: Theory of Industrial Organization. Cambridge, Mass, MIT Press, 1988

Relethford J: The Human Species: An Introduction to Biological Anthropology. Mountain View, Calif, Mayfield, 1990

Chapters in Edited Books

Bernstein IS, Gordon TP, Rose RM: The interaction of hormones, behavior and social context in nonhuman primates, in Hormones and Aggressive Behavior. Edited by Svare BB. New York, Plenum, 1983

Ellis L: Neurohormonal bases of varying tendencies to learn delinquent and criminal behavior, in Behavioral Approaches to Crime and Delinquency. Edited by Morris EK, Braukmann, CJ. New York, Plenum, 1987

Goodkasian GA: Confronting domestic violence: The role of criminal court judges, in American Justice: Research of the National Institute of Justice. Edited by Siegel LJ. St. Paul, Minn, West, 1990

Some Special Notes

Authors—no periods after initials and no commas separating an author's last name and his or her initials.

Year of publication—placed near end of reference.

Titles of articles—capitalize only first word: do not capitalize after a colon.

Titles of books and journals—no underlining or italicizing.

Titles of most journals—abbreviated according to rules used widely in the field of medicine (the letter "J" stands for "Journal of" or "Journal of the").

Paging—pages for specific chapters in edited books are not identified.

Guidelines and Recommendations for Preparing Research Reports

This appendix provides some basic rules and suggestions for writing a research report and other technical and professional communications. For additional information, see the suggested readings at the end of this appendix.

Overall Format and Style of a Research Manuscript

Research manuscripts should be double-spaced throughout (so that readers can make comments and corrections easily). Manuscripts should simply have a staple or paper clip in the upper left corner (most binders make it difficult for readers to keep the material open to the page being read and to make comments in the margins).

As a rule, research report writing should be in the past tense (i.e., what others have found, and what was done in the research study to be reported). One exception would be in proposing a study that has not yet been conducted. Proposals should be in the future tense. The other exception would be near the end of the manuscript where suggestions are made about where future research on this topic should go.

If a manuscript includes one or more tables or figures, these should be put at the end of the manuscript after the reference section with each table or figure on a separate page. Do not use any table or figure that is not specifically referred to at least once in the body of the manuscript. Immediately following the paragraph containing the first reference to table or figure, the following insertion should be made:

——————————————————

Table XX (or Figure XX) about here

——————————————————

The reason for this style is that manuscripts that actually get published usually have the tables and figures specially typeset or processed. Only when the article is finally laid out in the journal will the tables and figures be inserted close to where they are discussed in the body of the article.

The Basic Format for the Initial Pages

All manuscripts should contain a title page and a second page devoted to the abstract. On the third page, the title (but not the author) is repeated, usually a few spaces down on the page, and then the body of the article begins.

The title page should contain the following items of information: the title (usually about a fifth of the way down on the page), and the author(s) and his, her, or their institutional or work affiliation (about midway on the page). In addition, near the bottom of the title page should appear a running head (i.e., some shortened two- to four-word title for the article that will then be printed at the upper right corner (outside the regular margins) of each subsequent page of the manuscript. One reason for this running head is to ensure that pages are never mixed up with some other manuscript. Another reason is that some journals have manuscripts reviewed "blind" with respect to who wrote them. Since the author's name only appears on the title page, this can be done simply by removing the title page before sending a manuscript out for review. Also near the bottom of the title page should appear any acknowledgments that the author(s) wishes to make (such as thanking those who helped in data collection or who read and critiqued drafts of the manuscript).

The abstract, on the next page, should not exceed 250 words. (This 250-word limit is the length of an average typed page containing 1 1/4 inch margins all around.) Most journal editors prefer abstracts of 100 to 150 words in length. The word *Abstract* is normally underlined and centered near the top of the abstract page.

No attempt should be made in the abstract to review the literature. Rather, the first sentence or two should explain the purpose of the study. Then a sentence or two should inform the reader of the nature of the sample and procedures that were used, followed by another sentence or two about the nature of the findings. Finally, one or two sentences should inform the reader of the implications of the findings.

The Body of the Manuscript

You may recall from Chapter 6 that a research report consists of the following sections (and subsections): Introduction (literature review plus statement of the problem), methods (description of the sample or population and procedures), results, and conclusions. Unless the report is exceedingly short (i.e., two to four double-spaced typed pages), these sections (and sometimes the subsections) should be individually identified. The only section that is often not identified is the introduction, since it obviously leads off the body of a research report and ends where the methods section begins. The name of each section of a report is centered, often with underlining, with the first letter of each important word capitalized.

Here are some brief suggestions to keep in mind when preparing each section of a research report.

Introduction

Using a proper citation style (see pp. 82–84), the introduction begins by informing the reader of what is currently known about the subject to be investigated. Many judgments must be made about how detailed this introduction should be. The following factors should be weighed in making these judgments: (a) How much relevant literature is there? (b) Are the readers already familiar with the nature of the findings in this area? (c) Is the journal for which the manuscript is being prepared more likely to publish a long or a short article on this particular topic? (d) How much detail is needed to document the necessity of the study you wish to undertake?

In preparing a literature review, here are some things to bear in mind: Scientific studies are judged on the basis of how well they can be seen as logical extensions of studies that have preceeded them. Failure to demonstrate a firm grasp of the relevant literature will substantially diminish the chances of your manuscript being taken seriously by reviewers.

Generally speaking, the more active others have been in an area prior to your own study, the more of a challenge it will be for you to prepare a comprehensive literature review. However, even in areas that have received little research attention, you can often find numerous articles with some relevance to your particular study.

Because it can take you several months to read material relevant to a research topic, it is important to take notes while you read. Many scientists keep such notes in a special file—nowadays often computerized—subdivided into numerous detailed categories. Each note should contain information about the finding of interest and about where the finding was published so that it can be properly cited.

The statement of the problem (or the hypothesis) often consists of one or two sentences, and rarely does it exceed a paragraph. The statement of the problem almost always appears at the very end of the introduction.

Methods

It is the obligation of the researcher to tell readers everything that is important about how data were collected, so that, if readers choose to do so, they can replicate your study. Thus, you should state where and how the subjects for the study were obtained, how many there were, and their basic demographics. Describing the demographics of a sample can often be done within a paragraph or two, or sometimes it is helpful to organize this data in a table.

In presenting the procedures used to obtain information specific to the research topic, the writer should describe all research instruments. If a questionnaire was used, some key questions might be presented verbatim, or the reader might be referred to an appendix that contains a copy of the research instrument.

Results

Deciding what results to present is often a challenge, even to seasoned researchers. It is not uncommon for a researcher to uncover many interesting and unexpected findings. Some of these may be quite tangential to the initial purpose of the study. If this happens, you must decide whether to abandon your original study, or to write a second report in which the tangential findings are reported. You should avoid the temptation of including in the results everything that was found, regardless of its relevance to the stated purpose of your study.

Keeping this caveat in mind, you may still be uncertain about how much detail to provide. Here is some advice that you should consider in making these decisions:

1. Try to put yourself in the place of the typical reader. How much detail would most readers want in order to make sense of what your study found?
2. Try to identify with the editor and with the reviewers of your manuscript, keeping in mind that most journals can only accept a fraction (usually less than half) of all the manuscripts submitted to them. From their vantage point, would the limited space of the journal be well spent by looking at what your study found? If there is a significant amount of trivia and even half-baked "filler" in the results section, an affirmative answer is unlikely.

Conclusions

In this final section of the body of the manuscript, the writer usually tries to give the reader (a) a summary of the results, (b) an impression of the overall significance of the findings, and (c) advice on the direction of future research (and what pitfalls to avoid).

Following the Body of a Research Manuscript

After the body of a research report, the following sections should appear: the reference section, any tables, any figures, and any appendixes.

Advice on Writing Styles for Research Manuscripts

Few scientists appreciate long-winded answers to simple questions. Probably the biggest mistake that novices make in preparing research reports is failing to write and rewrite their reports until the most meaningful information is presented in as few words as possible. For more specific advice on writing styles, see Appendix D.

Tailoring a Research Manuscript for a Specific Journal

Before writing a research report for a specific journal, it is a good idea to read that journal's *style sheet*. Style sheets are usually one-page outlines of the following information as it pertains to that particular journal:

A. Where manuscripts are to be sent.
B. A statement of the type of manuscript the journal usually publishes.
C. Basic citation and referencing style to be used.
D. Number of copies of the manuscript to be submitted.
E. Whether or not a submission fee is required.

Style sheets are usually published once each year (or sometimes in each issue) in the front or back of the journal, or they may be obtained by writing to the journal editor.

Suggested Reading

Barzun, J. (1985). *On writing, editing, and publishing* (2nd ed.). Chicago: University of Chicago Press.

Powell, W. W. (1985). *Getting into print: The decision-making process in scholarly publishing.* Chicago: University of Chicago Press.

Basic Guidelines for Professional Writing in the Social Sciences

This appendix provides advice on writing styles, especially when addressing social science audiences. Most of the advice will be pertinent to papers written for social science courses, although the advice is particularly tailored for writing social science research reports. Students should read through this section before starting to write a research report, and once again after having completed a draft to make sure that none of the relevant points were missed.

Never ask someone to read your first draft. One of the biggest mistakes made in writing professionally (including writing class papers) is to assume that a good report can be written the first (or even the second) time through. After all, if you can clearly say what you did and found, why is it not possible to just write it that way too? There are several problems with this reasoning: First, communicating in writing is often more of a challenge than doing so orally because the communicator cannot use gestures to augment what is being said and the audience cannot ask questions when they do not understand. Second, if you were to record and play back an oral account of what someone had found in a research study, you would find that many potentially important aspects of the study were skipped. The more complex and technical the research is that one tries to describe, the less likely it is that a clear and accurate description of that study can be given the first time.

Learn to compose on a word processor. For those of you who have not yet tried it, few everyday experiences will be as awe-inspiring as when you first learn to use a computer like a typewriter. Within a few hours, you will learn not only how to type and save each draft as you refine it, but also how to delete sentences, move paragraphs around, and even check your spelling and grammar. Nothing that you ever learn is more likely to advance your ability to write well than learning how to compose your thoughts on a word processor.

In this connection, if possible, use a word processing program that carries the capacity to check your spelling and grammar. Research has shown that the use of word processing programs with grammar check subroutines can substantially improve people's ability to express themselves in writing (see suggested readings at the end of this appendix).

Have a "critic" read your manuscript. It is not cheating to have people read over your paper and point out where the meaning is unclear or your train of thought is hard to follow provided they do not rewrite it for you. When you ask them to do this, emphasize that you are interested in knowing where it might be improved, *not* in knowing how good they consider it.

Avoid sentences that are too long and too short. Compare the following two paragraphs:

> Do not write a lot of short sentences. They become irritating to read. An occasional one is alright. However, one after another is not. Numerous short, choppy sentences suggest that the writer has not thought through very well what he or she is trying to say.
>
> Although there is nothing wrong with an occasional short sentence, several of them strung together become irritating to read. In addition, stringing together numerous short, choppy sentences indicates a lack of careful organization by the writer.

Notice how the sentences in the second paragraph tend to flow more than in the first, and how they suggest that the writer has carefully organized his or her thought into a tightly integrated argument, rather than simply thrown a bunch of half-baked thoughts together for the reader to try to sort out.

While striving to avoid numerous short sentences, take care in constructing more complex sentences. If they are not well-organized and well thought out, longer sentences can confuse and lose the reader.

Avoid one-sentence paragraphs as well as paragraphs longer than one page. Typically, the first sentence in a new paragraph should contain the most general statement that a writer wants to make about a particular idea. Subsequent sentences then elaborate on and qualify this initial sentence. Numerous one-sentence paragraphs suggest that the writer is not really organizing his or her thoughts as much as simply throwing them out in a haphazard fashion.

At the other extreme, you should not have lengthy paragraphs (i.e., in excess of a page). If you have drafted a paragraph that is unusually long, go back over it and look for ways that it could be divided into two separate sets of arguments or lines of reasoning, or look for how sentences can be dropped, shortened, or combined with others.

When using a pronoun, be sure that the referent is clear. Sometimes a writer will use such pronouns as "this" and "these" without clarifying for the reader what is being referenced. Use words such as "this" or "these" only to refer to concepts named in the same, or occasionally a preceding paragraph.

Avoid the use of contractions in formal writing. Saying "wasn't" instead of "was not" is usually not considered acceptable in formal writing.

Maintain a tone of objectivity. Never assert that "this study proves such-and-such." A writer's credibility can be undermined by exaggerating the conclusiveness of the evidence. Recall that, whereas most theories and hypotheses are made with respect to broad universes, they are usually tested with samples of a few hundred (see pp. 213–214). Such phrases as "The evidence suggests" or "The data are consistent with the conclusion" are more reflective of reality than phrases such as "It is now a fact" and "My study makes it obvious that. . . ."

Minimize first-person references, especially when there is only one author. Instead of stating "I collected the data" or "I believe such-and-such," it is preferable to say "The data were collected in such-and-such a way" or "Current evidence would lead one to believe." While publishers of scientific reports vary, many prefer that a single author refer to himself or herself as "The present writer" or "The present investigator" rather than as "I."

Vary your sentence structure. Do not begin most of your sentences in the same way (e.g., "So-and-so said that . . . ," "This study showed that . . ."). Try varying the structure of your sentences. For example:

Following prior studies in this area, so-and-so attempted to determine if . . .
Given the evidence that such-and-such is true, the present study was undertaken to . . .
Should studies continue to confirm the relationship identified in this study, the conclusion would be that . . .
Despite assertions to the contrary, this study found that . . .
As might be suspected, the research indicated . . .

Make sure that the meaning of each statement is clear. "The males scored lower on this variable" does not make clear who the males were being compared to (e.g., females). Likewise, the statement "Studies have shown that child abuse in such-and-such a country has become greater" fails to do two things. First, it has not identified the time frames being compared. Second, there is no indication as to whether the sheer *number* of cases has increased (likely to happen in countries with a population increase or the *rate* of abuse has increased. A rate would be obtained by dividing the number of abuse cases by some risk factor (e.g., the number of children in a population who were still living with their parents).

Minimize the use of underlining (or boldfacing) for emphasis. Most of your ideas should be sufficiently emphasized by the way you organize and structure your sentences, not by underlining key words or phrases. In other words, you can begin sentences with such phrases as "It appears important to emphasize that" or "To underscore the main finding of this study, we found that." On the other hand, underlining (or boldfacing) should be used when a term is defined for the first time.

Special Comments on Citing and on Typing

Citing References

Recall from Chapter 6 that, especially in the author-date citation style, there are two basic ways to make a citation. One refers to the author(s) in the structure of the sentence, and the other does not. Here is an example of the same citation made in these two ways:

A study by Jones (1963) found that . . .	One study found that . . . (Jones, 1963).

Either variation is acceptable, although when discussing several studies at once, the second alternative will make a sentence more readable.

In citing articles, avoid mentioning the author's first name or institutional affiliation (i.e., "at such-and-such university"). This practice differs from what you would do if writing a "science review" for a popular magazine. Two main exceptions are: (a) Two individuals with the same last name cited in a single report, and (b) Reference to a historical figure, especially if he or she has a common last name. Also, authors who are cited in research reports (and other technical writings) are not referred to as Mr., Ms., Dr., or Professor, but merely by their last names.

Typing

Indent 5 spaces to begin each paragraph.

Space twice after the period at the end of each sentence.

Double-space all manuscripts throughout, unless there are instructions to do otherwise.

Suggested Reading

Becker, H. S. (1986). *Writing for social scientists: How to start and finish your thesis, book, or article.* Chicago: University of Chicago Press.

Hartley, J. (Ed.). (1992). *Technology and writing.* London: Jessica Kingsley. (This book contains a review of recent evidence suggesting that computers can help people improve their writing skills. Most of this help comes in the form of "grammar check" programs that are now part of most word processing packages.)

GLOSSARY*

ABAB experimental design

[15] A type of reversal before-after no control group experimental design. In this design, an independent variable is withheld, imposed, and then again withheld and again imposed over the course of four time frames. This design uses either one subject or a single group of subjects.

Abstract

[2] A brief summary of a research report or other scientific article. Publications containing collections of such summaries also go by this name.

Additive rule (or Addition rule)

[5] The rule that states that the likelihood of some events is the sum of certain individual probabilities. For example, the probability of getting a one or a two any given time you role a die is equal to the sum of their individual probabilities (i.e., $1/6 + 1/6 = 1/3$).

---

*Note: This glossary can be used not only to check the meaning of social research method terminology, but also as a study guide. To use it as a study guide, place a strip of cardboard over the left side of each page in the glossary, and read each definition that is preceded by a bracketed number corresponding to the chapter that you are studying. Put a light pencil mark to the right of any definition you fail to match with the correct term. Wait a few hours, and then go back over the marked definitions a second time, erasing the marks if you are able to correctly name the term the second time through. Repeat this process until all the pencil marks have been erased.

Italicized words that are used as part of a definition are themselves also defined in the glossary.

Adoption study

[16] A type of quasi-experimental design used to help answer nature-nurture questions. This design takes advantage of the fact that adopted children have essentially two sets of parents. By comparing the behavior of adoptees with both sets of parents, researchers have been able to estimate the relative influence of genetic factors as opposed to family environmental factors on the behavior.

Aesthetic appeal

[14] One of the criteria by which the elegance (or merit) of a scientific theory is judged. It has to do with how beautiful a theory seems to be.

After-only experimental design

[15] An experimental design involving at least one experimental group and one control group, but only one time frame.

Allied disciplines

[1] Academic disciplines that have much in common with the social sciences, especially in research methodology. They encompass journalism, advertising, marketing, business, and home economics. A thin line may be drawn between these disciplines and the near social sciences such as education, ethology, psychiatry, public health, and sociobiology.

All-points-anchored response scale

[8] A type of response option given to subjects in which all the responses that can be given are presented in word form. The most widely used form of this type of response option is the *Likert scale*.

Alternative hypothesis

[5] A hypothesis that there is some type of difference or relationship with respect to two or more variables. It is also called the *research hypothesis,* and is considered contrary to the *null hypothesis*.

Analysis of variance (ANOVA)

[5] A statistical test used to estimate the probability that two or more distributions and their accompanying means are significantly different from one another. It is more detailed than a t-test.

Anecdotal evidence

[20] Evidence based on impressionistic testimonials without solid scientific backing.

Animal model

[14] A type of scientific model in which nonhuman animals are found to possess a trait similar to or the same as one found in humans. Then research that would not be possible with humans are conducted with these animals.

Anthropology

[1] The study of humankind. It has at least two major branches, one dealing primarily with the physical aspects of human evolution, and the other pertaining to the diversity of human cultures.

Applied research

[20] Research that has immediate practical applications. This type of research is the opposite of *basic research*.

Archaeological data

[9] Largely qualitative data derived from excavating prehistoric (or early historic) human remains and artifacts.

Archival data [11] Quantitative data that have been collected by others, usually as part of the functioning of an organization. Such data is often subjected *secondary analyses.*

Arithmetic average (see Mean)

Artifacts [9] Physical things that humans have modified for some aesthetic or useful purpose.

Ascetic morality [19] Morality having to do with a variety of arbitrary standards of conduct. Contrasted with *social morality.*

Attrition (see Sample attrition)

Augmenting interactive effects [15] The effects in an experiment in which the impact of one independent variable is enhanced by interacting with a second independent variable.

Author-date citation style [6] The most common method for citing prior publications within the body of a scientific article or book. It denotes the author(s), and the date (and sometimes the page numbers). The other main citation style is called the *numbering citation style.*

Average [3] The central tendency with reference to a variable. Three main types are recognized and used in science: the *mean,* the *median,* and the *mode.*

Basic research [20] Research that is undertaken to increase scientific understanding, not to help solve some practical problem. Also called *pure research.*

Before-after no control group design [15] An experimental design involving two or more time frames, but only one group of subjects. This design can also be used with a single experimental subject.

Behavioral science (see Social science)

Behaviorism (and behaviorist movement) [20] An approach to social science, especially psychology, which emphasizes that a researcher's attention should focus on objective aspects of behavior rather than mentalistic-cognitive processes. This approach helped to promote more rigorous evaluations of clinical treatment programs.

Bell-shaped curve (see Normal curve)

Bimodal [3] A frequency distribution curve with two peaks.

Bivariate statistics [4] A category of statistics in which two variables are compared or correlated.

Bogus pipeline   [10] A method for helping to ensure the complete candor of research subjects when responding to questions on sensitive topics. With this method, subjects are deceived into believing that the researcher is using sophisticated electronic equipment to determine whether or not the subject is being completely honest.

Burt, Cyril   [18] A psychologist who devoted much of his career to determining the relative influence of genetic and environmental factors on human intelligence. A few years after his death in the 1960s, assertions surfaced that he may have fabricated some of his data. Although several recent publications have vindicated him, many scientists still regard some of his work as fraudulent.

Carry-over effect   [20] In an experiment, the lingering effect of an independent variable beyond the time frame during which the independent variable was imposed.

Causation   [4] The idea that some events induce (or provoke) other events.

Census   [12] A survey that includes (or at least comes close to including) 100% of the members of a population, either directly or indirectly (such as through another household member). The word itself derives from the fact that most of these surveys are conducted once every ten years (at the beginning of each new decade).

Chagnon, Napoleon   [9] An anthropologist who has conducted much ethnographic research among tribal people in South America's Amazon Basin.

Chi-square (X^2)   [5] A statistical test used to estimate the degree to which two or more proportions (e.g., percentages) are significantly different from one another.

Chosen sample   [13] All the subjects initially selected for a survey (as opposed to an *obtained sample*).

Citation   [6] In scientific writing, the act of referring to another written work in the text of one's own manuscript.

Classical Experimental Design [15] A basic experimental design involving subjects being assigned to at least two groups, an experimental group, and a control group. In such a design, the dependent variable is measured during at least two time frames.

Clinical evaluation research   [20] One of the two main forms of evaluation research. It is concerned with the effectiveness of treating persons who voluntarily seek help for mental or physical illnesses or for interpersonal problems.

Clinical sampling   [12] Another name for *event sampling*.

Cluster sample	[12] A sample containing elements of random sampling, but that is distinguishable from random sampling in significant ways. In this particular form of sample, sampling frames come in two or more "layers," the number of which varys according to whether simple or multistage sampling is involved.
Coding	[8] The process of deciding how data will be entered into a standard format for analysis.
Cohort	[4] A group of subjects with some significant lifetime event(s) in common (e.g., all citizens of Iowa born during the 1970s, all Americans who got married during the Great Depression).
Coleman, James C.	[20] A sociologist who has conducted research on the effects of different forms of education on academic learning. Most recently, he has been instrumental in comparing the educational achievement of students attending public and parochial schools.
Comparison group	[16] A group of subjects in a quasi-experiment who serve the same function as a control group, but are not assigned in a random fashion.
Conceptual definition	[2] A definition that uses other words to convey the meaning of a concept. It is the type of definition one commonly finds in a dictionary. This kind of definition is the opposite of an *operational definition.*
Concurrent (comparative) validity	[7] The degree to which a new operational measure appears to be valid relative to one or more better established operational measures.
Confidentiality	[18] The assurance that is given to subjects in a research project that their responses will not be disclosed to anyone outside of the research team working on the project.
Conjunctive items	[8] Items (questions) presented in a questionnaire or an interview that ask subjects to respond to more than one variable at a time (e.g., Do you consider capital punishment uncivilized and immoral?).
Constant	[2] An empirical phenomenon that does not change within a particular study. In other words, this phenomenon only assumes a single value or intensity. Its opposite is called a *variable.*
Construct validity (see Theoretical validity)	
Content analysis	[11] A study based on the analysis of the frequency of various words and phrases in written documents.
Content validity	[7] Validity judged in terms of whether or not a method for measuring a variable seems reasonable as a way to measure the variable. It is also called *face validity.*

Continuous variable	[2] A variable with gradual variability, such as age or weight (regardless of how the variable happens to be measured). The opposite of this type of variable is a *discrete variable*.
Control group	[15] A group of subjects in an experiment that are exposed to an independent variable in a typical way, or to a normal degree.
Convenience sampling	[12] A sampling method wherein subjects are obtained "all at once" in relatively large groups, such as having all students in a particular class complete a survey questionnaire. Such methods of sampling are among the most widely used nonprobability sampling methods in social science.
Correlation	[4] A widely used set of statistical analysis procedures for determining whether variables are related to one another, and if so, in what way.
Correlation coefficient	[4] Numbers, ranging between −1.00 and +1.00, that reflect the degree to which two variables are related to one another.
Correlation matrix	[17] A tabular array of correlation coefficients that shows how all variables in a data set are related to one another.
Correlational statistics (see Correlation)	
Counteracting effect	[15] In an experiment, the tendency for one independent variable to eliminate the effects of a second independent variable.
Criminology/criminal justice	[1] The study of criminal behavior and of the sociolegal system that functions to help curb criminal behavior, and to arrest and punish criminal offenders.
Criterion variable	[17] A variable in a multivariate statistical study that a researcher is treating as a possible effect (also called a *dependent variable*).
Cross-fostering experiment	[16] A special type of experimental design used with nonhuman animals that is similar to adoption studies in humans. Both types of research designs are used to address socalled *nature-nurture questions* with regard to behavioral traits.
Cross-over design	[15] An experimental design involving at least two time frames and two groups of subjects, but, unlike a classical design, all groups receive exposure to both the independent and dependent variables, only during different time intervals.
Cross-sectional survey	[12] A survey undertaken only once (as opposed to a *longitudinal survey*).

Cross-test reliability   [7] A type of reliability in which the primary aim is to demonstrate that two or more measures of some variable substantially correlate with one another.

Curvilinear relationship   [4] A relationship between variables that is something other than linear.

Debrief   [18] The process of fully informing subjects about the nature of a study after their participation is finished. It is particularly common in studies involving varying degrees of deception.

Demarcated linear form of an end-anchored continuum   [8] A type of end-anchored response continuum in which subjects are allowed to respond at five to nine positions along a line with only the two most extreme response categories identified by some term. The most common version of this response continuum is the *semantic differential scale.*

Demographic variable   [2] An important category of social science variables used to help describe human samples and populations. Examples of such variables include age, sex, marital status, religious affiliation, and social status.

Dependent variable   [15] In experimental research, this is a variable that is possibly being affected by changes in the independent variable. In nonexperimental research, this is a variable that is possibly changing in response to some other variable.

Descartes, Rene   [4] A mid-1700s French philosopher-mathematician who first described how geometric shapes could be represented with equations. This gave rise to such fields of mathematics as algebra and calculus, and even laid some of the intellectual foundation for correlational statistics.

Determinism   [1] The unproven (and unprovable) assumption that natural (including social) forces, rather than supernatural or ''free-will'' forces, are responsible for whatever phenomenon one is attempting to explain.

Diagnostic research   [20] Applied research undertaken to assess the extent to which specific symptoms exist in some clinical population. Such research is similar to *epidemiological research,* except that the latter is concerned with general populations rather than clinical populations.

Diagrammatic (structural) model   [14] A scientific model in which a geometric sketch (or actual physical object) is used to help explain a phenomenon. Such models are usually used as part of a scientific theory.

Discrete variable   [2] A variable with two or more categories into which it can be divided (e.g., sex and religious preference). These variables are usually measured at the nominal level. The opposite of this type of variable is a *continuous variable.*

Dispersion	[3] The degree to which scores tend to be "tightly" or "loosely" scattered about some measure of central tendency. The most widely used measure of this concept is *standard deviation.*
Double-blind experiment	[15] A special type of experimental design used with human subjects to help control for the so-called *placebo* (or *expectancy*) *effect.* With this design, subjects first agree to take part in an experiment, and then are randomly assigned to the experimental or control groups, and neither they nor the persons who have direct contact with them know whether they are the experimentals or controls.
Dummy variable	[17] A continuous variable that has been measured nominally, usually with only two calibrating units. Such variables are sometimes included in multivariate statistical analyses.
Economics	[1] The social science that specializes in studying financial and business activities.
Education	[1] One of the near social sciences that specializes in understanding the transmission of knowledge, particularly in academic settings.
Elegance	[14] The quality or merit of a scientific theory.
Empirical	[1] That which may be seen, tasted, heard, smelled, or felt; the experiences upon which all scientific knowledge is grounded.
Empirical objectivism	[19] The philosophical view that an objective, knowable universe exists.
Empirical relativism	[19] The philosophical view that nothing is really true (or false) except within the cultural-historical context in which it is perceived. Also called cultural relativism.
End-anchored response continuum	[8] Any of three types of response options given to subjects in which only the most extreme response options have a specified meaning. All of the intermediate response options are simply numbers or lines. An example of such a response option would be to say to subjects: "On a scale from 1 to 10, with 1 being the least desirable and 10 being the most desirable, how well do you like the following foods?" The three forms of this type of response continuum are the *demarcated linear form* and two *numeric forms* (the write-in and the circled form).
Epidemiological research	[20] Applied research undertaken to assess the extent to which a social or health problem exists in some population.
Equational (or mathematical) model	[14] A scientific model in which an equation is used to help explain or describe a phenomenon.

Ethnographic Atlas
[11] A data bank derived from hundreds of individual ethnographic accounts. It is used by social scientists to test numerous cross-cultural hypotheses about human behavior. Also called the *Human Relations Area Files* (HRAF).

Ethnographic research
[9] The name given to research that involves visiting a specific society and recording one's observations, usually without the aid of any formal data recording format.

Ethnology
[1] An aspect of cultural anthropology that specializes in studying and comparing human cultures in individualized detail.

Ethology
[1] One of the near social sciences. It specializes in studying animal behavior in naturalistic settings to better understand how the behavior may have helped a particular species to adapt to its environment.

Evaluation research
[20] A major type of applied research that is undertaken to assess the success of a program designed to deal with some significant human problem.

Event sampling
[12] A sampling method that typically samples every instance of a hard-to-observe event (or rare condition). An example would be to interview every person who comes to a physician's office with a specific condition. It is also called *clinical sampling*.

Event-specific alignment study
[16] A special type of time series quasi-experimental design that can be especially powerful in answering causal questions. In this design, all of the instances in which the independent variable is imposed are aligned at a single point. Then observations are made of the dependent variable during standard units of time leading up to and following the imposition of the independent variable.

Expectancy effect
[15] Any outcome resulting strictly from a subject anticipating what is going to happen (also called the *placebo effect*). An experimental procedure sometimes used to reduce the confounding effects of this phenomenon is called a *double-blind experiment.*

Experimental control
[17] Control that is achieved over variables by randomly assigning subjects to one or more experimental and control groups. It can be contrasted with *statistical control.*

Experimental group
[15] The subjects in an experiment that are exposed to an independent variable to an unusual degree.

Experimental research (or Experimental design)
[15] Research in which a scientist systematically manipulates a variable suspected of being a cause of another variable, and then documents whether predicted changes in the second variable actually occur.

Experimentals (see Experimental group)	[15] A name used to describe members of an experimental group.
Ex post facto quasi-experimental design	[16] A research design that simulates an after-only experiment. The only important deviation from a true after-only experiment in this design is that subjects comprising the control group are "constructed" after the experimental group has already been exposed to an independent variable.
Exposure group	[16] Subjects in a quasi-experiment who are comparable to an experimental group in an actual experiment.
Eysenck, Hans J.	[20] The psychologist who wrote a major review article in the 1950s on the effectiveness of psychotherapeutic counseling techniques for treatment of mental illness. He concluded that there was little evidence to support the view that these techniques were effective for serious forms of mental illness. His article, although widely criticized, provided a major impetus toward an increase in rigorous evaluation of clinical programs.
F	[5] The symbol used to represent the number (or coefficient) derived from calculating an analysis of variance statistical test.
Face validity	[7] A method for assessing validity that is based on common sense or subjective judgments. It is also called *content validity*.
Factor analysis	[17] A type of multivariate statistics that is used to classify responses to large numbers of items (such as questions in a questionnaire) into categories, usually called factors.
Factor loading	[17] A term used in factor analysis to refer to the degree to which a particular item comprising a factor epitomizes that particular factor. It is expressed by a coefficient ranging from 0.00 to 1.00.
Factorial experimental design	[15] A type of experimental design involving only a single time frame in which there are at least four groups of subjects exposed to at least two levels of at least two independent variables.
Falsifiability	[14] The degree to which one can imagine the conditions under which a theory could be empirically disproven. The easier it is to imagine such conditions, the more elegant the theory is said to be.
Feasibility research	[20] Research undertaken to determine the availability of resources needed to implement a plan to deal with a human social or health problem.
Field research (field studies)	[9] Research that is conducted in the environment in which the subjects being studied normally live (as opposed to laboratory research or research based strictly on responses to a questionnaire). Such research may be either qualitative or quantitative in nature.

Fill-in-the-blank response option	[8] A type of response option in which subjects are asked to respond to a question by writing in (or uttering) a limited number of words (usually one or two) without the list of options being presented. Examples of variables often obtained with this type of response option would be religious preference and place of birth.
Focus group research	[9] A type of largely qualitative research in which a dozen or so subjects are convened in small samples from some population to discuss a specific topic such as a commercial product or political candidate. The purpose is to give researchers an impression of the strengths and weaknesses of the product or candidate.
Fossil	[9] Chemically transformed physical remnant of a formerly living creature.
Frequency distribution	[3] A type of graph or table used to represent how a single variable is distributed within some sample or population of interest.
Galton, Francis	[4] One of the key individuals responsible for developing the modern concept of correlation. Also see *Karl Pearson.*
Generalization	[14] A broad statement about the nature of reality (usually derived from the findings of several studies).
Geography	[1] The study of how human activities impact, and are affected by, the forces and the features of the surface of the earth.
Goodall, Jane	[1 & 9] An anthropologist who has conducted largely qualitative field research among chimpanzees since the early 1960s. Much of her research has been funded by the National Geographic Society.
Grab sampling	[12] One of the crudest methods for obtaining a sample for a research study. Typically, it involves standing in one location and trying to interview (or observe) whoever happens along (such as at a shopping mall or a convention booth). This method is also called incidental sampling and straw polling.
Group matching	[16] A sampling procedure used most often in quasi-experimentation for obtaining a comparison group. This procedure is designed to ensure that the comparison group is, on average, similar to an exposure group (except with regard to the independent variable).
Hawthorne effect	[15] A biased outcome in an experiment caused by the extra attention and reinforcement inadvertently given to subjects.
Historiographic data	[9] Largely qualitative data based on documents or testimonials about past events.
History	[1] The discipline that specializes in studying accounts (especially written accounts) of past human events.

H₀	[5] The symbol used to represent the *null hypothesis.*
Human Relations Area Files (see Ethnographic Atlas)	
Hypothesis	[5] A tentative statement about the nature of empirical reality that may or may not be true.
Independent variable	[15] A variable in experimental research that is manipulated by a researcher. In clinical experiments, this variable is sometimes called a treatment variable.
Index publication	[2] A publication that lists articles and other published material in a specific area, but without providing abstracts for each article.
Indirect observations	[11] Data that the individual performing a particular analysis was not responsible for collecting. The three main forms of such data are *archival data, content analysis data,* and *meta-analysis data.*
Individual matching	[16] A sampling procedure used most often in quasi-experiments for obtaining a comparison group. This procedure is designed to ensure that each individual member of a comparison group is similar to each member of an exposure group.
Informant	[9] An individual who helps provide a researcher, especially in a qualitative study, with information about the social group being studied.
Informed consent	[18] The act of volunteering to take part in a research project after being told the nature of the study and any possible risks it may entail.
In-house document (or In-house publication)	[20] A publication whose circulation is largely confined to the agency that produced the document. Many evaluation studies of government programs are never publicized beyond the release of such documents.
Institutional Review Boards	[18] Boards established in universities and hospitals in the United States (and in many other countries) to pass judgment on the ethical acceptability of research involving human subjects. They are also called human subject protection committees.
Instrument (see Research instrument)	
Interactive effect	[15] An effect on a dependent variable that is due to the joint actions of two or more independent variables that does not occur when one of these variables acts alone.

Inter-item (intra-test) reliability	[7] A method for assessing reliability that involves comparing scores on part of a multi-item measure of a variable with scores on another part of the same measure. The most widely used form of this method is called the *split-half reliability.*
Inter-rater (inter-judge) reliability	[7] A method for assessing reliability that involves comparing the judgments of two or more raters (or judges) of the same trait.
Interval level measurement	[2] One of the four levels of measurement. In it, the calibrating units must be arranged in a specific order, and a prescribed distance (usually equal) must exist between each calibrating unit.
Interval sampling (see Systematic sampling)	[12] A type of random sampling that involves taking sampling units from a sampling frame at designated intervals (e.g., every tenth name in a directory).
Introduction	[6] The name given to the beginning of the body of a research report. It is typically subdivided into two parts: the *review of the literature* and the *statement of the problem* (or the *hypothesis*).
Inverse correlation	[4] A correlation in which increasing values of one variable are associated with decreasing values of another variable. It is also referred to as a *negative correlation.*
Item	[8] In the context of a research questionnaire, any sentence or phrase used to elicit a response from a subject (also called a *question*).
Jensen, Arthur R.	[19] A psychologist-educator who published a summary of evidence in the late 1960s dealing with average racial differences in scores on tests of intellectual ability and performance.
Journal	[2] The general term for a periodical that reports scientific (or other technical) information.
Kuhn, Thomas	[14] A philosopher of science who has offered an explanation of how science develops from a pre-paradigm phase, in which members of a discipline spend considerable time debating how best to approach their discipline, to *normal science,* the period after a single paradigm has formed.
Law of diminishing returns	[5 & 12] The term applied to the fact that the larger one's sample already is, the less one reduces random sampling error by adding a new sampling unit.
Laws (see Scientific laws)	
Levels of measurement (or calibration)	[2] Levels at which variability in variables may be measured. Four levels are recognized: nominal, ordinal, interval, and ratio.

Levels of significance   [5] The degree to which a probability of error is being risked when declaring a finding statistically significant. Thus, if a finding is declared significant at the .01 level, a 1% chance of doing so in error is being risked.

Likert scale (usually pronounced Lick′ ert)   [8] Any of a variety of usually five-point all-points anchored response options of the following form:
>   SA—Strongly Agree
>   A—Agree
>   N—Neutral, Undecided
>   D—Disagree
>   SD—Strongly Disagree

Linear relationship   [4] A relationship (or correlation) between two variables in which the regression line is, or is assumed to be, straight. The opposite of this would be *curvilinear relationships*.

Literature review   [6] One of two components of the introduction to a research report. It is the part of a research report in which the writer presents a summary of prior research and theory on a particular topic.

Load, loading (see Factor loading)

Local universe   [14] A collection of all the instances of some phenomenon within the confines of what a researcher could reasonably hope to ever study (as opposed to a *universe as a whole*).

Longitudinal survey   [12] A survey undertaken in the same population during two or more periods of time. At least three different sampling procedures are used in these surveys: panel, nonpanel, and partial panel.

M   [3] A symbol used to represent the mean.

Matching   [16] In an experimental or quasi-experimental design, a method of selecting control or comparison subjects without random assignment.

Mead, Margaret   [9] An anthropologist who, in the early part of the 20th century, conducted ethnographic research, especially among villagers in the Samoan Islands. In recent years the accuracy of her research findings have been seriously questioned.

Mean   [3] The result of adding up the values (or scores) for some variable for a group of subjects, and then dividing the total by the number of subjects. It is also called the *arithmetic average*.

Measurement error   [7] Error in the results of a research study caused by a failure to measure a variable accurately; as opposed to *random sampling error*.

Measure of dispersion	[3] A univariate statistic that describes how much variation exists around a central tendency. Examples include such things as ranges, standard deviations, and variances.
Median	[3] The point above which and below which half the subjects are found with respect to some variable.
Meta-analysis	[11] A study that collectively analyzes the findings of several individual studies of some phenomenon.
Methods	[6] The section of a research report immediately following the statement of the problem (or hypothesis). This section is comprised of two subsections: description of the *sample* and description of the *procedures.*
Milgram, Stanley	[18] A social psychologist who undertook a series of experiments in the 1960s to help assess people's tendencies to follow orders, even when doing so required hurting others. The design of these experiments raised serious ethical questions.
Mode	[3] The highest point in a frequency distribution. If there are two such points, the distribution is said to be *bimodal.*
Model	[14] A theory or a major component of a theory that can be presented in some simplified graphic, equational, or physical form, or that can be demonstrated with some nonhuman animal subjects instead of human subjects.
Moral relativism	[19] The view that no moral standards of conduct are common to all societies. Instead, morality is seen as the product of ecological circumstances in which a society develops, or of special interest groups (usually those in positions of power) operating within a society.
Moral universalism	[19] The view that moral standards of conduct are universally accepted in all human societies.
Multi-item scale	[7] A way of measuring a variable by combining the responses to two or more questions.
Multiple regression	[17] A category of multivariate statistics. It is used to assess how two or more predictor variables seem to influence a criterion variable, with or without control variables being held constant.
Multiplicative (or multiplication) rule	[5] The rule that states that the probability of two independent events is equal to the independent probabilities of these two events multiplied by one another. Thus, the likelihood of turning up a 4 with two consecutive roles of a die is solved by multiplying each individual probability. Thus, $1/6 \times 1/6 = 1/36$ (or .0278).

Multistage cluster sampling

[12] A type of cluster sampling that involves several stages or "layers" in the sampling process.

Multivariate statistics

[17] A category of correlational statistics in which three or more variables are interrelated. The main categories are *factor analysis, partial correlation, multiple regression,* and *path analysis.*

Murdock, George

[11] An anthropologist who was instrumental in collecting information from hundreds of individual ethnographic accounts into a single *Ethnographic Atlas.*

n (for a sample) N (for a population)

[3] A symbol for the number of subjects in a study.

Naturalist

[9] A scientist who studies living things in their natural habitat.

Nature-nurture issue (or question)

[16] Having to do with the relative influence of genetic as opposed to environmentally learned factors on human behavior. This is one of the most fundamental issues in the social sciences.

Near social sciences

[1] Disciplines that, for various reasons, are not normally classified as social sciences even though they share much of the same knowledge and research methodology with the social sciences. These disciplines are education, ethology, psychiatry, public health, and sociobiology.

Negative correlation

[4] A relationship in which increasing values of one variable are associated with decreasing values of another variable. Also called an *inverse correlation.*

Nominal level measurement

[2] One of four levels at which a variable may be measured. It is the level in which names (or arbitrary numbers) are assigned to each calibrating unit, and the calibrating units may be arranged in any order.

Nonclinical evaluation research

[20] Applied research undertaken to assess the effects of programs designed to help groups of people all at once (as opposed to *clinical evaluation research,* although the line separating them is fuzzy).

Nonpanel longitudinal survey

[12] A longitudinal survey in which an entirely new group of subjects is picked from a population each time the survey is conducted.

Nonprobability sampling method

[12] Any of several methods of sampling that normally should not be relied on to yield samples that are representative of the universe from which they were drawn. It is the opposite of *probability sampling method.*

Normal curve

[3] A frequency distribution in which equal proportions of observations for a variable are found on each side of the mean as one moves a prescribed distance away from the mean. This type of frequency distribution is also called a *bell-shaped curve.*

Normal science	[14] A stage in the development of a scientific discipline characterized by having most of its practitioners agreeing on a common paradigm.
Null hypothesis	[5] An hypothesis made about reality in which no relationship or no difference is posited.
Numbering citation style	[6] One of the two main methods for citing prior publications in a scientific article or book. This citation style involves placing a number (usually in superscript) immediately following a statement or passage. The other main citation method is the *author-date citation style.*
Numeric form of end-anchored response scale	[8] The form of the end-anchored response scale in which subjects respond by writing any number between two stated extremes (e.g., between 1 and 10). Only the two most extreme responses are anchored.
Objectivism (see Empirical objectivism)	
Obtained sample	[13] The subjects who are actually included in a survey. This group of subjects is the result of the chosen sample minus the sample attrition.
Occam's razor	[14] Referring to the simplicity or parsimony of a theory. The name is derived from an 18th century scientist who spent considerable time simplifying other scientists' theories.
On-going evaluation research design	[20] A type of evaluation research that focuses on some aspect of organization functioning, and for which there is no projected point at which the evaluation will be stopped.
Open-ended response option	[8] A type of response option to questionnaire items in which respondents are given essentially no guidelines or boundaries for responding to a researcher's question.
Operational definition	[2] A definition that describes in specific empirical terms how variations in a concept may be observed. The opposite of this type of definition is a *conceptual definition.*
Ordinal level measurement	[2] One of the four levels at which variables may be measured. It is the level in which one assumes that each calibrating unit will appear in a specific order, although the distance between each calibrating unit may be irregular.
Outlier	[3] An observation whose value is extremely deviant relative to nearly all other observations.

p (or the p-value)   [5] A letter used to represent the probability of error associated with a statistic. The closer this number is to 0.00, the more likely it is that a particular set of observations will be deemed statistically significant.

p <   [5] A symbol for representing "the probability is less than."

p =   [5] A symbol for representing "the probability is equal to."

p ≤   [5] A symbol for representing "the probability is equal to or less than."

p >   [5] A symbol for representing "the probability is greater than."

Panel longitudinal survey   [12] A type of longitudinal survey in which the same group of subjects are used each time the survey is conducted.

Paradigm   [14] An interrelated set of assumptions about the nature of the phenomenon to be explained that provides a conceptual framework within which one or more scientific theories are formulated. This set of assumptions may be thought of as existing at an even higher level of abstraction than the concept of a *theory*.

Parsimony   [14] Another name for the simplicity (or Occam's razor) of a theory.

Partial correlation (Partialling or Partial regression)   [17] A type of multivariate statistic undertaken to identify a cause-and-effect relationship between two variables while the presumed confounding effects of one or more control variables are statistically removed from the relationship under scrutiny.

Partial panel longitudinal survey   [12] A type of longitudinal survey in which some of the subjects are new each time the survey is conducted, while other subjects were in one or more of the previous runs of the survey.

Path analysis   [17] A type of multivariate statistic undertaken to construct a visual model of how a set of variables may be causally linked in a chain leading to a final outcome.

Pearson, Karl   [4] A social scientist who developed the most widely used formula for calculating correlations.

Philosophy   [1] The discipline devoted to understanding the meaning of life, the nature of good and evil, and the limits to human knowledge.

Piggybacking   [18] Unwarranted inclusion of someone's name as the author of a publication. A form of fraud.

Piltdown Skull hoax   [18] The most famous example of scientific fraud in anthropology. It involved the supposed discovery of a human-ape skull in England around the turn of the 20th century.

Placebo effect (see Expectancy effect)

Plagiarism [18] Intentional representation of someone else's writings or ideas as one's own. A form of fraud.

Political science [1] The social science that focuses on the study of political institutions and processes.

Polygraph [13] A type of apparatus used to measure various physiological indicators of emotional stress (e.g., palm sweat, increased heart rate). From these measures, inferences are made about the likelihood that a subject is lying. These apparatuses—popularly known as lie detectors—are sometimes used to detect deceptive responses in social science research.

Population [12] A naturally existing collection of some phenomenon (usually a collection of people or other living creatures existing in a designated geographic area at a given point in time). This term is more or less synonymous with the concept of a *universe* in the field of statistics.

Positive relationship (or Positive correlation) [4] A relationship in which increasing values of one variable are associated with increasing values of another variable.

Post-exposure time frame [15] In an experiment, this is a designated period of time during or following subjects' exposure to an independent variable.

Precision [7] The degree to which the measurement of a variable is "fine grained" versus "coarse grained."

Predictive accuracy [14] Having to do with how well a theory can be used to predict some set of phenomena. It is generally considered the most important criteria by which the elegance of scientific theories are judged.

Predictive scope [14] Pertaining to how broadly a theory can predict in the sense of the number of hypotheses that can be derived from it. It is an important criteria for assessing the elegance of scientific theories.

Predictive (or criterion) validity [7] A type of validity in which the measurement of one variable is assessed in terms of how well that variable relates to some other variable in a way that makes sense. For example, if people's attitudes toward religion proved to be unrelated to how often they went to church, one would have to question the validity of the attitudinal measures.

Predictor variable [17] A variable that is treated as a cause (or independent variable) in multivariate statistical research.

Pre-exposure time frame [15] In an experiment, a designated period of time during which a dependent variable is measured prior to subjects being exposed to an independent variable.

Prehistoric	[1] That which occurred in some geographical area prior to the existence of written records.
Pretesting	[8] The process of administering a questionnaire to would-be subjects before giving it to actual subjects.
Primary analysis	[11] The analysis of data for which the data were primarily collected. As opposed to *secondary analysis.*
Primatology	[1] Usually considered a branch of physical anthropology that specializes in studying primates (other than humans).
Probability of error	[5] The probability that a particular observation (based on a given sample size) was due to chance.
Probability sampling method	[12] Method of sampling that can be relied on to yield samples that are representative of the universe from which they were drawn.
Probability theory	[5] A set of mathematically derived principles that can be used to estimate the probable outcome of various events (not to be confused with a scientific theory).
Procedures	[6] One of the subparts of the methods section of most scientific research reports. In this part, researchers disclose the treatment of subjects in order to obtain the data (e.g., asked subjects to complete a questionnaire).
Prospective quasi-experimental design	[16] A quasi-experimental design in which the independent variable is measured more or less at the time it is taking place, as opposed to being measured retrospectively.
Psychiatry	[1] One of the near social sciences; it specializes in treating persons who are diagnosed as mentally ill. Unlike clinical psychologists, who also are involved in treating mental illness, members of this profession typically hold a medical degree.
Psychology	[1] The study of behavior, cognition, and emotions. It is a major social/behavioral science.
Public health	[1] One of the near social sciences; it is devoted to improving the health of human populations not by treating individual patients, but by improving the collective behavior of people and the general environment in which they live.
"Publish or perish institutions"	[18] Universities (and some hospitals) at which a heavy emphasis is placed on research and publishing, as opposed to teaching (or patient care). Many professors working at these institutions understand that job security is dependent on their rate of publication.

Pure random sampling [12] A sampling method that precisely conforms to the definition of random sampling (i.e., every member of the universe must be given an equal chance of being selected each time a new sampling unit is picked).

Qualified moral universalism [19] The view that a core group of moral standards of conduct (social morals, as opposed to aesthetic morals) are universally accepted in all human societies.

Qualitative observations [9] Scientific observations that are not recorded in any standardized coding format.

Quantitative observations [10] Scientific observations that are recorded in a numeric or some other standardized coding format.

Quartiles [3] The result of dividing a frequency distribution curve into fourths.

Quasi-experimental design [16] A research design that approximates an experiment. It includes *ex post facto* and *time series* designs.

Question [8] In the context of a research questionnaire, any sentence or phrase used to elicit a response from a subject. It is sometimes called an *item* or a questionnaire item.

Questionnaire [8] Any research instrument on which respondents provide information about their lives and behavior.

Questionnaire item (see Question)

Quota sampling [12] A sampling method that usually involves grab sampling with the stipulation that a certain proportion of the subjects must have certain characteristics (e.g., equal numbers of both sexes). Sometimes this sampling method is incorporated into cluster sampling methods.

Random assignment [15] The process of relegating a pool of subjects to two (or more) groups in an entirely unprejudicial way. The purpose of this procedure is to ensure that a researcher has two (or more) groups of equivalent subjects before one group is exposed to an independent variable to an unusual degree.

Random digit dialing [12] A special type of random sampling method used only in telephone surveys. Once the first three digits (the prefix) used in an area to be sampled has been entered into a computer that has been connected to a telephone via a modem, the computer can be programmed to dial the last four digits at random.

Random sample [12] A sample that has been drawn from a population in which every member of the population has an equal chance of being picked. This sampling method is normally one of the surest ways of obtaining a representative sample.

Random sampling error   [13] Error in the results of a survey which can be reduced by increasing sample size. Such error can be contrasted with *systematic sampling error.*

Range   [3] The result of subtracting the lowest from the highest value for a variable within some data set.

Ratio level measurement   [2] The "highest" of the four levels of measurement. It not only stipulates that there should be a specific (usually equal) distance between each of the calibrating units, but that there be a point at which the variable disappears (designated as zero). Weight is a variable normally measured at this level.

Reference   [6] In scientific writing, it involves indicating the author, title, etc., of a publication so that others may locate and read it.

Regression line   [4] The line that comes closest to intersecting all the points in a scattergram.

Regression plane   [17] A plane that comes closest to intersecting all the points in a cubical (rather than two-dimensional) scattergram.

Reliability   [7] The degree to which the measurement of a variable tends to be stable and consistent over time.

Replication research   [19] Research undertaken to verify the findings of some prior research report.

Representative sample   [12] A sample whose members have characteristics of the population in the same proportion as does the population as a whole. Such a sample is an ideal toward which researchers aim, and may be approximated using various sampling methods.

Reprint   [2] A copy of an article that has been printed by the publisher separate from the particular issue of the periodical in which it appeared. In a broader sense, it also includes photocopies of scientific articles.

Research hypothesis (see Alternative hypothesis)

Research instrument   [6] Any tangible object used in the collection of scientific data. The most common type in social science research is the questionnaire.

Respondent   [8] A human subject in a research project who provides information through a questionnaire or an interview.

Response option   [8] A set of options given to subjects for responding to a question.

Results   [6] One of the main sections of a research report. In it, the researcher reveals details about what was found.

Reversal experimental design	[15] Any of a variety of before-after no control group designs involving three or more time frames (e.g., ABA, ABBA, ABAB experimental designs).
Review of literature (see Literature review)	
s²	[3] A symbol for variance, which is mathematically defined as the square of the standard deviation.
Sample	[12] A subset of some population.
Sample attrition	[13] Subjects who are selected for a survey, but who either cannot be contacted or decline to be studied.
Sample size	[5 & 12] The number of subjects (or sampling units) in a study. It is often represented with the letter N or n.
Sampling error (see Random sampling error)	
Sampling frame	[12] A complete list of all the members of the population (or the source for such a list). All random sampling methods require working from this (with the exception of *random digit dialing* methods).
Sampling unit	[12] Any member of a sample.
Scattergram	[4] A graph used to represent how two variables are related to one another. It is generally used with variables that have been measured at the interval or ratio levels, and is sometimes called a scatterplot.
Scenario item	[8] An item in a questionnaire that includes describing some hypothetical situation that the respondent is asked to imagine before responding to a question.
Scientific law	[14] A statement about what should always occur under a prescribed set of conditions.
Scientific model (see Model)	
Scientific paradigm (see Paradigm)	
Scientific theory (see Theory)	
SD	[3] One of the symbols used to represent standard deviation.
Secondary analysis	[11] The analysis of data that a researcher did not participate in collecting.

Self-selected sample	[12] A sample that is highly dependent on subjects taking the initiative to be involved. An example of this type of sample would be a survey based on the calls that television viewers make to register their opinion on some topic.
Semantic differential scale	[8] A type of end-anchored linear response scale. It was originally developed by Charles Osgood.
Semi-field observations	[10] Observations, usually of nonhuman animals, that are made in enclosures much larger than a normal cage.
Serendipitous observations	[9] Observations of events that were completely unanticipated by the researcher.
Shared variance (or Common variance)	[4] The degree to which variation in one variable is associated with or attributable to variation in a second variable.
Σ	[3] One of the symbols used to represent standard deviation (usually for a population rather than a sample). In the Greek alphabet, this symbol is called a lower case sigma.
Simple cluster sampling	[12] A type of sampling in which a researcher randomly picks a few clusters of sampling units within a universe (e.g., a few dozen church parishes within the United States), and then uses all the members of these parishes as the sampling units.
Simplicity	[14] One of the criteria for judging the elegance of a theory. It is also referred to as *parsimony* and *Occam's razor*.
Single-subject experimental design	[20] One of the adaptations of before-after no control group experimental designs. In it, only one subject is utilized. It is most often used in clinical evaluation research.
Snowball sampling	[12] A sampling method in which subjects are recruited and then asked to help to recruit additional subjects.
Social morality	[19] Morality having to do with how people should interact without intentionally harming one another. As opposed to *ascetic morality*.
Social science	[1] A term that refers to all disciplines that have as their primary aim to better understand behavioral and social phenomena.
Social work	[1] The social science discipline that specializes in helping a society's poor, disabled, and disadvantaged citizens to function more efficiently within the society.
Sociobiology	[1] One of the near social sciences, which specializes in studying the biological underpinnings of social behavior.
Sociology	[1] The study of social behavior, social institutions, and societies in general.

Solomon four-group experimental design	[15] A specialized experimental design involving a minimum of two experimental groups and two control groups. One of the experimental and one of the control groups is exposed to the independent variable without any preexposure measurement of the dependent variable, while the remaining two groups are exposed to the independent variable as in a classical experimental design.
Split-half reliability	[7] The main type of intra-test reliability. In it, scores on one half of a multi-item scale are correlated with scores on the other half of the scale.
Spontaneous recovery	[15] The tendency for an individual to seek help for both medical and behavioral problems when they are close to or at their worst. This makes it probable that often after seeking help, people will report improvement. Clinicians need to guard against interpreting such changes as evidence of the effectiveness in their treatment.
Spuriousness (or Spurious relationship)	[17] Refers to a relationship that is only coincidental in nature. The term is commonly used in multivariate statistics as being the opposite of cause-and-effect relationships.
Standard deviation	[3] The most widely used measure of dispersion about the mean, particularly for variables that are normally distributed (or nearly so).
Statement of the problem	[6] One of the components of a research report. In it, the writer succinctly states the *hypothesis* to be tested (or, less formally, the question to be addressed).
Statistical control	[17] Control that is achieved over a variable by using *multivariate statistics* rather than using *random assignment* or *matching* procedures.
Statistical probability	[5] A mathematical estimate of the likelihood of some event, usually based on various established laws of probability.
Statistical significance	[5] A precise estimate of probability that certain observed differences or relationships are too great to be the result of mere chance.
Statistics	[3] A branch of mathematics used by scientists to represent averages and dispersions with reference to variables, relationships between variables, and probabilities that various observations are due to chance.
Stratified random sampling	[12] A special type of random sampling that makes it possible for groups with low representation in a population to be more highly represented in a sample.
Student's t-test (see t-test)	
Subject	[8] A human or other animal used in a research project.

Summative evaluation research design	[20] A type of evaluation research in which the effectiveness of a program is assessed after the program has been completed (as opposed to an *on-going evaluation research design*).
Sunset laws	[20] Laws stipulating that various social programs will be automatically terminated unless active steps are taken to renew them. In this way, programs that fail to be proven effective have a greater chance of not being perpetuated.
Survey	[12] Any research study that examines an empirical phenomenon without disturbing it. This term is particularly appropriate if the aim of the study is to determine the prevalence of some phenomenon within a population over a specific time frame.
Systematic (or Interval) sampling	[12] A random sampling method that involves taking sampling units from a sampling frame at designated intervals (such as every tenth name in a directory) or at designated positions (such as the third name from the top of each page).
Systematic sampling error	[13] Error in the results of a survey that is in a specific direction relative to the true population mean. In studies of human subjects, this type of error usually results from inappropriate phrasing of questions or poor response options. Unlike *random sampling error,* this type of sampling error will not be reduced by increasing sample size.
t	[5] The symbol used to represent the result of calculating a t-test.
Tasiday hoax	[18] A fraudulent claim made in the 1970s of having found a stone age tribe still inhabiting one of the Philippine Islands.
Telescoping	[13] The tendency that subjects have to include events that happened prior to a time frame specified by a researcher. In other words, if asked if they were a crime victim in the past year, many include instances that happened 13 or 14 months ago.
Test-retest reliability	[7] A method for assessing reliability in which the primary aim is to demonstrate consistency in scores obtained by the same measurement procedure in at least two different time frames. An example would be to give a group of students the same exam separated by a week's time and then determine how well their two scores correlated.
Thematic surveys	[13] Surveys that focus intently on a single topic.
Theoretical model	[14] Basically, a ''mini-theory'' or a theory derived from a larger (grander) theory.

Theoretical (or Construct) validity	[7] A type of validity that so far is infrequently used in the social sciences. However, in the case of very precise and powerful theories, one can often tell how valid a measure is for a variable by how well the measurement of that variable is related to numerous other variables. If the relationships are not as the theory predicts, the measurement of the variable must be invalid.
Theory	[14] A set of statements about the nature of reality from which testable hypotheses may be derived.
Third variable problem	[4] Refers to the fact that whenever simple relationships between variables are observed, the reason for their being related could be the result of some "third variable" that was not included in one's study.
Time frame	[15] The length of time during which the dependent variable is monitored for any effects of exposure to the independent variable.
Time series design	[16] A type of quasi-experimental design that most closely resembles before-after no control group experiments. This design involves tracking a dependent variable over two or more time frames in a single group of subjects (and sometimes just a single subject) and observing whether the dependent variable changes in response to changes in an independent variable.
Tolerance limits	[5] The degree of risk one is willing to take when declaring a relationship or group difference statistically significant. As a rule, researchers do not risk more than a 5% chance of error in declaring a finding statistically significant.
Treatment variable (see Independent variable)	
Truth	[14] A repeatedly confirmed hypothesis. Because the concept implies finality, and because scientists tend to be tentative and probabilistic in their thinking about empirical reality, most researchers avoid using this term except in casual conversation.
t-test (or Student's t-test)	[5] A statistical test used to estimate the probability that two means are significantly different from one another.
Twin study	[16] A type of quasi-experimental design used to help answer nature-nurture questions. It takes advantage of the fact that humans give birth to two types of twins (identical and fraternal), and that identical twins share twice (i.e., 100%) as many genes as do fraternal twins (i.e., 50%).

Type I error   [14] The error a researcher makes when he or she rejects the null hypothesis when it is in fact true.

Type II error   [14] The error a researcher makes when he or she accepts the null hypothesis when it is in fact false.

Unexplained variance   [17] Variance in a criterion (or dependent) variable that cannot be accounted for by one or more predictor (or independent) variables. This term is commonly used in multivariate statistical studies.

Unit of analysis   [11] The delimiting boundaries that will be used in a study. For example, comparing different cultures often requires fairly arbitrary boundaries between cultures (e.g., Should Native Americans be included in a study of American culture?).

Univariate statistics   [3] Statistics that are applied to one variable at a time (e.g., *averages* and *measures of dispersion*).

Universe   [12] A complete collection of some phenomenon (see *population*).

Universe as a whole   [14] A collection of all instances of some phenomenon throughout time and space (as opposed to a *local universe*).

Validity   [7] The degree to which the measurement of a variable is, in fact, measuring that variable.

Variable   [2] An observable (or empirical) phenomenon that can take on different values or intensities (as opposed to a *constant*).

Variance   [3] The standard deviation squared.

Verifiable   [1] One of the characteristics of the scientific method. It assumes that nearly everyone has the same sensory apparatuses, and can therefore cross-check the accuracy of someone else's observations.

Weighting   [12] A set of methods for mathematically adjusting survey data after having been collected to make the data more representative of its intended universe. The procedures require basic information about the universe as a whole, such as that derived from census surveys.

$\overline{\textbf{X}}$ [3] A common symbol to represent the mean.

$\textbf{X}^2$ [5] The symbol used to represent the number (or coefficient) derived from calculating a chi-square statistical test.

Yeasaying items   [8] Questionnaire items that are phrased in ways that tend to compel respondents to answer in the affirmative.

Zero-order (simple) correlation matrix   [17] An array of correlation coefficients showing how many variables in a study are interrelated. This type of matrix serves as a springboard for most multivariate statistical analyses.

SUBJECT INDEX

A

ABAB experimental design, 229, 317
abortion
  accuracy of self-reports on, 192
  measuring attitudes toward, 106–7
abstract publication
  electronic (computerized) searches
    of, 26–28
  manual searches of, 25–26
  use of, 24–25
academic ability/achievement
  anxiety and, 155
  based on institutional data, 150
  government financing of private
    education and, 271
  public schools vs. parochial
    schools, 257–58, 270–71
  race and, 299–301
  tests of, 299–300
accident proneness
  meta-analysis of, 155
accidents
  motor vehicle, 318
accuracy of measurement
  about abortion, 192
  about child molestation, 192
  about drug use, 192
  assessment of, 89
  subject anxiety and, 95–96

activity levels
  sex differences in, 155
additive rule
  statistical probability and, 63
ADHD (see attentional-deficit
    hyperactivity disorder)
adoption studies
  as a type of quasi-experimental
    design, 249–51
  combined with twin studies, 250
  cross-fostering experiments and,
    250
  of genetic influences upon
    behavior, 249–51
adversarial nature of qualitative and
    quantitative data, 143
advertising/advertisers
  social science research and, 9
  surveys conducted by, 164
aesthetic appeal of a theory, 204–5
after-only experimental design, 225–27
age
  at marriage, 150
  criminality and, 150, 209
  of researcher and scientific fraud,
    288
  reaction time and, 137
  seat belt usage and, 141
aggression
  dominance and, 142
  measurement of, 114–15

nonhuman animals and, 210
  pornography and, 142
  selective breeding experiments
    and, 248
  technological advancement and,
    122
agrarian societies
  marriage patterns and, 153
alcohol
  preferences and heredity, 248
  prenatal exposure to, 244
alcoholism and drug abuse/addition
  adoption studies and, 250
  Alcoholics Anonomous treatment
    for, 243
  nonhuman animals and, 210
  treatment of, 287
all-points-anchored response options,
  105
alternative hypothesis
  vs. null hypothesis, 68–69, 214–15
altruism
  theory of, 208–9
American Rifleman, 268
American Sign Language
  use of among apes, 127
analysis of variance (ANOVA), 70, 72
Anasazi
  cannibalism and, 137